ABOUT THE AUTHOR

Felicity Lawrence is an award-winning journalist and editor who began writing about food-related issues nearly thirty years ago. *Not On the Label* won the Guild of Food Writers' Jeremy Round Award for best first book in 2005 and a special commendation in the Andre Simon Awards 2004. Lawrence has twice been awarded the Derek Cooper Award for Investigative Food Writer of the Year, has twice been shortlisted for Specialist Reporter of the Year in the British Press Awards, and has been commended in the Paul Foot and Martha Gellhorn prizes. She is special correspondent for the *Guardian* and lives in London.

Not On the Label

*What Really Goes into the
Food on Your Plate*

FELICITY LAWRENCE

PENGUIN BOOKS

For Matt, Cecy, Anna and Ellie, and
those who have shared secrets

PENGUIN BOOKS

Published by the Penguin Group
Penguin Books Ltd, 80 Strand, London WC2R 0RL, England
Penguin Group (USA) Inc., 375 Hudson Street, New York, New York 10014, USA
Penguin Group (Canada), 90 Eglinton Avenue East, Suite 700, Toronto, Ontario,
Canada M4P 2Y3 (a division of Pearson Penguin Canada Inc.)
Penguin Ireland, 25 St Stephen's Green, Dublin 2, Ireland (a division of Penguin Books Ltd)
Penguin Group (Australia), 707 Collins Street, Melbourne, Victoria 3008, Australia
(a division of Pearson Australia Group Pty Ltd)
Penguin Books India Pvt Ltd, 11 Community Centre, Panchsheel Park, New Delhi – 110 017, India
Penguin Group (NZ), 67 Apollo Drive, Rosedale, Auckland 0632, New Zealand
(a division of Pearson New Zealand Ltd)
Penguin Books (South Africa) (Pty) Ltd, Block D, Rosebank Office Park,
181 Jan Smuts Avenue, Parktown North, Gauteng 2193, South Africa

Penguin Books Ltd, Registered Offices: 80 Strand, London WC2R 0RL, England

www.penguin.com

First published 2004
Revised edition 2013
001

Set in 11/13pt PostScript Monotype Bembo
Printed in Great Britain by Clays Ltd, St Ives plc

A CIP catalogue record for this book is available from the British Library

ISBN: 978-0-241-96782-9

www.greenpenguin.co.uk

Contents

Introduction

It is nearly a decade since the first edition of *Not On the Label* emerged from a series of investigative journeys I had taken around the global food business.

Those had been shaped partly by my personal experience. I had worked for a couple of years in Pakistan on the Afghan border and, having been isolated from Western culture for a long stretch, on my return I found myself looking at it through different eyes, as though for the first time. Having lived among refugees in an area where food could never be taken for granted, the contrast back in London was dramatic. Here people struggled with overeating and the diseases of excess rather than the diseases of malnutrition and hunger.

The march of the supermarket across our food culture, well under way when I left, was almost complete by the time I came back. There was a cornucopia of plenty at every journey's end but the destination mostly seemed to be a retail car park. Seasons, so prominent in the bazaars of Central Asia, had been abolished in favour of a permanent transcontinental summer time on the high street. It looked awesome. It had removed the daily grind of shopping that had consumed the time and energy of women (mostly) of the previous generation. I wondered if a genius in a white lab coat had invented it while I was away.

But there was something missing from this way of producing, selling and consuming food that seemed to reflect a deeper societal malaise. Human interaction had been reduced to a hurried minimum. There was no scent and little taste to much of the fresh food on offer. The infinite variety on the aisles so often turned out to be just fifty variations on the same over-processed combinations of denatured commodity ingredients high in salt, sugar and fat, despite being packaged and marketed as different brands. There was so much waste.

For all the sophistication of food production in Europe, there was a sense of loss. Independent shops and markets were disappearing. Unpackaged, unprocessed food that had not passed through the mill of big chains was hard to find, and even harder to find at an affordable price. Farmers struggled to make a living. The system was a miracle of logistics and a response to our ever busy and changing lifestyles, but in gobbling sandwiches furtively at our desks, wolfing fast food on the run or throwing together a meal of pre-cut chicken and ready chopped vegetables to consume in front of screens, much of the cultural significance of shared meals had been sacrificed. And in those places where meals were given time and significance, it was at the other extreme. Foodie feasts and high-end restaurants were so hung up on provenance you practically needed a bank loan to indulge in their dishes. I remembered the simple meals from communal bowls set on a Baluch carpet in a refugee's mud house, where the business of eating was serious. It wasn't just about refuelling as efficiently as possible, it was the focus of human exchange. The simplest things could be the most delicious. Sitting together over food was where adults shared news and views, where children learned to communicate, to defer to the needs of others and were socialized.

Oddest of all, given this abundance and all the technology that created it, everyone back home seemed worried about their food. Food poisoning had been a regular part of life abroad in an under-developed and war-torn region, but why did so much anxiety surround food even in the affluent West? All the hi-tech hygiene and computerized traceability systems of which the industry boasted seemed unable to keep a series of crises in their complex global chains at bay. Each of these revealed the dysfunction at the heart of our food system.

The foot and mouth epidemic of 2001 had been the background to much of the original research for *Not On the Label*.

The horror of seeing millions of sheep and cattle immolated in funeral pyres on our television screens each night had led to a brief period of intense questioning among politicians and experts about the way we farmed. Rural communities were left decimated by it, but otherwise, once the crisis was over, in many ways it was back to business as usual. In 2013 the industrial-scale adulteration of beef with horsemeat has once again turned the spotlight on all that is troubling about the way we eat today.

The response to *Not On the Label* was overwhelming and humbling. It seemed to tap into profound concerns many people felt about the nature of the global food business – concerns about animal welfare, about our health, about the destruction of the countryside, about inequalities at home and injustice in trade abroad – that had been widespread but largely ill-defined. As I travelled around from farms to factories and from pack-houses to lorry depots around the world, I discovered why beef and pork waste ended up in chicken products, why a third of apples are thrown away, why bread is full of air and water. It became clear that children getting fat, motorways clogged with juggernauts, ravaged fields in Europe, starving smallholders in Africa and migrants working in appalling conditions were all connected; they were the interrelated parts of a system in which a handful of powerful corporations had achieved unprecedented control over what we eat and where we buy it. The inequities and failings of the food system turned out to be both symptom of and mirror to those of the world's wider political economy. The deterioration in conditions at the bottom of the chain is in stark contrast to the increased concentration in wealth at the top of it. And the gap has kept growing.

I was only able to bring to light much of what I uncovered thanks to the efforts of experts and those on the ground who had fought to right the system over many years. Health campaigners, aid agencies, union organizers, environmental activists, concerned officials, and alternative farming and producers' organizations had all prepared the way and pointed me to what

I needed to see. The book then became part of a grassroots movement to fight back. I received hundreds of letters and emails from people kind enough to tell me how they had changed their way of eating and shopping or even their whole lives after reading it. There have been campaigns since, many of them with celebrity support, that have put some of the issues firmly into the mainstream. TV chefs have thrown their energies and the power of their medium into trying to save fish, make chicken happier, banish junk from schools and improve the diets of those who are marginalized. The real food movement looked as though it was getting into full swing. Then the financial crisis of 2008 threw everything off course, and it became clear how few of the fundamentals of the power structure had altered.

How we produce our food, whether there is enough of it, whether people can afford it, whether it keeps us healthy or makes us sick, who uses the resources it takes and who makes the money from it, these are truly vital questions. It is no co-incidence that many of the largest aid agencies have now chosen to focus their efforts in development on campaigns to map and change the globalized food system. The answers today are as unsatisfactory as they were when I first wrote *Not On the Label*. Some of the details have changed, people are much more aware of the problems and failings of Big Food, but sadly the criticisms still stand.

The industrial chicken I described as being routinely con-taminated with the nasty food-poisoning bug campylobacter is not as likely to be so today, it is *more* likely to be, with 65 per cent of retail packs of fresh chicken now carrying the bacterium, over a quarter of them contaminated by high concentrations of it. Fresh poultry still makes around 500,000 people in the UK ill each year, sending many of those to hospital. The number of companies who now process animals for our meat continues to shrink as the sector becomes more and more concentrated in fewer and fewer abattoirs. The factory where I worked under-cover on the chicken line has been sold by the family company that had owned it for decades to one of the largest poultry groups in the country as the primary processing sector continues to become more concentrated.

It is easier to find a well-reared chicken now than when *Not On the Label* first appeared but it will set you back £15–20, and the way the majority of chickens are grown and processed has changed little, although the poultry farmers say they are more squeezed than ever. The risk of resistant disease spreading from intensively produced animals to humans remains a serious concern, heightened by the outbreaks of bird flu that were predicted and have now happened.

The chlorine washes used on fresh bagged salad that I first described put customers off so much that bags of prepacked leaves washed in spring water are now available, at a price. The exploitation of migrant workers who produce the crops, however, continues, as does the liberal use of pesticides to attain cosmetic perfection. A brief period of trying to raise labour standards has been followed by a deterioration in conditions for many as the recession has taken hold. Conditions among many of the migrants working on salad crops in Spain were as bad as anyone could remember when I revisited to make a film for the *Guardian* in 2011. Those migrants are driven to leave their countries and head to Europe, partly by conflict, as always, but increasingly also by crises over food in their own countries. Their ability to live and feed their families at home has been reduced by the effects of climate change and loss of crops, and by huge spikes in food prices made more volatile by deregulated financial speculation in agricultural commodities.

The chapter on bread explored the debasing of our staples and the disproportionate effect that has on those on the lowest incomes. There has been a huge revival in interest in real bread since, with its very own campaign group promoting healthier loaves made without chemical improvers. Sales of white sliced bread have fallen slightly. However bread as a category has remained one of the battlegrounds in which retailers fight price wars to win our custom. Where white sliced has been replaced, it is mostly with other kinds of breads such as wraps and pittas that are equally stripped of the nutritional value available from whole grains. Meanwhile British Bakeries, whose factory I toured, is now part of the heavily indebted private equity group Premier Foods, which has taken over several iconic British brands. The food poverty I met in London's East End when investigating the breadline there is deeper than ever. In these austere times of sharply rising food and fuel inflation and stagnating incomes, half a million people have become dependent on handouts from foodbanks in the UK, the world's seventh richest nation.

The plight of African coffee farmers, unable to make a living from their crop while other parts of the chain are highly profitable, has not improved in a decade. The large transnational roasting and trading companies have increased their control of the supply chain, and speculation in agricultural commodities markets has made prices highly volatile here too. A brutal restructuring is taking place, made worse by the fact that climate change is altering the height at which coffee can be grown, driving smallholders off their land but leaving them with no alternative livelihoods.

The process of big retailers crushing smaller independent shops has accelerated, so even fewer areas have butchers, bakers or greengrocers. The big four supermarket groups have rushed into the vacuum left by this hollowing out, opening small 24/7 branches in the spaces left on boarded-up high streets. While the return of groceries to shops in food deserts is welcome, albeit run by the same handful of supermarkets and with some higher prices than in their main stores, our choice of retailer has narrowed again. Farmers' markets on the other hand have burgeoned. The desire for a different kind of system is widespread, but the recession has already placed these under pressure. Meat and dairy produce from animals reared slowly on grass is more expensive than that from animals fed a fast-food diet of heavily subsidized grains. The former may have a healthier nutritional composition, and the farming methods involved in the latter may mean we all pay in different ways later, but with wallets feeling the pinch many people are not able to make the best choice.

I am pleased to say that my dissection of the ready meal led to some supermarkets removing additives and fillers from their products. Less happily, that process of cleaning up has sometimes meant hiding additives more deeply so that they are no longer on the label, or finding alternatives that are equally nutritionally bankrupt but sound less scary, rather than substituting real fresh whole foods that are nourishing. Marketing foods high in fat, salt and sugar to children on TV became subject to restrictions; however the food industry has become adept at bypassing them through social media or online viral marketing, or simply by advertising junk foods during the breaks in adult programmes such as talent shows that count huge numbers of children among their audience, shows that were lobbied out of the restrictions by special interest groups.

So the journeys in *Not On the Label* still tell the hidden story of our food. This revised edition includes all the chapters from the first, and begins with a new chapter on the horsemeat scandal. The persistent ills of the system are all too clear in this latest saga of the mass adulteration of what we eat. The underlying drivers have not been addressed; sadly neither have the other realities of our transnational corporate way of producing it. The forces, economic, political and cultural, that led us down the path of degraded, industrialized food remain. As pressure on the planet's resources grows, and diet-related diseases reach epidemic proportions across the globe, change seems ever more urgent.

The fight for a better, fairer way for food was never going to be easy or quick. The struggle goes on.

1. Horse

There was more than a touch of comedy to the horsemeat scandal of winter 2013. Thousands of old nags had been passed off as beef, probably for years, in millions of cheap frozen beef burgers, ready meals and school dinners all around Europe.

Shoppers had been duped; supermarket and manufacturing reputations had been minced; and the cast list of food industry players proclaiming themselves innocent victims of fraud just kept growing longer and longer. It included some of the best-known brands, the sort we love to hate for colonizing our diets and being so powerfully ubiquitous, from Burger King to Birds Eye, from Nestlé to Tesco. As with all the best whodunnits there were suspects galore, although no one could say who the perpetrators were, nor where the crime had taken place, nor even what the implements to effect it had been.

But no one had died from eating horse. Some cultures would not have objected to consuming it anyway if they had known. The French have always eaten *cheval*. Pubs and restaurants started serving 'filly mignon' as a stunt. Look! Horse! Lovely stuff. There is nothing necessarily illegal about flogging dead horse, so long as you declare it. (And so long as you don't mince it. Lumps of horse are fine but cross-border trading in minced horse is very specifically illegal in the European Union. Perhaps someone somewhere in Brussels had known something all along.)

But even a little sleight of hand over species seemed widely acceptable. A well-known Amsterdam steakhouse owner was reported to have admitted he had been selling horse as beefsteak for sixty-three years and no one had complained; in fact they had lapped it up. His business thrived on his belated confession.

The jokes came thick and fast. 'Shamburgers is an anagram of that most famous Irish racehorse Shergar's bum'; 'Burger King has changed the cheese in its burgers from Cheddar to masc-a-pone'; 'A Findus beef lasagne is almost an anagram of "Feed us fine able nags"';'Complaining about horse in discount burgers?You're lucky there's meat in them at all ...'

The unflappable head of the Irish Food Safety Authority (FSAI), Professor Alan Reilly, the man who had been brave enough to be the first to conduct official tests and find equine DNA in products made by some of the biggest names in Irish beef processing, said that discovering that beef burgers made for Tesco were in fact 29 per cent horsemeat was 'like winning the Lotto'.

British MPs were more than a little sceptical about this 'luck of the Irish' when they interrogated him before parliament and wanted to know 'why all roads lead to Ireland?' What in fact did the Irish know when? And where was it Reilly's compatriot and previous head at the FSAI had recently gone? Of course, to lead a body called Horse Sport Ireland.

You couldn't make it up.

A company that had supplied beef adulterated with horse-meat to Sodexo, one of Europe's biggest catering companies, turned out to be owned by the Queen's Master of Horse, Lord Vestey and family. The French transnational caterer, which served schools, the armed forces, care homes, hospitals and prisons, was a little coy about owning up to this royal link, as were Vestey and the British government. But then, embarrassing joke, Sodexo had also provided meals to Royal Ascot. Could Her Majesty and her noble lord have actually eaten horse while simultaneously watching horse racing together? Who knew? Anything might be possible in this new world of racy recycling. Vestey Foods protested they were innocent dupes, supplied by a meat dealer from London's Smithfield meat market, and that their Ascot ingredients were not affected.

The dealer was an elected member of the corporation of the City of London, but innocent dupe too nevertheless. He declined to say who had supplied the meat to him.

Meanwhile one Dutch trader, a convicted fraudster called Jan Fasen who was accused of being part of a chain of horse 'laundering' across Continental Europe, turned out to be operating through a trading company registered offshore in Cyprus with a tax-haven vehicle in the British Virgin Islands. It was called Draap, which is *paard*, the Dutch for horse, spelled backwards. They were having a laugh.

Draap's *paard* had ended up, via a French trading group, Spanghero, owned by a company called Poujol, in a Luxembourg factory, Tavola, which made beef (or horse) ready meals for a northern French food processing giant called Comigel that supplied Tesco, Findus and others around Europe.

The horse seemed to have come from Romania originally, and although tabloids were quick to blame a surplus of old cart horses in backward eastern European states that they implausibly claimed had only recently discovered the car, the French authorities later confirmed that the horsemeat had left respectable Romanian horse abattoirs correctly labelled. If horse had begat beef, it had happened elsewhere. Eastern Europeans were a scapegoat convenient to our prejudices but not in the end the main villains of the plot. Meanwhile global food supply chains turned out to be as complicated as, but rather less well recorded and discoverable than, bloodlines.

An Irish horse slaughterer, caught at its Tipperary cutting plant packing horsemeat in boxes labelled in the Czech language as 'beef', assured the authorities it wasn't a scam. Both the UK-based trader buying it from the factory and his eventual customers were fully aware they were getting horse. They had asked for horse and they were paying for horse. They had ordered those very eastern European labels too. Fraud? Ach no, not at all, everyone knew. The B&F Meats factory was found out after the horsemeat scandal had broken, when the Irish Department of Agriculture inspected in February 2013 as part of its investigations. It closed the factory when its inspectors found the 'Czech beef', but the weakness of regulation seemed to make it a struggle to take it too seriously. The department's report in March expressed concern at B&F's wilful act of mislabelling, but a week after the February visit the company had been allowed to get back to the business of deboning mares as usual while the authorities wondered what to do about the spot of bother over the translation of Irish horse into eastern European cow. The Czech authorities, meanwhile, had imposed a substantial fine on their end of the chain within weeks.

B&F's owner, Ted Farrell, had told an Irish parliamentary committee three years previously that it ought to relax the rules on slaughtering horse for human food consumption rather than rejecting horses just because they had been treated with veterinary drugs at some point in their lives.

Farrell had been supported at the committee by Ted Walsh, one of Ireland's most successful racehorse trainers, who was flush from triumphs at recent racing events at the time. Slaughtering horses for meat was 'a great way out for a fellow with a horse that should be put down', he said. He wanted the rules relaxed too. Where's the harm in a bit of old racehorse?

And he hoped, by the by, that the committee members had had a flutter and placed a few winning euros on his own horses.

Yet for all the humour, being a saga with Irish beginnings, the horsemeat scandal was also one shot through with a deadly seriousness. If you wanted a catalogue of all the ways in which our global food system has become profoundly dysfunctional and unfair, horsegate would provide a reasonably comprehensive one.

It would turn out to be a tale of excessive corporate power, of businesses that had become too big for governments to challenge, and transnational chains too long to be held to account. It would show a system in which Big Food had wielded its political influence to roll back the state, had lobbied for and won deregulation in the name of free markets, only to create markets that were not free at all but captured by a few. It exposed the routine adulteration of our food, both legal and illegal, and the glaring social and health inequalities that persist in the quality of diets.

Horsegate was also a manifestation of patterns of consumption that were unsustainable – economically, socially, environmentally – not just in the long term, as the global population grows and demand increases, but even in the short term, as economic and climatic shocks hit home.

Horse! the unfolding drama, in other words, revealed the stark realities of modern capitalism. Shot through with irony, it was more Irish tragicomedy than good clean fun.

At the root of the scandal was an attempt to defy the rules of economics.

The products testing positive for horse were all bottom-of-the-range discount foods. With one exception, that would turn out to be notable, they were frozen foods made from frozen ingredients, not fresh meat. The beef burgers were of the kind that sell in the plain white packaging supermarkets have adopted in recent years to make the subliminal claim that this is honest-to-goodness no-frills value. The ready meals were of the frozen bargain variety. Much of the material also went to food service companies who sold it on to public institutions whose budgets were being cut and to fast-food outlets selling all-in meals for a few pounds. These are not generally the sort of things foodies or posh people buy. There was a distinct class element to horsegate.

Horse-burgers were clearly a product of our neoliberal times too. Just as the economic boom had been built on highly artificial financial derivatives and junk mortgages for those who couldn't afford them that promised nevertheless to magic money out of nothing for every player in the game, so cheap food had been built on turning junk commodity ingredients into highly profitable 'added-value' meals. So long as it was labelled, there was thought to be no great role for the regulator here. Let the buyer beware.

Seriously cheap beef burgers depended on maintaining the

illusion that you can buy meat at less than the minimum cost of production for months on end, package it up and pass it on down a long chain in which everyone adds to the cost by taking their margins, and still sell it dirt cheap to the consumer. The super-value beef burger turned out to be the art of the economically impossible. It was a con.

At the time of the scandal the raw material for a decent beef burger cost at least £3.80 per kilo (£1.73 per pound) on the wholesale markets. That was the price of beef trim of the sort that would make a burger that was 85–90 per cent lean from reasonable quality offcuts from the carcass once the most valuable cuts such as fillet and rump have been removed – the sort of burger you might make at home. You could move upmarket and use even higher-quality meat, but £3.80 per kilo was the baseline for a burger that was actually proper beef with a reasonable ratio of fat to lean. That meant that the cost price of decent mince in a quarter pounder would be about 43p, before you factored in anything for the manufacturer's and retailer's labour, energy, transport and capital costs. The frozen economy burgers of the sort that turned out to contain surprise horsemeat were selling at £1 for a pack of eight: that is about 12p per thin burger, or the equivalent of 25p per quarter pound.

The motive for substituting cheaper ingredients somewhere in the supply chain was never really in question.

The price of beef on commodity markets has been at record highs in recent times, reflecting the perfect storm of elements that make food security one of the world's most pressing but unaddressed problems.

In 2010, the Food and Agriculture Organization of the United Nations' (FAO) index of meat prices rose to a twenty-year high.

Beef prices were up again 20–30 per cent in the following two years.

Prices have been driven up by a number of converging pressures which are likely to increase rather than abate. There has been a rapid growth in demand for livestock and meat from emerging economies such as China and Latin America, as their populations become more affluent and switch to a more Westernized, animal-protein-based diet. The cost of grain has also soared in response to increased demand from a growing global population and shortages provoked by the impact of climate change. The extremes of weather from drought to flood associated with global warming have repeatedly decimated harvests in key grain-producing areas. Intensive meat production has itself ironically contributed greatly to climate change, agriculture being one of the main sources of greenhouse gas emissions and livestock being estimated to be responsible for 80 per cent of agricultural emissions.

Unlike cattle raised slowly on natural pasture, today's intensively reared animals are fattened quickly on grains – incidentally a generally inefficient way of producing food energy if you are concerned with feeding the world. Cattle reared this way consume many more calories than they produce in the form of meat because they waste most of the energy and protein value of their feed in digestion and bodily maintenance.

The rush to replace oil with biofuels, spurred on by subsidies and government mandates, has diverted vital crops to fill the tanks of cars rather than feeding people, and this has increased food prices. Globally, 15 per cent of maize production (and 40 per cent of maize grown in the USA) and 16 per cent of the production of rapeseed, soya beans, sunflower and palm oil, go to biofuels. On top of that farmers have faced enormous rises in other costs, since so much of modern agricultural inputs are dependent on fossil fuels and determined by the price of energy, from fertilizer to tractor fuel and energy for animal housing. The global recession gave a brief respite from the upward spiral of oil prices, but no one expects the energy on which our mechanized and industrialized global food system has been built post-war to become cheap again.

In a market that functioned properly, you would expect rising prices to help bring supply and demand into balance, as more farmers found it profitable to produce beef, but near-monopoly powers and subsidies have long distorted the UK and European markets. Despite high global prices, many British beef farmers were receiving negative returns in the years just before the horsemeat scandal; they were selling their animals at less than the cost of production. A typical British beef farmer rearing a steer through the three-year cycle from calf to fattened animal for slaughter was losing 26p per kilo or around £100 per cow, and that's without even accounting for the value of unpaid family labour on the farm or the value of the land. The price they were being paid had gone up, but their costs were going up faster.

In this, beef simply reflects a wider pattern. The average UK farm income had fallen by 14 per cent in real terms between 2011 and 2012. And deeply troubling for any longer-term future, the median age of farm holders was fifty-nine years.

It was not that the price of meat to consumers had not gone up – it had, and at a rate much faster than overall consumer price inflation. In fact there was a marked spike in the price of fresh meat in the UK in 2008, coinciding with the financial crisis, and further spikes each year after that. By autumn 2011 wholesale prices were nearly double what they had been in 2008.

But who was getting the benefit of those prices was not clear.

Supermarkets wield such power it is not unusual for a processor to agree to produce foods at a loss for a period as a way of winning business. These are not free markets but oligopolies, in which a handful of big chains across Europe control access to consumers, whether it be in fast-food or grocery shopping. (See Chapter 6: Apples and Bananas).

The last two to three decades have seen an extraordinary concentration in processing and manufacturing too, with repeated mergers and acquisitions leading to three or four companies dominating each main sector from milk to beef, from poultry to bread. The trend has been inexorable, an inevitable response to the concentration of retail buying power. The only way a processor can stand up to the negotiating clout of a major retailer is by wielding a similar power.

Just like other food sectors, the European beef processing

industry is dominated by a handful of players. The Irish ABP Food Group – the initials derive from Anglo-Irish Beef Processors – is one of the major players, perhaps the largest, slaughtering around 1 million cattle a year.

As a private unlimited company it does not publish accounts, so accurate market shares are not available. Its owner is the Irish beef baron and property magnate Larry Goodman, whose controversial dealings with Saddam Hussein's Iraq and key Irish ministers some twenty-five years previously had helped bring down the Irish government. That saga had been one of the great political scandals of the modern Republic's history. Today Goodman's group is estimated to have an annual turnover of around €2.5 billion and annual profits in recent years of around €80 million. It employs 2,500 people in the Republic and 8,000 in total in Britain, the Netherlands and Poland, in divisions which include pet food, rendering and byproducts, and renewable energy from fat as well as beef processing. Around 50 million Europeans are said to buy ABP products every week.

Born in the Irish border town of Dundalk, Goodman had built up his empire in the tough environment of the Troubles. It had collapsed once, its assets handed over to the banks, but he had bought it back and built it up again. The Tesco 29 per cent horse-burger had been made by a Goodman company.

Other big players in European beef processing at the time of the scandal included Dawn Meats, another Irish-based company, with an annual turnover of around €1 billion and whose business spans processing, manufacture of frozen burgers and ready meals, meat trading and dealing in hides and rendering. Its founding directors came from another big family name in Irish beef, the Queallys. Dawn Meats held the contract, worth €300 million over five years, for processing beef for McDonald's burgers in Europe.

Neither Dawn Meats nor McDonald's were implicated in the horsemeat scandal. Other businesses owned by the Queally family were, but they were entirely separate corporate entities from Dawn Meats.

The Dutch-based poultry and red meat giant Vion was also a big packer of beef at the time. It was not caught by horsegate either, but it had struggled to make money in the UK and was already in the process of divesting itself of its red meat operations there as a result. It sold them to a company that was already one of the biggest suppliers of poultry to UK supermarkets.

With this sort of concentration, if you are a farmer you have precious little leverage over who slaughters your cattle and what price they pay you.

Paradoxically this unhealthy market concentration had also left both supermarkets and processors exposed.

The big abattoirs had been under constant pressure from supermarkets to keep prices down and to produce special offers for shoppers. With food inflation taking off just as household budgets were shrinking due to the recession, the retailers were struggling to put prices up any further without sales falling. In an era of impatient capital, when returns in traditional manufacturing and retailing sectors such as food had been required to match the dizzy returns seen in the financial sector, any dent in growth was swiftly punished by shareholders.

The average duration of shareholding in UK-listed companies had fallen from about five years in the mid-1960s to about seven and a half months at the end of 2007. Senior executives' rewards are pegged to their share prices. In this climate, there had not been much room for taking the long view of investment in what was best for a business or nurturing a really sustainable food supply.

The way Tesco's financial results around the time of the horsemeat scandal were portrayed showed how great the pressure was. It was being pilloried in 2012 for its first reported fall in profits for twenty years. This 'disaster' meant Tesco managed only £1.1 billion profit in UK trading in the first half of the year.

Although the supermarkets denied it, the relentless need for growth even in deeply recessionary times inevitably fed back in to the negotiating practices of their buyers.

Processors' trade bodies were constantly complaining that their members were not being allowed by supermarkets to pass on their unavoidably increased costs. But equally supermarkets, whose own business model is so dependent on the extravagant use of energy for centralized distribution, just-in-time delivering and refrigeration, were seeing their costs rise unavoidably too. Moreover they did not have many options if they became unhappy with a processor. It would be nearly impossible to delist one of the largest of these without leaving a huge hole in supply.

Farmers have been crushed between the two forces. Despite the fact that the UK has all the natural conditions for livestock production, and that supermarkets are clear that their customers want to know that their beef is sourced not from any old commodity market trader but directly from the British Isles, the size of the national beef herd is declining.

By 2012 the total number of cattle in the UK was at its lowest for eighty years. (The UK gets about half its beef from suckler cattle herds and half from dairy herds, but the pattern has been the same in dairy farming.) Beef and veal production was 6 per cent down on the previous year. Just when maximizing production might be considered essential to our food security, we were heading in the opposite direction. This decline in the national herd was mirrored in the other main producing countries – the US herd was also at its lowest level ever.

It was in the middle of this squeeze on everything, from shoppers' wallets, farmers' incomes, processors' margins and supermarkets' profits, that the special offer economy burger found its place. The hubris shown by the powerful forces controlling our food supply was about to meet its bathetic nemesis in a patty made of horse.

The special offer frozen economy burger may look just like the economy burger on sale at a higher price the week before; its packaging will probably be the same. But that's precisely the trouble with junk foods. They rarely own up to their secrets.

In fact this special offer frozen economy burger was often made to a different specification under special contract to a supermarket. I was told by industry insiders that contracts such as these were being renegotiated as often as every six months. No surprise then that it became a race to the bottom. Rather than agreeing a contract price based on costs plus a margin for profit, the special offer economy burger was generally constructed down to a price fixed by the retail buyer.

So what was in a pack of them? I asked a key player in the business of supermarket meat to explain how the process might work. Unsurprisingly, he did not want to be identified.

Economy beef burgers, he explained, tend to have a meat content hovering around 60–65 per cent, but by law a product with that description need be only 47 per cent cow (as opposed to horse or pig or whatever bargain-basement ingredient a rogue supplier happens to have on hand). So the knock-down burger tends to have more fat and more water in its specification than the full price burger (water being the cheapest ingredient of all and nicely heavy with it). The meat itself, that 47 per cent legal minimum bit, isn't just what you and I think of as meat – that is, lean muscle meat – but is allowed to contain fat, collagen and connective tissue in the same proportions as they naturally occur in the cut being used.

So if a manufacturer wants to make a really cheap beef burger – he can't afford to run at a loss for too long, and even the powerful supermarket buyers recognize this – he can look up a cut such as beef brisket. That's on average 32 per cent fat, 19 per cent connective tissue and 3 per cent collagen. And yes, collagen is what you are thinking of, the stuff film stars inject into their faces to make them look smoother than they really are, and it's a top tool in the cheap meat industry's box. So the 'meat', which is less than half the burger already, can in fact be up to one third fat.

Manufacturers used to use desinewed meat to eke out products such as these. Desinewed meat is made up of the bits of flesh left on the bones after cutting, which are then cleaned off by water pressure. It was less of a slurry than mechanically recovered meat, and a UK speciality until the EU told British processors to get in line with other European countries and stop using it in April 2012. With this source of cheap protein gone, substitutes had to be found.

Typically, once this sort of special burger contract was in place, my industry sources told me, the manufacturing company would put out a call for bids from meat traders to supply meat at a price it had named. If meat in Ireland and the UK was too expensive, they would source elsewhere, Holland and Belgium being favoured countries to find cheap stocks.

During a promotion a manufacturer might be told by the supermarket buyer that it could add extra fat, maybe around 20 per cent extra, which is legal so long as it's declared as added fat on the label. Beef fat on average contains 6 per cent collagen. So you can whack in a bit more collagen while you are adding extra fat and help bulk your product up. The crucial thing to understand is that economy foods at rock-bottom prices such as these are a reconstruction of deconstructed parts, bought around the world from wherever is cheapest. Exchange rate fluctuations might affect where you want to buy your components from week to week. The raw materials are mostly frozen commodity goods, with a freezer life of a few years. Any cows to which they were once connected will have been pushing up the daisies a long while back.

When a meat processor is constructing this special offer product to meet a particular price, he and his supermarket buyer also know they have to hit the percentages laid down in the regulations. Factory tests checking for meat content involve a computerized measure of what's called visual lean. Public analyst tests check for protein content. The knock-down burger, with its payload of fat and water, might tend to be a little light on protein, so the manufacturer might add concentrated proteins in various forms. It makes it harder for analysts to detect products that are short on their declared ingredients. These proteins might be extracted from boiled-up bits of animal even the French wouldn't eat, such as hide or gristle and other offcuts, which are then dried and ground down to a powder that can go into a 'seasoning' or 'carrier' mix. They might alternatively be extracted from animal waste by chemical hydrolysis. The ingredients of the carrier mixes themselves do not have to be broken down on the label where they are considered 'incidental' to production. Experts suspect these protein powders are the explanation for much of the contamination of burgers with undeclared pork at low levels that was found. Or extra proteins might come from soya protein isolate.

The other handy thing about protein concentrates is that they bind in water, cutting production costs and making sure the burger doesn't shrink too dramatically when cooked. But added water tends to dilute the flavour. Added fat tends to separate out. So you need ingredients to add meaty flavour and colour to your special offer burger and to act as emulsifiers. Favourites among these for meat products are yeast extracts and barley malt. Yeast extracts are useful because they have a meaty flavour and good water-binding and emulsifying capacity. Here's a list of the benefits claimed for barley malt used in meat processing from an industrial ingredients supplier's website:

Clean label benefit *[i.e. you don't have to list anything that sounds nasty or unnatural on the label]*

Added value and cost reduction *[you can use less meat by using a cheaper bulking agent]*

Enhanced, richer, premium appearance, colour addition *[makes all that whitish fat you've added look more like proper meat]*

Seasoning carrier *[you don't have to list those other things you've put in]*

Sweetness addition *[all heavily processed foods targeting our infantilized palates must be sweet]*.

Dextrose is also often used to help create browning. It can make the burger taste too sweet but then that effect can be counteracted by a generous dose of salt or other flavourings.

The labels on bargain-basement burgers found to contain horse had a pattern to their ingredients, containing 'meat' at around 60 per cent, bulked up with 10 per cent onion, added water, added beef or pork fat, soya protein isolate, yeast/sugar extract, barley malt extract and various other spice extracts/flavourings.

Some of the same principles applied to frozen ready meals. In fact the damage-limitation PR company hired by Findus to talk away its horse crisis admitted to me, when pushed, that the meat in some of its beef lasagnes had been 100 per cent horse, but argued that since the meat was only 15 per cent of the total meal its significance was diminished. The principal ingredient by weight in the Bolognese part of its beef lasagne was water, thickened by corn starch, the flavour helped by both colouring and sugar.

Not all supermarket and fast-food beef burgers are made this way. To understand how the top end of the market worked I visited Scotbeef, one of Scotland's largest red meat manufacturers, and a fourth-generation family-owned company that processes more than 100,000 cattle a year.

It has a short chain that is the antithesis of the long globalized trails that produced the economy burger. It buys live animals directly from approved, mostly local, farmers with whom it has built up relationships over decades, and slaughters them itself. It makes burgers only from meat from its own abattoir. 'We don't trade at all. If we need more meat, we kill more animals,' its managing director, Robbie Galloway, explained.

Its burgers are made with forequarter meat and meat trim cut off its own carcasses. The family tried to set up a frozen burger line a decade ago to take advantage of a booming market but could never put in a price low enough using its own meat to win a big tender, according to Galloway.

The company had been supplying Marks and Spencer for more than fifty years and also had a McDonald's contract. The relationship between processor and its powerful customers was not always easy: 'It's like a marriage, both parties have to work hard at it, and there may be times when no one is speaking to each other, but it's a question of trust,' Galloway told me. As we watched the production line at the Bridge of Allan abattoir and packing factory, he also pointed out that 'if you steal from farmers in the prices you pay' you generally see the cost to your own business at some later point.

A continuous belt was moving animals from stunning and slaughter through evisceration, past government inspectors and on for cutting, then in to giant chill rooms for maturing. Meanwhile, carcasses from a few days earlier were shunting on again into the bright white boning hall where sixty-five specialist butchers in chainmail protective clothing and gauntlets, sheaths of knives and steels hanging from their waist, were removing the main cuts and the trim from the quarters. Other than the brutal reality of the moment of bloodletting after stunning, it was extraordinarily sanitized and clean.

About sixty cattle an hour passed through the industrial shed that was as scrubbed as an operating theatre, and where around 200 employees in their whites, 70 per cent local and 30 per cent eastern European, worked a double shift. Stainless-steel work platforms on hydraulic lifts, high-pressure water hoses and vacuums, and power-cutting tools have here taken most of the gore and much of the heavy labour out of what can be notoriously dirty, dangerous work. There was almost no smell, only the loud hum of the chilling machinery, punctuated by a regular klaxon warning that a carcass was on the move and about to come round the corner at you. Investment in safe machinery and a unionized workforce added to costs but had created decent jobs for those in the area.

A short, tightly controlled supply chain costs more than buying meat on the spot markets too. Marks and Spencer is prepared to pay because its brand trades on quality in food rather than matching the prices of discount and cheaper supermarkets; McDonald's, having suffered immense damage to its reputation over its sourcing of cattle in the McLibel trial in the 1990s, puts a premium on knowing exactly where and how its beef burgers are made.

The main protection against fraud comes from a sophisticated computer system of tagging everything from beginning to end. Since the BSE crisis, all cattle have to have passports recording their movements. A series of barcoded labels identifying the animal are attached and repeatedly scanned and cross-checked as the carcass moves through the factory, so that each cut can be traced back to a particular animal and the time it is killed.

A further process of weighing everything in and out gives a 'mass volume balance' figure that can be checked by external auditors to ensure nothing extraneous has been introduced.

It is not impossible to cheat but it would take a determined effort and sophisticated double book-keeping computer software to do so. Privately, several in the industry suspected that at least some of the horse fraud must have involved double book-keeping at some points in the chain. They had come across the practice in supply chains in developing countries where factories have been caught with one set of production records for the auditors and another set that reflects reality.

Scotbeef's burger operation is located on the outskirts of Glasgow. Sealed, tagged and barcoded meat is taken from its slaughterhouse, in vans that have also been sealed, direct to the site for further processing. The secret of a top-of-the-range burger is to handle the meat as little as possible, leaving it with the open texture achieved in a domestic kitchen rather than the heavily emulsified, toothpaste-tube texture of bargain frozen versions with their added fat. The more you mince and bind the meat and fat, the more rubbery the final product. So the meat is briefly minced, passed through an extruder and shaped into burgers, and that's it.

Well-made factory burgers like these cost up to four times what the special offer economy burgers were being sold for.

Instead, at the bottom of the range, the legalized adulteration of meat products had become the norm. Yet, despite the substitution of junk for real ingredients, the economics of the permanent clearance sale still did not add up. An analysis from data provided by the Office of National Statistics of the prices that were being charged on the high street shows why.

While fresh beef prices on the supermarket shelf had almost doubled since the crash, and risen faster than overall food inflation, frozen burger prices fell from mid-2009 until by spring 2010 they were roughly tracking food inflation. In 2011 they undercut it and were being sold at average prices that matched what they had been pre-crash.

Meat was more expensive but people had less money, so supermarkets sold them burgers for less. A large retailer can cross-subsidize loss of margin in one type of food by increasing margins on others whose prices are less well recognized and therefore less sensitive. For those further back in the process, cross-subsidy wasn't so easy.

Legal adulteration to keep the price down had gone as far as it could. Small wonder perhaps that at some point in the long supply chain of frozen blocks of raw materials being moved around Europe someone turned to fraud.

The attraction of horse as the form of this fraud, apart from its cheapness, was explained to UK MPs in a committee session by an executive from one of the Irish companies found with horsemeat on its premises.

Horses tend to have very little fat on them, and give a very high proportion of lean, especially if they have been trained for racing or have been disposed of by someone who hasn't been able to afford the cost of their feed. If you were mixing horsemeat with cheap fat from beef in a box of meat it would increase your visual lean and protein content nicely.

The opportunities for fraud in a frozen burger, however,

turned out to be far more numerous than even experts had imagined. The Goodman ABP Silvercrest factory that supplied Tesco with its 29 per cent horse beef burgers was, according to the Irish Department of Agriculture report, using 'multiple ingredients from some forty suppliers in production batches, and the mixture of ingredients could vary in every half-hour production batch'.

The consultancy and accountancy company KPMG pointed out that in fact in some forms of meat production there were hundreds of points between farmer and end consumer at which things could go wrong. 'Many companies use supply chains that revolve around a web of international partners . . . one study has shown that from conception to consumption there are more than 450 critical control points. It means that there are opportunities at almost every step of the way, such as at the abattoir, the processing plant and at the point of packaging, where checking needs to be done, not just at the end of the production line.'

Just how far adrift the industry had become is perhaps indicated by the size of the war chest Tesco had announced to bolster its red meat supply chain around the time of the horse-meat scandal. It had said it was investing £25 million to develop more direct relationships with farmers.

The Food Standards Agency (FSA) Low Income Diet and Nutrition survey records that those on low incomes eat significantly more burgers, kebabs, meat pies and meat-based ready meals than average. They also consume far less fruit, vegetables and wholemeal cereals, and so miss out on the protective effect of foods high in nutrients.

Despite the industry's claims to being the innocent victims in all this, the real victims, as with so much of today's globalized food production, have been those at the end of the chain, those on the lowest incomes who disproportionately eat these sorts of processed meats, those who most need good nutrition but are palmed off with inferior food instead: growing children who are fed them in schools, the sick and the elderly who are offered them in hospitals and care homes, students with no cooking facilities.

Industry may have reaped the whirlwind but the price is paid by us all, in the soaring health bills arising from our ever increasing rates of diet-related disease, again disproportionately suffered by those on low incomes.

In our post-crash era of austerity, it was ordinary people struggling to pay their bills who were hit hardest, just as they had been by the fallout from the financial crisis. They and their children had been fed a diet of counterfeit junk. Real beef too expensive? Let them eat horse! Horse buried in a heavy disguise of obesogenic, artery-clogging, blood-pressure-raising fat, salt and additives, bulked up with water, processed to an unidentifiable emulsion before being extruded to form what passes for food. To add insult to injury, while the rest of the chain took its profits and its executives collected their bonuses, they had been sold not just horse but knackered horse at that.

That there was a problem with a glut of unwanted horses in Ireland was known to both the UK and the Irish governments at least two years before the horsemeat scandal. Before the financial crisis Ireland had seen a boom in the breeding of thoroughbreds for racing. With stud fees reaching over £100,000 for the very best horses, it had, along with speculative property development funded by dodgy bank loans, become something of a national pastime. After the crash, with the Irish economy on its knees, there were suddenly lots of owners who could no longer afford their animals. Professional horse trainers had always been straightforwardly ruthless about disposing of foals and yearlings that looked unlikely to make the grade for racing. Now they were joined by amateurs and pet owners falling on hard times. There had been a six-fold increase in the number of horses slaughtered at government-licensed abattoirs since the recession took hold. But those were only the official Irish records.

The Ulster Society for the Prevention of Cruelty to Animals

(USPCA) had reported in 2010 that large numbers of neglected horses were being corralled to meet a demand for horsemeat from the mainland UK. Its officers saw them being collected in the dead of night and followed some of them from Northern Ireland to a slaughterhouse in England.

One of the things that leapt out later, when supermarket victims put their investigators on to the scandal, was that the locations of those companies on the Irish side of the water implicated in the supply of horsemeat were heavily concentrated around the border areas between north and south. This was territory notorious for smuggling, particularly through the era of the Troubles, when organized crime involving unlawful movement of animals, drugs and arms across the border had been inextricably linked with fundraising for paramilitaries. Animals might be moved over the border and back through the night, claiming subsidies in one territory and then in the next. No one was wanting to stir up paramilitary history, but there was a growing sense that the enforcement agencies might have known some of what was going on with meat but decided to let it play out because of bigger politics.

The horse passport system, designed to keep a check on animals and any drugs they might have been administered, was widely known to be open to abuse. In theory each horse acquires a passport at birth, and its veterinary history is written in it, so that it can only enter the human food chain once an official inspector at a slaughterhouse has checked that its record is free of certain drugs.

Most horses, and racehorses in particular, are at some point in their lives administered phenylbutazone, an anti-inflammatory drug so common it is sometimes called horse aspirin. However in humans 'bute', as it is known, can in rare cases cause a potentially life-threatening illness, aplastic anaemia, or bone marrow failure. Since it is not known what triggers the illness, it has not been possible to set any safe level for bute residues in human food. Doses from horsemeat are likely to be very low, and the government's chief medical officer stressed that any health risk to humans was also very low. Nevertheless, horses that have been treated with bute, even long previously, are banned from food.

In practice the passport system was in chaos. Some owners do not bother to register horses at all. Those that do can choose between over seventy horse passport issuing agencies. The documents can be faked with a cheap printing set. There have been so many variations on them through the years it is very hard for inspectors to be sure whether the passports they are shown are genuine or not. Once an animal has been slaughtered the passport is returned to the issuing agency, but with increasing frequency the issuers were reporting that animals that were already dead had been killed again, or that they had never issued the passport in the first place.

The USPCA had warned that thousands of horses were being given false passports and new microchips to get round the ban on veterinary drugs in the food chain. It thought around 70,000 horses in Ireland were unaccounted for.

Other animal welfare charities had also noticed that the tripartite agreement between the UK, Ireland and France, which allowed horses for breeding purposes to be moved freely between the three countries without health certificates, was being abused. World Horse Welfare, which works closely with port and other enforcement authorities, had been warning government for some time that the ease with which horses could be moved across borders had made the horse trade attractive to organized criminals who were transporting them not for breeding, as intended by the agreement, but for slaughter and were using them as cover for other illegal activities including smuggling. In fact the movement of horses of low value from Ireland to the UK mainland was taking place on such a scale that it only made economic sense, given the cost of transport, if the horses were being sent for slaughter. These were the sorts of poor horses that fetched only £5–10 as live animals at market but could be turned into £450–500 worth of meat.

A lorry full of live animals is hard to inspect at ports; tight rules to protect customs officials' safety mean it can only be done in certain circumstances. The result was that lorries were often waved through.

Aintree racecourse played host in 2011 when the relevant charities convened a meeting of officials from the UK Department of Environment, Food and Rural Affairs (Defra) and representatives from trading standards to discuss their fears. The Irish Department of Agriculture was invited to attend but did not.

In the end it was the Scottish authorities which moved in on one gang of suspects. In October 2012 they secured the conviction of loyalist horse dealer Laurence McAllister from Country Antrim and Kieran Murphy, originally from South Armagh, who were found guilty of trying to smuggle over £500,000 worth of cannabis from Scotland into Northern Ireland through Belfast port in their horse lorry. The drug haul was concealed in bags of molasses between the horse stalls. McAllister had been tracked on two occasions transporting unfit horses and donkeys, some without passports, from Northern Ireland into Scotland for disposal in the UK; cannabis was part of the return load. He was later also found guilty of animal cruelty offences and of smuggling prescription-only veterinary medicines. Some of the animals he had been shipping over were seriously ill with chest infections, wounds, sepsis and diarrhoea.

Ireland was not the only country where there was a glut of horses. The USA had indulged in its share of overbreeding, and about 100,000 American horses are slaughtered for meat every year. Since the US banned killing horses within its borders in 2006 they have been trucked to abattoirs in Mexico and Canada to be dispatched before being exported. About 70–80 per cent of horsemeat of US origin is sent to the EU, most of it arriving via Belgium, which has become a favoured conduit.

The US horse trade has been bedevilled by the same problems with falsified documents, horses sold for meat when they have been treated with drugs banned in the food chain, and weak enforcement of legislation.

Efforts to tighten up the horsemeat trade globally have been lackadaisical however. The EU stopped collecting data on the slaughter of horses in 2008 when a voluntary agreement was made that member states would gather information individually. Since then, no country has made its figures available.

As far as the UK and Irish authorities were concerned, since virtually all of the produce was exported to Continental Europe, it merited only a low priority.

So, far from sorting out the mess over passports and tightening up the registration of horses, the UK government had given up on it in 2012 when it withdrew funding for the National Equine Database, effectively closing it.

In its drive to roll back the state and cut public spending, the Conservative–Liberal Democrat coalition government had weakened regulation and enforcement elsewhere too. The rhetoric of cutting 'red tape' by removing inspection and testing went back to previous administrations – the Labour government had been keen on leaving the food industry to police itself too – but the coalition brought a new zeal to 'light touch regulation'.

In 2010 it put into action the Conservative election promise to have a bonfire of the quangos – all those government bodies that were just so much burden to business in its eyes. One of the targets was the Food Standards Agency. The FSA had been set up as a non-ministerial government department in the wake of the BSE crisis, when it was recognized that if the UK wanted a reliably safe and healthy food supply it needed a single body, independent of industry and politicians susceptible to its lobbying, to oversee all aspects of food quality and authenticity. But the FSA had been rather too successful in many ways, particularly in naming and shaming the food industry over excessive salt, fat and sugar in its products, and in pressing for traffic light labelling on processed foods which would be easy for consumers to understand. A powerful lobby group against the labelling scheme, led by Tesco and Kellogg's, had helped persuade the

Conservatives that the agency was getting in the way of business interests and should be eviscerated. Ideologically, its action on public health was no longer in favour either. To the Tory mind, eating well was a matter of individual choice and personal responsibility and no business of the state. The FSA's remit over nutrition and the quality of food was taken away and given to the Department of Health. Policy on labelling and the composition of food was taken off to Defra. The FSA was left in charge of food safety. When horsemeat hit, thanks to this neoliberal thinking, there was a real muddle about who had responsibility for what.

Cuts had taken their toll elsewhere. Licensed slaughterhouses across Europe are required to have an official vet in attendance when slaughtering takes place – in the UK most of these vets used to be directly employed by the government, but many are now supplied under contract to the FSA by a private company. The majority of factory vets are highly skilled migrant workers, British trained vets generally preferring not to practice their animal skills in the killing context. These vets can be put under intense pressure by abattoir managers, when stopping a production line even for a few minutes can cost thousands of pounds.

Plants over a certain size are also required to have a meat hygiene inspector. But a trend to deregulate and leave industry to police itself had seen numbers of inspectors fall from 1,700 at the height of the BSE crisis to around 800 in 2013. Smaller cutting plants of the sort where much of the horse must have been chopped up and the cold stores through which it must have passed are no longer subject to daily inspection either.

Enforcement of labelling and checks to see that supermarkets and food outlets are actually selling what they claim to be selling largely fall to individual local authorities and their trading standards officers. The FSA did not even have the powers to force industry to test for horse or reveal its results. Other than a small testing programme of its own, it depended on companies alerting it voluntarily. Local authority budgets had been slashed too. There had been 743 jobs losses in trading standards at council level between 2009 and 2012.

Horsemeat was a fraud waiting to go undetected.

With hindsight, it was clear that there had been abundant raw material available for large-scale adulteration of the food chain with horse. But finding the route by which the wrong species had trotted in proved an intractable task.

Ministers in the UK and Ireland declared quite early on in the scandal that the adulteration had been Europe-wide and probably at some points in the plot involved organized international criminal networks. The European law enforcers Europol were called upon to investigate. The City of London police fraud unit, more used to tracking crime through webs of corporate structures and false accounting, was given the task of unpicking the UK connections. Experts in the meat trade told me that the way the scandal developed, with reported outbreaks of horse spreading rapidly across borders like a contagion that had taken hold long before it was diagnosed, suggested criminal elements involved were interconnected in some way, using the same methods of operating, either co-operating with each other or working in parallel having carved out overlapping turfs. Part of the difficulty was pinning down the crime itself. There was nothing wrong with selling horsemeat, only with failing to declare it or passing it off as something else. So it was not just a question of establishing who had owned and sold what to whom, but who had labelled it and as what. Since most of the horse had already bolted and been consumed, the task was doubly difficult. The impossibility of policing such global and complex networks began to dawn.

It was when I was chasing some of these undeclared links in the chain that a few pieces fell into place unexpectedly.

Activists from an animal sanctuary sent me information on lorry movements from one of the UK's main horse abattoirs in Cheshire to the Continent.

The Red Lion slaughterhouse had already achieved a certain prominence before the horsemeat scandal broke. The animal sanctuary Hillside had planted hidden cameras in key parts of the abattoir and recorded three of its Polish slaughtermen apparently abusing horses and breaking the rules as they killed them. Animal rights campaigners had organized protests outside the abattoir.

The FSA had suspended the slaughtermen's licences when shown the footage and was carrying out further investigations, with a view to prosecuting, which were not complete at the time of the horsemeat scandal. Local sources had also told me that these Polish workers were living in caravans next to the site in very poor conditions themselves. The company told me it was carrying out its own investigation into the welfare abuses, but said the living conditions of workers were none of its responsibility since employees organized their own accommodation.

I knew too that the Northern Irish horse dealer convicted of animal cruelty and cannabis smuggling, McAllister, had been followed making his deliveries to England. Sources engaged in enforcement told me they had evidence that Red Lion was the final destination of some of his loads. A man claiming to be part of a criminal gang operating in Northern Ireland had also told the BBC that he had delivered horses with forged papers to the abattoir on several occasions.

The Turner family who owned it denied ever knowingly receiving deliveries from McAllister and said it had never knowingly taken in or slaughtered horses that were unfit or had forged passports.

In fact I discovered that the abattoir had been on the FSA's radar for some time. Horses passing through it had tested positive for the banned drug bute, which meant that some slaughtered animals had had false or inaccurate passports. Chasing the horses after they had gone had been a bit of a run-around for the authorities. At the time, tests for bute on slaughtered horses were taking three weeks. One horse that came back positive had been purchased by two premises nearby in the UK for personal consumption, according to the abattoir. But when officials went looking for one part of the bute carcass, said to have been returned to a Lancashire farmer for his own hotpot, it was nowhere to be found. Others had been exported and eaten abroad before the alert has been raised.

The abattoir felt it was being made a scapegoat by the authorities. Its lawyer, who unusually had also been the official vet at the site in previous years, said that every horse entering the plant was minutely scrutinized by FSA veterinary staff, and only passed for slaughter once they were satisfied its passport was genuine and it was fit for consumption. Shortly after this, the FSA ordered the plant to halt killing on the grounds that its premises had failed to meet all the required standards. It continued to buy horses for slaughter, sending them instead to another abattoir whose owner had been arrested early in the horsemeat scandal but allowed to resume trade, and brought them back to Red Lion to debone and cut them before export. The company that owned Red Lion, High Peak Meat Exports Ltd., was later charged with seven offences under the food and hygiene regulations. The FSA allegations were that it had allowed the meat of three horses to be put on the market when it was unsafe, had failed to provide information to trace a horse and had failed to comply with detention notices relating to three horses. High Peak Meat Exports' solicitor said the allegations covered nothing other than technical issues at the plant and it was confident it could defend them.

The animal sanctuary's footage showed the family's refrigerated lorries being loaded at night and setting off for the Continent. I combed through the tracking data from the previous year and checked the places they stopped. I then went to visit the key addresses. The trail led through the port of Harwich to Holland and a meat cutting plant in the city of Oss, south of Rotterdam. Oss is near the main trans-European network of motorways that have made this part of the Netherlands the principal corridor for industrial food production and trading. With its easy container ship access, and government support for innovations in hi-tech processing, the Low Countries have become something of a hub for the adulteration of meat, legal and otherwise. I recognized the Oss address. It was a factory owned by Willy Selten, a Dutch meat processor who had been ordered by his authorities to recall 50,000 tonnes of meat distributed in the previous two years to more than 500 companies across Europe, including eight in the UK and one in Ireland, because he was unable to show records of its origin.

The Turners had been making deliveries of horse carcasses to Selten. They said that all the horses they had sold him had been correctly labelled as horse and were legal, although they acknowledged that one had been subject to a recall having tested positive for bute.

With the help of a Dutch meat union official I arranged to talk to one of the eighty-five Polish migrant workers who had been paid to cut up the horse at Selten's factory. Jan (not his real name) was nervous, as were most of his fellow workers. They had suspected some of their work might have been unlawful, although they were fully entitled to work in the EU. As migrants whose jobs and accommodation depended entirely on the boss, they had not felt free to report irregularities.

'Everything passed through my hands: beef, horse, old meat that stank, sometimes even "fresh" meat but it wasn't exactly fresh . . . Yes, I cut horse. I suspected there was something wrong but I just did what I was told to do,' Jan told me.

He and the others explained through their union representative, Michiel Al, how the laundering had allegedly taken place. Horsemeat was processed at the end of the day, after the normal shift had finished and the plant had been cleaned. Workers were then tasked with cutting the horse deliveries and mixing them with beef, some of it defrosted from consignments with labels as old as 2001. They had to cut out 'green' putrid beef, which smelled so bad that they could keep working only by tying towels around their faces. They also described having to endure brutally tough working conditions and filthy, overcrowded accommodation.

The mixing and repacking of horse had gone on for at least five years at the Selten plant, they claimed, and Jan told me he had been involved in cutting up horsemeat there himself for two and a half years. The horse trucks would come from England and Germany each week, and for every ten to fifteen parts of beef about four of horsemeat would be mixed in.

'The worst meat was always processed in overtime or on Saturdays, not on the normal shift. We'd do it to earn a bit extra. Overtime was paid in cash in envelopes,' he said.

The meat would then be repacked and relabelled, some of it as organic beef, according to his friends.

Jan and the others were employed on unlawful zero-hours contracts and paid about €500 a month less than the minimum required by Dutch regulations for the meat sector, according to Al. The Polish men described regular accidents at the factory in which workers were seriously injured by butchering knives. They alleged that a Dutch worker would treat injuries in the canteen but that the company made no effort to take employees to hospital when necessary, leaving this to their Polish colleagues.

As with so much work in today's food production around the world, the jobs they described were not secure, steady ones in reasonable conditions, but depended on the economics of the black market and illegality. Changing shifts, cash in hand, exposure to danger, these were the terms of employment that had allegedly replaced and undercut the hard won rights of the locally employed workforce.

The Poles were housed by Selten in mobile homes on a campsite or in a rented farmhouse in the village of Nistelrode, where the Dutch businessman has his own fine farmhouse home surrounded by fields of horses.

When the factory was raided as part of the horsemeat investigation, the Polish workers suddenly found themselves without a job and without money, although they were still required to pay rent. At that point, fifty of them had joined the union, which had been supporting them since.

Al said conditions were very poor and overcrowded when he visited the Poles in their accommodation. Six to eight workers slept in bunk beds in each mobile home. At the farmhouse, walls were brown with grime and the floor was crammed with mattresses. Jan told me there were up to thirty workers living in the four-bedroomed house and in a neighbouring property. This had been another consistent feature of today's food sector employment. Ordering 'just in time', so that you do not have to tie up money and space in holding stock, is highly efficient for the big retailers, but it has created a need for a highly mobile pool of labour to turn on and off without notice to meet constantly fluctuating demand, and this casual labour has to be accommodated somewhere. The need is met by migrant workers, desperate enough to take it, most often found living in squalor in rural areas, fuelling the resentments of the local population.

When I visited the landlord, a former pig farmer who had been unable to make money from farming and had turned to the more lucrative business of real estate instead, he said he thought there were twelve tenants per house and blamed the Polish men themselves for the overcrowding, for not being clean and for chain-smoking and drinking beer. He also thought Selten was being made a scapegoat unfairly – everyone was at it, passing off horse as beef. Selten had just been unlucky and got caught, he claimed.

Selten's lawyer rejected several of the workers' allegations when I put them to him. Horse had been mixed with beef to meet specific orders but only for ten months and it had never been relabelled as beef, he claimed. Where meat was old it was being recycled for pet food, he said, adding that workers were paid the legal minimum wage and wanted the flexibility of zero-hours contracts and cash for overtime.

He admitted that small injuries were treated in the canteen

but in serious cases workers went to the doctor with a colleague. The Polish workers were responsible themselves for cleaning their accommodation and 'some had stayed for years without complaint'. In fact, all the workers were invited and came to family and company parties. 'The atmosphere was top!' he told me.

Shortly after my visit, Willy Selten was arrested and questioned on suspicion of false accounting and fraud. The prosecutor's office said that the business had allegedly received 300 tonnes of horsemeat from England, Ireland and the Netherlands in 2011 and 2012 but its accounts only recorded beef. Tests on more than 150 samples of meat labelled as beef taken from the factory by the Dutch Food Safety Authority had found horse DNA in 21 per cent of them.

Selten delivered to supermarkets, meat processing factories and butchers throughout Europe. The Dutch, UK and Irish authorities declined to say more precisely who they were. How much they knew about what they were handling was almost impossible to establish.

Horse had been turned into beef by some miracle of transubstantiation, it seemed. But for advances in science and DNA testing, the miracle would probably still be going on.

The scandal had burst into the open in the middle of January 2013 when the FSAI published the results of tests it had commissioned towards the end of the previous year on samples of beef burgers and ready meals being sold in leading supermarkets in the Republic. It had found undeclared horse DNA in over a third of the beef burger samples and pig DNA in 85 per cent of them. Tesco's frozen Everyday Value burgers were top of the league with their 29 per cent horse content. The majority of the beef ready meals, from cottage pie to curries and lasagne, also contained undeclared pig but not horse, although that picture was to change later as more tests were carried out.

Until then, as far as anyone knew, enforcement bodies and supermarkets had not tested for horse in beef products, because it had apparently not occurred to them it might be there, although they did know quite a bit about how pork was infiltrated into meats of other species (see Chapter 2: Chicken).

This stunning news of industrial-scale, illegal adulteration of the food supply sparked the largest regime of food testing in recent times. Everyone professed themselves shocked and very sorry that they had let customers down unwittingly. They all said they had had no idea that they were selling horse.

The beef burgers, sold in branches of big name European supermarkets Tesco, Lidl, Aldi, Iceland and Dunnes Stores, had been manufactured in one of three factories, two in Ireland – Silvercrest Foods in County Monaghan, and Liffey Meats in County Cavan – and one in the UK – Dalepak in North Yorkshire. Both Silvercrest and Dalepak were part of Larry Goodman's ABP group. The adulteration that had taken place within his group of factories was on such a significant scale, and his businesses were so much at the heart European processing, that it could not be brushed off easily with an apology that the adulteration was unwitting.

Liffey Meats was owned by another Irish beef family of long standing, the Mallons, also on the country's rich list.

These were not bit players but key figures in the industry.

Moreover the factories involved supplied not just those retailers whose products had been caught already by the Irish authorities' tests, but almost all the leading UK supermarkets. The concentration in the processing sector meant they were all sourcing from the same small pool. Those not already named could not be confident that they would not be drawn in.

Goodman's Dalepak factory in Yorkshire not only made burgers for Iceland, which had already been found to contain traces of horse, but also made minced meat products for Waitrose, Sainsbury's and Asda. The Silvercrest factory produced for the Co-op and Burger King as well as Tesco.

Of these companies, only Sainsbury's escaped unscathed.

Waitrose tests on beef products gave it the all clear on horse but its beef meatballs, made by another Goodman factory in Scotland, turned out to be up to 30 per cent undeclared pork.

Co-op beef burgers from Silvercrest tested as nearly a fifth horse. Burger King's offerings from the same plant were found to contain horse at trace levels too.

Much later, as companies worked through a great queue of sampling on products that had been withdrawn as a precaution from the beginning, Asda frozen mince from the Goodman Dalepak site in Yorkshire tested as 29 per cent horse as well.

Other products made elsewhere were implicated too: Tesco's meatloaf, for example, made by Eurostock, a Northern Irish company in County Down. Eurostock had fought previous legal battles with the Northern Ireland Department of Agriculture, and then the Food Standards Agency, which tried to stop it processing beef heads under rules about BSE risk material. Eurostock took the agency to judicial review, arguing that since the heads were imported from Ireland, UK BSE rules did not apply. The long-running case was settled in a confidential agreement. Eurostock said it was shocked at finding horse in its supply chain and welcomed the investigations.

Once retailers and big brand manufacturers started testing all their beef lines, their European supply chains were drawn in. More and more companies had to admit that horse had passed through their hands. Ikea, Nestlé, Findus, Bird's Eye, Carrefour, Monoprix, Auchan, Taco Bell, their manufacturing subcontractors and more joined the ranks of the embarrassed.

The global food chain was both so extenuated and so interconnected that a horse-burger in a little known county in Ireland could send shockwaves to the furthest corners of Europe.

But it was hard to pin down what had gone wrong and where.

Liffey simply said the contamination of beef burgers at its plant had been at very low levels and that it had traced the source to imported ingredients which would be replaced.

It was not the first time the company had been caught up in controversy. Established by the Mallon family, its founding and current director Frank Mallon had been convicted in 1996 as a farmer for possessing and administering banned hormones to cattle. The company had also had battles with the Irish Department of Agriculture, including one that had led to suspension of work at a factory over irregularities in 1993.

That was the past though, and the Department of Agriculture concluded that since the equine DNA found in the original tests had only been at very low levels and no subsequent tests had found horse, there was no need to investigate Liffey further.

ABP admitted that its Silvercrest factory had strayed from its contracts and used meat from suppliers who had not been approved by its supermarket and fast-food customers. It blamed rogue managers at the one plant operating without the knowledge of headquarters for this, and insisted that no one at the company had knowingly processed horse.

Information about how the chain of supply further down the line fitted together was tightly controlled and emerged only bit by bit. Industry was reluctant to identify other parties, partly for fear of being sued and partly to contain the damage; the authorities were also fearful of being sued and concerned to avoid prejudicing any future prosecutions.

ABP at first pointed the finger to Continental suppliers of raw materials, believed to be in Spain and the Netherlands, for introducing horsemeat to its factories but gradually the focus shifted to meat said to be Polish.

ABP said it had bought meat of Polish origin, which it believed was the source of the adulteration, from an Irish trader, Martin McAdam, based nearby in the border area of County Monaghan. McAdam imported meat and ran a fleet of refrigerated lorries to distribute it. He, like ABP, insisted he had no idea he had ever handled horse. However neither ABP nor McAdam could agree what volume of meat had been ordered and delivered between them and neither had any idea horsemeat was involved. Later McAdam lodged a claim in the High Court in Dublin against ABP for defamation, which ABP said it would fight.

Then McAdam was named in connection with another consignment that turned out to be 80 per cent horse.

This meat had been detained by chance at a cold store owned by a supermarket burger manufacturing company called Freeza Meats on the other side of the border in Northern Ireland a few months previously. A UK local authority environmental health officer had visited the Newry-based factory on a routine inspection and been suspicious: according to the head of the FSA in Northern Ireland some of the boxes of meat in the consignment had no labels at all; some had 'Polish' labels but they didn't seem right; and it wasn't clear from the accompanying documents who owned the meat or where it was going. Freeza Meats said this was a consignment it had just been looking after briefly 'as a goodwill gesture' for McAdam. It had no idea it was giving a home to horse. The frozen meat had ended up in limbo in the Freeza Meats cold store because it had been rejected by another meat processor, Rangeland – not because it was horse, it had no idea about that, but because it was the wrong size for its machines. When the UK authorities checked the 'Polish' labels on this meat with their increasingly indignant Polish counterparts they said they were fake. When they defrosted it, some of the meat turned out to be Irish horse, stamped with Irish abattoir labels. McAdam said he had bought meat, which he thought was beef, from a UK trader with the helpful name of Flexi Foods, but said he hadn't even set eyes on it, trade in frozen blocks being by and large an electronic affair, and he'd paid beef prices so he couldn't have known it was horse. Flexi Foods was raided; it said it had no idea it had handled horse but was co-operating with enforcement agencies.

Rangeland was based in the Irish border area of County Monaghan too, not far from Goodman's Silvercrest factory. It admitted that it had found horse DNA at levels of 75 per cent in another batch of meat it said it had bought from McAdam for manufacturing that had been labelled once again as frozen beef trimmings of 'Polish' origin. This load had not been used, it said, although it had had no idea it contained horse. But then shortly afterwards, it admitted that it had found between 5 per cent and 30 per cent horse in frozen burgers it had sent to UK caterers and wholesalers. It had had no idea those products contained horse either.

According to the Irish Department of Agriculture, Rangeland had rejected a consignment of frozen meat that had been sourced by another UK-based trading company. In the UK parliament this trader had been identified as Norwest Foods of Cheshire, and Norwest was said to have been returning it to the Netherlands to Willy Selten, the factory owner arrested on suspicion of laundering horse with beef, whose workers I had interviewed. Norwest declined to comment on whether it had had any idea it had handled horse. Norwest had on separate occasions supplied ABP with meat from Selten, according to ABP. The Irish Department of Agriculture said it was McAdam who had sourced this load, rejected by Rangeland from the UK company. No I didn't, said he. And we never dealt with Rangeland, said Norwest.

And this was the pattern. Like a tense game of pass the parcel, responsibility for consignments involving huge frozen blocks of meat seemed to be handed round and round, with layers of labels and wrapping and documents that hid a surprise inside, but no one was quite able to say who had had what, nor who had handled any fake papers around it, when the music stopped. The authorities were only allowed to rip open a share of the parcel while it was in their hands on their territory. If the layers of paper still covered what was in the middle, too bad, it had to be passed on to the next jurisdiction; it was no longer their turn.

Hoping to draw a line under the scandal, ABP suspended and later sacked the rogue Silvercrest managers, and sold the plant and its burger production to another Irish beef processing company.

The source of 'Polish' meat at ABP's Yorkshire factory that turned out to be horse had not been fully explained.

Media headlines died down; the political steam had evaporated from the crisis.

But UK retailers and manufacturers were increasingly concerned that the full truth would never be known. They feared that if no one got to the bottom of how the fraud had worked in the British and Irish part of the chain, malpractice might go to ground for as long as the spotlight was on the industry, only to mutate and re-emerge again later in some new form.

They were frustrated too at the speed with which things were progressing compared to the investigations on the Continent. The French authorities seemed to have been able to unravel their part of the plot very rapidly and publicly. The French consumer minister was remarkably forthcoming, in fact. Legitimately processed Romanian horse had ended up as 'beef' in manufacturing in northern France thanks to the Cypriot-registered Dutch-owned Draap company, which had been responsible for the trading, but it was the southern French meat processing company Spanghero which had applied the beef labels to around 750 tonnes of horsemeat, sending it on to be used in 4.5 million ready meals sold in thirteen countries. Spanghero had made more than €500,000 (£430,000) profit from it.

By contrast, four months on in the UK and Ireland and the way through the horsemeat morass seemed as clear as a path through a peat bog.

I was being told by sources in UK enforcement that where supply chains crossed jurisdictions they were not getting enough co-operation. Industry victims reported that their own efforts to find out where their meat had come from were being frustrated beyond the immediate suppliers with whom they had legal contracts. Officials and meat buyers hoping for a full flow of information on how the supply chains connected were meeting what they described as 'an Irish wall of silence'.

The Irish government vigorously disputed this account of its activities. A spokesman for the Department of Agriculture, Food and the Marine (DAFM) told me it had conducted a comprehensive investigation with its own special unit and the police and had passed information about traders and other intermediaries in the supply chain outside its jurisdiction to Europol and other EU states in a fully transparent manner. It was, after all, the Irish who had blown the whistle on a pan-European scandal, it pointed out. Its investigation had concluded that the adulteration of beef with horse and any mislabelling of products had not taken place within the borders of the Republic.

The place many of these tensions were played out in public was the UK parliament's Environment, Food and Rural Affairs Committee (Efra). MPs called a series of witnesses before them in an attempt to unpack the parcel of horse.

One of the first to appear was the head of the Irish Food Safety Authority, the lotto-winning Tesco-horse-burger-exposing Professor Reilly.

It was widely believed by industry that he must have been acting on a tip-off about serious irregularities in the Irish beef sector when he commissioned his original tests. The British secretary of state for environment and food, Owen Paterson, said as much in his account to the UK parliament at the beginning of the crisis, and told MPs he in turn had heard as much from his Irish counterpart, the minister for agriculture Simon Coveney. But Irish officials subsequently denied there had been any intelligence or that Coveney had said there was. Reilly had also commissioned DNA tests for horse using new methods that, while cutting edge and generally considered reliable, were not formally accredited. These were methods able to detect DNA of the wrong species at exceptionally low levels. Even if horse was not being processed at the time the samples taken were being manufactured, but had passed through a factory in a batch before, it would be picked up in traces. It looked to outsiders as though the authorities had been determined to spread the net as far as possible and had known just where to look.

This impression, that something was known but had been kept quiet, was strengthened by the news two months into the investigation that a further Irish company, QK Meats, with cold stores in a small town called Naas in County Kildare, had belatedly admitted that it had tested some consignments of 'Polish-labelled beef trimmings' the previous year and found several contained horse DNA. It had known about horse in its supply chain since June 2012 and yet had not thought to report it, even when tests in October, November and December 2012 found horse again. QK is part of the Arrow Group, controlled by the Queally family, who are also directors of another beef processing company within the group, Dawn Fresh Foods. (The same Queallys are directors of Dawn Meats, the company that had the contract to supply McDonald's, but that is an entirely separate entity and did not source any of its meat from QK.) The dramatis personae were beginning to look like a Who's Who of the Irish beef plutocracy.

QK was named by Birds Eye as the source of adulteration of its beef ready meals. Dawn Fresh Foods' UK operation, which also received its meat from QK, was found to have supplied horse in pies to Lancashire schools. In fact, QK said it had mixed 'Polish-labelled' raw materials with other ingredients at a rate of between 10 per cent and 40 per cent when processing frozen minced meat for a range of customers in six countries as well as for its own manufacturing subsidiary.

Why was it testing for horse in the first place? It would only say there had been mumblings in the trade about some raw material with Polish labels being suspect. It did not test deliveries from all of its nineteen different suppliers of Polish meat, however, only those coming from nine of them.

If QK had heard mumblings about horse, what had the FSAI known? Why did it test for horse specifically, and not dog, say, or zebra or seagull?

A key member of the Efra committee, Labour MP Barry Gardiner, who had been a former minister in both the UK agriculture and Northern Ireland departments, had a theory. It was backed up by notes of conversations between the Irish food safety chief and his English counterpart in London, in which Professor Reilly had said that his minister's agenda was to protect the Irish beef industry.

The beef sector is one of Ireland's largest industries, worth nearly €2 billion in 2012. It employs almost 100,000 farm families and 8,000 workers in processing. The transition from an economy based on primary agriculture exporting live animals – and people alongside them as emigrants to the UK – to a more industrialized economy exporting added-value meat, with the creation of factory jobs in processing, had been a key part of the development of Ireland through the previous decades. Irish governments had supported it both with policy decisions and with hard cash in development grants to the big beef companies. Irish beef processing was intimately tied up with Irish nationalism. Upsetting its power base would have considerable economic and political effects.

Gardiner put it to Professor Reilly that his random tests for horse in beef burgers were anything but random. He had used a test method he knew had not been accredited and therefore could not be used in court in any subsequent prosecutions. He tested to such a low level of sensitivity that he would catch even the smallest traces of horse. In other words, the tests were a warning shot to the Irish beef industry, Gardiner maintained during the committee session. It was known that funny stuff was going on with horse. 'You wanted them to clean up their act, but you didn't want to destroy the Irish industry in the process, and your minister would have been furious with you if you had. So you developed a way of managing to square the circle,' he suggested.

'That's a fantastic theory,' Reilly replied in his soft Irish burr, 'but it's not true.'

The committee wanted to hear too from the companies which had handled and processed horse.

When you peeled back through company accounts, directors, incorporation dates, shareholders and addresses, it turned out that many of the businesses being named had historic connections with each other. Past history was no evidence of current malpractice, but it did at the very least raise questions that needed to be asked. Efra called on some of the cast to give evidence. It was an invitation several felt able to refuse.

The bells had begun to ring with two of the principal characters at Freeza Meats, the Northern Ireland company on whose premises a large consignment of frozen horse had been found, and with the Irish beef processor called Rangeland, which had also found horse in its supplies.

Freeza Meats' founding director was Eamon Mackle. The man listed as its sales and marketing director at the time of the first horse DNA test results was Jim Fairbairn. These two had been identified in a major Irish public inquiry into allegations of serious illegality in the beef industry in the 1980s, specifically at Goodman companies, and in efforts to cover them up. The inquiry, known as the Beef Tribunal, had sat for three years and reported in 1994.

The evidence it uncovered was a huge political scandal in the Republic at the time. It had been set up to investigate allegations made in the Irish parliament and a *World in Action* television documentary in 1991 that Goodman's companies had committed a number of frauds to claim European subsidies that had involved faking documents, cheating customs officials, having their own bogus official stamps made to misclassify carcasses illegally, including stamps of other countries, passing off inferior beef trimmings as higher grade meat and falsifying weights on meat boxes. In addition the Goodman group was alleged to have practiced institutionalized tax evasion through the use of fake invoices and tried to cover it up when it was exposed. The inquiry was also charged with investigating whether Goodman, who was a donor to the political parties, had been improperly favoured by the Irish prime minister Charles Haughey, the then industry minister and later prime minister Albert Reynolds, and the EC agriculture commissioner, a former Irish agriculture minister, Ray MacSharry. Many, although not all, of the allegations of wrongdoing were substantiated in the final report. The Irish Department of Agriculture was exposed for being at best incompetent in failing to prevent fraud. Although Goodman was shown to have extraordinary access to government at the very top, he and ministers were exonerated of impropriety in their dealings, with one notable exception. When a package of around £30 million in state grants to the Goodman group to help expand its business was being negotiated, the government had 'wrongfully and in excess of its powers' directed the Irish Industrial Development Agency to drop clauses which tied the payments to job creation. Apart from that the judge found that Goodman had access almost at will to ministers because his beef company was so important to the Irish economy – it accounted for approximately 4 per cent of Ireland's GDP – and supporting it was seen as being in the national interest.

The tribunal's report had been a 1,400-page rambling affair printed without summary or index, with conclusions on individual allegations threaded through pages and pages of detail. When the horsemeat scandal blew up, it was hard to find and even harder to penetrate, as I can vouch having ploughed through it all.

But those who did read it found a detailed account of the former roles of Mackle and Fairbairn. Fairbairn was a senior executive in Goodman's Anglo-Irish Beef Processors' (AIBP, as it was then known) international division in the 1980s. Mackle, a Dundalk-born man like Goodman himself, had been running a couple of AIBP's factory boning halls under a contract.

Throughout this period the European Common Agriculture Policy was providing subsidies to keep beef prices artificially high within the community by taking surplus beef off the market and into intervention stores. As leading European beef processors, Goodman's companies were entitled to claim many millions of pounds in these subsidies and make their contribution to the beef mountain. Beef of the required grade would be

boxed and placed under the control of customs in approved cold
stores and then EC subsidies and export refunds were paid out
to the company for it.

Mackle had been named in the tribunal in connection with
fraudulent claims for these subsidies at one Goodman factory in
Waterford in the late 1980s while he was managing its boning
hall. The weights on boxes of meat for which the subsidies were
claimed had been consistently inflated and cheap trimmings had
been substituted for the proper grade of beef. When the fraud
was uncovered by customs officials a gang of men, known to
other employees as 'the A-Team', who worked under Fairbairn's
division and were sent as a sort of flying squad to repack and
re-label meat when needed, were alleged to have been dispatched to try to cover up the fraud.

A witness to the tribunal claimed that Fairbairn was involved
in concocting a panic plan to take boxed beef of the right weight
and grade from another AIBP factory in Cahir, Tipperary, and
swap it overnight for the dodgy boxes in the Waterford cold
store. A detailed map of the chill rooms and where pallets were
stacked, together with details of the official veterinary seals they
needed to match, was produced. The witness described, in a nar-
rative that was not without comic touches, how the A-Team had
come with the substitute load in lorries but had parked up at the
pub nearby because officials were still in the cold store. Fairbairn
denied that any of this plan had been conceived let alone exe-
cuted, but the judge ruled that he was lying and it had been
drawn up.

AIBP said that Mackle as the subcontractor was to blame, and
that it hadn't checked his work, alleging the changes had been
made without its knowledge. Mackle and Goodman's business
parted company and Mackle went off to pursue his own meat
trade interests.

Another incident detailed in the tribunal stood out for the
almost comic cheek of the cat and mouse game played with
government officials by executives of Eirfreeze, another Good-

man company cold store in Dublin Harbour, and the A-Team drafted in to work there secretly on a night job re-labelling meat. The officials, having been repeatedly fobbed off and told either that work had finished, was happening next door, or not all, came back unannounced and eventually caught the team applying bogus stamps to a consignment of beef that had been sent over the border from the north to be repacked for shipping to Morocco. Even though the ink from the stamps was still wet, the AIBP manager tried to deny that new ones had been applied.

The tribunal noted several instances in which Goodman companies had commissioned fake official stamps to apply to consignments of meat, for which it said there could be no innocent explanation.

The tribunal also judged that there was clear and deliberate policy by management at another plant to misappropriate tonnes of intervention beef, property of the Department of Agriculture, and sell it on to supermarkets over a long period.

Goodman maintained he had not known of these illegal activities, and the tribunal said it had not found evidence that he had, nor that they were institutionalized across his businesses.

The Efra committee looking at horse adulteration knew of the Goodman group's record and wanted to ask questions. Labour MP Barry Gardiner quizzed ABP's current chief executive Paul Finnerty: had Mackle and Fairbairn engaged recently in similar activity to that of the 1980s, repacking and re-labelling what turned out to be horse at Freeza Meats? Was the A-Team back at work? Finnerty said he had no knowledge of the A-Team, and objected that it was unreasonable to go back over twenty-five years.

Goodman also had a record of being the secret beneficial owner of meat companies which appeared to be separate entities. The true ownership of some companies had only emerged during proceedings to salvage the Goodman group when it faced bankruptcy. Goodman was a key exporter of beef to Iraq to feed Saddam Hussein's army in the 1980s. The Irish government ran a system of export credit insurance, of which Goodman's group was the main beneficiary, to cover the risk of Saddam defaulting on payments. But in the late 1980s officials recommended that the insurance was becoming too risky to provide. Goodman lobbied hard for it to continue and Albert Reynolds decided, against all the professional advice the Fianna Fail-led government had been given, that it would maintain the insurance cover. Moreover its ceiling would be more than doubled. If Saddam failed to pay, Irish taxpayers would be exposed to millions in payments. Coalition partners later cancelled the insurance in 1989 when it became clear it was underwriting not new production of Irish beef but old meat Goodman was taking from the EC beef mountain and other countries. When Iraq invaded Kuwait and sanctions were imposed, Saddam did default on what he owed. The Goodman group, which already had huge debts to the banks, was left severely exposed and close to collapse. Its business was seen as so key to the economy that the Irish parliament was recalled from its summer break to rush through emergency legislation amending company law, which gave Goodman protection from his creditors. The group went in to examinership rather than bankruptcy.

During the examinership into Goodman companies, it emerged that Goodman secretly owned other meat interests. One of his assets back then was listed as Rangeland Meats, in which he had a substantial hidden shareholding through a nominee company in Liechtenstein.

A director of Rangeland had appeared before the Beef Tribunal to explain how Rangeland had boxed meat for Goodman's Iraqi contracts and to testify that although the Iraqis had not been sent fresh halal beef, as specified in their contracts, they had known this was the case.

Although entirely separate companies today, Efra committee member Barry Gardiner wanted to check whether there was still any hidden link between Goodman and Rangeland. Did

Goodman currently hold any undeclared interests in Rangeland? No, ABP's Finnerty said.

Gardiner also wanted to know whether anyone was doing the sort of risk analysis that involved examining the corporate structures and beneficial ownerships of other companies that were part of the official horsemeat investigation. For example, he said in another committee session, the owners of Norwest, which had supplied ABP with meat from Selten, included Ray Mac-Sharry Jnr, son of the former Irish agriculture minister of the same name. Ray MacSharry Jnr had worked for Goodman's AIBP during the period investigated by the Beef Tribunal, and then left at the end of 1992. He continued to work in the meat processing industry and set up his own meat businesses. His interests in Norwest were held through a network of Irish companies. Did Goodman have any stake in Norwest? Gardiner had asked the ABP boss. No again, Finnerty replied, denying any connection for the third time.

Gardiner was persistent. Goodman had worked in the past through a hidden group of companies known as the Cork companies in which his interests were held via nominees in various tax haven jurisdictions including Liechtenstein. Were they still in existence, or if the Cork network had gone, was it replaced by any similar structure that held secret shares in meat processing companies?

No, Finnerty replied, all ABP business was done through ABP. ABP later reiterated that the Cork investment companies no longer existed and that ABP had no investments or corporate relations of any sort with any of the other companies caught up in the horsemeat saga.

At another session of the committee it was the turn of UK agriculture minister David Heath to be quizzed. Gardiner outlined what he said appeared to be the modus operandi in the chain being investigated by the UK, Ireland and Holland. It looked as though Irish horsemeat came up over the border into

Northern Ireland. It was mixed with other meat and re-labelled with fake Polish labels. That sort of re-labelling activity, Gardiner continued, had been one of the specialities of Jim Fairbairn in the 1980s. The re-labelled horse and beef was shipped back across the border to ABP and Rangeland, he added. How did the UK agriculture minister hope to get to grips with this degree of complexity in inter-country transfers, repackaging and relabelling, Gardiner asked Heath. It was indeed very complex, the minister replied, and would be part of the government's review of the saga.

In response to my inquiries about these points, ABP sent a statement expressing surprise that I should think it appropriate to repeat allegations from the 1980s, which it said had no relevance to the current horsemeat scandal. 'Those issues were fully addressed by the report of the Beef Tribunal after an exhaustive investigation. It found that there was no institutionalized fraud or abuse at AIBP factories, It also found that there were no improper payments made to politicians. Not a single complaint was made to it by any customer of AIBP ... We have made it clear we never knowingly bought horsemeat ... as far as ABP Food Group is concerned, if equine was deliberately introduced in to the food chain, then we were among those who have suffered as a result of such activity.'

The company also pointed to the statements made by the Irish agriculture minister Simon Coveney in the Irish parliament that he knew of no breaches of law or food safety standards that were uncovered at Silvercrest, nor of any evidence that Silvercrest was knowingly importing horsemeat.

It later told me that there was no relationship between ABP and Freeza Meats, with which it had not traded for over twelve months.

The committee asked Larry Goodman to come to give evidence in person but he declined, saying he had nothing useful to add to what his chief executive had already told them. Ray Mac-Sharry Jnr refused the invitation to come too. Norwest and MacSharry declined to comment when I approached the com-

pany. Rangeland said that the only shareholders in the company
since 1999 had been members of the Lucey family. It added that
the Department of Agriculture had concluded that it had not
knowingly bought or used horsemeat in its production process.

Eamon Mackle also turned down the committee's invitation,
but Jim Fairbairn did agree to appear. He said when he got there
that he had just retired from Freeza Meats and he declined to
respond to any questions relating to the tribunal and his record
at that time.

My own inquiries for the *Guardian* as to whether there were
any links between Goodman companies and his old team now
at Freeza Meats had been met with a denial, a refusal to comment on the Beef Tribunal and a legal threat: 'Freeza Meats has
suffered greatly over the past few months through no fault of its
own and jobs have been lost as a result of the collateral damage
brought about by reckless media commentary. The company
stands over its comments that Freeza Meats is an independent
business which has no links to ABP or Larry Goodman, not
now and not ever. Any attempt to suggest otherwise is false
and will result in legal action.' The company also reiterated
that none of its own products had tested positive for horse.

The company had lost its order for Asda beef burgers, said to
be worth around £2.5 million a year when the FSA found horse
on its premises. It also lost other potential orders worth £3–4
million. Several supermarkets sourcing from ABP Silvercrest had
come to Freeza looking for a clean break and a new supplier
when the Tesco horse-burger tests were revealed, but the FSA
finding of horse in the consignment it was storing put an end to
any prospect of those. It reckoned it had suffered enough.

But Fairbairn's evidence to the committee did throw some
light on the current scandal. The price of raw material for mince
products had doubled in the past two and a half years; you had
to look for the cheapest you could find, he explained. Freeza's
suppliers in Ireland included ABP, Dawn Meats, Liffey Meats
and, in the UK, ABP, Vestey and others. In fact Freeza had

dealings with quite a number of Goodman factories, Fairbairn was happy to say to MPs.

Also on the committee's invitation list was Patrick Coveney, the chief executive of a processing company called Greencore, although he too declined to attend. Patrick Coveney happened to be the brother of the Irish minister of agriculture Simon Coveney. Greencore had been sucked into inquiries over the curious incident of the Asda fresh beef Bolognese.

Until this point, all the products found to contain horse had been cheap frozen foods made from large blocks of frozen meat that is traded transnationally and can be kept in cold stores for years. The ownership and paper trail of the meat in these complex chains is often separate from the physical movements of the blocks. It was easy to see how horse could be buried in the middle of a 25kg frozen lump going into manufacturing. But then, for the first time, a month after all hell had broken loose with the first findings of horse from the Irish FSA, at a time when everyone knew that supermarkets were testing all their beef products, this fresh meat product became implicated. Asda's tests on its fresh beef Bolognese sauce found it to contain 5 per cent horse. Asda fresh sauces were supposed to be made with fresh meat, recently killed, from the UK and Ireland. How could equine material have got in there? Who would try to infiltrate it under the nose of the biggest food surveillance operation in recent times?

The sauce had been made for the supermarket group by Greencore. Greencore said it had bought the raw material for it from one of Goodman's ABP factories, not from the Silvercrest one with its rogue managers but from an ABP factory in Nenagh, Tipperary.

When it published its report on the horsemeat scandal the Irish Department of Agriculture said it had carried out a full examination of records at ABP Nenagh and had 'found no evidence that pointed to equine contamination originating in the plant'. Subsequent tests by Greencore on the batches of sauce all came back negative. So the department concluded that no further investigation of ABP Nenagh or Greencore was warranted, and stated that Asda's initial concerns no longer applied. ABP stressed that it had been able to trace all the raw material in its chilled meat business right back to the farms that had produced the cattle. Greencore and ABP believed that Asda's tests that found horse in this fresh meat were simply 'mistaken', a false alarm over something that had not in fact ever happened. Asda, which had commissioned the tests from one of Europe's leading labs, remained clear that its concerns did still apply and that significant levels of horse DNA had been found in its sauce from Greencore. It was all a bit of a mystery, a riddle that looked set to remain unsolved.

The Coveney brothers were adamant that there was no conflict of interest raised by the case. Greencore's Patrick Coveney said that while his company was headquartered in Ireland the bulk of its operations were in the UK, where it was regulated, so there was no conflict with his brother being the Irish minister. The Department of Agriculture in Ireland pointed out that far from suffering from conflicts of interest it had been the Irish authorities that had uncovered the horsemeat scandal in the first place. The adulteration had taken place right across Europe, but it had been Dublin that had found it.

And so investigations continued. Sales of frozen burgers had slumped by 43 per cent as shoppers remembered that an American fast-food invention was not the only meat you could eat. Supermarkets began to take more interest in short, local supply chains, but they would need at least the three-year cycle from calf to fattened bullock to bring them on full stream. Processors forswore long complex trading arrangements.

Meanwhile, in terms of the players, there was not much radical change. The Silvercrest factory had new managers and immediately won back its lost Burger King contract. The other companies had mostly gone straight back to work. The big supermarkets had continued to source fresh meat from ABP throughout. There would be more tests and more audits now, but otherwise it was business as usual, except in one important respect. Any retail or manufacturing company that wanted to be sure they would get beef rather than horse in their burgers or mince now expected to have to pay more to the processors who had landed them in horse trouble in the first place. You had to laugh.

The small matter of uninvited pork in beef had largely been forgotten. I realized then that I had been brought all the way back to where *Not On the Label* had first started. Of course all this had happened before. With chicken . . .

2. Chicken

It was the scald tank that got me in the end. I had expected trouble in the slaughter room, but we'd moved through there without incident. We'd already passed the electrocution bath and I'd slipped easily enough round the neck cutters slicing through carotid arteries. There wasn't as much blood as I'd feared.

I had been smuggled into a large chicken factory by a meat hygiene inspector who was worried about standards in the poultry industry. We were gazing into a hot-water tank into which the dead birds were being dipped at the rate of 180 a minute, to scald the skin and loosen the feathers before they went into the plucking machine.

It was 3 p.m. and as at many factories the water was only changed once a day. It was a brown soup of faeces and feather fragments and at 52°C 'the perfect temperature for salmonella and campylobacter organisms to survive and cross-contaminate the birds', the hygiene inspector pointed out. We moved on to the whirring rubber fingers which remove the feathers. 'Plucking machines exert considerable pressure on the carcass which tends to squeeze faecal matter out on to the production line. It only takes one bird colonized with campylobacter to infect the rest. The bacteria count goes up tenfold after this point,' he continued. I found myself wondering who had done the counting.

'But free-range and organic birds . . .' I started to ask without wanting to know the answer.

'. . . nearly all come through the same plants, yes. There's no difference except that in plants which process organic birds you can tell the organic ones. They are used to being allowed to run about a bit and so they try to escape when they are shackled.'

We went outside. There, towering stacks of birds in crates,

delivered earlier in the day by a procession of juggernauts, were being given a chance to calm down before being shunted into the slaughter room. They need to settle for the men to be able to pick them up by their feet and hang them upside down on the moving belt on which they begin their journey through the factory process.

The crates are made of plastic mesh with holes. The birds, which have typically been kept indoors all their lives, in eighteen-hour-a-day low light for maximum productivity, tend to panic when they are caught and taken into the fresh air and daylight for the first time. As they open their bowels, the faeces fall from the crates at the top down through the tower on to those below.

'Pretty daft, isn't it?' the inspector said.

Two thirds of the chicken on sale in UK supermarkets is contaminated with campylobacter. Campylobacter causes a nasty kind of food poisoning with severe, often bloody, diarrhoea. Although some worrying new strains of salmonella have been appearing recently, salmonella incidence generally has been falling, largely thanks to the vaccination of flocks, but food poisoning is still rising inexorably in this country, and chicken is the most common source of infection. Campylobacter can be killed by thorough cooking. Nevertheless the rise in the incidence of campylobacter infection in people mirrors the rise in chicken consumption.

'There isn't a great deal they can do when birds arrive at the factory with campylobacter in their gut. There are so many opportunities for cross-contamination,' Janet Corry, research fellow in food microbiology at the University of Bristol, told me. She had been generous with her time but sounded impatient with journalists writing exposés about chicken. 'Look, if you are going to process poultry at that price, there's not much you can do. The important thing is that they are killed humanely. The factories are designed to get them through fast. People want cheap food.'

Wander down the meat aisles of any supermarket and sure enough you will find mountains of chicken being sold at unbelievable prices. They're always there now, on 365-day 'special' offer. Chicken breasts: buy one, get one free . . . Chicken thighs: three for the price of two . . . Whole birds: half price.

We spend a much lower proportion of our income on feeding ourselves than previous generations. In the 1930s the average proportion of income spent on food was 35 per cent; today it is less than 10 per cent, although for the poorest fifth of the population the figure is still around one third. It is certainly true that we expect meat to be an affordable, everyday food in a way that our grandparents would never have done. Few of us have time or inclination to spend the hours needed to turn the offcuts that were traditionally the source of cheap meat into delicious meals. We want prime cuts we can cook fast.

Thanks to intensive factory farming, the industry has been able to deliver. Chicken is cheaper than it was in the 1980s, and we're buying five times more of it, spending £2.5 billion a year. Supermarkets have played their part in the deflationary process too, as chicken has become one of the weapons in retailers' price wars. But being able to buy a whole chicken for not much more than the price of a Starbucks cup of coffee comes at a cost.

The story of meat reflects the revolution that has taken place in our food system since the war. Chickens, like other animals, have become industrialized and globalized. We no longer know where they are produced or how they are processed. By the time we buy them in aseptic little packages, or processed into convenience meals, we have lost any sense of their origin. Until I worked in a chicken factory, I had no idea how the links in the chain fitted together. I am an enthusiastic cook, yet the extent to which processing has been transformed even in my lifetime had passed me by. It was an undercover stint in November 2001 with one of Britain's leading chicken processors in the West Country that first introduced me to the impact of that industrialization. What I needed to know was not on the label.

I had joined the twilight shift, at £4.50 an hour, reporting secretly for the *Guardian* newspaper, because I had been tipped off that the poultry being packed there as fresh British chicken breast for a supermarket was not what the retailer thought it was. The Devon women who packed poultry day in day out jokingly called it the Chicken Run. First you passed the guard in his sentry box on the unlit footbridge over the main railway line. The night trucks rumbled along the tracks below you as you crossed into the searchlights on the other side, where vast, windowless sheds loomed out of the mist. The darkness rang with the clanking of fork-lifts and the air was heavy with the smell of burning fat.

The Devon factory was owned by Lloyd Maunder, a family firm and leading supplier to Sainsbury's for over 100 years. It produced not just fresh chicken but West Country and organic poultry for the supermarket as well. Inside it was what is called a state-of-the-art fully integrated plant.

The vast majority of the 820 million UK chickens we eat each year are now processed in huge factories like this which combine an abattoir with cutting, packing and labelling the meat before it is transported directly to supermarket distribution centres. Over half the chicken farms in the UK are directly contracted to the factories too, rearing chicks delivered to them from the factory hatcheries, although British poultry farmers are increasingly struggling to stay in business in the face of cheap imports, particularly from Thailand and Brazil. The wholesale meat markets, supplied by independent farmers, around which a network of traditional butchers was built, now represent only a fraction of the trade.

The Lloyd Maunder website boasted 'total control and traceability', but I had been told by a worker at the factory that the 'traceability' claimed for the chicken had broken down – chicken breasts from Dutch crates were being repacked with new use-by dates and sent out with British red tractor logos for a Sainsbury's special offer.

Each EU-approved factory has its own health mark with

which to stamp any meat it handles. Batches are also given barcodes. These marks are designed to make sure all meat can be traced as it moves through the system. It's a complicated paper trail but making sure the system of health marking works is vital to protect the public.

In recent years environmental health officers have uncovered large-scale frauds where unfit chicken, condemned either for rendering or pet food, has instead been recycled back into the human food chain in vast quantities. Inspectors employed in the factories by the government's Meat Hygiene Service are supposed to reject any meat which is not properly health-marked. If the traceability had broken down, it would be a serious matter.

Before we started our evening's work, we had to be trained in hygiene and safety. There were a dozen or so of us: a farmer who could no longer make enough money from his farm and was taking a night job so that his family could stay on the land; an English teacher and a couple of other men who were there to earn extra money after their day jobs to pay for their children's Christmas presents; and a handful of Devon mothers made redundant from another chicken factory which had succumbed to global competition the previous week. They had trussing and cutting skills and came to work each evening once their children were home from school, 'to pay for the PlayStations and Game Boys and bikes the kids need to keep up with their peers', as Linda, their supervisor from the old factory, put it with a roll of her eyes.

Our trainers seemed to have a pretty clear grasp of the economics of the industry. 'Competition is what it's all about these days.' The big chicken manufacturers want to become bigger. 'They seem to be after a monopoly. But maybe that's not such a bad thing, if we're going to stand up to the power of the supermarkets. Perhaps you don't know, but when a supermarket wants to do a BOGOF [buy one, get one free offer, pronounced bog off] it's not just them that pays for the extra, it's us,' she told us conspiratorially, as she showed us some slides about not picking your nose and the importance of washing your hands. We then had to watch a Sainsbury's quality assurance video that included an earnest woman in a white lab coat measuring the length of a carrot with a ruler. At the end we had to sign a statement that we had watched it. 'That covers Sainsbury's for due diligence if anything goes wrong,' the trainer explained. As the food chain has become longer, protecting themselves from being sued if safety breaks down at any point is of prime importance to the big retailers.

'The biggest complaint we get from customers these days is about product going off. Perhaps that's to do with the way we all shop in our cars. Or perhaps it's the way we keep pushing sell-by dates,' the trainer joked.

This was a reputable company and we were run through benefits, career prospects and equal opportunities. We were warned against discrimination on racial or religious grounds. 'We've got Afghanistans [sic], Yemenis, Kurds, Kosovans, Croats, Serbs, Lithuanians, Africans, you name it. And we take into account their religious needs. Oooh yes, it's all Rama-dama-ding-dong round here,' she said.

A final warning from the trainer. Don't pilfer. Someone had been sacked not long before for taking bin bags. And don't trade in illegal substances on the factory floor. Someone had been caught for that too, and Customs and Excise were planning to come back, possibly undercover. 'It could be one of you here now,' she grinned as she scanned the room. I smiled inanely.

Then we were off to be kitted out with green boots, white coats, hairnets and helmets – blue helmets are managers; white, regular workers; green, rookies. We passed the staff noticeboard displaying the excellent official score given to the factory for hygiene that month, and a warning that a customer had complained of finding a whole Marigold glove in a portion of chicken drumsticks.

Then we went through the washing and disinfectant lobby

to scrub our hands and drag our boots through the foot wash, passed down a narrow white-walled corridor, through the heavy doors and into the main packing and cutting area.

The plucked and chilled chickens came in here upside down, thousands of them swinging by their feet from the continuous, spiralling belts of metal shackles that started in the abattoir and wound around the ceiling of the huge cutting hall, where production lines stretched into the distance. Disco music blared out above the noise of machinery, and the decapitated birds jerked and dived above our heads in macabre syncopation. Some were dropped off whole on to the trussing line, others bobbed along to have their wings sliced off. Legs and torsos danced on, all limbs, no tops, until they too were chopped off by the machines and dropped on to a packing line. This was where the labour-intensive bit started, since for supermarket orders the pieces have to be arranged by hand on plastic trays before going back into machines which wrap them and label them with prices and barcodes. The carcasses came on to a different track, with a metal fist through their innards.

Breasts had to be cut off by hand. A chain of Central Asian-looking workers were first tearing off the skin, then quickly flicking their sharp knives through to the bone and slicing the breasts away.

The Devon ladies, who were warm and raucous, had taken me with them to truss chickens on plastic trays because you got more money for that skilled job and they were trying to cover for me. I was no good at it. My hands were freezing. I was too slow off the mark changing and by the time I reached the glove dispenser the handwarmers had run out. An old hand from another section eventually took pity on me. 'Psst, what size are you?' She had a quick look over her shoulder, then reached down her leg and found me a pair from the stash in her wellies.

The packing lines displayed orders from the supermarket, crossed out and changed several times during the day. Processors risk losing their orders if they fall short of the supermarkets' requirements, which can fluctuate considerably, but in general the supermarkets are under no reciprocal obligation to pay if they want to cut back at short notice. An alert to supervisors on the labelling machine explained Sainsbury's new policy on barcodes and gave a clear indication of the balance of power between retailers and suppliers. If the barcode cannot be scanned at the till first time, the processor will be warned. Second offence: £500 fine; third offence: £1,000; fourth offence: £3,000; thereafter a Kafkaesque-sounding 'possible volume restructure'.

The night shift, when we moved into it, was a hardcore of foreign workers, many of whom spoke no English. The Devon mothers had returned to their homes and I had moved over to sliding breasts into trays, rough side down, good side up, curled over so those stringy bits couldn't be seen.

Then there was an unexpected pause. The chickens from the factory's own slaughterhouse had stopped winding through. The supervisor in charge of the line climbed up the huge ladder to the glass eyrie in the roof from where the managers could watch the workers below. We were given an early break. When we got back, a couple of dozen Belgian and blue Dutch crates filled with vacuum-packed breast fillets had been pulled in. We were set to packing those instead.

The crates were labelled GMB Meats, 'use by 25 November'; the vacuum packs said the same, 'use by 25 November', and carried the GMB Meats name. GMB Meats is a cutting plant in Wolverhampton which does not slaughter its own birds but buys them in from other British processors and imports from Belgium, Holland and other countries. The old health marks had been torn off but clear traces, saying Platte Kip (the Flemish and Dutch for chicken fillet), remained on the crates. The new health marks did not have batch numbers, making it difficult to trace their origin.

The vacuum packs were cut open and tipped on to the conveyor belts. Several chicken fillets fell down through the gaps and stayed at our feet while we packed into Sainsbury's trays for the next couple of hours.

There was a bit of aggro on the line by then. The clingfilm wrapper kept jamming and the Lithuanian next to me was indicating fairly forcefully that my elbows were taking up too much space. Further down the line workers were sticking a Buy One, Get One Free label on each pack as it emerged from the wrapper, before it trundled on to get its British red tractor logo and a new Sainsbury's label with a 'sell by 27 November' and 'use by 27 November' date stamp.

Sainsbury's had told me the previous week that all its fresh meat was 'completely traceable' to inspected and approved slaughterhouses which did not use subcontractors. When we confronted the company with our evidence it said that it was 'shocked' that a supplier had broken their agreement and used another company to cut its chicken without its knowledge. 'We pride ourselves on the integrity and traceability of our food, and take this extremely seriously.' It added that the chicken had undergone the usual tests and posed no health risk to customers. The company said it would completely review its meat-buying and introduce changes. Senior sources told me this did happen.

The tangle that is UK food and labelling law also became apparent. It would not actually be illegal to label foreign meat with the British red tractor logo, which in law means 'British farm standard', not necessarily produced in Britain, although of course most customers would be surprised to discover that. The use-by date on the giant vacuum packs I had helped to repack would have legal status and could not be changed if they had been intended for a caterer (as GMB Meats told us they were) but not if they were for an industrial customer repacking them. Putting the fillets in new packs with different dates might mean that the 'fresh chicken' was eight days old, but it would still have met Sainsbury's specification. Lloyd Maunder, having been asked by us to check, said at first that chicken from GMB was only ever packed for catering customers who did not specify a required country of origin. GMB did not seek to claim the meat was British, saying only that it came from EU-approved sources. Lloyd Maunder subsequently said that it had packed GMB chicken for Sainsbury's, explaining that it did very occasionally use other processors to cut its own birds for Sainsbury's, and that that was what had happened in this case. Officially, it could only do this with advance notice, yet Sainsbury's did not know what had happened. Lloyd Maunder's representative said that the company employed the highest standards of care in the operation of its business with its customers. When it had completed an audit of the factory after my investigation, Sainsbury's said it was satisfied that everything was in order. Trading standards officials said they had found nothing to investigate. Sources at the factory said that changes had also been made there.

Sainsbury's subsequently informed me that they refuted any implied or stated suggestion that Sainsbury's sold chicken with altered use-by dates or that they or one of their suppliers extended the original specified use-by date of chicken. They also said that chicken at Lloyd Maunder was repacked into Sainsbury's packaging and that the date on the first packet referred to a 'repack-by' date, and that the date on their own packaging was the 'use-by' date for customers. In 2008, the Lloyd Maunder family sold its business to one of the largest UK poultry processors, 2 Sisters Food Group.

Those working on the frontline of enforcement in the meat trade feared that the system of health marking generally had broken down and was no longer sufficient to protect the public. Just how vital traceability is became clear when the pet-food scandal came to light. The late Sue Sonnex, a chief environmental health officer in Derbyshire, remembered clearly the day in December 2000 that recycled pet food entered her life. An anonymous caller had tipped off the council that a company on its patch, Denby Poultry, was taking condemned chicken – diseased and contaminated birds from big factories which should have been sent for rendering or to be turned into pet food – and trimming it, washing it with bleach, and cleaning it up before selling it back into the human food chain.

For the next two years the lives of Sue Sonnex and her colleagues were dominated by the attempt to unwind the complicated threads that linked Denby to over 1,000 other food manufacturers, wholesalers and retailers around the country. Sonnex wanted to know not just how far the chicken had gone but, more importantly, why the system allowed such abuses. Environmental health colleagues in Rotherham had discovered a similar scam to recycle pet food and achieved a conviction in 2000, but the tentacles of that operation reached far and wide and there had not been the money to pursue them. Other cases were coming up in other areas. It seemed to be the tip of an iceberg of meat laundering.

Sonnex quickly realized the weaknesses of the inspection system. Investigators found health marks belonging to one major factory and supposedly unique to it lying around in another cutting plant. The marks had been faked – easily done – in the Denby case. Denby Poultry Products was a pet-food processing plant in Derbyshire registered to receive low-risk waste for use in pet foods. But it was laundering both low-risk waste and high-risk waste carrying hepatitis, Staphylococci and E. coli-septicaemia back into the human food chain. It sold cleaned-up waste to another company which applied illegitimate health marks to it before selling it on to other companies. The owner of Denby Poultry, Peter Roberts, known in the trade as Maggot Pete, was found guilty in his absence at Nottingham Crown Court in 2003. He is thought to have fled the country. Five other men pleaded guilty to conspiracy to defraud.

The official vets employed at meat factories are meant to oversee inspection of poultry, including waste. Because of the shortage of local vets, at the time large numbers of young female Spanish vets were being employed; today many are from eastern Europe. They can feel isolated and intimidated, and are often ignorant of British law. Many of the abuses take place at night after the inspectors have gone home.

Meat from the companies involved in the recycling had ended up, via major manufacturers Perkins and Shippams, in chicken products on the shelves of Tesco and Sainsbury's and in Kwiksave, and in schools and hospitals around the country, triggering food hazard warnings in April 2001. They had been unwitting victims of the scam. The retailers all have audit systems which are supposed to detect any abuses, but they had failed to pick up the problems.

Many environmental health officers were unconvinced that measures taken by the Food Standards Agency to control the illegal trade would be effective. They required factories to stain with blue dye all 'high-risk' poultry waste, that is, birds that are diseased. But they did not require the staining of 'low-risk' waste, in other words meat that is bruised, or has failed quality tests. The new system left the door open to abuse, according to Sonnex. It depended on poultry processors separating the different types of waste. Officially inspectors have only fifteen minutes a month allocated to supervising this part of the factory process, in plants that work twenty-four hours a day, seven days a week. The big pet-food companies which use low-risk waste for cat and dog food lobbied hard against staining and won the day. Commercial interests were also at work when it came to recalling products from companies caught up with the supplies of recycled meat. Two leading manufacturers initially refused to recall their products even when they were told they had been buying from a company which was laundering pet food. Only when threatened with naming and shaming did they co-operate.

But it was the economics of the globalized poultry industry that were at the root of the problem, according to Sonnex. When she interviewed the big processors who had failed to comply with regulations on disposing of their waste, they complained that they were being squeezed so hard on price by the retailers and operating on such tight margins that paying to get rid of the waste was often the final straw. The pressure applied by the major supermarkets to fund special offers and price drops was often cited as the factor that had pushed them into cutting corners.

'Five major poultry houses were offloading their waste – these were big-name companies – to save on disposal costs. The meat was laundered through an unlicensed cutting plant and sold for about 40p per kilo to a licensed plant which gave it a health mark. It sold it on for £1.50 per kilo. Then it went through brokers selling it at a bit more and on to food manufacturers who are selling chicken products at £15 per kilo. The raw material is worth so little it makes economic sense to ship it hundreds of miles. It's more profitable than drugs. Everyone can take a piece. We'll pay a fortune for processed junk but we won't pay anything for high-quality raw ingredients,' Sonnex explained.

If we are ignorant of how our fresh meat reaches us, we are even further removed from understanding which bits of animals go into the processed meats that have become ubiquitous. I, like many a harassed working parent, have fed my children their favourite chicken nuggets, thinking that the white meat they contained must be healthier than the fattier red meats in hamburgers. It was Sue Sonnex who first enlightened me on the true origins of the chicken nugget. During her investigation she had been shocked to find a manufacturer making nuggets almost entirely out of chicken skin. The label is not likely to tell you, but of course what the factory I worked at and all the others like it are involved in is a division of parts that transforms a cheap bird into profitable 'added-value' goods. Our recently acquired habit of just buying chicken breasts leaves all the other parts to be disposed of. While Europe is big on breasts, the Japanese prefer thighs. The feet are a bit of a fetish in China, and gizzards often go to Russia. But that leaves the carcasses and mountains of skin. So the skin is shipped around the world to make chicken nuggets.

It was while following the trail of the chicken skin that I found the answer to another puzzle: why the mention of Dutch catering chicken makes the industry so twitchy. I went first to a reputable organic manufacturer to understand the process of making nuggets.

Gary Stiles had spent his life in the meat trade and owned a small factory in Wiltshire. I watched with him as an army of small, perfectly formed nuggets marched along a conveyor belt. At one end of the factory line a pulp of half-frozen meat and skin went into a giant stainless-steel hopper. Minced and mixed beyond recognition, it was then extruded through a small tube on to metal plates. These pressed it into pale pink nugget shapes which trundled on down the belt. Through a dust bath of flour and seasoning they went, before being lowered under a sheet of constantly pouring batter. Then they passed through a tray of scattered breadcrumbs and into a vast vat of boiling oil for thirty seconds. As they emerged, workers in white coats, blue hairnets and white boots caught them, bagged them in plastic, and posted them back for the last rites. The belt carried them into a nitrogen tunnel to take them down to freezing point and finally out into a cardboard box, labelled with Stiles's own-brand Pure Organics For Georgia's Sake or Tesco organic chicken nuggets, according to the orders of the day.

Stiles explained that you need some skin to keep the nuggets succulent. He reckoned that 15 per cent was about right. Mixed in that proportion with breast and dark meat, it matched what you would get if you were eating a whole bird and he knew exactly where his chicken skin came from. Like the rest of his meat, it was bought from two organic farms he knew personally. Unlike some other manufacturers, he didn't use more skin than that, and he didn't use mechanically recovered meat (MRM) which is obtained by pushing the carcass through a giant teabag-like screen to produce a slurry of protein, which is then bound back together with polyphosphates and gums. He didn't add large quantities of water, nor did he use other additives that some manufacturers use, such as soya proteins to restore the texture of meat, or emulsifying gums to stop the mix separating out again, or flavourings and sugars to make up for the lack of meat. But the trouble is, once you've minced bits of chicken to a pulp, that pulp could be anything from anywhere. With other manufacturers, sometimes it was.

When Leicester trading standards received a complaint from a member of the public about the quality of some nuggets, they decided to test twenty-one samples from seventeen different shops, including the major supermarkets.

In one third of the samples the label was misleading about the nuggets' content. One pack of nuggets contained only 16 per cent meat, 30 per cent less than it claimed. (And skin, of course, counts as meat.) The trading standards officials were unable to identify the brands involved for legal reasons – one company disputed their tests. Instead, they gave a warning to the worst offender. That was in 2002. Subsequent tests showed that the manufacturer had not changed its ways.

That trading standards were not able to do more to stop the abuse is a reflection of the imbalance of power in the food business – small local authority enforcement departments with very few resources are pitted against panoplies of lawyers from the food industry.

Looking elsewhere in the chain it became clear that doctoring of our processed foods had not only become commonplace, it was also in many cases perfectly legal. Water is routinely added to catering chicken, together with additives to hold it in. If you've ever eaten a takeaway, a ready meal or a sandwich containing chicken, the chances are that you will have consumed chicken adulterated like this.

The Netherlands is the centre of the tumbling industry, the process in which the bulking up of chicken takes place. Dutch processors import cheap frozen chicken from Thailand and Brazil through Holland's ports. The meat has often been salted, because salted meat attracts only a fraction of the EU tariff applied to fresh meat. The processors defrost the meat, and then inject a solution of additives into it with dozens of needles, or

tumble it in giant cement-mixer-like machines, until the water
has been absorbed. The tumbling helps dilute the salt to make the
chicken palatable, so as well as avoiding substantial taxes, the processors can make huge profits by selling water. Once the chicken
has been tumbled and/or injected, it is refrozen and shipped on
for further processing by manufacturers or for use by caterers.

The story gets even less appetizing, as I discovered when I
met John Sandford, leading trading standards officer in Hull
City Council. He thought nothing could surprise him any more.
Like many an unsung local authority hero, he had spent over
twenty years sustained not by a large pay packet, but by a York-
shireman's sense of humour and dedication to honesty, as he had
tried to keep up with the poultry trade. He was aware that they
knew a trick or two, but when he saw some test results from the
public analyst's laboratory in the autumn of 2001, he was nevertheless amazed. The chicken breasts he and his colleagues had
collected for testing contained pork.

His investigations had begun in 1997 when trading standards
officers were contacted by a restaurateur who couldn't get his
chicken, bought from a wholesaler, to cook properly. It fell to
Hull Council to test it and they found it contained 30 per cent
added water. Sandford began puzzling over how the processors
had managed to get so much water to stay in the chicken. Why
didn't the water just flood out when it was turned into a takeaway or a ready meal or a chicken nugget? The chicken was
from Holland. Some time later Sandford discovered that there
was gossip among the producers in the UK that some Dutch
companies had new methods of adulterating their meat. The
FSA had been alerted to it. Now the authorities had to prove it.
Sandford knew it would be a slog. 'When they realize you are on
their trail, they just change their specification to disguise what
they are doing in different ways. They are multi-million-pound
companies with limitless money to spend on technology.' Sandford had a budget of £20,000 a year to spend on laboratory tests.

The breakthrough came when the laboratory he used in

Manchester was able to develop new DNA testing which could pinpoint protein from different species of animals. The first DNA tests on further samples of Dutch catering chicken – well-known brands which you can find used widely in takeaways, pubs, clubs, Indian, Chinese and other ethnic restaurants across the country – showed up the pork, and lots of water.

The FSA announced the results of the tests at a press conference in London in December 2001. Some of the samples of what were being sold as chicken breasts were in fact only 54 per cent chicken. Nearly half of the samples contained less meat than they claimed and were mislabelled. Most had originated in Thailand and Brazil. They had been exported to Holland where they had been pumped full of water, salts, sugars, gums, flavourings, aromas and other additives which would hold the water in, even when the chicken was cooked. But instead of using the old trick of phosphates to hold the water in, the processors were using a new, little understood one, based on hydrolyzed proteins.

Hydrolyzed proteins are proteins extracted at high temperatures or by chemical hydrolysis from old animals or parts of animals which are no use for food, such as skin, hide, bone, ligaments and feathers. Rather like cosmetic collagen implants, they make the flesh swell up and retain liquid.

The FSA public line at this point was that adding water to chicken was not in itself illegal, so long as the meat and other ingredients that had gone into it were accurately labelled when sold by wholesalers. Adding proteins from other animals would not be illegal either. Their main concern was that the chicken was not being correctly labelled. 'The added water, protein and other ingredients do not have food safety implications,' it said. The fact that by the time you and I eat it in a restaurant or canteen, the chicken has no label on at all, and that we would have no idea that we were not eating real chicken, seemed not to count. On this occasion it was left to a colleague of John Sandford's from trading standards to condemn what he saw as an outrageous consumer fraud.

Shortly after this some documents came into my hands that suggested there was considerably more going on behind the scenes. What the FSA and the lab had been looking for was not just chicken adulterated with pork, but – much more troubling – chicken adulterated with beef waste. The possibility of BSE in chicken meat had raised its ugly head.

If the Dutch processors were injecting chicken with hydro-lyzed proteins extracted from cow material, as these documents suggested, which bit of the cow were they coming from? If the processors were cheating and not declaring the presence of bovine proteins on the label, how could they be trusted to be following the regulations on removing certain high-risk cattle materials from the food chain? Would the process of hydrolysis kill off any infective BSE prions?

The baton had passed to Ireland where the Food Safety Authority in Dublin, tipped off by the English FSA, had started its own testing on chicken. Using a private lab with different and more sensitive DNA testing techniques, it found what it had been looking for: undeclared bovine proteins in chicken breasts from Holland, and lots more pork in chicken labelled 'halal'. Since much of the chicken was destined for ethnic restaurants where pork would be abhorrent to Muslims and beef to Hindus, it presented considerable moral dilemmas.

At this point, the authorities in England and Ireland were not really aware of what was going on. Until they knew the source of the bovine proteins, they could not rule out the theoretical risk of BSE. They hoped that the beef waste being used was col-lagen from hides, which would not present any safety risk – that was what the processors were saying. But the Dutch authorities, through whom the English and Irish were obliged to work, were being extraordinarily slow in checking the source of the proteins back down the chain. Sandford and the scientific experts at the FSA were becoming increasingly frustrated.

By now I knew from documents I had seen and conversations with expert sources that chicken adulterated with beef waste was also circulating widely in the UK and almost certainly being used in the manufacture of other chicken products, such as nuggets and ready meals. (The giveaway sign that your chicken has been adulterated is a slightly spongy texture.) We ran a piece in the *Guardian* saying so.

I had also been sent technical papers showing that the Brazilian poultry industry, working together with a Danish company, had developed the technology to extract hydrolyzed beef proteins from cattle blood and bone – BSE-risk materials in Europe – and were marketing their new technique for turning water into money to companies in eastern Europe.

The English FSA's public response was that their tests had found no evidence that the adulterated meat was circulating in the UK, and that in any case hydrolyzed beef proteins being used by the Dutch were derived from hide. There was no safety risk. It was a labelling issue, since it would be legal so long as it was correctly labelled.

I was beginning to wonder if I would ever escape the subject of chicken, as were my *Guardian* colleagues, who had taken to clucking as they walked past my desk. The BBC's *Panorama* team were keen to take the investigation further and it made sense to join forces with them. I had traced the production of hydrolyzed proteins back to factories in Germany and Spain. *Panorama* began secret filming. Their evidence was shocking.

They caught a Dutch additive supplier and a German protein manufacturer on video boasting that they had developed undetectable methods of adulterating chicken with waste from cows. The cow proteins were mixed into additive powders which were then injected into the meat, mostly chicken breasts, by poultry processors so that it could take up as much as 50 per cent water. But they were able to break down the DNA of the cow proteins to such an extent that the authorities' tests would not find it. Proteins extracted from chicken waste could also be used, but the reason for choosing cows was that the raw material was even cheaper. The owner of the Dutch company which mixed the proteins into powders for the chicken processors to use told the undercover reporters that for more than ten years the industry had been extracting hydrolyzed beef proteins to inject not only into chicken but also into other meats such as ham. At least twelve companies in Holland were using the new undetectable hydrolyzed proteins. The owner of the German company said that the material for the beef proteins was cow hide from Brazil and that Brazil was BSE-free, but he declined to show the undercover reporters the process by which they were extracted.

At first the FSA maintained the line that it was a labelling issue, but then decided it was a major scandal and fraud. The industry says some added water is vital for technical reasons, to prevent the chicken from drying out. Despite a pioneering investigation by its own scientific experts, the FSA was hamstrung by the fact that in European law there was nothing illegal about what the Dutch were doing so long as they put it on an obscure label somewhere. A multi-million-pound hi-tech industry had been, and still is, able to import cheap frozen Thai and Brazilian chicken, doctor it with animal waste, and sell it to restaurants, institutions and manufacturers across Britain. It had run rings around the authorities for years. A study by the FSA in 2008 found that proteins of beef and pork origin were still being used in frozen chicken processing and not properly declared. My industry sources told me in 2013 that the problem had never been successfully tackled. Industry was still adding up to 40 per cent water to frozen chicken, and it was only after the horsemeat scandal that any serious efforts were made to enforce tighter rules on tumbling imported salted poultry meat. Processors already knew how to beat the tests. Who knows how far the technology had spread? I saw sales literature from additive companies offering protein mixes for all kinds of meats and for fish.

The more you ship food around, the easier it becomes to hide this sort of fraud. Most shoppers, when asked, say they prefer

British meat because they want a short and accountable supply chain. But the structure of the globalized food industry is making it increasingly difficult for all but the largest British poultry farmers and processors to make a living. Farmers are going out of business in droves, and the processing side of the business is seeing rapid consolidation.

A chicken farmer, who may also have invested £1 million or more in chicken units with computerized feeding systems, may only make 1–2p profit per kilo for his birds. In the late 1980s chicken farmers received just over 30 per cent of the retail price of chicken, but today they are lucky to get 20 per cent. British chicken processors, whose factories require substantial capital investment and have high labour costs, are often working on margins of less than 1 per cent. If they cannot deliver the price the supermarket wants, retailers can also use the stick of sourcing abroad, from Europe where the value of the pound to the euro can favour Continental farmers, or from developing countries where costs are lower and standards may not be so good.

It is only by keeping volumes high that conventional farmers and processors here can survive. Two thirds of chicken farms in the UK now consist of units of 100,000 birds or more. But that makes them dependent on the people who were squeezing their margins in the first place – the big retailers. They are the only people who buy in sufficient volume.

The story is not unique to chicken. Pig farmers and processors suffer similar problems. In the 1990s a British pig farmer made £9 profit per pig, in 2002 he lost an average of £3 per pig. Neither poultry nor pig farming receives subsidies. Only the biggest and most intense producers can compete. This is one of the consequences of our obsession with cheap meat. The constant drive to increase yields leads to ever greater intensification. As the trade has globalized, the same trend is now being seen in developing countries. Small poultry farmers in Brazil and Thailand are being squeezed out by huge factory farms. It is a pattern that can be observed in most food sectors, from vegetable farming to confectionery manufacture. But where livestock is involved, the almost irresistible drive towards industrialization has particular consequences. The price is paid in animal welfare and vulnerability to disease.

The modern broiler chicken has been bred to fatten in the shortest time possible. (The name derives from a combination of the two traditional methods of cooking chicken: boiling and roasting.)

The broiler farms divide the year up into a series of eight-week cropping periods. Each 'crop' of chickens takes forty to forty-two days to grow from chick to 2kg bird ready for slaughter. One week is taken to clean and disinfect the sheds before the next crop is begun – the units are not cleaned during cropping, so that after two to three weeks the wood shavings on the floor of the sheds are completely covered with poultry manure and the air is acrid with ammonia. Everything is automated. Computers control not just the heating and ventilating systems but also the dispensing of feed and water. The feed and water are medicated with drugs to control parasites or with mass doses of antibiotics as necessary.

Sheds these days typically hold 30,000–50,000 birds. Space and heating cost money, so the more birds you can pack in, the greater the yield. The UK government guidelines currently advise that there should be a maximum stocking density of 34kg of bird per square metre of floor space. In fact a survey conducted by Compassion in World Farming in 2001 found that only Marks and Spencer stipulated this as a maximum. Most other supermarkets permitted stocking densities of up to 38kg per square metre. This allows each mature chicken an area smaller than an A4 sheet of paper. By the time the birds reach the end of their lives, the sheds are so crammed that they can hardly move. Animal welfare groups have regularly video-recorded signs of acute stress in birds including feather-pecking and cannibalism of dead chickens. Mortality rates are high, at 1 per cent a week seven times higher than in egg-laying hens. Once the shed is carpeted with chickens, it can be hard for the stockman to see all those that have died before the others start feeding on them. New European regulations that came into force in 2010 reduced maximum legal stocking densities slightly, but countries could opt out and in the UK densities remained roughly the same.

Two companies – Ross Breeders and Cobb – supply 80 per cent of the breeding stock for commercial broilers around the world. Much research has been devoted to genetic selection to produce the most efficient bird. The RSPCA, which says that it sees the suffering of broiler chickens as one of the most pressing animal welfare issues in the UK today, produced a little pamphlet, called *Behind Closed Doors*, which showed the effect of that genetic selection. More eloquent than any description is a series of matching pairs of tiny photographs in the margin of each page. The top photograph shows a normal egg-laying hen taken at intervals of a few days, as it grows from chick to maturity. Underneath is a parallel picture of the broiler chicken taken at the same intervals. By day nine, the broiler chick's legs can barely keep its oversized breast off the ground. By day eleven, it is puffed up to double the size of its cousin. It looks like an obese nine-year-old standing on the legs of a five-year-old. By day thirty-five, it looks more like a weightlifter on steroids and dwarfs the egg-laying hen.

In 1957 the average growth period for an eating chicken was sixty-three days and just under 3kg of feed was required for each kilo of weight. By the 1990s the number of growth days had been reduced to forty-two to forty-three, and little over 1.5kg of feed was required. The industry is working to reduce the lifespan still further. Free-range chickens have some access to the outdoors, and must be kept at slightly reduced stocking densities and be reared more slowly so they are fifty-six days old at slaughter. Organic chickens have even higher standards of welfare and take twelve weeks, or eighty-seven days, to mature.

But genetic selection to produce birds that work like factory units of production creates serious health problems – their bones, heart and lungs just cannot keep up. A large proportion of broilers suffer from leg problems: you can tell when you buy a chicken from the hock burns – dark red patches – on the leg around the knee joint. The industry disputes just how much of a problem lameness is. A study in 1992 by the University of Bristol found that 90 per cent of UK broilers had a detectable problem and over a quarter of birds had leg problems severe enough to affect their welfare. The industry had done its own survey and said that fewer than 4 per cent of birds had significant problems, but did not make the research available in the public domain.

Lameness is not just a welfare problem. Birds that sit in fouled litter and cannot stand up suffer more skin disease. Deaths from heart attacks or swollen hearts that cannot supply enough oxygen to the birds' oversized breast muscles are also common. If these diseased birds make it to the processing factory, inspectors are supposed to weed them out along with DOAs (dead on arrivals), but with chickens moving through at 180 or more a minute, some slip through. A 1996 *Which?* survey of chicken on sale in leading supermarkets found several birds with severe bruising, disease and skin infections.

Because broilers grow unnaturally fast, those which are kept for breeding – and are therefore not slaughtered at six weeks but allowed to reach sexual maturity at about fifteen to eighteen weeks – have to be starved, otherwise they would become too big to mate.

Factory farming in these sorts of conditions is heavily dependent on the use of drugs to prevent or treat disease. Pigs, chickens, laying hens, sheep, calves, dairy cows and farmed fish all receive regular dosages of antibiotics either through injection or in their food and water. By the end of the 1990s about 450 tonnes of antibiotics were being used on farm animals in the UK each year – about the same quantity as on humans. Many of the antibiotics given to farm animals are the same as, or related to, antibiotics used in human medicine.

Farmers were first allowed to feed livestock antibiotics as growth promoters fifty years ago, just ten years after this life-saving class of drugs first became widely available to tackle human disease. By wiping out competing bacteria in the guts of chickens, the antibiotics speeded up the rate at which the birds absorbed food and grew. They also acted as a prophylaxis against the diseases common in factory-farmed chicken.

Scientists took their time arguing about the impact of the use of antibiotics in animals on the effectiveness of these drugs for humans. Many were extremely alarmed by their overuse; others were less convinced of the dangers. But international bodies agreed that at the very least it made sense to be cautious. In 1999 the government's Advisory Committee on the Micro-biological Safety of Food (ACMSF) said: 'Much of modern medicine depends on the control of infection with antibiotics and if this were to become largely ineffective, it would have calamitous consequences ... We believe that giving antibiotics to animals results in the emergence of some resistant bacteria which infect humans.'

The EU banned an antibiotic called avoparcin for use in ani-mals in 1997 because of the likely development of resistance in humans to the related antibiotic vancomycin. But its legacy remains. Because it was given in low dosages to chickens in feed or drinking water, it didn't kill bacteria completely but allowed some to survive and develop resistance. Now we are facing vancomycin-resistant enterococci – that is, superbugs in humans which cannot be treated. Vancomycin is the most powerful human antibiotic available, the last line of defence for patients with the hospital superbug MRSA.

In 1998 the UK poultry industry said it would remove all growth-promoting antibiotics from feed voluntarily, ahead of a European ban which came into force in 2006. But by 2003 it had become clear that one in five producers had quietly slipped back into the habit. Richard Young, an organic farmer and expert adviser on antibiotic use to the Soil Association, worked out that something fishy was going on. Overall antibiotic use actually increased rather than decreased after the voluntary ban. Many producers had found that their birds were falling ill without the growth promoters and resumed administering them. Others had switched to far greater use of therapeutic antibiotics prescribed by vets. I saw production sheets from a large chicken factory, sent to me anonymously, which made clear that its chicks, both free-range and indoor-reared, were still routinely given antibiotics in their water.

The 2003 FSA survey of chicken found that half of the salmonella and half of the campylobacter detected in retail samples were resistant to at least one antimicrobial drug, and nearly a quarter to several other drugs which are needed to treat humans when they are infected by these food-poisoning bugs. By 2013 the UK's chief medical officer was warning of the dire threat posed by rising levels of antibiotic resistance. Dame Sally Davies told parliament that we face an 'apocalyptic scenario' where people going for simple operations in twenty years' time will die of routine infections because we have run out of antibiotics. Their overuse in human medicine is a huge and acknowledged problem, but the UK government was still choosing to argue over the contributory role of their overuse in livestock farming. Denmark, the Netherlands and Sweden had introduced programmes to reduce antibiotic use on farms but Defra had argued against taking significant measures at EU level because it could increase production costs for the industry.

Ironically, while industrial farming has risked compromising the effectiveness of antibiotics for humans, its heavy drugs use has not prevented regular and catastrophic outbreaks of disease in intensively reared animals.

Some 2,000 British pig farmers went out of business between 1998 and 2002. For many, the beginning of the end was the arrival of swine fever. The disease spreads through intensive pig farms like wildfire, and devastated the UK industry in 2000. Mark Hayward, a pig farmer in Suffolk, was badly hit. His farm was not infected but nearby ones were and he was banned from moving his animals. 'It's very, very infectious and very nasty – you get vomiting, wasting, high fevers, sudden death. You go into a pen one morning and two or three of them are ill; by the end of the day the whole pen is ill. We worked like shit to keep the disease off our land. But we couldn't move our pigs for five months.'

They couldn't sell the pigs that were reaching their full weight, and they couldn't turn off the relentless production cycle of sows in pig giving birth. 'We were stacking up three hundred and fifty pigs a week with nowhere to put them. It was horrendous. Three hundred pigs in pens where there should have been a hundred. They were fighting. It was so distressing staff started to leave.'

Swine fever was an early warning that the regulations on importing illegal meat and treating animal feed were not being enforced. It cost Mark's farm, which never caught it, £100,000.

Nearly a quarter of a million pigs in his part of the world were destroyed. Just fifteen months later, the warning unheeded, foot and mouth struck. It was first spotted on pigs in an abattoir in Essex, but by then animals which had been trucked all around England had spread the disease. From the Welsh hills to the Lake District, from the weald of Essex to the moors of Devon, animals had to be slaughtered. The countryside was burning with the funeral pyres of sheep and cattle. The army had been called in and the government had been forced to postpone its chosen date for a general election.

It was the turn of the Dutch army to be called out in February 2003. Avian flu had broken out in the eastern province of Gelderland. It enforced a ban on movement in a desperate effort to stop the disease spreading through the intensive poultry units in the Netherlands. By April it had spread to Belgium. Exports of eggs and chickens were banned. By the time the Germans had caught it in May and started sealing their roads, over 30 million Dutch and Belgian chickens had been destroyed. A Dutch vet had also died, having caught the disease from an infected bird, briefly sparking fears that the virus could mutate and trigger a flu epidemic in humans.

It is not a coincidence that European farmers have lurched from crisis to crisis like this. Our methods of farming livestock intensively and of moving animals vast distances make them particularly vulnerable to epidemics of disease. For centuries traditional farms were mixed, partly to take advantage of the virtuous circle of plants feeding animals whose manure could then feed crops, but also as an insurance against the risk of disease. Farm diseases are usually quite specific, and attack one type of livestock or crop. The best way to prevent them is to avoid keeping too many of the same animals together in one place, and to rotate them so that the cycle of diseases and parasites is broken. Organic farmers know this. Once a disease does strike, just as isolation works with human illness, so keeping animals away from contact with other animals of their type is the best way of controlling it. Modern systems of monoculture do the opposite. Meat and livestock are not only regularly transported around the world but also kept together in great crowds in the same place year after year. By the time a disease has been noticed, it has often taken devastating grip.

The final cost of the foot and mouth outbreak of 2001 has been estimated at £8 billion, although the true financial cost to rural economies as large parts of the countryside were effectively shut down is incalculable. Some 4 million animals were slaughtered, although just 2,000 cases of foot and mouth were confirmed. The earlier BSE crisis, caused by feeding old cattle back to herbivore cattle in the pursuit of maximum yields, cost British farmers £1.6 billion in lost export markets alone. The UK poultry industry escaped the European epidemic of avian flu in 2003, but it was back on red alert in January 2004 as the disease struck again, this time cutting through flocks in south-east Asia and claiming lives as it spread to the human population. The World Health Organization warned that if the bird virus mutated and attached itself to human flu, the consequences would be devastating. Imports of meat from Thailand were banned by the EU when it emerged that the Thai government had been covering up the fact that its flocks were infected. The strain of flu was particularly virulent and the *Lancet* said that if it became contagious among people, the prospect of a worldwide pandemic was 'massively frightening'.

In 2007 it was the UK's turn when an outbreak of bird flu H5N1 occurred at a poultry factory in Suffolk, owned by leading brand Bernard Matthews. H5N1 is the virulent subtype of flu virus responsible for a potentially deadly strain of flu in humans. The cause of the outbreak was not established, but the fact that the company regularly transported poultry products between the UK and Hungary, where there had also been an outbreak, was thought significant. In 2013, Bernard Matthews suffered another outbreak of a less alarming strain of avian flu at a factory farm for breeding birds in Suffolk. The risks have not gone away.

3. Salad

In an idle moment I decided to reconstruct the contents of a 99p bag of washed and ready-to-eat salad. Of course you are not meant to do this, the whole point of bagged salad being that we are too busy to wash our own lettuce leaves, let alone count them. But I wanted to know how many you get for your money. Erring well on the side of generosity, I reckoned that for roughly £1 I had bought two leaves of frisée, one leaf of red radicchio, and two leaves of a pale green crunchy variety of lettuce. This portion was livened up by eighteen tiny whole leaves and seven torn pieces of dark green leaves about the size of a 2p coin.

Bagged salads did not exist before 1992. Now two thirds of households buy them regularly. The value of the UK salad vegetable market had in fact grown by 90 per cent between 1992 and 2002. By 2002 it was worth £1.25 billion – more than the total value of the sliced bread market, or the breakfast cereal market.

This does not mean we are eating 90 per cent more salad – volumes have grown only by 18 per cent over the same period – just that the food industry has found ways to make much more money out of salad.

Time was when we ate lettuces in summer and, following our northern European seasons, switched to root vegetables and brassicas in winter. But now, thanks to global sourcing and advances in packaging technology, we have got used to the idea of eating a variety of salads all year round.

Modified-atmosphere packaging (MAP) can now increase the shelf life of prepared salad by over 50 per cent, making it possible for supermarkets to sell us washed and bagged salad from around the world. Lettuce and salad leaves are harvested from fields in the UK, southern Europe or the USA one day and reach a packing house either the same day or a day or two later if imported. The salad is cut or separated out into individual leaves by gangs of workers, then washed, often in chlorine, dried and sorted before being packaged in pillows of plastic in which the normal levels of oxygen and carbon dioxide have been altered. Typically, in MAP, the oxygen is reduced from 21 per cent to 3 per cent and the CO_2 levels correspondingly raised. This slows any visible deterioration or discolouring. The salad is then trucked to a supermarket's distribution centre where it will be dispatched for delivery to the stores. The MAP keeps it looking fresh for up to ten days. Some lettuces imported from the USA are kept fresh in MAP for up to a month.

Unfortunately, some research published in 2003 in the *British Journal of Nutrition* suggested that this new invention to prolong shelf life and provide us with convenience while multiplying profits might actually destroy many of the vital nutrients in salad.

A team of researchers and volunteers at the Rome Institute of Food and Nutrition had conducted an experiment. They took lettuce grown by a co-operative and gave it to volunteers to eat on the day it was harvested; lettuce from the same source was then given to volunteers to eat after it had been packed in MAP straight after harvesting and stored for three days. Blood samples of the two groups were analysed after they had eaten the salad. The researchers noted that several antioxidant nutrients – which protect against ageing, degenerative disease and cancer – such as vitamin C, vitamin E, polyphenols and other micronutrients – seemed to be lost in the MAP process. The volunteers who had eaten the fresh lettuce showed an increase in antioxidant levels in their blood, but those who had eaten lettuce stored for three days in MAP showed no increase in antioxidant levels. The researchers noted that nutrient levels fell at a similar rate in lettuce stored in normal atmospheric conditions, the difference being that a lettuce stored normally showed signs of limpness after a few days whereas with MAP the illusion of freshness is preserved.

When the results of this trial were published, they provoked a defensive debate among packers in the UK. Jon Fielder, director of a company called Waterwise, which sells ozone-based disinfecting systems to salad packers, wrote to the trade magazine the *Grocer* saying that it couldn't be the MAP that was to blame for destroying nutrients.

It is commonly acknowledged that MAP does have an effect on the depletion of nutritional value of salad, however it is the chlorine used by most UK packaged salad producers in the washing process which has a far worse effect on consumer health. In most cases, the salad leaves are immersed in water with chlorine which is an oxidizing disinfectant. The chlorine level is usually maintained at a minimum of 50mg per litre – twenty times higher than in the average swimming pool.

In fact the Italian researchers had not used chlorine, so the MAP must have been responsible for the nutrient loss, but it was a helpful addition to public knowledge to have the industry view on chlorine washes.

Chlorine washes leave surface residues of chlorinated compounds on lettuce, and because of this the process is banned in organic production. Some chlorinated compounds are known to be cancer-causing, but there appears to be little research on those left on foods treated with doses of chlorine, the process having evolved in an ad hoc way.

'As well as disinfecting out the bugs, they disinfect out the taste of fresh leaves, as anyone who has eaten salad straight from the garden knows,' Fielder points out. But it is controlling bugs rather than preserving taste or nutrients that wins most attention. As Fielder says, 'In a litigious society, and with the prospect of damage from bad publicity, no supermarket dare risk having E. coli food-poisoning bugs on the salad they sell.'

There appears to be good reason for supermarkets selling pre-washed salads to worry. Between 1992 and 2000, the period in which bagged salads took off, nearly 6 per cent of food-poisoning outbreaks were associated with ready-to-eat salads and prepared fruit and vegetables. In 2000 two serious outbreaks of salmonella poisoning in the UK were traced back to lettuce. One person died as a result.

Once the market started growing so rapidly, the government's Public Health Laboratory Service (PHLS) decided to monitor bacteria levels in salads. A study of refrigerated ready-to-eat salads sold at retail stores in the UK in 1995 found that 6.5 per cent contained listeria, and 13 per cent E. coli bacteria. A further PHLS survey in 2001 found salmonella in five samples and high levels of listeria in one sample of ready-to-eat salad from three major supermarkets. One of the samples containing salmonella also contained E. coli bacteria. Fuller investigation subsequently uncovered an outbreak of salmonella poisoning in different parts of England and Wales caused by the salad. The majority of the samples were fine but, as the authors of the study pointed out, the new methods of packing raised new dangers.

Effective decontamination of ready-to-eat vegetables is difficult . . . there is increasing concern regarding the microbiological safety of such products and the effectiveness of current methods.

Food-poisoning incidents related to salad vegetables have occurred since – one in the UK in 2007 was traced to basil, and a fatal one in Germany in 2011 turned out to be the result of contamination of bean sprouts, although it was Spanish cucumbers that wrongly came under suspicion first and were destroyed by the tonne.

E. coli bugs are usually spread from human or animal faeces, either from the unwashed hands of farm or packhouse labourers, from manure that has not been properly composted, or from contaminated water. Good hygiene practices are essential to controlling them. But Jon Fielder, even as someone who sells disinfecting technology, says, 'The longer the factory chain the harder it is to control contamination. I always feel I should wash the lettuce I buy even if it is bagged and ready-to-eat.'

It might seem obvious that ensuring that those who work with fresh prepared foods are healthy, have access to proper sanitation at all times, and are well trained in good hygiene is vital. Standards of hygiene in factories and packhouses themselves are generally high and meticulously monitored. But in almost every other respect the system of employment that prevails in the food industry today militates against decent conditions.

The preparation and packing of fresh foods such as salad are now dependent on cheap, casual labour. That cheap labour has been largely provided by migrant workers. The labour-intensive business of sorting, washing, cutting and packing leaves and other fresh produce by hand could not be done without them. Many of them, however, are now living in this country in appalling squalor.

Casual and frequently itinerant labour has gone together with agriculture for as long as anyone can remember. In Britain, from the early nineteenth century, gangmasters were contracted to collect labour from the villages around farms to bring in the annual harvest. The 1867 Agricultural Gangs Act defined a gangmaster as a person 'who hires Children, Young Persons or Women with a view to their being employed in Agricultural Labour on Lands not in his own Occupation'. Until the 1980s, the work was often done by women in rural communities to earn a bit of extra money while looking after the family, or by students taking temporary summer jobs on farms. But in the last few decades the whole nature of the industry has changed.

Advances in agricultural science have helped extend the British season well beyond the old holiday times. Many farms are no longer simply places where food is grown, but sophisticated industrial complexes built around packing sheds and lorry parks. When they are not harvesting and packing their own produce, the big farms today are trucking or flying in supplies from abroad and packing them. The majority of the fresh food we buy is now wrapped in plastic. The need to pack fresh produce has been driven not so much by consumer demand as by the supermarkets' requirements, for barcode scanning at the till or for the food to be protected while it is moved around centralized distribution systems, for example.

Supermarkets are now open long hours, seven days a week. Packhouses operate twenty-four hours, seven days a week, partly because farmers wanting to supply the supermarkets have had to make substantial investment in packing and labelling machinery to meet their specifications and need to work the capital as hard as they can, and partly because supermarket ordering systems demand complete flexibility from suppliers.

At the same time, long working hours, and greater numbers of women going out to work, have led to an increased demand for convenience from time-pressed shoppers. The combined effect has been an explosion in this new form of economic activity. Other industries with such year-round demand do not depend on a casual and shifting workforce, but the food industry has stuck to the old nineteenth-century systems.

Labourers are often needed at very short notice and for long and unsocial hours. A report by the House of Commons select committee for Environment, food and rural affairs (Efra) described the system. A supermarket might, for example, find that during hot weather its sales of salad have increased dramatically and will place an order with a supplier to provide extra washed lettuce later that day. The packhouse suddenly finds it needs an extra thirty or forty staff for the day and asks its gangmasters to provide them. The gangmaster may subcontract the order for workers if he doesn't have enough people on tap. The risks of meeting changing demand are thus transferred from the retailers to the workers.

Supermarkets rarely have written contracts with farmers or packhouses promising to buying certain quantities, although farmers are obliged to commit to supplying certain amounts to

them. The farmers are both required to take the loss on any surplus and to meet any shortfall at their own expense by importing
if their own harvest does not meet demand. This is what happened in the summer of 2003. The exceptionally hot weather
caused much of the UK lettuce crop to mature at once, leaving
major producers with a shortfall on their commitments to supply supermarkets in subsequent weeks. They had to make up
quantities by air-freighting in lettuce from the USA and selling
it at a considerable loss. The market price for a head of lettuce
went from roughly 30p to 80p. Some supermarkets continued
paying farmers the lower price agreed at the beginning of the
year, but were able to hike their own prices in the shops because
of high demand and shortages. When the farmer's profits are
under such intense pressure, one of the few things he or she can
still control is the cost of labour. The prices paid to farmers are
nowhere near the cost of carrying a permanent workforce large
enough to cope with fluctuations in demand.

The work is hard, as agricultural labour has always been, often
in freezing conditions in refrigerated plants. Industrial injuries
are common. The pay is unattractive and never guaranteed. Small
wonder that the need for labour is no longer met by the indi-
genous population. Instead, large numbers of migrants have
filled the gap.

I first became involved in the issue of migrant labour when
the *Guardian* published my description of the Devon chicken
factory where I worked packing chicken for Sainsbury's (see
Chapter 2: Chicken). Its staff included eighteen or so different
nationalities. There was no suggestion that any of these were
illegal workers, but shortly after the piece, I began to get phone
calls. Did I know about the fifty Russians in the Portakabin on
a meat factory site in Derbyshire? Or the dozens of Russians
also in Portakabins packing salad leaves in Hampshire? Could I
look into the streams of untaxed minivans full of foreigners
going to farms and packhouses in the Vale of Evesham? Most of
the calls were anonymous tip-offs, some of them clearly moti-

vated by xenophobia, but others not. Some were from people disturbed about the conditions they could see migrants were being housed in. Others were from people worried that their own jobs and pay were being undercut by exploited illegal labourers being paid less than the minimum wage. One was from a farmer who said he couldn't pay people properly any more: he was being undercut by rivals who, he felt, were only able to accept the supermarkets' demands for constant price reductions because they were using illegal labour; he faced the choice of doing the same himself or going out of business.

After that I visited factories, farms and packhouses in many areas, or simply talked to local people who could see what was really going on; to local Immigration officers, who were not officially allowed to talk to the press but who feared that casual employment had been handed over wholesale to criminal gangs calling themselves employment agencies; to farmers who feared they would lose their contracts if they said publicly what they were prepared to admit privately, that it was almost impossible to recruit sufficient casual labour legally to meet supermarkets' endlessly fluctuating demands; to packhouse managers who talked about the frequent Immigration raids on illegal workers in their *last* jobs; to trade union organizers in food companies who witnessed it all happening, including in one case a police helicopter buzzing around a chicken factory while illegal migrants, who appeared to have been tipped off, legged it through the fields. I also talked to many migrants and visited them where they lived.

What became clear was that the scale of migrant labour in the food industry was much larger than anyone was prepared to acknowledge, and that a very substantial proportion of that labour was being employed illegally. The Efra committee said it was appalled that no attempt had been made to assess the extent of illegal activity in this area. Doug Henderson, chief executive of the Fresh Produce Consortium, who appeared before the committee representing the producers, admitted that it was 'a

very large black economy ... a dreadful situation' and that the
problem was deteriorating. He also said that VAT, tax and insurance scams provided 'a huge opportunity for very substantial
fraud ... that has encouraged the criminalization of the activity'.
Don Pollard, who did extensive research for the T&G Union on
exploitation of workers in agriculture and food processing in
the latter half of the 1990s, estimated then that at least 50 per
cent of workers were controlled by gangmasters, with perhaps as
many as 100,000 people being involved.

But by the 2000s, the numbers looked much higher. Operation Shark, a pilot investigation into illegal labour carried out
by government departments in 2002, covered the whole of the
fish processing industry in Scotland. It targeted the big labour
agencies supplying thousands of workers to gut, fillet, cut and
pack fish, much of it salmon for the major retailers. It sent a
counter-fraud unit to raid a large fish company with half a dozen
factories supplying supermarkets. It found that over 50 per cent
of the workforce of 100 people at one factory were foreign. Of
those more than one third were in the UK illegally. Of the local
workforce, 10 per cent were claiming benefits they were not
entitled to. The factory was working three shifts, and the foreign
workers were doing either twelve hours or double shifts of sixteen hours a day, seven days a week. They were being paid less
than the minimum wage, though exactly how much was hard to
tell, since the gangmaster was deducting accommodation charges
as well as tax and insurance. The result of Shark was that two
health and safety orders were put on fish companies to curb
excessive hours. Two gangmasters had their contracts worth
£8 million and £1 million a year terminated. But at the time of
writing no other charges had been brought.

David Jackson, the former police officer in charge at the time
of the government's Operation Gangmaster, the overall programme of which Shark was a part, said that these figures were
representative of conditions they had found throughout the
fish processing industry. By definition, it is impossible to know

how many people work illegally. But what was not in any doubt was that exploitation of these labourers was not the exception but the norm.

Authorities investigating the illegal use of labour in the food and agricultural industries could see a pattern emerging right across the country and feared it bore the hallmarks of a series of mafia operations. 'The MO [modus operandi or method of operation] of the gangmasters is so similar across the country, from the south of England to the north of Scotland, making use of the same sophisticated techniques to exploit loopholes in UK law, that we suspect there is some dominant controlling mafia, with mafias from different countries having carved out particular areas,' one senior official explained to me. The only ones who appeared to operate differently were the Chinese gangs, who had descended in large numbers on King's Lynn and seemed to have cut out the middle men.

The mafia-style system works like this: gangmasters set themselves up as 'employment agencies' in the form of one or more limited companies. They are usually small companies with two to three owners but often with turnovers of £8–10 million a year. They recruit workers from abroad, sometimes being involved either directly or indirectly in smuggling them in and providing them with false documents. The migrants will often have been charged huge sums to be brought here and some are in debt to the gangmasters when they arrive. The gangmasters may use a core of legal workers from EU countries or students from eastern Europe and the former Soviet bloc given permission to come under government schemes for agricultural employment as a cover. So, for instance, Portuguese workers are used as cover to bring in Brazilians on fake Portuguese IDs. The gangmasters then provide workers with housing and transport, which not only ensures that the workers remain completely dependent on them but also provides a way of disguising the fact that they are paying less than the minimum wage. They charge the packhouses, factories and farmers the going rate, and deduct tax and insurance from the workers' pay packets, even when it has nowhere legitimate to go because the workers are on fake IDs. This ensures that the books of the companies they are supplying with labour are kept clean. The gangmasters then go bankrupt before paying tax and insurance or VAT, which are collected retrospectively. It is quite common for them to declare themselves bankrupt owing between £1 million and £3 million in unpaid tax and insurance and VAT, much of which will have been moved offshore and thus be inaccessible to UK authorities. Once they have gone into liquidation they frequently reappear as phoenix companies, with the same directors supplying workers to the same sites just days afterwards but trading as a new employment agency under a different name. Clone companies are also created which provide subcontracted labour to the mother company, partly as a way of disguising the frauds further but also to get round restrictions which prevent bankrupts being directors of other companies.

Violence and crime of other sorts go hand in hand with these illegal employment activities. Intelligence briefings on gangmasters included details of the Azerbaijani Stanley signature – the slash of the knife that goes up from the back of the shoulder and down across the chest – and Kalashnikovs on farms, used to keep workers in order. Intimidation and punishments are meted out to both legal and illegal workers. Sometimes intimidation turns into murder. At least two murder investigations in 2004 appeared to involve the murder of one migrant worker by another. Some gangmasters were known to be involved in running prostitution and drug-smuggling rings. Protection rackets had also grown up around this activity. Workers described these to me. At one house in southern England, for example, new arrivals were befriended by an eastern European runner for a gangmaster. After a few weeks he would return to the house with thugs armed with knives to collect any cash from wages that had been hidden under mattresses. Few migrant workers are able to open bank accounts. No one complained for fear of being shopped to the Immigration authorities.

Not all gangmasters are criminal. But it was becoming very difficult for honest ones to compete. When I asked experts working in the territory to name a good gangmaster I might interview, they only ever came up with one person – Zad Padda. He was a second-generation Asian gangmaster based in Birmingham. He said that failure to grasp the nettle was making it harder and harder for people like him who wanted to operate within the law to survive. He supplied mainly Pakistani and Yemeni workers to horticultural companies in the Vale of Evesham, paying £1 million a year into government coffers in tax and insurance. He was advising the government on systems to check labourers' documentation and had introduced language courses and training for migrant workers. But he said that unscrupulous operators could always undercut him. According to one source, the unofficial going rate for labour was about £2.50–3 a hour in his area at a time when the minimum wage was £4.20. 'It all comes down to price. If that's the only basis on which you buy your food, you'll end up with illegal labour.'

While there had been much trumpeting by the Home Office and other government departments of raids which had caught illegal workers, actually arresting and successfully prosecuting those who ran the system proved more difficult. The workers not only bore the brunt of the appalling conditions but suffered the punishment too.

An enforcement officer in East Anglia expressed the frustration many working in the area felt. 'A local gangmaster has been to Lithuania to recruit directly. We know that. We also know there is plenty of violence – there have been court cases to deal with attacks by illegal migrants on other migrants, people being burned with hot irons, blackmail and extortion, that sort of thing. Individuals get deported – you'd be amazed how many pay slips have names like Marilyn Monroe on them. But no one seems to be able to get the big fish. Because the employment is devolved to a gangmaster, it's the gangmaster's legal responsibility to check the papers. But all the employer has to do is show that he checked the papers and "believed" they were genuine. They are very easy to fake. It all comes down to money at the end of the day. I go to the supermarket and I want the cheapest price. That's where the chain starts, with all the competition to cut prices.'

Most of the workers involved were too frightened to speak out. But I spoke to many, just by approaching them in the workplace, who described this system exactly. Most would not give their names for fear of being deported or of violent retribution.

Even those who were in the UK legally were often too afraid to complain or were unaware of their rights. But many Portuguese workers, who as members of the EU were entitled to work here, were able to give a clear picture of the prevailing conditions in the food industry. Although they could in theory be employed directly by the packhouses and factories, in practice they rarely were. They were dependent on the gangmasters for housing as well as jobs, since few local people were prepared to rent direct to them. Moreover, without the gangmasters' transport they could not get to the jobs, which were in remote rural areas with shifts often starting at night or very early in the morning.

Both supermarkets' representatives and the farmers' union denied that they benefited from the low wages paid to illegal workers. The suppliers argued that since they paid the gangmaster the going rate, not an illegal cut-price one, the system did not enable them to cut down on labour costs. But what it did enable them to do was turn the supply of workers on and off like a tap, and keep the tap running when they needed to, well beyond any legal limit on maximum hours. The supermarkets had driven down prices and transferred the risk to suppliers; they in turn saved money by not carrying the spare capacity that flexibility really demands.

The UK supermarkets are of course working in a global market. The drive to lower prices comes from international competition as much as anything. If you wanted evidence of the impact of supermarkets' price wars on wages, none could be clearer than that from the USA. Even the pro-business magazine *Business Week* was moved to question in a cover story whether Wal-Mart, which owns Asda in the UK, had become too powerful. Wal-Mart, it said, had relentlessly wrung tens of billions of dollars in cost efficiencies out of the retail supply chain, passing savings on to shoppers as bargain prices.

With a global workforce of 1.4 million, it plays a huge role in wages and working conditions worldwide . . . However, Wal-Mart's seemingly virtuous business model is fraught with perverse consequences. On average, in this staunchly anti-union company, America's largest private employer . . . sales clerks pulled in $13,861 a year in 2001. At the time, the federal poverty line for a family of three was $14,630.

In the autumn of 2003, 70,000 grocery workers in southern California went on strike as supermarkets tried to freeze or lower wages in order to compete with forty Wal-Mart supercentres due to open in the state. A *New York Times* editorial summarized why this apparently distant industrial relations problem affected us all.

The supermarkets say they are forced to lower their labour costs to compete with Wal-Mart, a non-union, low-wage employer aggressively moving into the grocery business. Everyone should be concerned about this fight. It is at bottom about the ability of retail workers to earn wages that keep their families out of poverty. Wal-Mart's prices are about 14 per cent lower than other groceries' because the company is aggressive about squeezing costs, including labour costs. Wal-Mart uses hardball tactics to ward off unions . . . workers are already only a step – or a second family income – from poverty. Wal-Mart may also be driving down costs by using undocumented immigrants. Last month, federal agents raided Wal-Marts in twenty-one states [and now the company] is facing a grand jury investigation.

The undocumented workers were employed through an agency, and Wal-Mart denied knowingly using illegal labour.

In the UK, with its much stronger employment legislation, the impact of price wars had been passed further down the line. It has not been the regular workforce employed by the super-markets themselves that has felt the squeeze, but the casual labour that works for the suppliers to whom so much of the business risk has been devolved.

I was often asked where all this went on, as if it were confined to small pockets of the country. It suited sections of the media to characterize these workers as 'bogus' or 'failed asylum seekers'. In fact the labour was and still is constantly moved around and fits no easy categorizing. Workers move in and out of different sectors, and in and out of legality. They may be students allowed to work only twenty hours who work longer, or seasonal work-ers who overstay their visas, or asylum seekers not allowed to work, or economic migrants who have entered the country il-legally and have no intention of claiming asylum. As David Jackson of Operation Gangmaster put it: 'It might be south-west for mushrooms one week, flowers in Lincolnshire the next, then greenhouse produce in Lancashire, then fruit in Evesham, salad in Sussex, cockles in Scotland, and so on.' Packhouses and food processing factories are everywhere and the conditions are the same right across the UK.

The pattern of employment is the same right round the country. Sometimes the scale of it is hidden within larger con-urbations – the labourers of Evesham, for instance, are mostly transported from Birmingham; those in the south-east may be brought out to work from London. It is in East Anglia that the impact of today's system of food production on migrants and the communities in which they find themselves is most clearly seen. The flatlands of the Fens are among the most productive agri-cultural areas in England, and the network of small towns around them have become the packhouse capital of the UK. Far from any large city which might provide labour or housing, the scale of economic migration here has been highly visible.

Thetford was typical: a small town in the middle of Norfolk, surrounded by lowland heaths and wetlands. Its prosperous market square reflects its past glory as Anglo-Saxon capital of East Anglia and more recently as home of Thomas Paine, the eighteenth-century radical and champion of the abolition of slavery.

The Red Lion, the old coaching inn in the main square, was known as 'the Portuguese pub', where the migrants who provide the labour to many of the food factories, packhouses and farms in the region congregated in their brief moments of leisure. It was here that I met Joaquim. He had been employed by a gangmaster packing vegetables and salads in the Norfolk factories for a few years. He was Portuguese and here legally but he was nervous. Some of the people he had worked for had used violence on others. There were things he didn't want to talk about.

The first factory he worked at – a big company supplying supermarkets – was staffed by a mix of legal Portuguese workers and illegal Russians and Ukrainians. The supervisor would always give more work to the illegals – and they in turn would give him backhanders to make sure they could get work or the best positions on the production line. There was a lot of corruption, so if work was slack, as it often was when supermarket orders were suddenly cancelled, you wouldn't get any. It was piecework and if you worked really hard, you could earn £400 a week. That was when they decided to change the system so the maximum you could get was £200 a week. 'I was on a carrot line, sorting them by appearance. You could get good at it. You couldn't stop when you had done your eight hours though, you had to carry on till the order was finished. After that I worked in a salad factory. It was a good company but the hours were unpredictable, and then a gangmaster offered me a bit more money for driving a minivan, taking workers to the packhouses, so I did that. The vehicle had no tax or insurance and was supposed to take twelve but we'd drive eighteen. It had no MOT and the steering was dodgy, which was a problem because we had to turn right on a roundabout into the packhouse. There weren't any windows, so that people couldn't see who was inside. Sometimes you would get a warning that Immigration were coming, so then you would make sure there were no Russians or Brazilians that day, only Portuguese people.

'I would be charged thirty-five pounds a week to share a tiny room and in some jobs after all the deductions I only got sixty pounds in my pocket a week even though I worked long hours.

'One of the gangmasters would boast that he could take any woman to bed. He'd say the women had no choice because they were illegal. There was an attempted rape in one house – there's lots of sexual harassment, but this was serious assault. One of the women in the house who was legal rang the gangmaster and threatened to go to the police. So he told her she was sacked over the phone and then came round to evict her.

'The orders would come suddenly and you would be taken to the factory. But then if there was no work you would be taken back to the house after just a couple of hours. You might work for one factory packing from six a.m. till one p.m. and then get taken to another factory for a four p.m. to ten p.m. shift. There was a lot of violence to enforce the regime. In the first three months I saved nothing. It was easy to blow your money at the weekend on drink. Then I decided I had to get out of the trap and be very disciplined. I worked sixteen hours a day and saved everything to escape.'

The Red Lion was one of Fatima's haunts. Fatima was fiftyish with dyed dark hair and bright red lipstick. Her plucked eyebrows had been redrawn half an inch higher on her forehead so that her expression is one of constant amused astonishment at her predicament. She had been trying to organize Portuguese workers locally into a union to fight for their rights, but when her gangmaster found out, she was evicted without warning from her accommodation in Thetford. She managed to get her-self a caravan in a field to live in and was happy to have escaped the tied housing which made her so dependent on the gang-master. He had put her in a house with ten South African men he used as his enforcers and she didn't feel safe. There was lots of sexual harassment by the Portuguese supervisors at work. The gangmaster was then arrested and charged with not paying tax and insurance, she said, and the business and workers were handed over to another gangmaster, but one of the managers was the same as before. When I met Fatima she was working through the new gangmaster doing twelve-hour night shifts, six days a week, with no overtime payments, for a printer who printed the labels for supermarket ready meals. When she com-plained that it was too cold to work in the factory, she was threatened with a beating. She had decided to go home. 'There is a lot of racism,' she said. 'It's horrible here.'

There were 4,000 Portuguese workers living in Thetford and the surrounding areas and an unknown number of Brazilians. The first wave of Portuguese migration was followed by another of mostly Polish and Lithuanian workers when several eastern European countries acceded to the EU in 2004. Fatima was friendly with many of them and took me on a tour to meet them. In one small house in a 1970s estate in nearby Brandon, a town serving more food factories, she introduced me to Agost-inha. Agostinha was a survivor, a big Portuguese woman in her mid-thirties with lots of bleached blonde hair, a deep voice and a ready laugh. She and Jose, her Brazilian husband, younger by several years, were sharing one small bedroom in the house with her ten-year-old son Pedro, who went to the local school. There had been eight living in the house the week before, but three of the Brazilians, a couple and their little girl, also at a local school, had just been deported. The bailiffs had called to collect debts left by previous tenants, South Africans. The landlord had threat-ened to evict Agostinha, but the police had intervened.

They paid £100 a week for their one bedroom, and the

landlord's usual terms were pasted up by the front door: £7 per bed per night. He kept a key and came in whenever he felt like it, sometimes at night, to check up on them. Agostinha showed me her room, rushing round with air-freshener spray before I went in, apologizing for the mess. The room was jammed with their possessions – suitcases, piles of clothes and shoes, a bowl of fruit, cuddly toys, a homework folder, a few ornaments, a small double bed and a child's single bed in the corner. Everything was as neat and ordered as it could be in such a tiny space.

Over a communal Sunday lunch she had prepared for everyone in the house, Agostinha told me about her work experiences. She was first employed cutting and packing salads at the factory nearby. The lettuce would come along the line for them to cut, different ways for different clients, one way for Tesco, another way for McDonald's. Then they'd put it back on the belt to go for washing in a rolling carpet of water and chlorine. As it came out you picked out the bad leaves and packed the good ones. The chlorine burned your eyes but everything was very clean. Then there was work for a while, trussing birds, at a chicken factory supplying the major retailers. Agostinha developed wrist pain but was told to carry on working and did so for three weeks while in pain. She says that the factory manager told her it wasn't a problem and that she must work faster. But then it got too bad to continue and they sent her home. The local doctor had diagnosed tendonitis and she was on the waiting list for an operation on her hand at the NHS hospital. She was given no sick pay by the gangmaster despite having paid tax and insurance. She had been told by social security that she would be receiving state benefits soon.

She also told me about 'a guy at one of the gangmasters, Junior, everyone knows who he is, he's the one who fixes the Brazilians' papers. You pay three hundred pounds to a lawyer through him and everything is taken care of.' They charged the Brazilians to come to England – many of them had sold houses and cars at home to pay – and then they shopped them after a few months when they owed them wages. It meant they could make more money charging the next lot to come. This brutal practice was a recurring theme among the migrants I spoke to.

I wondered what it must be like for Agostinha's son Pedro, witnessing all the coming and going, and living in such cramped conditions. 'He cried nearly every day for the first year, there was such a lot of racism at school, kids would keep telling him he was the son of a bitch and should go home.' She actually wanted to go home, but her husband's papers were stuck with the Immigration office in Croydon. They were taken by Immigration officials who raided the house looking for a South African who wasn't there. Since Jose was now married to her, he was perfectly entitled to be in the country, but despite making the trek to London twice Agostinha had been waiting a year to get them back so they could travel. She laughed at the craziness of it all. 'Well, do you want us or want to get rid of us?'

Teresa, by contrast, was pale, thin and seven months pregnant. She and her husband Joao lived slightly north of Thetford in Watton, another small Norfolk town, along with several other Portuguese workers. Joao's eyes were bloodshot with exhaustion, and he seemed to shrink into his fragile frame. Their tiny one-bedroomed flat was up a metal staircase, along a corridor with a filthy carpet and bare live electricity cables hanging from the ceiling. Teresa had been unable to work recently, having suffered from serious depression, which was being treated by the local GP. But she had done shifts in many of the food factories and packhouses in the area, always working through gangmasters because that was the only way she and her husband could get housing. She did a spell at a canning factory where they cut labels off supermarket cans that had been dented and put new labels on top to cover the dents. She'd work on the potato packing lines at weekends. The worst job her husband had was in the cat food factory where the gangmaster would have them picked up with Chinese workers for night shifts, dragging everyone in, just so that a supervisor could line them up and walk along pointing with his finger: 'You, you, you and you' and then send the rest home without work. During a period without work Joao had to sell his gold wedding ring to buy food.

A Portuguese friend in the town had had her car vandalized, and another Portuguese couple had been attacked in the street one night, so Teresa was fearful of going out. The flat was expensive – £80 a week – and after long hours in his current job in a duck processing factory Joao was left with £60 a week after all the deductions. But at least they weren't living with rats any more. When they complained about conditions to one gangmaster they were evicted. They were told by the Citizens' Advice Bureau in King's Lynn to go to the council because they were homeless, but were too frightened to do so. If was known that you caused trouble, you wouldn't get the jobs. They were however on the council's social housing register.

One of the local doctors in Thetford, Dr Giles Smith, wrote to the Efra select committee asking why no one could stop the gangmasters recruiting people. His practice had some 700 Portuguese on its lists, as well as Russians and Chinese. Dr Smith told me he had seen increasing evidence of migrant workers doing long hours and night shifts in vegetable factories becoming 'long-term sick'. 'They are being abused and overworked. Quite a few have industrial injuries and get dumped on the sick system. They then apply for housing from the local authority. I feel for them, but I feel for the services the NHS is trying to provide too. We're hanging on by our fingernails. My colleagues and staff are spending vast amounts of time sorting the problems of non-English speaking patients. The strain on the infrastructure – medical, police, education, housing, sewage, roads – is intolerable. There is huge resentment in the town. I fear there is going to be tribal war.'

He proved right. In 2004 hours of violent rioting outside the Red Lion pub followed England's defeat by Portugal in the European football cup. A mob of over 200 local youths surrounded the building and hurled missiles at its windows while shouting racist abuse. About forty Portuguese workers and their families barricaded themselves inside for over two hours while police struggled to bring the crowd under control. Eight were injured that night and ten young men were later jailed for the attack.

The Efra committee, after hearing at length evidence from retailers' organizations, farmers, unions and others, reached the damning conclusion that

the dominant position of the supermarkets in relation to their suppliers is a significant contributory factor in creating an environment where illegal activity by gangmasters can take root. Intense price competition and the short time-scales between orders from the supermarkets and deliveries to them put pressure on suppliers who have little opportunity or incentive to check the legality of the labour. Supermarkets go to great lengths to ensure that the labels on their products are accurate. We believe they should pay equal attention to the conditions under which their produce is harvested and packed ... supermarkets cannot wash their hands of this matter.

MPs also said they were 'appalled by the lack of priority given to what is supposed to be the government's coordinated response to illegal activity by gangmasters'.

When I first started writing about the plight of migrant workers in Britain's food factories and packhouses in the early 2000s, the general assumption was that exploitation did occur, but in isolated incidents and was down to a few rogue gangmasters. To those on the ground, however, it was clear that problems were widespread and growing. We kept finding examples of egregious abuse in mainstream factories, including particularly troubling cases such as debt-bonded labour packing fruit for Tesco in a supplier's factory in Lincolnshire. I came back to the subject in my second book, *Eat Your Heart Out*, and the more I interviewed migrants around the country the more common themes emerged: they were at the mercy of agencies that held power over their everyday lives, and they were nearly all physically afraid because of their routine exposure to violence and intimidation. Much of the business was run by agencies closely linked to not just illegal labour but other forms of crime, including people-smuggling, money-laundering, identity fraud, drug-trafficking and prostitution. But government ministers either had no idea of the scale of the problem or chose not to see it.

It was later accepted that at least 500,000, and probably more, migrants were in this country illegally, many of them employed in the food and catering business. Their lack of legal status made them particularly vulnerable.

Then the Morecambe Bay tragedy of 2004, in which twenty-three Chinese cockle-pickers, trapped by the tide on quicksands were abandoned by their gangmasters and drowned, made it impossible to ignore the exploitation anymore. New legislation was hastily introduced through a messy private member's bill to licence gangmasters.

The first inspection for the Gangmaster's Licensing Authority (GLA), carried out in 2007, was on a company where I had previously investigated illegal labour. Bomfords, in the Vale of Evesham, supplied more than 50 per cent of the big supermarkets' spring onions and more than a quarter of their green beans and fresh peas, as well as asparagus. All seven gangmasters supplying labour to Bomfords were found by the GLA to be breaking the law and had their licences suspended after the inspection. One had its licence revoked with immediate effect on the grounds that its workers were in danger and were being intimidated. They were Poles and other eastern Europeans.

It had been common knowledge in the industry for years that the hourly rates for workers Bomfords offered its gangmasters made it all but certain that those gangmasters would be breaking the law. At a time when the minimum wage was £5.35, a gangmaster complying with the law on minimum wage, national insurance, sick and holiday pay would have to charge at the very least £6.27 per worker per hour. And that's without any allowance for the gangmaster's costs or profits. If you factored in the gangmaster's administration and overhead costs, the minimum rate would have needed to be nearly £7. But the industry's Association of Labour Providers reported that Bomfords was paying just £6.10 per hour.

Bomfords had substantial debts. After the inspection Bomfords had to employ more workers to harvest and pack its supermarket vegetables directly on significantly higher rates. A few months later it went bust. The economics of supplying the supermarkets had stopped working for it. It owed growers, including farmers in Africa, about £18 million. Some of them were highly distressed and contacted me.

One of the reasons Bomfords was able to supply vegetables more cheaply than others, and the supermarkets in turn were able to sell them more cheaply, was that it didn't pay as much for its labour as others. The business model of cheap fresh food which supermarkets have used to establish their dominance has in other words depended on illegality and exploitation.

In Bomfords' history you could see a supermarket system laid bare: a system on the one hand capable of checking that every last bean and asparagus tip conforms to an exact size and shape, a system capable of tracking when, where and by whom they were packed, yet on the other unable to spot that every gangmaster sending workers to a major supplier was breaking the law.

Even where companies were complying with the law, the necessity of being the lowest cost producer led to a race to the bottom, in which the minimum wage fast became the maximum wage.

The impact of this sort of flexible labour market on social cohesion in Britain has been considerable.

The resentments were simmering even before the financial crisis. After it, with the economy in deep recession and youth unemployment around Europe at record levels, the anti-immigration lobby and the far right has been resurgent.

Yet even now, the reality that the global movement of goods

and capital has driven mass migrations is not fully acknowledged. Nor is the fact that dominant transnational food retailers, manufacturers and processors have created a system which I believe is dependent on exploitation – and at its worst new forms of slavery – even as their profits have risen dramatically.

This is how globalization has worked: it has widened the gap between the rich and the poor. Large companies have captured the value of the food market and have benefited from lower labour costs. The affluent have been able to maintain their time-pressured lifestyles thanks to a plentiful supply of cheap food and services supplied by underpaid migrants, but they did not ask for this and many are not comfortable with it.

The GLA achieved some success but was never sufficiently resourced to tackle the problem of illegal employment and exploitation properly. Unions, most notably the Transport and General Workers' Union, and its new incarnation Unite, have worked intensely to persuade British factory workers that their best hope of protecting their own jobs and conditions is to make sure everyone including migrants is organized and receives the same pay. Supermarkets have been shamed into paying more attention to labour conditions in their supply chains. I was told by my sources that the abuses in the food sector were beginning to be a little less pervasive by 2008 but then the economic slump put things into reverse. The GLA survived the 2010 coalition government's bonfire of the quangos, but only just. Its already meagre budget was to be slashed by nearly a fifth by the end of the Conservative–Liberal Democrat-led parliament. In response to complaints from agribusiness it had been instructed to be more 'light touch' in its regulation and inspection of farm businesses and packhouses. It will have no money to be anything else.

A raid I was invited to join in late 2012 gave an indication of how great the need for the GLA's work remains. In a joint operation with Kent police and the Serious Organized Crime Agency (SOCA), the GLA moved in to liberate more than

thirty Lithuanian workers who were alleged to have been traf-
ficked into the UK. They were said to have then been kept in
debt bondage, forced to work up to seventeen hours a shift,
bussed to farms the length of the country to catch hens through
the night, sleeping in vans for days at a time, some weeks not
paid at all, and, according to workers' testimony, kept under control by Lithuanian enforcers with threats of violence and on
occasion actual physical assault. They described not even knowing where they were going, but trying to find out from the GPS
system at the front of the minivan. They claimed they were
refused toilet stops on journeys and that in between jobs they
were kept for hours in the vans at roadside parking places. The
conditions they reported met official UN definitions of modern
slavery.

The gangmaster company was a member of Freedom Food,
the welfare scheme licensed by the RSPCA. Six dogs, including
some fighting breeds, which the migrants claimed were used to
intimidate them, were taken from a separate property into the
care of a local branch of the RSPCA.

The gangmaster business supplied the workers to Noble
Foods, one of the UK's largest processors of eggs and chickens.
Noble was at the time promoting its own brand of 'happy eggs'
on primetime television with an advert that showed its hens
leaping for joy at their lovely conditions to the Olympian sound-
track of *Chariots of Fire*. Noble also supplied premium free-range
eggs to McDonald's and the leading supermarkets. The company's chairman, Peter Dean, has been a key Tory party donor.

When asked what measures it took to ensure standards for
workers, as opposed to the hens in its supply chain, it said in a
statement: 'Noble Foods is one of many companies within the
poultry industry that has used [this gangmaster]. After being
notified of the action taken by Kent police we immediately
ceased using this organization. As the police investigation is
ongoing it would be inappropriate for us to comment further.'

The *Guardian* asked the gangmasters to comment on the

allegations but they too declined because of the police investigation. Their licence was revoked with immediate effect. They were appealing at the time of writing. The Lithuanian alleged to be the 'enforcer' was out of the country at the time of the raid and avoided arrest. No charges have been brought.

McDonald's also declined to comment and referred us to Noble Foods. A Tesco spokesperson said: 'As a founder member of the Ethical Trading Initiative, we are committed to decent working conditions on all the farms and factories in our supply chain. These allegations are clearly shocking. We will continue to work closely with the GLA, our suppliers and others to ensure good practice throughout the sector.' The other retailers also said that they took the allegations very seriously and were co-operating with the enforcement agencies.

The RSPCA's Freedom Food company said individual licence holders were responsible for ensuring animal welfare. There are no specific labour standards in its licence terms, but where a member does anything which would bring Freedom Food or the RSPCA into disrepute then the membership agreement makes provision for suspending or cancelling a business's membership. 'Should these shocking allegations regarding workers prove to be true then Freedom Food would enact this provision,' it said.

When the English outdoor salad season comes to an end in late October, much of the production moves to Spain. Several large English producers have acquired farms there, mostly in the Murcia and Andalucía regions, to enable them to guarantee year-round supplies of salads to supermarkets.

Spanish farms are also the source of many of the Mediterranean vegetables such as peppers and aubergines sold in British supermarkets, along with tomatoes, cucumbers, celery, out-of-season broccoli and organic produce. Quite apart from the climate, the costs are lower there.

EU structural funds have helped create this new horticultural industry. They have paid for a motorway network to be driven right through Spain, so that refrigerated lorries scarcely have to leave the dual carriageway as they plough from Almeria in the south to the further reaches of northern Europe.

The land is arid, and the regional governments are proud of their 'miracles', saying that like the Israelis they have made the desert bloom. The dramatic economic growth has transformed an area that was until recently among the poorest in Europe. English literati travelling through it in the 1950s and 1960s never failed to mention the destitution they saw. Thanks to intensive farming, the Almeria area alone now produces nearly 3 million tonnes of fruit and vegetables annually, mostly for export to the UK, Germany, Holland and Belgium, earning £1 billion in export revenue a year. But the success story is already losing its varnish. There is talk of EU social funds being needed to pay for a planned abandonment of some of the lands where the soil or water is most polluted. Its critics say the 'miracle' is ravaging the area.

I arranged to meet Hector Gravina early one morning in a hotel favoured by British package tour companies on the Costa Blanca. The Spanish organic farmers' association was running a conference here and I had been told there would be a chance to meet the chief of agri-environment from Spain's Ministry of Agriculture, along with other leading academic experts. Everything had been done by email, with the timings left rather vague, so I wasn't quite sure who I was looking for. I was scanning the crowds of passing holidaymakers when a short, wiry man, with a dramatic scar slashed across his forehead to his beetling brows, official conference bag slung across his shoulder like a bandolier, enveloped me in a great bear hug and a swirl of roll-up cigarette smoke. '*Hola!*'

Standing back for air a few minutes later, I took in Hector Gravina, a veteran campaigner from Spain's Friends of the Earth: black leather jerkin, black trousers, long-sleeved red T-shirt, close-cropped black hair, left in a little mop on top, with a tiny pigtail curling down his neck behind, and the remnants of a goatee beard on his chin.

'You have chosen a good day. Our tour bus is going round one of the most beautiful nature reserves of Spain. I can show you the most intensive agricultural production in the country, the fields of plastic, and then you see organic lettuce being grown in the shadow of the farmhouse that inspired our great playwright, Garcia Lorca, to write *Blood Wedding*. But first we will have it from the horse's mouth, let's catch the man from the ministry . . .'

The chief of agri-environment, Manuel Ariza, a substantial, jowly man, had just arrived in the lobby. Hidden behind his black sunglasses, his eyes gave no clue to his sympathies when I asked what he saw as the main issues for Spanish agriculture, but traces of a good breakfast were just visible on his shirt, hinting at a man who enjoys his food. 'Agriculture is three per cent of our total GDP. Intensive farming represents fifty per cent of the total agricultural area. It is mainly concentrated in the Mediterranean arc. We are Europe's California,' he said as solemnly as a text-book, then his whole body heaved with laughter. 'So we have all their problems, problems with water – pollution of coastal waters, exhaustion of ground water, problems with soil degrad-ation . . .' Then he disappeared into his official car while we piled on to our bus.

We drove along the coast, where any gaps in the line of hotels were filled with cranes and construction sites for new apart-ments and golf courses. Then we passed into a dramatic landscape of desert rock, blazing with light and stunning shadows. 'The Sahara is creeping up, you can see how intensive agriculture has accelerated the process and where the hills have lost any ground cover,' Hector pointed out.

At Níjar, the sea of plastic greenhouses began. The green-houses did not look like greenhouses so much as old army tents, an invasion of plastic sheeting pitched over wooden or metal poles that stretched as far as the eye could see. The plastic was greying and drooping, opaque with dust and splashes of chemicals. There was no visible greenery. Agrochemical adverts appeared like milestones at regular intervals. All the big companies are here – Bayer, DuPont, Monsanto, Syngenta. Here and there diggers were at work excavating soil that had become saturated with chemicals or so exhausted by the cycle of three harvests a year that it was no longer economical to farm it and new soil had to be brought in.

This is the driest part of Europe and the water supply is indeed at crisis point here. Unlike the olives, almonds and other traditional crops of the region that used to be farmed on mixed holdings with sheep and goats, horticultural crops are thirsty, and salads the thirstiest of them all. Intensive agriculture has competed with the tourist industry to be the most extravagant user of water. The groundwater has become polluted with pesticides. The water table has been infiltrated by the sea as a result of over-extraction. Excessive use of chemical fertilizers has led to nitrate levels that are in some places ten times higher than World Health Organization safety limits.

The nitrate problem is not confined to Spain. Intensive farming in England has also polluted groundwater, damaging the ecology of streams, rivers and lakes and ruining coastal waters. Some 55 per cent of the country has recently been designated as 'nitrate vulnerable zones'.

Much of southern Spain has already run out of drinking water. The tourist and farming industries currently depend on aqueducts bringing water from rivers further north. But now those supplies are inadequate too. The Spanish government proposed a grandiose plan to divert part of the Ebro river to bring water from the north of the country to the south to feed the lettuce and other vegetables, which involved building over 100 dams, 1,000 kilometres of canals and pipes at a cost of €18 billion.

Hector had been among the 1 million protestors who took to the streets in March 2002 to campaign against the plan, in one of the greatest public displays of anti-government sentiment in Spain since the days of General Franco. The project would have threatened the Ebro delta, Europe's second largest wetland. It was eventually abandoned in favour of an alternative proposal to construct fifteen vast desalination plants in the south, which would bring their own environmental difficulties. Meanwhile, many farms in the south had taken to extracting water illegally to get round government restrictions.

Our tour bus eventually emerged from the plastic wasteland into one of the last remaining nature reserves on the Cabo da Gata, and stopped in front of the romantic ruins of a farm, with old drystone walls marking out terraces of gnarled olive and wild fig trees. Much of the land here was abandoned in the 1960s, when the Spanish migrated in their thousands to escape the grinding poverty that went with living on its poor soil. No one wanted to go back to the good old days.

I caught up with the man from the ministry again and asked him what he thought would happen in the coming years. 'Of course this intensive vegetable production is not sustainable. We will have to switch back to rotating crops. Olive production is sustainable here.' He bent down to admire a desert snail with beautiful markings, and invited me to join him in the official limousine. 'The chemical companies started to promote products, the farmers started to misuse them, the plants grow in excess, they need more water, the farmers are thrilled, but you can't go on doing that, taking three or four crops a year from soil. Over time the exploitation of the land will shift. Mediterranean vegetables will move to the Maghreb where the laws are less stringent – European countries have already invested there, it's cheaper and there is still beautiful land there. We'll grow more organic and farm more extensively. There'll be warranties against residues for produce from outside the EU – we'll test more and reject produce with pesticide residues, so it will be safe – but no warranties for the environment ...'

I said that not many British government officials would be

quite so outspoken. 'Ah well, I've survived a few governments. I'll take the risk. That is my personal opinion of course, not necessarily the view of my government. Now, where's lunch . . . ?'

We had stopped in the middle of the nature reserve, at a viewpoint over the scorched and rugged hills. The men had brought out a paella dish the size of a paddling pool and placed it over a camp fire and were emptying a 5-litre can of local organic olive oil into it. Ariza took a swig of chilled beer and continued the argument: 'Globalization of food is not the answer. It is a system designed by finance people and lawyers. Of course, individuals will have to change.' The prawns were going into the paella at this point – Ariza leaned over and inspected the label on the box. 'It says "Produce of South Africa",' he laughed. 'No, but I am optimistic for Europe. The environmental problems will be brought under control in the West and the USA. They will be passed on instead to poorer countries. The real problem will be with the petrochemical companies. They will have to find their money elsewhere.'

There was little sign of that at the time. The byproducts of the refining of crude oil – the plastics that made the greenhouses, the toxic pesticides that were applied to the plants – were heavily promoted. It was still common practice in Spain to rely heavily on chemical disease control. There has been some move towards biological pest controls since.

The pristine-looking leaves we have acquired an appetite for cannot achieve their cosmetic perfection without a little hi-tech help, particularly when they are grown outside their normal season. Intensive monoculture of salads with extended seasons of cropping allows the buildup of pests and diseases in the soil. There has been a correspondingly rapid increase in pesticide usage. Salad leaves are particularly likely to contain pesticide residues. Lettuce appeared on the 'persistent offenders list' for pesticide residues compiled by the Consumers' Association from government data, in the company of apples, celery, grapes, fresh salmon, pears, peaches and nectarines, strawberries and wholemeal flour.

Most large producers in the UK are fairly coy about what pesticides they use. So I spoke to an agricultural technical consultant who worked with the agrochemical industry in Spain. He explained the system to me on the condition of anonymity.

'Lettuces have a two-and-a-half to three-month growing period here in Spain. They are sprayed every week with a mixture of fungicide and insecticide except for the last two weeks. There is lots of pesticide resistance, so the products we used last year were completely different to the ones we were using five or six years ago. Some of them are very toxic. For example, we treat the lettuces with dithiocarbamates as a preventive – the English seem to use a lot of these. They are very hazardous. But there's a fungus called sclerotinia that can suddenly flare up where you have had intense cropping of the same lettuces in the same place. This monoculture allows a lot of funguses and pests to flourish. It is devastating, you can lose half the crop. With the plastic hothouses it's bad too, they are all so close together, pests spread through those crops like wildfire. I also have to advise growers to use more pesticides than I would like because if there is just one tiny aphid, their whole crop can be rejected by the supermarkets. If you want something so perfect that you can't even see one tiny aphid on it, as though it came not from the soil but from a factory, of course you have to use much more pesticide.

'Many of the seed varieties the supermarkets want are patented. The seed companies have developed hybrids in consultation with the retailers. They cost a lot, so once you've invested in them as a farmer you can't afford to take risks. The seed companies give you a whole agrochemical recipe to go with them, so of course you follow it. (The agrochemical industry has seen rapid concentration in the last few years with a series of mergers and takeovers. Six top companies (see Chapter 7: Coffee and Grains) accounted for 75 per cent of the $134 billion-worth of agrochemical sales worldwide in 2010. They have also moved heavily into the seed industry and now control about 30 per cent of it, in what for them is a virtuous business circle. Many seeds now come with a seed 'dressing' of pesticides already applied, which is a major contributor to the increase in pesticide use, according to Barbara Dinham, director of Pesticides Action Network UK.)

'Because lettuces grow first from a few outer leaves, with the heart developing later, the outside leaves are where the nitrates and pesticides are most concentrated. By the end of a crop cycle they can have been treated with eleven or twelve doses of pesticide as well as several fertilizer applications. More and more lettuces are sold by the supermarkets as hearts only. This conveniently removes the contaminated outer leaves as well as allowing them to charge for a "premium product".'

Most supermarkets and producers will say that pesticide usage is being reduced as companies are encouraged to switch to 'integrated crop management' (ICM) in which instead of routinely spraying, farmers make more effort to diagnose and treat problems as they arise. When *Not On the Label* first appeared the government programme of tests for pesticide residues had lettuce as a priority for annual checks since it was such a persistent offender. The Pesticides Safety Directorate's (PSD) survey of lettuce bought in 2001–2 showed that nearly one in five lettuces exceeded maximum residue levels and 6 per cent contained pesticides not approved for use. The PSD considered that in two cases the pesticide levels presented 'possible safety risks' but no action was taken because the growers had followed the manufacturers' instructions on the label.

Lettuce remains on the official surveillance list. In 2007 a residue of a chemical, chlorothalonil, which is not approved for use on salad in the UK, was found on two samples of lettuce above statutory maximum residue level (MRL). Chlorothalonil is classed by the Pesticide Action Network as a 'bad actor'. It is highly toxic, and may be a carcinogen and endocrine disruptor, one of a class of chemicals which interfere with hormones.

In subsequent years up to and including 2011 a residue of thiamethoxam, another chemical which is not approved for lettuce, has been found. Thiamethoxam is one of a class of chemicals called neonicotinoids, which are suspected of causing a devastating decline in bees.

The government's survey of pesticide residues in early 2011 found that over half of retail samples tested contained residues of multiple pesticides, with two samples containing seven types of residue. These included carbamates, which work on the nervous system in a similar way to organophosphates. None exceeded the MRL and the Pesticide Residues Committee concluded none of the residues detected would be expected to have an effect on health.

While in recent years, in response to consumer concern, supermarkets have made efforts to take some of the most troubling pesticides off the lists of products their growers may use, producing perfect blemish-free and insect-free leaves without chemical props has proved very difficult.

The government's Central Science Laboratory records overall usage of pesticides in the UK. Its 2011 reports on chemical use in lettuce crops notes: 'The demands from major retailers, in terms of the quality of crops purchased, are extremely high and, as a consequence, the use of biological control agents, insecticides, fungicides and disinfectants need to match these requirements.'

They also record that 60 per cent of lettuce and leafy salad crops grown under glass or plastic in the UK were treated more than four times with pesticides, and 20 per cent were treated four times. Less than a fifth of indoor lettuce was left untreated with chemicals, and on average these crops received three doses of fungicide, two of insecticide and one of herbicide during the growing season. Outdoor lettuce received on average three doses of insecticides, two of fungicide and two of herbicide, with only 2 per cent of lettuce grown outdoors remaining untreated with chemicals.

The Pesticide Action Network has drawn up its own list of foods most likely to contain residues of endocrine disruptors from test results published by the European Food Safety Authority. A growing body of scientific evidence has linked these endocrine disruptors, which alter hormonal systems, to chronic diseases including obesity and diabetes, to decreased fertility, and to hormone-related cancers such as breast and prostate cancer. Lettuce is the worst offender, closely followed by tomatoes, cucumbers, apples and leeks.

The effect of pesticide residues on our health is disputed. The government's Pesticide Residues Committee says that most residues are present at such a low level that they do not 'present a concern for consumer health'. The FSA's advice is that while about 40 per cent of fresh fruit and vegetables contain residues, they typically occur at very low levels, that is, at parts per million, and that people eating small amounts of pesticide residues in their diet are not at risk. It does however recognize concern over the so-called 'cocktail effect' of residues from different sources and asked the government's committee on toxicity to look into the risks. The committee concluded that it was extremely difficult to assess the risks because the data was not available, but highlighted groups of chemicals of specific concern. These include insecticides that work by blocking nerve receptors – the organophosphates and carbamates; certain fungicides; and the range of chemicals which are endocrine disrupters – in other words, precisely the sort of residues that have been found in salad.

The committee on toxicity agrees that endocrine-disrupting chemicals may be implicated in declining sperm counts and increasing rates of breast and testicular cancer. A Royal Society report also said that it was sensible for pregnant women to minimize their exposure to endocrine-disrupting chemicals.

Other experts are less sanguine. Dr Vyvyan Howard is a leading toxicopathologist at the University of Ulster and a former member of the government's advisory committee on pesticides, who has studied the effects of pesticides on unborn children. He points out that the average Briton has between 300 and 500 chemicals in their body which were not present fifty years ago. 'We have substantially changed the chemical environment of the womb. Pregnant women are now exposed to completely novel molecules that their grandmothers were not. Quite a number of these are capable of hormone disruption and it takes only extremely low doses to cause effects.' He believes there is ample evidence that the pesticide cocktail effect is producing enormous change. Exposure to endocrine disrupters in the womb could be one of the reasons for the much-decreased age of puberty in girls. Early onset of puberty is linked to breast cancer later in life. In the 1960s women had a one in twenty chance of getting breast cancer, now it is one in nine. Dr Howard recommends minimizing exposure to pesticides on a precautionary basis.

The problem for the supermarkets is that despite their protestation that they are doing everything to cut down on pesticides, they are on a chemical treadmill. Friends of the Earth campaigns on pesticide use in food and says that the retailers' demand for cosmetic perfection forces farmers to use more pesticides than they would otherwise.

Meanwhile, a briefing paper on the Spanish horticulture industry written for Defra noted: 'A heavy reliance on chemical pest and disease control is still standard practice among Spanish growers.'

From the Costa Blanca, I moved east, on my first trip in 2003, to see the Almerian miracle at its most intense, along the Costa del Sol.

Roquetas de Mar, like every other resort town along Spain's south coast, has been swallowed up by its *urbanizaciones*. An uninterrupted strip of time-share tower blocks in Malaga pink and Moorish beige competes with wall-to-wall package-holiday hotels to cover every inch of the seafront from here to the next town in either direction. Their balconies point towards the Mediterranean where jaunty straw parasols, painted brochure blue, shade rows and rows of yellow sun-loungers along the beach.

For a few euros you can take a toytown train inland a few hundred yards. It toots up the main street of bars with its central reserve of palms and carefully tended shrubs just as far as the roundabout where the barren desert intrudes again, and then turns straight back down to the front. Alternatively, you can tour the high rises in traditional horse and cart, complete with sing-ing driver in sombrero.

You can buy your place in the sun here for as little as €65,000. A few chunks of plaster have already fallen off some of the new tower blocks, but in the brilliant light and haze of cheap sangria, no one's noticing. Arsenal v Liverpool is showing on Sky at the Colossimo pub where Brits enjoy an early-morning pint, and *Waf-feln mit Kirschen* are being served to Germans in the café next door.

Less than a mile away, on the other side of the roundabout, the good road, and with it the world of holidays, comes to an abrupt halt. Drive over the patch of rough ground beyond, and you find yourself plunging instead into the sea of plastic greenhouses that have drowned the wide coastal plain for miles around.

I came up here on my first night in Roquetas, having been warned to take care. It's easy to get lost in this featureless land-scape. The roads through the hothouses all look the same after a while – a maze of cracked tarmac corridors fading into unmade edges. But what the friendly advice had meant was this is another country. It is a segregated universe, alarming to locals, that stretches for miles across the province of Almeria and into neighbouring Murcia in which 70,000–90,000 or more migrant labourers live. They squat by the side of the roads for hours, from dawn till dusk, in the hope of being picked up for work on the vegetables.

I had arranged to meet Gabriel Ataya, a Senegalese organizer for the Rural Workers' Union, and his friends here on the edge of town where the migrants have colonized old houses aban-doned by the Spanish.

It was dark and there was no more hope of work that day, but there were still people by the roadside, refusing to give up. Some of them were slumped against telegraph poles, snatching sleep, others stared listlessly at the ground, raising their eyes briefly at each passing van.

Outside Ataya's house, a tall black man, hearing me call out in French, came up and begged for food. He told me his name was Drame Diongo. He had arrived from Senegal one month before, having left his family and paid a man in Dakar about £1,000 to borrow his papers. He'd queued every morning by the road for work but had never got picked by the Spanish farm owners. He hadn't eaten for two days. He was big and looked strong, but his weary voice was hard to catch. He had no idea why he didn't get picked and asked me what I thought.

Perhaps it was that his jeans, specially saved for and bought for his new life, looked too new; perhaps it was that his beard and Islamic cap made him look like a caricature of a terrorist, or perhaps it was just that he didn't speak Spanish. I suggested Ataya might be able to explain how the pecking order worked.

Inside Ataya's single-storey, rough-plastered old house, it turned out that Ataya knew Drame and had already helped him. Several other men appeared to have adopted the house too and drifted in and out of the sitting room past the large sacks of rice in the hall, while I talked to Ataya's friend Spitou.

Spitou had been a Spanish teacher in Senegal, but he had had to support two families since his brother died and found he could not survive on his official salary back home. He managed to get a visa from the French embassy in Dakar which he was able to use to come to Spain: 'It's easier for people like me to get visas because I had a good job.' He too was tall, with handsome, even features and a soft voice. He had worked for nearly three years on farms where they grow tomatoes for export to the UK and Holland. The work was never guaranteed but when he was needed he was paid €30 (about £20) for eight or nine hours' labour – the daylight hours – thinning the fruit so that the tomatoes left on the vines would grow uniformly, and harvesting. It's backbreaking work and unbearably hot as the temperature is usually 45–48°C under the plastic. The irrigation water, which comes in a huge new pipe, is computer-controlled, mixed with pesticides and fertilizers and constantly drip-fed to the plants to keep them healthy, but there's no drinking water for the workers. The boss knew Spitou by a false identity, and Spitou was paying tax and insurance, but against this false identity, on another man's papers.

'The boss doesn't care but he wants to stay the right side of the law. The police don't bother you if you stay here in the agricultural area, but if you stray into town it's another story,' he said. 'You feel persecuted on all sides. You have no papers, so you limit your movements; you fear being stopped and deported, so you hide. You can take no leisure, you cannot be yourself. You give up all idea of yourself. Many people break. We survive by supporting each other and by remembering the injustice.'

I asked him why, when conditions were so hard, he stayed. His eyes filled with tears. 'I cannot go back. I have paid to come. The borders are closed. You cannot come and go and come again. I cannot save, I have just enough to send back each month for my responsibilities.'

The tears were slipping down his cheeks now, just visible as they gleamed in the half-light of the lamp, and he paused to steady his voice. But he didn't want to stop. 'Every night when I go to sleep I dream of home, of my children, of my friends. There is never a day when I do not wake up dreaming of my home, but I expect to be here as long as the West is better off than the South.'

Ataya wanted to take me out to meet the English-speaking migrants who live nearby. Spitou cycled off into the night with a cheery wave, the homesickness my questioning had brought to the surface suppressed once more, the bicycle a sign of success, while we wandered down a narrow lane which twisted between abandoned houses along the edge of a patch of wasteland. A few old lamp-posts cast a weak, sulphurous-yellow light at irregular intervals. Electricity cables had been strung loosely across the street and between the low roofs. The moon was just beginning to wane in a clear sky, and the sounds of a warm African night came from glassless windows all around. The end of one house had been converted into a makeshift shop-cum-telephone exchange selling a few essentials – pieces of soap, oil, sugar, chickpeas, Dettol and lightening body lotion. Along one wall was a line of wooden phone booths for those who wanted to call home.

Sammi from the Congo had come to buy cigarettes, and conducted a trilingual conversation in Spanish, French and English, swaying slightly as he sized me up with his huge bulging eyes. He was wearing an old English cloth cap, and a tweedy-patterned cotton shirt-jacket over a scruffy polo shirt. He adopted a mock county drawl – 'Eeoohh, how interesting' – when he was told why I was here, but declined to talk to me further because he'd 'had a spot of bother' in Madrid and it might be better if he didn't. 'Allow me however to introduce you to Jacqueline. She is the fine lady in charge of giving a good time to everyone.'

Jacqueline was from Nigeria and was dressed in an Adidas bomber jacket and skintight short trousers over an ample frame. Her straightened hair was dyed pinkish-red on top, and crimson toenails peeped out of impossibly high platform sandals. She mostly worked in the big tomato-packing factory up the road, putting tomatoes into boxes for export to England, Belgium and sometimes Australia. The money's good when there's work, sometimes €40 a day if you work twelve hours. But sometimes there's no work, then you have to make do where you can. Her two children were back home, looked after by her mother. 'Does their father help?' I asked. 'How would I know? I'm here,' she shrugged.

Breakfast at the hotel on the beach next morning was a self-service, flat-rate, €6 buffet, constantly replenished from 8 a.m. until 11 a.m. Here the chefs were on display behind a giant hot-plate frying fifty eggs at a time, flipping 100 pieces of bacon as they turned a sugary brown. The white bread rolls were stacked like a game of sticks, so high that you couldn't remove one without disturbing the whole pile. There were twenty different kinds of pastry and a dozen processed cereals. Buckets of baked beans sat next to platters of meat. And yet this free-for-all plenty had induced a kind of frenzy. We were pouncing on the counters like hunters, cutting across one another, grabbing tongs, barging for plates. There was no conversation but every third body spoke the same story – here were the diseases of affluence, the epidemic of obesity afflicting Western nations, writ large.

There was a diet counter where people trying hard to lose weight were loading their plates high with 'reduced-calorie' cheeses and slabs of liverish-pink 'low-fat' sausagemeat, filling their bowls with tinned fruit cocktail, and inspecting the labels of artificially sweetened yoghurts ('New! Added calcium for healthy bones!').

A humming electric cube delivered ersatz orange juice, with its tell-tale 'mouth-feel' of flavourings and sugar, even though fresh oranges grown nearby cost only a few cents. Eastern European waitresses moved silently up and down the tables clearing away plates as fast as eaters pushed them aside.

Out in the foyer, the big-name package tour companies offered day trips – 'to the Carrefour supermarket for retail therapy … here you shop to your heart's content' – and to the Sunday market where you can 'buy a little bit of real Spain' to take home.

Sunday is in fact still a day of rest in Spain. This was the only time I could meet the migrants who live right in among the greenhouses, when the farm managers were away having their traditional long family lunches. So I had to forgo the market and my piece of real Spain and head back to the sea of plastic instead.

I found I could navigate my way through the plastic maze by using the dozens of billboards advertising agrochemicals as markers. I took a left at the DuPont sign for 'Lannate r' systematic insecticide with triple action for complete crop security.

There are few trees and no fields here. All is grey and dusty brown, except where the endless line of sheeting is broken here and there by large rubbish tips on to which hundreds of brightly coloured chemical containers have been dumped.

I wandered over a fenced-off dump and gingerly kicked the containers. Some still had dregs left in them. Here were the big brand names again. Others were recognizable for the notoriety of their active ingredients. Endosulfan, a persistent organochlorine pesticide, acutely toxic and an endocrine disrupter. Metam sodium, a soil fumigant that acts as fungicide, herbicide and worm killer, also acutely toxic; Metomilo, a carbamate – highly toxic. There were dozens I'd never heard of, and lots of emptied cartons of nitrate and phosphate fertilizers, and ground disinfectants, all displaying their hazardous chemical warning signs and instructions on careful disposal. The Spanish government has been trying to improve its record on waste, but these were still awaiting attention.

On the next road along, mountains of rubble and soil excavated from the greenhouses when the land has become exhausted had been dumped on another tip, along with old contaminated plastic sheets and more pesticide containers. A farmer had driven his white van to the middle of the tip where he was feeding his sheep plant waste, the tomato vines and pepper stalks collected from the greenhouses once the crops have been harvested. The practice is banned because the plant waste contains chemical residues which then accumulate in the animals' fatty tissue, thus building up in the food chain, but it's common all the same.

The next dump a few miles on looked like the entrance to hell. A huge crater had been carved out of one end by diggers, a heap of spoil was being turned at the other, and plastic and concrete debris was everywhere. A foul smell of rottenness was rising up from it. On one edge of the pit there was a small pile of broken wood that looked as though it was part of the heap, but as I got closer, five men emerged. This was their home. They were all Moroccan. Half a broken door and a few uneven planks had been lassoed to some dead tree branches and shorn-off water pipes. A torn boat tarpaulin, black with oil and smoke, had been tied over them. A scavenged mattress on top provided a desperate bulwark against wind and rain. Inside they were cooking their Sunday lunch. One of them checked the flat bread they had made and wrapped in a towel before tucking it up in their bed to prove, while a pot of couscous and herbs simmered on a stove of bottled gas. A pair of jeans, an anorak and track-suit bottoms hung from a line of nails hammered into the cardboard walls, over a row of photographs from a mail-order fashion catalogue. Upturned vegetable crates did for furniture. Hanging by the door was a broken child's blackboard, chalked with Arabic and Spanish – they had been giving one another lessons.

They had all arrived in boats, having paid the going rate of £1,000 to intermediaries to secure a place with the smugglers. They had lived there in the shack for two and a half years, and three of them had managed to get official papers. They were legal. Most of them were in debt after their journey, their families back home providing surety. They had jobs on the big farm down the road. When there was work they earned €30 a day. If there was enough work, they ate, if there wasn't, they didn't. There was no water or sanitation, only closed irrigation pipes for the crops, so they collected water from a tank for agricultural effluent. They were often ill with headaches and stomach trouble.

What if the farmer discovered them here, I asked. Would they be forced to move on? 'But he knows, he comes to pick us up in the morning in his van,' they said. They were getting nervous, so I went back down towards the road, happy to escape the stench, and passed the water tank. It was scummy, with three empty pesticide containers floating in it.

After a few hours, your eyes become acclimatized and you can begin to distinguish the piles of rubble which are inhabited from those which are not. Any expanse of concrete is likely to have been made into a shelter. Those who had been there a short

time were still sleeping on upturned crates, lined with cardboard; those who had been there a bit longer had managed to
carry home stained mattresses from the tips. When it rained
most of them got wet. Apart from Mohammed.

Mohammed was a craftsman and an optimist. I found him on
a rubbish tip near some greenhouses of particularly fine construction, owned not by a small farmer but by a big company.
He shared the tip with about fifty Moroccans, who all lived in
rickety shacks of plastic. But Mohammed had managed to find
a rusty saw and had used it to build a hut from the pallets used
to transport crates of vegetables on juggernauts. It was good new
wood. He then covered the outside with a double layer of plastic
sheeting and lined the inside with carefully cut cardboard,
screwed into place with 'top-quality nuts and bolts'. 'It doesn't
leak,' he declared in triumph.

The bedroom was perfect for three men, so he invited his
uncle over from Morocco to join him. There was no water or
sanitation here either but he had found a way to tap into the
main irrigation pipe, a huge conduit of clean water running
alongside the greenhouses. With some nifty work with a nail and
a replaceable plug he had provided safe supplies for all of them.
'It comes out in a terrific gush,' he said, provoking laughter from
all the other men. He offered me the fried aubergine and corn
bread his friend was making for their Sunday lunch.

If they could survive here for five years and prove they had
been here that long by showing they have made regular remit-
tances home, these migrants would be granted residence. For
those with relatives already in Spain, it's quicker – just three years.

Abdel Majid had done two years already. He was thirty-seven,
dressed in American basketball shirt and plastic shoes. He had
worked on the cucumbers and tomatoes but he had only once
succeeded in sending money back to Morocco, so he might have
trouble proving it. The jobs had been erratic, but he was still getting up to queue by the roadside each morning. Home for him

was an abandoned Andalucian farmhouse, its roof long gone and its walls reduced to jagged teeth, that he shared with twenty-five other men. They had put plastic over the top, weighted down with stones, and made tiny tables from scavenged chair legs and old planks. Two of them were burning plastic and rubbish on a huge bonfire outside when I arrived, releasing acrid fumes. Abdel invited me to sit in his cardboard room and drink green tea. A young boy with him was making bread – his mother had taught him how to do it, wanting to give him a skill before he chanced his life in the boats. Hundreds of Moroccans drown each year trying to cross from Africa to Spain.

Abdel wanted me to know that they were respectable people. 'I do not live like this at home. It's true I have no papers. But we are quiet and law-abiding. We work hard and sleep a little. What do you think of all this, have you seen this before?' I did not know what to say. My French was inadequate to the task, leaving me silent. I had seen this before, but not since a visit to an aid project in the slums of Delhi over twenty years ago, and amidst all the African French and Arabic I was struggling to remember that I was in Spain, less than a mile from the Costa del Sol. So I borrowed Spitou's words, and said I thought it unjust, dangerously so, but that I was impressed by their dignity. Abdel smiled encouragingly before replying: 'I think of myself as a slave. I go to sleep dreaming of work. I live amongst the rubbish like a rat. But I remember that I am a man. Wherever I live, whatever anyone thinks, I am a man.'

About 40 kilometres west, the greenhouses of Roquetas merge with those of El Ejido. El Ejido is a small, conservative Spanish town inland from the coast, stranded in the sea of plastic. Its narrow, straight main street is lined with plane trees and unremarkable shops. But its outskirts are swollen with new construction built with recent agricultural wealth. The value of its horticultural production has tripled in ten years.

In the hour before dawn, nothing much was stirring in the centre. But up by the petrol station café on the new highway that skirts the perimeter, farm managers with flat caps and old-fashioned moustaches were downing a quick brandy. A police vehicle was already cruising up and down, its headlights catching the shifting shadows on the pavements. Its passing beam showed 100 or more people queuing on the edge of the road. They had been walking up for nearly an hour, arriving from all directions, first the early birds, mostly black men wanting to improve their chances by picking the best spots, then Moroccans, then white men and a few white women, mostly in pairs. As the sun rose and the traffic picked up, they shuffled forward a bit. Then a white van pulled up and stopped near the white men. A farmer got out and pointed at the four he wanted. They climbed into the van and set off for work. An ordinary car pulled up and a man got out to talk to the women. They turned away and he drove off. Another van pulled up, the crowd surged forward, a bit more aggressively now, and another five white men were chosen. Some moved down into the light thrown out by the bakery, just opened, hoping to be seen first next time. The rest waited. And waited. The police patrol passed by again. One more van came and took another three, who looked Moroccan. But then there was nothing for over an hour and a half. By 9 a.m. it was clear that most of the rest of the crowd would not have work that day. The police patrol car was back: the cue for the majority of them to fade away. But a few squatted down for the day, just in case.

In February 2000 there were three days of rioting in El Ejido. A Moroccan man with severe mental health problems stabbed a twenty-six-year-old Spanish girl to death. The killing followed the arrest of another Moroccan two weeks earlier for stabbing two agricultural workers to death. After the young woman's funeral, Spanish men marched through El Ejido shouting racist slogans. Then they went on the rampage burning shops and cars owned by Moroccans and attacking any migrants they found. It took more than three days to quell the riots, during which more than thirty people were injured. Moroccan workers subsequently organized a strike, demanding their rights. The disturbances shocked the government into issuing permits to many migrants. They also provoked a series of studies highlighting conditions. More than 90 per cent of the agricultural workers in the region turned out to be immigrants, and well over half of them had no access to drinking water or sanitation. Since then, according to some academics, such as Emma Martín Díaz, professor of social anthropology at the University of Seville, there has been a deliberate policy of segregation and harassment to keep migrants out of the town, but also a move to recruit more eastern Europeans who are less visibly different. 'This situation is only different from South African apartheid in that it is not sanctioned by law,' she says, a claim that I thought extravagant until I saw the conditions.

I had not expected to see any of the illegal migrants I had met in southern Spain again, but I was invited in 2006 to address MEPs in the European Parliament about the conditions I had seen and to my surprise and delight found myself sharing the platform with Spitou. He had managed to become regularized in one of the Spanish government's amnesties, and as soon as he had his papers he had started helping other migrants through the Rural Workers' Union. We kept in touch and in 2011 he warned that conditions were deteriorating once more. The credit crunch had led to the bursting of the Spanish property bubble and many migrants had been driven out of construction into the hothouses looking for work.

Tensions between migrants and local communities had been growing. The union feared a repeat of the violence and rioting that occurred in 2000 in El Ejido. Spitou explained that they had seen the warning signs in another town in the heart of the industrial production area, San Isidro, the previous October when a farmer was murdered in his hothouse store and locals immediately pointed the finger at migrants. Thousands protested in the streets following his funeral, brandishing racist placards picturing Africans as black sheep and saying: 'Immigrants: behave or get out!' It later transpired that the police were investigating the farmer's links to organized crime.

So I returned to the area once more and interviewed close to 100 workers in different groups in the course of making a short film for the *Guardian*.

Many of them were living as before without sanitation or access to drinking water. The cardboard shacks among the plastic hothouses still passed as home for groups of them, along with derelict farm buildings illegally rented out to others. The African migrants I met told me that they were often paid less than half of the legal minimum wage for working long hours in up to 45°C heat; some told of farmers withholding pay, knowing that they were illegal migrants and could not go to the police. Many talked of being harassed by local police if they went to the wrong parts of town.

The Red Cross had been handing out free food to thousands of them and its local co-ordinator, Francisco Vicente, described the conditions as 'inhuman'. The charity estimated that there were between 15,000 and 20,000 homeless migrants in the Almeria province alone, of whom some 5,000 were living in abandoned houses and shacks without running water or electricity. 'These are more "established" communities, which the Red Cross can at least reach. But the others are spread throughout town, sleeping near bank cash machines, or just on the streets. This is being hidden; people are not interested in making this public. I am not referring to only politicians. Sometimes it's society itself – the people – who don't stand up,' Francisco told me.

Spitou was also angry at the conspiracy of silence about the conditions. 'You don't find the sons of Spain in the hothouses, only the blacks and people from former colonies. The farmers only want an unqualified, malleable workforce, which costs absolutely nothing. Only one part of the business is benefiting from this. It's big agribusiness that wins. Everyone knows this system exists, this is untamed neoliberalism. It's the capitalists that win. And humanity is killed that way. This is slavery in Europe. At the door to Europe, there is slavery as if we were in the sixteenth century. But people have closed their ears to it.'

He was not alone in his sense of outrage. In San Isidro, I came across a group of nuns handing out emergency food to thousands more migrants.

Sister Purification, or Puri, as she was known, was one of four Catholic nuns from the order of the Merciful Sisters of Charity who lived there. She recalled how the first black Africans had come to the town in 2002. The detention centres in the Canaries that received migrants arriving illegally in boats from Africa were full. In order to process new arrivals, the Spanish authorities began flying those already there out to mainland airports to disperse them to areas where labour was needed. They hired a coach to take about thirty Africans from Madrid airport to the centre of San Isidro, where the driver was instructed to open the doors in Plaza Colonización, the main square, and simply release them. 'That was the first time black people came here,' she said.

'The government gave them absolutely nothing; no money, no papers, nothing, just told them, off you go. No one here knew they were coming. The local authorities washed their hands of them. The people in the town didn't want anything to do with them. We had no idea what to do,' Puri explained.

In the end, the nuns took the African men to a disused hothouse. Others began arriving and started building cardboard hovels under its dilapidated structure, until more than 300 people were living there in a makeshift slum without sanitation. 'The conditions were terrible, horrible, not human,' Puri recalled.

As more and more people came, the nuns began to worry about health problems. They found TB, Aids and hepatitis among the migrants, but knew they couldn't get proper medical help. They began taking those who were ill to abandoned farmhouses nearby to isolate them. 'We didn't have the means to provide more. The government was doing next to nothing.'

Then in September 2005 a huge fire broke out in the makeshift colony. Hundreds of Africans were driven out of the slum
as the plastic burned. The fire brigade and police arrived, but
once the fire was out they just left again and refused to help,
according to Puri.

The nuns used their own small cars to begin distributing
more than 300 men to places they knew migrants were already
sheltering in the area – in old farm buildings and underground
wells. But by 2 a.m. there were still 120 men with nowhere to
go, and it was decided that they should sleep in the main square,
with the nuns accompanying them for solidarity. 'We were there
three days. The town did nothing. The government did nothing.
I was crying with rage, with impotence and with indignation,'
says Puri.

In 2011 the feeding centre the nuns were running had more
than 4,000 recipients registered on its computer in this one
small agricultural community of 7,000 inhabitants.

'There have been five deaths of migrants in the last year here
from traffic accidents at night,' Puri told me. 'About eighteen
months ago an African worker died in one of the hothouses – he
had fallen into the water tank and couldn't get out. There was no
punishment for the farmer, no police questions,' Puri told us. 'I
am very conscious what we are doing is not a real solution. But
they know that at least if they are sick or desperate, we are here
to hold their hand.'

My updated report caused a furore in Almeria, with the local
newspaper dedicating pages, edition after edition, to denoun-
cing me. Local academics and the industry, which had been
reluctant to speak to me while I was there, wrote pointing to all
the improvements made in recent years – 20,000 or so migrants
granted residence to work in agriculture in Almeria, social policies granting them access to public services regardless of their
immigration status, programmes to promote integration, strict
rules on wages. The casual employment of illegal workers was
the exception to the rule, they assured me, and many farms were

family businesses in which the owners themselves worked. And yet there they were, available by the thousand to talk to any visitor who would listen.

The horticultural industry has made one of the poorest regions of Spain wealthy but it cannot survive without a large number of migrants. It requires not just cheap labour, but cheap labour in excess. In order to turn labour on and off at will, you need to have people waiting at all hours, frightened enough to be docile and grateful enough to do whatever they are offered.

Just as previous revolutions in trade have led to mass movements of labour from the land into new cities, so globalization has been accompanied by waves of migration. The free movement of goods across borders and rapid improvements in transport have inevitably gone hand in hand with the movement of people. Today's food industry has not just drawn people into Spain, the UK and the rest of Europe, but has seen migrations within developing countries too. I have visited food factories in Thailand and Kenya where a newly urbanized workforce serves the boom in global sourcing and food for export from spreading slums.

Global trade has created the potential for new wealth. But in Europe it is as though we have gone back to the dark days of the early nineteenth century. In the name of a 'flexible workforce', we have effectively thrown away two centuries of reforming legislation. We have bypassed the Factory Acts and employment regulations that were introduced to curb the abuses and excesses of the Industrial Revolution, so that its enormous contribution to the affluence of society as a whole would not be undermined by squalor and suffering.

We have allowed a structure to emerge that enables our shops to be resupplied at short notice by casual labourers picked up from the roadside whatever the hour in the Costa del Sol, or collected from their Dickensian housing in rural England. These workers are at the mercy of pecking orders as brutal as those in the turn-of-the-century American docks. We are told this has happened because people want cheap food.

The paradox is that our fresh food is not cheap any more. By the time it has been packaged and transported, and the retailers have added their margins, it is very expensive. Ninety-nine pence for a few leaves is a lot of money. But 99p for an unlimited supply of servants to wash and pick over it all, hidden not as in the old days below stairs, but in remote caravans or underneath plastic hothouses – that is cheap.

4. Beans and Asparagus

The link in the chain that connects fluctuating orders to casual labour around the world is the supermarket distribution centre. It is at the heart of a revolution which has swept away the old and varied structures that used to bring our food to us and replaced them with a new centralized system controlled by a mere handful of operators. Yet, like the call centre that crept into our collective consciousness long after it had rewritten the notion of customer service, the distribution centre effected its revolution without us noticing.

The jargon of 'supply-chain logistics' is as tangled and ugly as Spaghetti Junction. 'Efficient customer response', 'constant replenishment', 'just-in-time deliveries', 'vendor-managed inventories', 'factory-gate pricing', 'global standard inner unit and outer-case barcodes' – the phrases are hardly the stuff of bedtime reading, which perhaps explains why we knew so little about the stranglehold the major supermarkets were acquiring over the distribution of food.

This new system is miraculous in its scale, speed and efficiency, but it is built on a fatal flaw. It is dependent on the unsustainable use of that most politically volatile of substances: crude oil. Not only is our intensive farming dependent on the byproducts of petroleum for its raw materials – the agrochemicals and plastics it uses in proliferation – now even our most basic foods cannot reach us without burning up food miles. We have made our supply lines extraordinarily vulnerable.

It took three visits to different distribution centres before I could take in the complexity of it all. These were by and large not places where journalists were welcomed. It was after watching more than a tenth of one retailer's total fresh produce for the

UK move through just one depot in a few hours that the enormity of the implications sank in.

I toured the Safeway nerve centre at Aylesford in 2003, hot on the heels of the then transport minister, John Spellar, who was reportedly equally awed after his private visit. Aylesford was one of just six hubs from which that supermarket chain was supplying its 480 or so stores around the country, while its fate was being decided in the boardrooms of rival retailers. (It was subsequently taken over by Morrisons as the sector consolidated further.) From this depot, ten times the size of Wembley stadium, 170 38-tonne lorries were shunted into and out of 120 cavernous loading bays in an endless cycle, day and night, 363 days a year. The lorries transported up to 1.7 million cases of groceries a week and, with the rest of the supermarket's fleet, clocked up over 120 million kilometres a year.

Add together the millions of journeys made by the fleets of the grocery retailers and between them they accounted for nearly 1.3 billion kilometres on our crowded transport network in 2012. Between 1978 and 2000 the distance food was transported within the UK by lorry nearly doubled.

Between 35 and 40 per cent of heavy goods vehicles on UK roads today are involved in producing and distributing food, with a quarter of those lorries being related to the transporting of food itself, and the rest carrying goods needed to grow and process it. Thirty years ago many of them would simply not have been there.

The Safeway regional distribution centre (RDC) at Aylesford was not the biggest or newest centre but it was one of the first, in the late 1970s, to create this new centralized way of getting our food to us. All the major retailers rationalized distribution into similar operations and constantly centralized further, so that by 2013 some 93 per cent of supermarket stock was delivered via centralized distribution centres rather than direct to individual stores.

The depots for fresh produce are not warehouses – almost

nothing is held in stock. Instead, millions of boxes of goods are ordered 'just in time' from suppliers and fed in and out of the distribution centres along the motorway network within twelve hours.

But for the procession of lorries, you might not have noticed the Aylesford RDC. Off the slip-road at junction 6 of the M20, then up a side road, it was just another industrial shed, marked with a supermarket logo, doing something you had never much thought about. Then, when you drove up to the entrance, the scale of the place suddenly overwhelmed you. The guard in his sentry box was 10 feet above your car. The welcome sign near the barrier with its gantries of lights was not just in English but in French, Spanish and Italian, and was at juggernaut height.

At 9 p.m. the chill room, a giant refrigerated shed on the site, was working full pelt. In the darkness outside dozens of trailer-less cabs scuttled across the yard, casting unearthly shadows on the sheer floodlit walls. Steam from the ammonia refrigeration plant hung over the roof. Lorries constantly came and went, a hollow rattle signalling those speeding back empty, a heavy growl accompanying those hauling out fully laden. Inside, an army of men was demolishing piles of fresh food, pulled from the maw of containers docked to the side of the building. A thousand of them worked myriad shifts. The chicken tikka masala was in from Newark. Broccoli had made it from Spain. So too had iceberg lettuce, but that had been rejected and lay waiting for its Continental producer to truck it back. Imported salad, washed and packed in Lincolnshire that morning, was being stacked ten crates high.

As fast as the 'tippers' – men with fork-lifts – emptied pallets from the containers, so more lorries backed up to the bays and opened their doors, constantly replenishing the heaps. Then bar-row men, the 'pickers', ant-like in dark caps and black fleeces, trundled up on the snub-nosed lifting machines to deconstruct the piles. They carried off their loads in a continuous column.

Holding down the tillers of their electric barrows, they moved back and forth on tiny platforms. Like the automata in Fritz Lang's *Metropolis*, they followed no discernible orders, but appeared programmed to advance from one pile to another. They skated off round corners, stopped suddenly to avoid collision, reversed, side-stepped round one another and filed on.

The label on each crate was zapped with a scanning gun as it arrived, generating a string of new numbers in the glass control room. Numbered strips in the vast hangar represented each of the Safeway stores served by this centre, and the goods, choreographed by barcode, moved from the arrivals section to departure lanes.

To 9848 Peckham, sweet and sour chicken. To 7013 Gibraltar, mushroom stroganoff with rice. Sirloin steaks for 9847 Brighton. Bangers and mash for 7818 Guernsey. Some higher intelligence had divined how many cabbages would be required on a cold day in Cambridge and how many kievs would be consumed in Colchester.

The pickers worked relentlessly, silently. An evaporator threw out icy air with a constant roar and fans the size of aircraft turbo engines pushed it around. Occasionally the cold was pierced by the blast of dozens of horns. When a barrow dropped a load, the pickers responded with a prolonged honk of tribal derision. But the diversion was brief. The piles were accumulating again and could not wait.

Last to dock, between 10 p.m. and 11 p.m. each night, were the lorries from the consolidators. These are the companies that run separate sheds taking smaller deliveries from suppliers around the world and putting them together in categories before trucking them into the distribution centres. They came in constant flurries. The doors opened, the tippers zoomed up and back. There was a pause and much shaking of heads. One load had been piled too high by a consolidator keen to keep his costs down. Some of the boxes were crushed. To sort the good from the broken would require stopping, taking time, and that might hold up a lorry going to two or three stores. It would be quicker to reject the whole lot, but they'd save what they could tonight, they said. Once the final loads were unpicked the operation went into reverse. The loading of vehicles started. Now the supermarket trailers were backed up and filled with pallets. By dawn the following morning all the piles had gone from the lanes. There was no trace of the night's efforts. And then the cycle began again.

Up in the transport control room, Steve Bethel was the planning manager responsible for over 300 lorry movements a day. He was looking at a screen showing a map of the M25. Red and orange arrows were flashing all around it, warning that speeds were down to less than 5 m.p.h. here, 10 m.p.h. there. The log-sheets showed thirteen lorries out between 5 a.m. and 5.30 a.m., and another thirteen between 5.30 a.m. and 6 a.m., each with its time slot like traffic control at a busy airport. It takes half an hour to load a 38-tonne trailer and turn it round and the supply trucks had to be out on time. Bethel keyed a GPS command into his computer. Within seconds a marker appeared on the screen pinpointing the location of one of his lorries. If necessary, his next load could be reallocated to a driver who had not been held up.

Bethel was executing the 'Aylesford falldown', and the process is still replicated in other supermarket distribution centres around the country each night. Before the 1980s big supermarkets used to stock about 8,000 products, mostly delivered direct to each shop. Then hi-tech information systems and the humble wooden pallet combined to rewrite the system. Stacking pallets, which can be forked on and off lorries, dispensed with the need to load and unload individual boxes, while creating a centralized RDC removed the need for storage at the back of the shop. Then the retailers worked out a way to revolutionize the 'picking' at the depots. Instead of starting with an order from each store and gathering what that store needed from stocks kept in different parts of the warehouse, they started 'picking by line'.

Now each product line – bananas, let's say – comes in and is immediately distributed around the depot to lanes allocated to the different stores so that it can go straight back out. Where depots used to hold a day's stock of fresh food they now hold none.

All this is possible because instant information about stock is transmitted electronically from the computerized checkout tills back to the distribution centres and directly to their suppliers. Many of the products sold in stores are now delivered twice a day. This is the concept of 'constant replenishment'. Without the need for room for stock, a big supermarket store can now keep 40,000 or more products on its shelves.

The 'falldown' begins when a customer buys something in one of the stores. Scanning the barcode at the till creates a new order for the product. The information is transmitted to head office, electronically collated several times a day and instantly converted into a delivery schedule for the farmer or manufacturer for the following day. The supplier will have estimated how much food to produce, but will only get a final order a few hours ahead of the time he or she is expected to deliver to the depot. It might be in the evening for delivery early the following day, or at noon for delivery that night, for example. The orders can vary dramatically. A spell of good weather can, for example, double the demand for lettuce. Failing to meet a retailer's order in full can result in a financial penalty. Suppliers can find themselves losing thousands of pounds. But then unexpected rain might halve your order. If you end up with a surplus there's hardly anywhere else for it to go, since the big retailers control so much of the country's total market. Wholesale markets are a shadow of their former selves and are used to dump surpluses at a fraction of the price. The need for a workforce that you can turn on and off like a tap, and if necessary keep at it for as long as it takes to fulfil your order, becomes clear. I have sat in on occasion on the other end of the ordering process, listening as late-night demands for fresh produce that differ wildly from what was expected have been transmitted to farm packhouse managers burning the midnight oil in their offices.

This system has not only turned patterns of unskilled employment upside down, it has also imposed a huge strain on our transport infrastructure. It was one of the factors driving much of the expansion of road networks across Europe, and would continue to be so as new countries joined the European Union. Retailers have turned our motorways into their warehouses.

I had a further chance to test the dry statistics on food's contribution to freight on UK roads when I hitched a lift in a vegetable lorry travelling to the Asda RDC at Dartford, Kent. I had been watching the Christmas Brussels sprout harvest in Lincolnshire and wanted to see it right through the process. Asda felt unable to let me into their depot at such a busy time, but the 'consolidator' agreed to let me go along for the ride. Martin Tate was one of three men running a Lincolnshire fresh produce company. He organized a group of other growers to provide seamless supplies of fruit and vegetables to Asda so that the supermarket didn't have to deal with them direct. 'Asda doesn't have the time or experience to deal with that number of growers. We've built the relationships here and in Spain. It's about commitment, vision, passion. The two most important things are availability and value. Our business is to deliver the promise,' he explained. 'Spalding is central. We can hit all depots from here to Scotland and Cornwall with our fleet. Forty-four tonnes is the maximum UK weight limit. It was traditionally what you could carry on the road if travelling from a rail terminal to a port. 'Course that doesn't apply now. But you'll see, trucks aren't horrible big belching things any more.'

So it was that I found myself 12 feet up in the cab of Bob's articulated lorry. Air-suspension seats like armchairs, a nice little bed behind, acres of leg-room, spotless wrap-around windscreen, computer controls, it was an exhilarating £90,000-worth of machine attached to a 40-tonne trailer full of vegetables, sitting on an 800-litre tank of diesel.

You could live in there, and Bob practically did. He averaged 180,000 kilometres a year, he reckoned. He had been driving lorries for forty-three years, food trucks for twenty-five of them. 'There have been a few changes,' he said.

We negotiated our way out of small lanes near Spalding, giving way to international food lorries coming in the opposite direction, and settled in for the long, slow drive from the pack-houses of East Anglia to the Asda distribution centre on the edge of London. Down the A1, then the A14, M11 and M25. The traffic wasn't too bad because it was holiday time, but the speed limit for lorries, carefully monitored by the legally required tacho-graph, is 55 m.p.h., and we'd got ourselves behind a Nisa-Today lorry also doing 55 m.p.h. 'We're stuck staring at his backdoor for a few hours now, I won't be able to get past him.'

We idled away the time with a game, counting lorries going by on the other side of the carriageway. While we talked about the difference half a century has made to our supply chain, I tested how many of the lorries were to do with food. We scored a hat-trick of points instantly. Asda, Safeway and Iceland colours were emblazoned on the first three juggernauts to thunder by. Then came a vehicle from Bob's own company. 'That's four in a row,' I said, surprised.

Bob was nonchalant. 'Well, it would be. Before supermarkets came along and put them to sleep, I used to do the wholesale markets. Every town had its wholesale market. But there's nothing much in town centres any more. The depots get bigger and bigger. We'd be taking in everything grown locally round here. The time scale was the same. It'd be from field to the market one day and into the shop the next. But there were more corner shops then and we used not to get caulis in winter. There are no seasons any more. You don't look forward to the new season's potatoes now.'

'Look, there's a James Irlam lorry.' No refrigeration unit, so I guessed that wasn't food.

'No, you're right there. That's not food. That's the packaging for food. They're big in that. Everything's packaged now, isn't it?

When I was young we used to just put a hand in a sack if we wanted potatoes. But those packhouses, they employ no end of people. Eddie Stobart's big in packaging too – plastic, glass jars, you name it.'

Co-op. Tesco. Asda again on the other side of the road. Eight out of eight. Oh no, nine, there goes Padley's Frozen Veg.

'Everything is so big these days. There are a lot of jobs in it. Matthews. That's Bernard Matthews. The cars are the worst though. They are getting faster, we're going slower. Imagine what this road'll be like in ten years' time.'

Shopping for food has made its contribution to the increase in traffic too. We are in fact all driving further to buy our food. In the ten years between the mid-1980s and mid-1990s, the average distance travelled to shop went up from 14 kilometres to 22 kilometres as small and local shops came under pressure from out-of-town retail stores and closed.

'George Kime,' I called out.

'He's a Boston veg merchant. NFT – that's Northern Foods, they do a lot of distribution. Dairy Crest. Kenyon European translink. I don't know that one.'

Thirteen out of fourteen so far.

'You get a lot of European lorries now, taking more of our work – their petrol's cheaper and their labour's cheaper. The German Willi Betz is one of the big European food hauliers.'

Turners Temperature Controlled. That must be food. BOC, that's not. Fourteen out of sixteen.

'We do a bit of backhauling now – picking up some onions from a farm on the return journey rather than going back empty – but not much. Here we are, the M25, the biggest car park in the country.'

I had thought that Christian Salvesen lorries with their blue crosses on white were from some sort of Scandawegian pharmaceutical company but no, they do distribution for the retailers and recycling of supermarket waste, Bob assured me. Fifteen out of seventeen.

Bob did a long day, twelve hours or so and then a short one of eight or nine hours, four days a week. It was stressful with all the traffic and he wouldn't want to be starting out now, he said. There was a serious shortage of drivers. And the new working-time directive restricting drivers' hours would make it worse, he said.

We counted Fletcher Frozen Foods from Hull, several more supermarket lorries, then an Esso tanker before puzzling over TransAmerica Leasing. Bob didn't know who they were.

By the time we reached the Dartford bridge we were in thick grey fog. As we swept down into the Asda depot, the mystery was solved. We spotted two TransAmerica Leasing lorries parked up, waiting to unload.

Of course our food doesn't just travel up and down the UK. During the 1990s there was a 90 per cent increase in the movement by road of agricultural and food products between the UK and Europe. And we don't just trade in food we cannot produce ourselves any more. For example, whereas in the 1960s we drank milk we produced locally, today we both import it and export it. Importing a product as perishable and heavy as fresh milk might sound perverse, and it is not what supermarkets set out to do. But concentration of power in the processing and retailing sectors enabled the big industry buyers to push what they paid to farmers down below the cost of production. The manufacturing sector, which uses milk in bulk, was able to base the price it paid on global prices which take into account dried milk supplies and had also been below the British cost of production. British dairy farmers have been squeezed so hard that thousands have gone out of business, and the national dairy herd has declined so dramatically that there is now a shortfall in the supply of fresh milk.

International trade in food in fact almost trebled in the last three decades of the twentieth century. Caroline Lucas, the Green Party politician, called the phenomenon 'the great food swap'. She gave another example: in one year Britain imported over 60,000 tonnes of poultry meat from the Netherlands while exporting 33,000 tonnes of poultry meat to the same country. Live animals have not been spared this food swap. Some 44 million cattle, pigs and sheep are traded across the world each year. Millions more are transported long distances within countries and over borders. Our increasing dependence on processed food has also made its contribution. A ready-made lasagne can contain more than twenty different ingredients which may have come from all over the world.

The food industry meanwhile has lobbied hard to be able to use our roads even more. Many cities impose night curfews and other restrictions on lorries over a certain size travelling through residential areas. For example, Steve Bethel's juggernauts from the Aylesford RDC were only allowed into London on officially designated trunk routes. During my visit he and his colleagues gave me a taste of what some of the lobbying officials had no doubt received. 'We're a 24-hour operation and we're in residential areas, but more curfews are being imposed by local authorities. The deliveries are shoe-horned into shorter and shorter times. It creates rush-hour traffic jams. If we could reduce morning deliveries and bring more in at night, we could stop adding to the problem. Central government is in favour of it but local government isn't,' Dave Timpson, system effectiveness controller at Safeway, explained.

Steve Bethel later showed me a map of the London and M25 area. To deliver to his supermarket's Holloway Road branch from Aylesford, he could not take the direct route down the A2, a journey of 134 kilometres. Instead, he said, he had to send his vehicles all the way round the M25 up to the A1, then down again, which is 214 kilometres. 'It's a busy store, we go twice a day, or four times a day at the back end of the week. That's 58,000 extra kilometres a year. If you look at all the London stores, we're doing an extra 242,422 kilometres a year, just one way. Half a million extra kilometres in all! Think of all the extra congestion!'

I found myself asking the idiot's question: Why couldn't they deliver to Holloway Road from the north or operate smaller warehouses instead of trucking everything round and round the country? 'Because by going bigger we can reduce the cost of produce in the stores. And reduce congestion, of course.'

As I left them, it took me fifteen minutes to crawl up from the slip-road on to the M20. On the other carriageway, there was a 6-mile tailback, waiting to get on to the M25. There appeared to be no reason for the queues, just sheer weight of traffic. I passed endless supermarket lorries stuck in the jam on the other side. A Tesco lorry boasted 'You shop, we drop'. I passed under a bridge on which the traffic was tailbacked too. For a moment there were food lorries above, to the side, in front and behind me all at once. The juggernaut above sported a different logo: 'Why pay more?' The answer to this rhetorical question is of course that we already pay more, maybe not at the checkout, but in so many other ways.

The cost of this kind of distribution is not simply paid in human terms by those on the lowest incomes who are at the mercy of the erratic shifts it requires. It dramatically changes our environment. At the micro level it is part of a car culture that condemns us to living in traffic-clogged and polluted towns and villages. At the macro level it is a significant contributor to climate change.

There is a newish 'local' supermarket near where I live. It's on an awkward corner, a junction of two main roads, where one road narrows from two lanes to one on a major through route. These are old coaching roads into London, never designed for the weight of traffic, or for the size of lorries, they see today. The lorries have a habit of mounting the pavement and cutting the corner as they squeeze past cars turning right. When the supermarket juggernaut arrives to deliver, it blocks the road almost immediately so that an angry queue of honking commuters builds up behind. This sort of scene is familiar to most city dwellers in Britain. The explosion in freight in the last twenty years has had a dramatic impact on the quality of our lives. With rural lanes and suburban streets given over to 44-tonne lorries and cars, many parents feel the roads are no longer safe for young children to negotiate by themselves. Study after study shows that our children have much less freedom than previous generations, with the result that they are less active than ever before. It is fear of traffic as much as fear of 'stranger danger' that restricts them.

The possibility of shifting back to older systems of supplying local food to local shops has become more and more remote. The retailers have tightened their grip on the distribution of food in other ways. Ten years ago, the buzz in the logistics business was 'factory-gate pricing'. Manufacturers had until then largely transported their goods to the retailers, or if they were small companies without their own fleets they had paid logistics companies to do so, and then agreed a price with the supermarkets which included the cost of freight. But retailers, led by Tesco, wanted a new system to make their own transport systems more cost efficient. They began requiring suppliers to quote them a factory-gate price which excluded the cost of transport, so that they could then decide whether to collect in their own lorries or not. Even the major manufacturers blanched. The head of logistics for Unilever Frozen Foods, David Ingram, described the experience to the *Grocer*. 'We got the infamous letter asking for very detailed information on the costs in our supply chain – which made us nervous because we didn't understand why we were being asked. Tesco was underwriting its fleet to the tune of some £400 million, almost twice as much as anyone else was spending. It has a lot of empty trucks and wanted to see a reduction in core costs.' Eventually Unilever agreed to a reduced factory-gate price to the retailer. 'We didn't have our own transport fleet, so we had a flexible approach.' Unilever later described the scheme as hugely successful. Others were not so happy, however. Independent wholesalers pointed out that it would become less and less economical for manufacturers to run their own fleets, making it harder for them to distribute their goods to independent retailers.

Long-distance transport and longer and longer supply chains have not just made it impossible to keep track of the whole chain, as the horsemeat scandal showed, they have also inevitably had an effect on the quality of our food. For just as packaging has been found to affect the nutritional content of salad, so the distance travelled by fresh food appears to be taking its toll.

The FSA advised that frozen broccoli contains more nutrients than fresh imported broccoli that has undergone a long refrigerated journey. Their comments followed research by the Austrian Consumers' Association which found that the nutrient content of a whole range of 'fresh' imported vegetables was lower than frozen versions of the same produce. The vitamin content of frozen broccoli, peas, cauliflower, sweetcorn and carrots was significantly higher than in 'fresh' versions of the vegetables imported from Italy, Spain, Turkey and Israel.

Of course we have always imported food that we cannot produce ourselves, and the UK has not been self-sufficient in food since the late eighteenth century. But it is the scale of the shift in recent decades, brought about by supermarket sourcing methods and globalization, that causes concern. British self-sufficiency in food was at historic lows in the 1930s just before the Second World War, and policies during and after it made sure that the pattern went into reverse as we learned the hard way that our national security depended on being able to feed ourselves. The trend continued until the 1980s, when our self-sufficiency started declining once more. By 2006, only half of the food consumed in the UK was produced here, and while we exported £10.5 billion worth of food, feed and drink we imported £24.8 billion worth. Our biggest food trade deficit by sector was in fresh fruit and vegetables – we brought in £6 billion worth in 2006.

What is new is this supermarket-driven creation of a permanent global summer time and the volume of food being imported at times when we could in theory supply our own. Inside my 'local' store, at the height of the English apple season, there were

no apples from this country on sale, but instead varieties shipped
or air-freighted and then trucked from New Zealand, South
Africa, the USA and, slightly nearer home, from France. The
fresh vegetable displays offered asparagus and mangetout from
Peru, a journey of 6,312 miles; baby corn from Thailand,
6,643 miles; and green beans from southern Africa, 5,979 miles.

Even the organic movement, one of whose founding principles was sustainability, has been sucked into this system. Over
80 per cent of organic food now comes from abroad. Supermarkets depend on global sourcing of organic fruit and vegetables
and truck it around the country just as much as conventional
produce.

We have all become accustomed to the idea that we can have
any fresh food at any time of year. So we purchase Israeli or
Egyptian potatoes that have travelled over 2,000 miles when we
want 'baby' potatoes in the winter. We buy tomatoes from Saudi
Arabia, over 3,000 miles away, or broccoli from Spain that has
travelled nearly 1,000 miles to reach us.

Most of us imagine we are buying the freshest of new-season
produce this way. Ironically, the baby potatoes are quite likely to
have been in store for six months or more and not actually just
lifted from the ground – but do you know when the Egyptian
potato season is? (Or the Argentinean pear season?) I always
imagined the baby potatoes were new potatoes, but in fact the
label does not make that claim for them, often just calling them
'salad' potatoes. Just as English carrots can be kept well in cold
store from September to May, so some foreign crops can be
brought in from store over an extended period. The reason for
sourcing them abroad is not just related to season; it may be that
costs are lower in developing regions or that foreign climates are
better suited to particular varieties that retailers are promoting.
The ability of retailers to source food from wherever it is cheapest at the touch of a computer key has had a perverse effect.
Even when fruit and vegetables are in season in the UK, they
may no longer be available. The British Potato council estimated

that the UK imported about 350,000 tonnes of potatoes a year
in the early 2000s, many of these coming in even when British
potatoes were available. By 2012, during the June to October
season, the UK was importing 750,000 tonnes of potatoes.

UK growers have found themselves pushed out of business,
with the result that our self-sufficiency in fruit and vegetables
has fallen dramatically. In the last twenty-five years, it has dropped
to just 4 per cent in fruit, and 52 per cent in vegetables. Moreover, the need to transport produce long distances has skewed
the market to varieties that will travel and keep well. Taste, texture and variety have been sacrificed to permanent global
summer time. As has ripeness. Fruit that has to journey thousands of miles to reach us needs to be picked hard.

I'm not denying that this permanent global summer time has
its attractions. A northern friend whose childhood was spent
largely without the benefit of modern food supplies remembers
clearly the shock of first discovering that broccoli came not just
in yellow but also, when imported fresh, in vivid green. Nor am
I suggesting that we should never eat imported or out-of-season
food, only that if we understood the impact our choices made
on other parts of our lives, we might make slightly different
choices.

The concept of food miles was first articulated by a campaign
group called SAFE, the alliance for better food and farming,
now known as Sustain. The phrase itself was coined by Tim
Lang, professor of food policy, now at London's City University.
It was an idea that rapidly went viral, encapsulating as it did
people's growing concern about the wider impacts of the way
the food system was becoming globalized. It also became handy
shorthand for types of production and distribution you might
want to avoid.

It has become fashionable to dismiss food miles more recently
as an oversimplistic way of judging how sustainable different
types of produce might be. Distance travelled was never the only
criterion used by the original campaigners, but in any case I still

find food miles a useful starting point for thinking about whether I want to buy something or not.

The way we produce and distribute food makes a major contribution to greenhouse gas emissions and climate change. A UK government report puts the UK food chain's emissions at just under a fifth of the UK's total. An EU study has estimated that food accounts for up to 31 per cent of the greenhouse gas emissions associated with a typical European household's consumption. If you are concerned about your own footprint, your diet is an area in which you can make a difference. Roughly half of the energy expended in the food chain is used on the farm, another third in the home. No doubt the whole chain needs to be more efficient, but unless you want to turn off your fridge or stop cooking, it seems fair enough to challenge the 10 per cent that goes into packaging, and the 8 per cent that goes on transport and retailing.

Climate change was one of the food miles campaigners' most pressing concerns. American oil interests and their lobbyists may still dispute the link between global warming and greenhouse gas emissions, but almost all scientists are now agreed. Global warming is already under way and the impacts of man-made climate change are already being felt. The Intergovernmental Panel on Climate Change (IPCC), made up of some 2,500 of the world's leading experts on climate change, concluded in 1995 that 'the balance of evidence suggests that there is a discernible human influence on global climate'. The evidence has become even clearer since.

Since the Industrial Revolution, we have managed to increase the atmospheric concentration of carbon dioxide and other greenhouse gases by about 5 per cent. By burning fossil fuels in our cars, lorries, homes and factories, we have taken the level of carbon dioxide in the atmosphere from 279 parts per million at the end of the seventeenth century to 389 parts per million in 2012, a level higher than at any time in the past 420,000 years. The most rapid increases have taken place in the last twenty to thirty years and the rate of increase is still accelerating. Carbon dioxide emissions from the consumption of fossil fuel increased by over 20 per cent between 1980 and 1999. Methane and nitrous oxide levels rose dramatically too.

The result has been that global temperatures are rising as extra solar radiation is trapped at the earth's surface. Reporting in the middle of 2013 the United Nations agency on weather and climate, the World Meteorological Organization, said that the planet 'experienced unprecedented high-impact climate extremes' in the ten years from 2001 to 2010, the warmest decade since the start of modern measurements in 1850.

So far there has been a rise of about 1°C in temperature since the nineteenth century. This apparently small rise in temperature has already had a dramatic effect. Glaciers are shrinking, and permafrost melting. Sea levels are rising. Extremes of climate are becoming more common. Warm air holds more vapour than cold, so evaporation increases, causing drought, which is then followed by flood when the vapour finally condenses. As temperatures rise, wind speeds increase, and storms become more violent. Globally, 2010 was the wettest year since the start of instrumental records. As well as floods, the ten years from the beginning of the century saw droughts across the world, with some of the longest and most severe in Australia, East Africa and the Amazon basin. Tropical cyclones were reported to have killed nearly 170,000 people and to have affected more than 250 million, causing economic damage of $380 billion.

The IPCC has predicted that temperatures will continue to rise, increasing between 1.4 and 5.8°C over the next 100 years. Even at the lower end of the predicted increases, large areas of farm land will become unusable, and hundreds of thousands of species will be lost. At the higher end of predictions, it is sobering to remember that a global rise in temperature of 6°C triggered a global warming episode 250 million years ago that wiped out 95 per cent of all species.

The government's chief scientific adviser, Sir David King, has also warned of the particular effects of global warming on the UK. Writing in the journal *Science*, he said that climate change was a more serious threat to the world than terrorism. Britain could face thirty times the current risk of flooding by 2080, so that the sort of flood levels which have been seen only once in every 100 years would instead recur every three years. Millions more around the world would be exposed to the risk of flood, hunger and drought, particularly in poor countries, if consumption of fossil fuels continued to grow at present rates. He reiterated the climate experts' call for the world's developed economies to cut emissions of greenhouse gases by 60 per cent of 1990 levels, in order to avoid far more expensive and disruptive changes later. 'Delaying action for decades, or even just years, is not a serious option,' he said.

Such dire predictions from eminent and generally restrained sources tend to induce individual paralysis. They so clearly call for concerted international action. But the Environment Agency has pointed out that if every driver took one fewer car journey a week averaging 9 miles, this would cut carbon emissions from traffic in UK by 13 per cent. Transport of food within the UK alone – both in lorries and in shopping trips by car – makes a significant contribution (3.5 per cent) to total carbon dioxide emissions in the UK. We not only travel further now to shop but make our car trips to supermarkets more often. In the mid-1980s, it was an average of one and a half times a week; by the mid-1990s that had gone up to two and a half times a week.

In the first three years of the twenty-first century the value of food imported by air grew by nearly 50 per cent. Air freight has remained the fastest-growing method of transporting food. In terms of energy efficiency and damaging emissions, it is still one of the most worrying aspects of the food chain. True, it only accounts for 1 per cent of food-tonne kilometres but that generates 11 per cent of all food transport emissions. Fruit and vegetables were the largest category of commodity being imported this way. Choices about how we shop and where we source our food do make a difference.

The rise in air-freighting food began thanks to a hidden subsidy. Air fuel, unlike most petrol, is not taxed. This meant it could make economic sense to fly our food in from far continents at short notice, to meet the demands of the retailers' distribution systems or to fly food out to countries where labour is cheapest.

My favourite example of the phenomenon of food miles was a product I found at Marks and Spencer for a time which sold for £2.99. It was an elegantly small plastic tray of baby vegetables, each tiny bundle of asparagus shoots, miniature corn, dwarf carrots and leeks tied together with a single chive. The chives were first flown from England to Kenya. The plastic trays and packaging were flown out too. There, African women worked day and night on long and unpredictable shifts in refrigerated packing sheds, next to Nairobi airport, turning the green stems into decorative ribbons around topped and tailed Kenyan produce. Then they were cling-wrapped and air-freighted back to England again, a round trip of 8,500 miles.

The company supplying the chive bundles to Marks and Spencer was Kenya's leading exporter of cut flowers and vegetables to the UK supermarkets, Homegrown. One of its directors at the time was Rod Evans, who generously offered to show me how his company 'added value' to the hundreds of tonnes of green beans and other vegetables he grew for Tesco, Marks and Spencer and other supermarkets. Kenya was where the business of air-freighting food first took off, and Homegrown had been the first company to turn strawberries into a commodity traded year round, thanks to an extended African season. From a beginning piggybacking on half-empty tourist flights returning to Europe, Homegrown had gradually built up its volumes of food exports to the point where it could charter its own freight flights. The practice spread across the world, complementing the air pollution from our roads with noise pollution of the skies above us.

One of the mainstays of Homegrown's business was the green bean. (The company is now owned by the Swire Group and still supplies large volumes of beans and other vegetables to super-markets.) Evans described how the supermarkets emailed over the orders for what they wanted put on the flight from Kenya that night, depending on how much their computerized tills told them they had sold the day before. Once again, they could eliminate nearly all financial risk from their end of the chain. Like most other suppliers, Homegrown told me it had no writ-ten contract with the supermarkets specifying quantities. The orders could go up or down dramatically. 'They might increase by five or six coffins. At Christmas it can be a three- or four-tonne increase in one day for sliced or topped and tailed beans. You've just got to get on and do it or you lose the business,' David Wakaba, manager of the packing operation, told me. 'Cof-fins' is the name given to the crates in which the vegetables are transported the 4,250 miles to the UK. A flexible workforce to fill the coffins was essential.

Homegrown was one of the better employers in Kenya. It had worked with the Ethical Trading Initiative to look at labour standards and was regularly audited to see how it measured up. But Evans admitted he wouldn't want to be starting out again, trying to establish terms with the retailers. The pressures imposed by modern distribution systems and the retailers' demand for constant price cuts were considerable.

To air-freight delicate vegetables and fruits, you have to pack them. Not only was much plastic packaging derived from oil, the explosion in its use through the last decades of the twentieth century played a major part in creating a crisis over landfill. We were creating so much waste there was no longer enough space to bury it. A quarter of household waste was made up of pack-aging, with nearly three quarters of that food-related at the beginning of the 2000s, and packaging in the grocery sector kept growing until 2008. Eventually the government was forced to act – European Union directives on waste and the ratcheting up of taxes have helped increase the use of packaging that can be recycled, or made from degradable materials such as starch or chalk which do not depend on fossil fuels. There has been a drive to reduce the weight of packaging by making containers thinner and lighter. The industry has also signed voluntary agreements to tackle its profligate use of non-renewable resources. But in 2011 the UK was still sending 44 million tonnes of waste to landfill a year, of which over 14 million tonnes was waste food, drink and the packaging associated with it.

The late Dr Andy Jones put all this into context in his ground-breaking report *Eating Oil*. 'Transporting food long distances is energy inefficient. One imported basket of food could release as much carbon dioxide into the atmosphere as an average four-bedroomed household does through cooking for eight months.' There was particular irony in UK farmers being forced to import large quantities of lettuce from California during the normal British season in the summer of 2003 to meet supermarket orders. The record high temperatures and drought that afflicted much of Europe that year were widely seen as evidence of global warming and climate change. They had a devastating effect on harvests, and so producers resorted to the air-freight that makes such a damaging contribution to carbon dioxide emissions, which in turn will have contributed to more global warming. Jones also calculated that importing just one calorie of lettuce from California burns up 127 calories of fuel energy

Homegrown defended the food miles its produce clocked up. Its exports were making a significant contribution to Kenya's parlous economy. Moreover, because Kenya has the benefit of a warm climate, this sort of production is no more extravagant with fossil fuels than growing green vegetables in glasshouses in northern Europe through the winter months when farmers spend as much fuel on heating, it argued. That is true. The issue of food miles was never entirely straightforward. If you are considering energy use and emissions, you need to take into account not just distance travelled but also refrigeration during transport, farming methods and method of transport. In the last few years there has been much research into what is called the 'life cycle analysis' of different products which factors in these much more complex calculations than the simple measure of food miles. But the point is that when they become routine, both the out-of-season salad grown by artificial heat in winter *and* the air-freighted green bean represent an unsustainable use of finite fossil fuels and a contribution to climate change.

UK ministers made the same point as Homegrown, that Africa needed this type of production to help it develop economically. Deciding not to buy food from poor countries just because it had been flown thousands of miles would harm those most in need of our support. Added to this point more recently has been the argument that you could do more to reduce your own contribution to emissions by giving up meat than by eschewing air-freighted fresh food.

How far food export helps a country develop depends of course on how much of the profits from the trade are left in that country and how much of its resources – water, soil, land – are exhausted rather than left available for long-term use.

The clearest case I have found that explains this – because, unusually, the figures are available – is Peruvian asparagus.

The market in fresh asparagus out of season barely existed before the end of the 1990s. Now the UK is the third largest importer of fresh Peruvian asparagus, consuming 6.5 million kilos a year of this thirsty luxury crop that is air-freighted over 6,000 miles. The Americans are also great enthusiasts for it. Peru meanwhile has become the largest exporter of asparagus in the world, earning more than $450 million a year from the trade. Around 95 per cent of this asparagus comes from the Ica valley.

The Ica valley is one of the driest regions on earth. The expansion of the agricultural frontier in the region was made possible thanks to multi-million dollar investments by the World

Bank from the late 1990s onwards. In just ten years asparagus cultivation exploded to cover nearly 100 square kilometres of reclaimed desert. Some of the largest producers received loans from the World Bank's commercial investment arm totalling $20 million (£12 million) or more over that period. The trade created around 10,000 new jobs in a very poor area, albeit the majority of them filled by indigenous migrants. From 1990 Peru's GDP grew steadily too when trade liberalization and food for export took off. In 2008 it grew by 9.2 per cent, the eleventh highest rate globally, and its foreign exchange reserves were at record levels, a big achievement. But the rosy macroeconomic picture disguised the fact that it had not delivered benefits to some of the poorest; in the long term it was questionable whether the benefits to Peru would continue at all.

The trade has already provoked conflict because it is sucking the valley dry with shocking speed. When a benighted World Bank executive went to investigate complaints about the water shortages he was shot at.

The aid charity Progressio reported that by 2010 industrial production of asparagus in the valley was depleting the area's water resources so fast that smaller farmers and local families were finding wells running dry. Water to the main city in the valley was also under threat.

The asparagus beds developed in the previous decade required constant irrigation, with the result that the local water table had plummeted since 2002 when extraction overtook replenishment. In some places it had fallen by 8 metres each year, one of the fastest rates of aquifer depletion in the world.

Two wells serving up to 18,500 people in the valley had already dried up. Traditional small- and medium-scale farmers also found their water supplies severely diminished.

Juan Alvarez's experience was typical. His family had farmed in the Ica valley for four generations. He was employing ten people through the year, with up to forty jobs for workers in peak asparagus season, but he told Progressio those livelihoods were under threat.

The wells on his farm used to hit water at 55 metres, and he could pump 60 litres of water a second from them. Now some had dried out, and where there was still water he had to drill down to 108 metres and could extract only 22 litres a second even at that depth.

Alvarez told researchers: 'Agro exporters came with new government policies and tax exemptions. They bought water rights and started buying wells very far away. They have created jobs and that's important, but the reality is they are depleting the water resources and when the water is gone they will leave. But what future is there for us? We will never leave.'

For smaller farmers the crisis was even more acute. Elisa Gomez and her family owned a small farm next to one of the largest asparagus exporters and had to buy water for irrigation from the local canal, but the industrial production had made it hard to survive. 'We pay for water for fifteen days twice a year. But the soil is not as productive as before and dries out in just three days. Now the land is so dry the water drains away much faster.'

The rights to the wells in their part of the valley had all been sold to the exporter. 'Those of us who didn't sell land suffered water shortages, so many people were forced to sell anyway. The exporters just wait for people to get tired and sell them cheap dry land,' she said.

The large-scale exporting companies were not immune from the crisis of over-extraction either. They were facing rising costs for their water. They had been deepening existing wells, buying up old ones from neighbouring land and piping water across huge distances. Some were also alleged to have got round a ban on new wells by paying off officials.

One of the largest and most modern of Peru's fresh asparagus producers, which supplies 18 per cent of exports to the UK, spoke to Progressio researchers anonymously. It had received loans from the World Bank's lending arm. Its chief executive said that the water levels in some wells were falling by as much as two metres a year. All its wells were licensed and legal but he said regulation was weak and there was no inspection of what people extracted.

Competition for diminishing global resources is emerging as one of the most pressing concerns for business as well as development organizations. Leading retailers have told me privately that water shortages in the areas where they source fresh fruit and vegetables out of season is top of their list of priorities when they check how sustainable their businesses are. That is the environmental crisis they expect to hit hardest and fastest. Even retailers, having created this system, are having to worry about emissions, climate change, soil depletion and sustainable land use now too.

The water shortages on Peru's Pacific coast meanwhile are expected to get worse as climate change shrinks the glaciers that feed the Ica river system. The horticulture exporters in Kenya face their own water crisis.

Time and time again export-led growth has this effect – an increase in inequalities and a deepening of poverty for those at the bottom of the chain.

Would it be worth it, if the overall growth in Peru's GDP eventually produced a trickle-down of wealth?

Well, first, how much real wealth is being created for Peru?

A hearing of the US Congress's Ways and Means Committee in 2006 unintentionally provided one of the most succinct answers to this question I have come across. The Peruvian asparagus industry was up before the House to reassure representatives that any growth in imports to the US from Peru following free trade agreements would be in US interests.

For every dollar spent by a US consumer on imported asparagus from Peru, 70 cents stayed in the US, the industry explained. The money goes not to Peruvian farmers but to US supermarkets and wholesalers, and to US shippers, distributors, importers and storage owners. Just 30 cents stays in Peru.

But Peru doesn't even get the full benefit of that 30 cents, because a large portion of that amount comes back to the US anyway: it is spent by Peruvian companies (or the Peruvian subsidiaries of multinational producers) on US seed, US materials for processing, US fertilizer and US pesticides.

Even that's not the end of it, because Peruvian asparagus growers were enticed to the region with generous tax breaks. Agricultural exporters' profits in Peru are taxed (assuming of course that they aren't offshored) at just 15 per cent, half the national average paid by other industries.

Not much to trickle down then, and with the water rapidly running out, not much time for it to trickle anywhere either.

When you learn of the story behind such mass-market innovations as air-freighted Peruvian asparagus it is hard to feel the same about the product again. Food miles are indeed only part of the picture, albeit one that generally rings the right alarm bells. Professor Lang has more recently called for some sort of 'omni-standards' label that might weigh up all these things along with nutritional content of food and the social effects of its production.

For most of us wanting to get the shopping done it can all sound bogglingly complicated. Far better that the businesses that dominate these sectors should be made to take responsibility for their impact.

Given the urgency of the crisis threatened by climate change, worrying about whether one form of giving up is more efficient than another – avoiding excessive food miles versus cutting our meat consumption – feels wide of the mark too. We might need to do both.

Livestock production accounts for just under a fifth of global greenhouse gas emissions, according to an enormously influential FAO report published in 2006 called Livestock's Long Shadow. Dr Rajendra Pachauri, the chair of the IPCC, has suggested that by halving their meat consumption, people in Western countries would do more to reduce their CO_2 emissions than if they halved their car usage. Since our addiction to personal transport is hard to break, he proposed that people who cared about their children's future might want to gradually move to a few meat-free days.

If you share the typical British appetite, you work your way through more than 1.5kg of meat a week as part of your annual 80kg quota of flesh-eating. That leaves you behind your typical American counterpart – working his or her way through 125kg a year – but still near the top of the international league of carnivores.

The case for cutting out meat consumption has long been a compelling one from whichever perspective you look at it – human health, environmental good, animal welfare, fair distribution of planetary resources.

Intensive meat production is a very inefficient way of feeding the world. Farm a decent acre with cattle and you can produce about 20lbs of beef protein. Give the same acre over to wheat and you can produce 138lbs of protein for human consumption. If the grain that is currently used to feed animals were fed instead directly to people, there may be just enough food to go around when population peaks.

Replacing meat with more plant foods would also reduce diet-related diseases such as obesity, heart disease and some cancers, according to reports in the *Lancet*. Malthusian panics about how to feed the world are not new, but the question has added urgency now as available resources dwindle.

The received wisdom has been that meat is superior because it contains 'complete' protein with all the amino acids humans need for growth and maintenance. This hang-up about complete protein seems to be one of the reasons meat still holds its powerful attraction. Until recently it was thought that we needed to eat the eight amino acids we cannot synthesize ourselves in combinations at the same time to be able to make use of plant protein. In fact nutritional science has subsequently caught up with the wisdom distilled in peasant cuisines that depend on beans and grains, using meat sparingly as a flavouring, and found this not true. But this idea of complete protein being the master ingredient persists.

The gospel of protein, as Geoffrey Cannon, editor of *World Nutrition* describes it, has been preached by governments for more than 100 years for three reasons: 'power, empire and war'. Protein became the master nutrient because concentrated animal protein promotes growth in early life. 'This was a period when the most powerful European nations and then the USA were expanding their empires and preparing for mass wars fought by land armies. Growth in every sense was the prevailing ideology. Governments needed production of more, bigger, faster-growing plants, animals and humans.'

American soldiers reared on diets high in meat and milk from the Midwest came over to help win the war in Europe in 1917 and in 1941 and seemed to be like young gods because they were so tall, broad and strong, even though their parents might have been smaller immigrant peasants from Europe. The physical weakness of the poorly fed working classes in Europe was seen as an impediment to national growth. Increasing production and consumption of animal protein was a British national priority up to the Second World War, Cannon explains.

Meanwhile, over in Germany in 1938, the German army high command was testing out its new Wehrmacht cookbook, I discovered. 'The soldier's efficiency can be maintained only if the elements consumed in working are supplied through the diet. The body is continually using up its own substance which has to be replaced in the form of protein, the body-building material,' it declares. It had come up with the rather forward-thinking idea that reducing animal products would be more economically efficient, 'as these products must be manufactured in a round-about way from plant materials by the bodies of animals themselves. This is an extravagant use of food'. Moreover, stocks of meat would be hard to accumulate and transport by the invading army. So instead the Germans tested mass-feeding with protein from 'pure soya'. The infantry were given 150g a day of protein, with soya stuffed into everything possible, from liver noodles to goulash with brown gravy and sponge pudding with chocolate sauce, topped by rice and soya milk as a midnight snack. We don't need to inflict such delights on ourselves.

Today's official guidelines are that adult men need just about a third of that Aryan-building calculation for protein. But recommended daily amounts of protein remain a somewhat movable feast, subject to political influence. They depend on body weight, and have been adjusted as understanding has increased. What is clear, though, is that protein deficiencies are rare in developed countries and most of us, including vegetarians, eat much more than we need.

Joe Millward, professor of nutrition at Surrey University, has sat on several national and international expert committees that have drawn up recommendations on protein requirements. Vegetarians who eat eggs and milk 'have no nutritional issues at all', he says. Their protein intakes are not much lower than the average meat-eater's, and they get plenty of the micronutrients associated with meat, such as B12 and iron.

Dr Mike Rayner, director of the British Heart Foundation health promotion group, points out, in the book *The Meat Crisis*, that the average person in the UK is already getting about 31g a day of protein from cereals, fruit, nuts and vegetables including potatoes. The UK government estimates that the average woman needs 36g of protein per day and the average man 44g. 'If official recommendations are right, then we don't need to eat much more of these foods to meet them.'

Most people in this country and the US eat double the amount of protein they need. Excess is just broken down in the body for energy or stored as fat.

A shift in cultural attitudes towards meat consumption in affluent countries would undoubtedly help mitigate against climate change. But reducing air-freighted veg or steak fests are not mutually exclusive options.

There is another glaring danger in continuing a system in

which supplying even the most basic of foods depends on long distribution chains: as well as contributing to them, it is also highly susceptible to both oil and climate shocks.

Oil is one of the most politically charged of substances. Wars are fought over it. As pressure on supplies grows, the struggle for energy is likely to distort our decision-making and lead us into more conflicts rather than fewer than in the past.

Just how insecure our food system already is became clear when the UK had its own very British fuel crisis in 2000. As violence in the Middle East drove the price of crude oil to a ten-year high of $35 a barrel (a price which seems cheerfully low now that it is regularly over $100 a barrel), a handful of angry farmers and hauliers blockaded oil depots around the country in protest at petrol price rises. The government was caught on the hop and appeared to be in a state of alarming ignorance about how our food reaches us these days. *The Times* reported that the chief executive of Sainsbury's had written to the prime minister warning that the petrol crisis could leave stores without food in days rather than weeks. The public was accused of panic buying as staples disappeared from the shops. Their panic turned out to be a well-founded fear that food would run out more rapidly than anyone was admitting. A senior member of the government has since admitted privately that the country very nearly did run out of food.

In the end it was not a question of days, but just hours, according to the Federation of Bakers: 'We came very close to not getting bread out in the fuel strike.' Bakeries, like supermarkets, order 'just in time' these days and keep little in stock. 'If you haven't got flour, you can't make bread. The whole supply chain was suffering in the same way. But there was great confusion at the ministry [MAFF as it then was]. There seemed a complete lack of understanding about how reliant every part of the chain was on everything else. We were on the phone to them all the time, but the civil servants just didn't seem to realize how interconnected it all is. Then some fuel was released and we were put to the top of the pile so we could get the deliveries going. But we were within just a few hours of the country not having a loaf to eat,' John White, Federation director, told me.

In 2010 it was an extreme weather event, of the sort that we know will become more frequent, that led to the supply of root vegetables taking its place on prime minister Gordon Brown's Downing Street agenda. Milk was also in danger of running out. A prolonged cold snap had exposed the system's fragility once again.

About 80 per cent of all supermarket supplies of carrots now come from just 10 major packers in East Anglia, Scotland and the north of England. More than half the carrots the UK eats have to make their way from north-east Scotland, where the fields had been frozen, to centralized distribution depots and back out again to stores.

The UK's milk supply now involves some 60 per cent of our fresh milk travelling from farms around the country to six locations for processing before being trucked back hundreds of miles up and down motorways to customers.

Whereas in the recent past the carrot harvest would have been lifted at the end of the autumn and stored, now the carrots are kept in the fields through the winter, covered with thick layers of straw and dug up just in time to meet supermarket orders day by day. The fields were covered in 2 feet of snow. A mixture of panic buying and demand for warming meals saw orders double just when conditions were harshest.

There was no slack in the system. In East Anglia, growers had to throw labour at the problem to keep up. Sarah Pettitt, chair of the National Farmers' Union board of horticultural growers, estimated that her brassica company had seen a 100 per cent increase in its costs in the cold weather, like most other vegetable growers she knew.

For two weeks, Pettitt's broccoli could not be lifted. Extra workers, mainly Lithuanian and Bulgarian migrants, had been needed across East Anglia to harvest in snow-covered fields where mechanical harvesters were unable to work, and to run thawing lines in packhouses. Extra shifts had been required on grading machines to pick out damaged and rotten vegetables.

She said there was 'absolute frustration' among producers that the costs of keeping supply lines going were not being shared by supermarkets, which set prices up to a year in advance. 'We've been blowing our brains out to keep continuity of supply to them, but there's no suggestion that the costs will be repaid.'

The structure of today's milk industry had made it more vulnerable to bad weather too. Milk travels further to fewer, larger processors, which use larger articulated lorries that are less able to cope with even a slight deterioration in weather than the smaller tankers the Milk Marketing Board used to operate. 'It can be mayhem even when conditions aren't really that bad,' Nick Tyler, a large-scale dairy farmer with 600 cows in Wiltshire, told me. He had lost £11,000 worth of milk in a week when the leading processor's tanker failed to turn up because of the weather and he was forced to throw it away. It had subcontracted its logistics to a separate leading haulier. 'They didn't even phone, they just didn't turn up,' Tyler said. 'We'd salted the road to the dairy, and the feed lorries managed to get in, but they didn't come to collect.' He woke to face 4 inches of fresh snow the next day and a fight to work out which company, if either, would pay. His local supermarket, meanwhile, was repeatedly out of milk and rationing customers to one loaf of bread each.

Huw Bowles, director of the organic co-operative OMSCO, highlighted the problem. 'Forty years ago milk was processed closer to where it was produced and delivered back to the same area.' The drive to make industry logistics as economically efficient as possible has removed any slack. OMSCO has cut the cost of collection by 30 per cent in recent years with these efficiencies but at the price of less resilience. 'There are no spare vehicles any more. If the driving speeds are reduced by just ten m.p.h. on a nine-hour shift because of the snow, they just can't get round the whole collection; the whole route is affected,' he explained.

A couple of weeks of cold weather had suddenly put supplies under threat. The thaw came just in time. It did not look like a resilient system fit for the future.

5. Bread

The wholemeal bread from the supermarket in-store bakery felt springy, but as I cut it, the top of the loaf squeezed down to half its height like a damp sponge and stayed there. I pulled it back into shape, put a slice into the toaster and watched it pop up, light as anything again. I found myself wondering, not for the first time, how *do* they do that?

How do they take wholemeal flour, yeast and water and make the mixture into something like boiled flannel? Why isn't it more like the wholemeal bread you can buy, if you are lucky, from a local craft baker, or the stuff you make yourself at home, with its nutty taste and dense texture? The labels, when I have inspected them, have been curiously silent on the subject. They generally have just one added ingredient listed. Flour treatment agent.

'Boy, that's pouffy. There's a lot of air and water in there,' Elizabeth Weisberg, master baker at the Lighthouse Bakery explained, as she too squeezed the specimen I had brought her. 'How do they do it, well, they use chemical so-called "improvers" to put the air and water in, and fat, hardened fat, to hold them up.'

We were standing in the bakery at the back of the small shop Elizabeth ran with her partner Rachel Duffield in south London. The scent of dough and freshly baked bread drew you in from yards away. You had to queue for it, but that was part of the experience.

Rachel and Elizabeth toyed with the idea of running a delicatessen before setting up a bakery. Bread won in the end because they liked the idea of re-creating the ritual of buying your daily bread from a small local shop where everyone gets to know everyone else. It is a ritual that binds communities together, one considered so important to the fabric of society by the French that their government had taken action to protect small bakers. But it is a ritual that we have almost completely lost.

While you patiently waited your turn outside the Lighthouse, you had time to agonize over which of the thirty or so types of bread you would choose when you got to the front of the queue: would it be Gloucester rye or Old English spelt, seven-seed cob or stoneground wholemeal for the goodness of the whole grain? Or for the luxury of real white, would it be farmhouse or sand-wich, cottage or bloomer? A board outside told you that all the breads were made and baked on the premises daily without the aid of 'any artificial enhancers or chemical improvers'.

The queue moved forward slowly because Rachel knew nearly everyone, and she stopped to chat with them. Likely as not, someone would be holding up the front of the line mad-deningly while they gossiped with another customer they knew. But then you found yourself doing the same as someone familiar greeted you.

Out at the back, Elizabeth worked non-stop, getting up at three most mornings and baking right through the night on Fri-day for the weekend rush. Rachel and Elizabeth now run the Lighthouse bakery school in Sussex.

Trays of willow baskets holding balls of sourdough which had been started the day before went into an old steel oven for another day's fermenting before baking the following day. Eliza-beth pulled from a bucket a lump of baguette dough that had been proving for several hours. It stretched and drooped from her hand and then flopped on to the counter. She kneaded it gently with her knuckles, folded it to pull it back, pushed away, and gave it a quick roll with the heel of her hand. It was springy and soft, and although it looked wet, was dry to the touch. Knocking back like this redistributes the gas bubbles produced by the yeast, helps the gluten to develop and sets the yeast going again. Once replaced in tins, the dough started coming back to life. Then it would be left to prove and rest overnight so that it fermented slowly and acquired the full flavour that comes from the traditionally made loaf. This is how our bread has been made for centuries.

The only ingredients required are flour, yeast and water. Bread has sustained generations. It was called the 'staff of life' because, when well made from good-quality ingredients, it contains so many of the vital nutrients we need for good health, the essential fats, fibre, protein, vitamins and minerals (over twenty of them) and carbohydrates that our bodies need to function properly. Since staples by definition account for a large proportion of our intake, if the staple of the diet is healthy, it is much easier to ensure that the diet overall is healthy.

But bread made like this also needs time and space, and in mass manufacturing, time and space mean money. Only a tiny fraction of our bread is made this way now.

Look at the supermarket shelves displaying dozens of loaves, and you might think that you are confronted with unlimited choice, but the vast majority of the breads on offer have emerged from the same factories and been made by one industrial method. Perhaps instinctively we know this. We spend on average less than one minute in the bread aisle when we shop.

Like much of food manufacturing today, the bread sector has become highly concentrated. By 2003, eleven factory baking companies, or 'plant bakeries' as they are called, were making the vast majority of the bread we ate. By 2013, production had been consolidated into some fifty factories and just three giant companies dominated the £3.4 billion UK market, Warburton's, with the largest market share, Allied Bakeries, second with its Kingsmill, Burgen, Sunblest and Allinson brands, and the private equity company Premier Foods that owned the Hovis brand close behind. The three brands accounted for two thirds of the 11 million or so loaves we eat each day. But since the same companies also make supermarkets' own label loaves, these large plant bakeries in fact represented 80 per cent of the total market.

Supermarket in-store bakeries represent 10–13 per cent of the bread market. The lure of bread fresh from the oven is used by the supermarkets to pull customers in; it whets their appetites and encourages them to spend more. But the illusion of freshness can be deceptive. Figures are hard to come by, but the baking industry reckons that half of the big retailers' in-store bakeries are using 'prebaked' dough and 'baking it off'. In other words, their bread is made by one of the plant bakery companies, and partially baked at its factory, then simply finished off in the oven in the supermarket store. Many of the remaining in-store bakeries make their bread from 'premixes', with flour, yeast, fat and improvers already measured out by a factory, to reduce the level of skills needed by workers in the supermarket to a minimum.

That leaves around 7 per cent of our bread to be produced by high street bakers, but even that figure is misleading because only a small number of them are independent or genuinely bake from scratch, many depending instead on the same factory 'premixes' of flour and additives. There are only 4,500 individual craft bakers in the UK, an increase of around 1,000 since the first publication of *Not On the Label* and a reflection of the revival of the real bread movement, but still a tiny number, compared to about 35,000 in France.

At the beginning of the nineteenth century most bread was made in the home. But with increasing urbanization, long working hours and the high cost of fuel needed to keep ovens warm, the baking industry began to develop. In 1850 nearly all bakers were independent master bakers, who baked bread and sold it on the same premises. By the beginning of the twentieth century a few large factory bakeries were emerging – some, like J. Lyons, making bread for their teahouses, others supplying their own shops. The pace of change accelerated in 1932 with the arrival in England of Garfield Weston, a successful Canadian biscuit manufacturer. He started buying up independent bakeries and shops, importing Canadian wheat to supply them, and in 1935 he formed Allied Bakeries Ltd. Before that only the

Co-operative Movement in Britain owned both mills and bakeries; the other big millers, Spillers and Rank, had no bakeries. But now, finding their flour markets threatened, they also started buying up bakeries and shops, and established their own factory bakeries. The rush to integrate had begun. Smaller millers were gradually squeezed out, particularly after the war when government subsidies and price controls on flour were removed. Independent bakers struggled to compete with the larger companies which were taking advantage of the launch of commercial TV to promote their brands of bread to a nation just recovering from rationing and the nutritious but heavy wartime National Loaf.

Although the sector was rationalizing rapidly, the bread its factories produced was nevertheless still made in a way recognizable to home bakers: dough would be left to ferment and prove over extended periods. Then in the early 1960s a method evolved that revolutionized the centuries-old process. Researchers at the British Baking Industries Research Association in Chorleywood developed a way of making bread that had first been used in the USA. It dispensed with all the time and expensive energy required by traditional methods. Instead of allowing two to three hours' fermentation, they found that air and water could be incorporated into dough if it was mixed with intense energy at high speeds in mechanical mixers. Double the quantity of yeast was needed to make it rise; chemical oxidants were essential to get the gas in; and hardened fat had to be added to provide structure – without the fat, the bread collapsed in early experiments – but the process removed labour, reduced costs and gave much higher yields of bread from each sack of flour because the dough absorbed so much more water. Cheaper British wheats, with lower protein content than the North American grains that had become standard, could also be used.

By 1965 the Chorleywood bread process, or CBP as it was known, had become widespread. It could not be used for wholemeal bread because regulations prevented the addition of anything to wholemeal bread other than 100 per cent whole-meal flour, yeast, salt and water. But in the late 1980s, once the use of improvers had finally been permitted in wholemeal bread too, production of that switched to the same instant industrial process.

The technology of the chemical improvers on which modern bread depends has developed rapidly since.

Improvers had first emerged in the 1920s as 'yeast foods'. By the 1930s the industry had found that soya flour whitened bread and softened the crumb. Then, when chemical oxidants were needed to make the short, intense mixing in the CBP work, it made sense to incorporate them into a premix of additives with soya flour as the carrier for the chemical ingredients; most of the improver manufacturers in fact started out as soya flour millers. The improver or 'flour treatment agent' was also the logical way to add the fats needed in CBP breads.

Ingredients manufacturers and bakers regard their improvers as commercially sensitive and are not overeager to tell you what is in them. Bakers' technical handbooks, however, are an instruct-ive source.

They explain why industrial bakers have added specially hardened fats for years: the CBP requires the addition of a fat with a high melting point to give the bread structure. The fat has to remain solid at temperatures of over 35°C. Until the mid-2000s most bakeries used artificially hardened or hydrogenated fats. The fat also needs to be present in the dough in a highly dis-persed form, so manufacturers of bread improvers and other industrial baking ingredients blend hard and soft fat and either spray-dry it or disperse it through a carrier such as soya flour. Unfortunately it turned out that the process of hydrogenation created trans fats that increased the risk of heart disease, so grad-ually they switched to new methods of creating the right sort of fat for the industrial process. Now they mostly use a fractionated fat typically made from palm oil. Fractionated fat is made by cooling the oil until fat crystals form so that the solids can be separated out. This palm stearin used to be considered waste but then it was found to have the high melting point that is so useful in food manufacture. Its hardness is double-edged however. It is highly saturated, and has been associated in some literature with heart disease. Industrial ingredients such as 'organic palm short-ening' are about 50 per cent saturated fat.

The CBP also needs emulsifiers. These perform a similar function to the fat. They plug the gaps, enabling the dough to retain more air while also slowing down staling. The most commonly used group of emulsifiers in bread are the data esters, relatively novel and complex compounds, made from petrochemicals.

Double the amount of yeast is also used in the CBP to make up for the lack of fermentation time. Champions of real bread have suggested a link between this increase in yeast and its resi-dues and the rise of infections such as thrush, which is produced by the yeast organism candida albicans. But there is little research in this area.

Salt goes in to add flavour. Traditionally flavour develops dur-ing the fermentation time, so when you eliminate that you need higher levels of salt. Bread is in fact the biggest contributor of dietary salt in the UK, delivering almost a fifth of the total we consume in processed foods. The recommended daily intake for UK adults is a maximum of 6g, with the current average 8.1g a day.

Excess dietary salt can lead to high blood pressure, an increased risk of heart attack, stroke and kidney disease, as well as to other health problems. And the evidence shows that curbing dietary salt at the population level is one of the most cost-effective means of improving public health. The FSA had run a deter-mined campaign to make industry reduce salt levels, with the result that they fell by around 20 per cent in the decade to 2011. But there was still a wide variation in the salt content of similar products, with just 42 per cent of branded breads meeting the targets it had set of 1g of salt per 100g of bread or less. Supermarket own-label goods did better, with nearly 90 per cent of them on target.

Legislation has gradually been introduced to restrict some of the more damaging additives manufacturers used to depend on in the CBP. Potassium bromate, which was used for years as a bleaching and oxidizing agent but also destroyed valuable nutrients, has been banned, for example. The only oxidizing agent that may now be used during mixing is ascorbic acid, often labelled as vitamin C, although any vitamin C content is destroyed in the baking.

It took from 1927, when a government committee first recommended a ban, until 1998 to stop the use of flour bleached with chlorine compounds. Manufacturers liked chlorinated flour, not just because of the bleaching effect but also because it allowed higher levels of water to be added. When it finally lost these props the industry accelerated research into enzymes and other novel ingredients to find alternatives. The Associated British Foods group that owns Allied Bakeries, for example, also owns AB Enzymes, the first company to supply enzymes, or 'tiny invisible helpers' as it calls them, to the baking industry.

As enzymes are destroyed in the baking process they do not have to be declared on the label. Their use in food has increased rapidly, thanks to the introduction of gene modification techniques. Naturally occurring enzymes – proteins that speed up biological reactions – have been used in food preparation for centuries. The combination of pineapple and ham may seem a culinary travesty but it evolved because the enzymes in the fruit have a tenderizing effect on the meat. Since the 1980s, however, companies have been using genetic modification to mass-produce customized enzymes. Many of the enzymes used in baking today are produced by genetically modified organisms (GMOs). It is the microorganisms that produce the enzymes, however, rather than the enzymes themselves that have been modified.

A report in the technical journal *New Food* highlights some of the benefits of these enzymes. It describes how certain hemicellulase enzymes 'enhance bread volumes' and control the softness of doughs so that manufacturers can incorporate more water, 'giving high percentage volume increases with relatively low-grade flour'.

Getting water into the dough is one of the keys to profitability. The CBP white loaf is made with about 3 per cent more water than one made by traditional methods. When the government's Food Standards Committee looked at water in bread in 1978, the average percentage of water in a loaf ranged from 36 to 40 per cent. A subsequent study in 1986 found the average percentage had risen to 45 per cent.

The comparisons looked even worse when a traditional wholemeal loaf was put alongside a CBP wholemeal one. The CBP wholemeal had 6.5 per cent more water than the traditional loaf. Bread is sold by weight, and water is pretty heavy stuff.

Most of our bread is now made by the CBP. Over 80 per cent of it is wrapped and sliced and of that three quarters is white sliced. At the time of writing a white sliced loaf can be bought in a supermarket for just 47p.

Chemical wizardry and economic efficiency have undoubtedly produced cheap daily bread. Yet for all their power and despite all the new hi-tech methods to help them make money, the bakers were under pressure, as I discovered when I went to a large white-sliced bread factory.

The great silos and chimneys of the Erith bread factory looked imposing as I walked up the leafy hill towards them from the suburban station of Barnehurst in outer London's Bexleyheath. But close up, the factory entrance, set amidst nondescript housing, was modest enough, as was the assessment of our culinary aspirations displayed on its welcome sign. 'Consistent products, contented customers,' it announced above a rollcall of brand names – Hovis Great White, Mother's Pride, Nimble – that manage to sound both weighty and light.

The loaves that came out of here were certainly consistent. Ten thousand of them an hour, a quarter of a million a day, travelled in an endless line through giant mixers and moulders into the gas oven, following a schedule which allowed for no interruption from each Saturday afternoon until the early hours of the following Saturday morning, when the plant closed down briefly for cleaning and maintenance before winding straight back up again.

This was where 10 per cent of all of what was British Bakeries bread was made. (The Rank Hovis McDougall milling and bread group it was part of was bought by private equity group Premier Foods at the height of the credit boom, in a deal financed with £2.1 billion of debt. It had struggled post-crash under the weight of its borrowings, and was said to have considered selling the Hovis brand at one point. Relations with its workforce had been turbulent. The loss of the contract to supply the Co-op group had led to hundreds of job cuts. There had been disputes over pay cuts and the replacement of permanent workers with agency labour brought in on 'zero-hours' contracts, that is given work only as and when needed.) At the Erith factory when I visited 13 tonnes of fats and 12 tonnes of chemical improvers were used each week to turn 820 tonnes of flour into the sort of bread that can fill 1.5 million factory bread bags, marked either with the company's own brands or with own-label logos for the big supermarkets. Because the volumes were so enormous, bread has been one of the few foods that retains its own distribution system. Eighteen articulated lorries took the bread from Erith to the company's distribution centre at Dagenham for it to be trucked on to hundreds of supermarkets across the south of England, hitting a precise delivery window between 3 a.m. and 5 a.m. to miss the night curfews but still be in time for the stores' opening hours.

Nigel Dalmon, the site manager at Erith at that time, showed me around together with John White from the Federation of Bakers, the industry lobbying group. Dalmon had started in the baking business thirty-three years before, as an apprentice aged fifteen. We began in the store room. It was surprisingly small – the flour comes in throughout the day in a 'just-in-time' delivery system. Most of it was British. UK wheat used to be considered too soft for breadmaking, and harder American wheats with a higher protein content were favoured, but the CBP, and the ability to separate out and then add back in gluten from other sources, has made it possible to use a majority of homegrown grain. It was much cheaper because the EU subsidized British grain farmers, and imposed tariffs on imported wheat.

A solitary worker put on his mask and weighed and sieved ingredients from one yellowy plastic tub to another, stirring up a ghostly cloud of dust. The range of technical possibilities was engraved on a row of bins marked 'BB Longer Life', 'BB Improver', 'Gluten', 'Bred [sic] soy'.

We went into the main plant room beyond, muffling our ears against the din. Here conveyor belts rose and fell, turned and advanced through every conceivable angle and plane, shunting the bread through its different stages. At any one time there were 35,000 loaves moving through the factory in various states of being, and the machine must not stop. 'Hold up any one part of it for more than five minutes and you lose the whole plant,' Nigel explained. Pipes and tubes wormed around the ceiling carrying yeast from pumps and flour from hoppers to the mixers. Most of the mechanical shunting was mere marking of time, keeping the stuff moving while it warmed up or cooled down. To stop would require labour. There were 100 people on each shift, but for the most part they were invisible presences.

The actual bread mixing was over in a blink. This is the wonder of the CBP. It replaces hours of waiting while the dough ferments. Two industrial steel mixers were being fed 225kg each of flour, plus water, vinegar, salt, yeast and the contents of one of the yellowy bins – layers of powders of different textures and a large glob of greyish fat. Then the vast bowls vibrated furiously for just three minutes before swinging up high, turning and disgorging an enormous lump of instant dough like a giant ball of chewing gum.

The ball of dough emerged from the mixers to be rolled up into a hopper from where it fell down through a divider. It was allowed to recover on the belt for ninety seconds before passing into the moulder where it was squashed to a pancake, and passed through a set of knives to divide it into four triangular pieces, each on its own lane, for white sliced bread. Wholemeal is made in one piece but white sliced is made up from four pieces of dough because 'it gives a more open texture with less shadow which makes it look whiter'. Further along, the four lanes converged and were joined by another tier bearing empty tins on a belt which glided up from underneath to meet them. Once brought together, the loaf moved for fifty-four minutes through the prover, then on through the lidding machine – for the laying on of lids – flat-top or dome depending on the supermarket client, or top left open for the independent sector. From there the bread passed on into the oven where tracks carried it back and forth past rows of gas burners for a precise twenty-one minutes.

The greatest expenditure of energy goes into cooling. The loaves have to be cold before they can be sliced or they collapse, and it takes 110 minutes to bring them down to the right temperature to pass through the high-speed blades of the slicer and be received into their plastic bags.

It was not good baking weather when I visited. The incinerating heat of a record summer and the blast of the furnaces had made it too hot. Nigel held a slice of bread up to the light. It had a few gas bubbles in it, yet looked uniform enough to me, but his practised eye was not happy. 'Our product has got to be the best on the shelf.' You can add more cold water but there's not much else you can do in a plant this size to keep the temperature down.

We walked past the coat-hanger-like racks of wrappers wearing the colours of the major retailers who have the white sliced loaves made here. I asked Nigel about the secret of the longer-life loaf. It is sprayed on the outside with either sorbate or calcium propionate – both antifungal agents which inhibit the growth of moulds. The latter has been associated with allergic reactions in workers. This factory uses the former, but not on its own brands of loaf.

I liked Nigel and John. Nigel was running an efficient factory providing good jobs. He was passionate about his staff and concerned about his neighbours' best interests. A keen cyclist himself, he was committed to doing something about the traffic nuisance caused by his lorries and shift workers driving to the factory at the crack of dawn – if only the council could get some public buses running at that time of day.

When we had finished our tour, we went upstairs to talk more about the pressures on the market.

Nigel offered me a plate of ham sandwiches on white bread.

'Your own bread?' I asked as I took a bite.

'Yes indeed.'

The bread was doing that curious thing sliced factory bread does, moulding itself to my teeth and the roof of my mouth and setting as though it were dentist's putty. I decided not to ask about the ham but worked furtively with my tongue, hoping to dislodge it without looking too rude, while Nigel and John sighed and tutted about the Atkins Diet.

The diet, a weight-loss programme originally devised ten years previously by an American doctor, Robert Atkins, had hit the bestseller lists again following an article in the *New York Times* magazine headlined 'What if it's all a big fat lie?' The *NYT* piece compiled evidence challenging the orthodoxy in the USA that excess consumption of fats in the diet was at the root of that country's current crisis of obesity, diabetes and heart disease. It posited instead the theory that the problem was an excess of carbohydrates, especially sugar and over-refined white flour, white rice and pasta, just as Atkins had maintained. Bread was in the firing line and that summer had become the season of culling the carbs.

The theory behind the Atkins Diet is that to lose weight you have to avoid foods that come high on the glycaemic index (GI). This is a system for measuring how fast a food triggers a rise in blood sugar and has been used for years by dieticians around the world working with diabetics. Put simply, we get energy from glucose in the blood, or blood sugar. When we eat carbohydrates they are quickly absorbed by the body and converted to glucose in the blood. Refined carbohydrates and sugars are converted fastest. But fats and proteins do not induce a significant rise in blood glucose.

Insulin is the hormone which transports glucose from the blood to cells, either for immediate use as energy or to be converted by the liver into glycogen (for short-term use in the muscles and liver), or to fat (for long-term storage around the body). The main chemical constituents of this stored fat are triglycerides and high triglyceride levels are a risk factor for heart disease and strokes. As the glucose level in the blood rises, the pancreas releases insulin, which reduces the blood-sugar levels. Simple sugars and starches from white bread, white rice, cooked potatoes and refined cereals are converted to glucose very fast. Fibre from unrefined carbohydrates meanwhile slows down the entry of glucose into the blood. Excessive consumption of refined carbohydrates overstimulates insulin production, leading to highs and lows of blood-sugar levels, which leave you feeling hungry and eventually cause the glucose-regulating mechanism to break down. The liver then converts more glucose to stored fat and you end up both overweight and with diabetes.

The GI takes glucose as the benchmark with a value of 100 and foods are rated high, medium or low depending on how they compare with that. White bread is a no-no with a score in the 70s, but wholemeal bread scores only 50 and stoneground wholemeal is lower still at only 30. How a food is grown and processed makes a huge difference, according to the exhaustive GI published by the *American Journal of Clinical Nutrition*, in which carrots from Romania eaten raw score a very low 16 but rate 92 when peeled and boiled by Americans.

Whatever the anomalies, Nigel and John could see that the propaganda war was running away from them. In fact there is surprising unanimity among nutrition experts, government advisory committees and diet gurus. Official health policy is that complex, as opposed to refined, carbohydrates should form a significant part of our diets if we wish to avoid the diseases of affluence that afflict industrialized nations, and that we should cut down on fats especially artificially hardened or saturated fats. Even Atkins, whose diet had been attacked by health experts for being high in fat, recommended wholemeal bread and whole grains once you have regained a decent weight.

The food industry, however, had been hoist on its own petard. Since most of the bread we buy is white sliced, it was hard for the big corporate bakers to argue back about GI ratings or the merits of wholemeal. So the industry maintained a line that there is no such thing as a bad food; a balanced diet is the key to health.

But the nutritional gulf between a well-made wholemeal loaf and a white sliced factory one is enormous. It's not just what goes into the white loaf, it's also a matter of what's been taken out.

The whole grain consists of an outer fibrous layer of bran; the germ (the embryo from which a new plant would grow); and the inner white endosperm. The bran contains the fibre, some protein, fat and minerals. The germ contains most of the oils, some protein and the highest concentration of vitamins and minerals. The endosperm is mostly carbohydrate and some protein. The oil of the whole grain has traditionally been one of the most important sources in the diet of essential fats, which are vital for healthy brain and nervous tissue function, but when whole wheat is milled to white flour, the most nutritious part of the grain is taken away.

There is method in this madness, however. The oil-rich germ can go rancid and requires more careful keeping. You can also make much more from grain by separating it into its constituent parts and selling it several times over. The holding groups of the baking and milling companies have included subsidiaries that are agricultural feed companies. It is no coincidence that baking companies have also made pet food. In fact, the pigs have the best of it. The wheat germ, in which the nutrients are concentrated, and the bran are sold as animal feed for the likes of them.

During the milling of white flour, over twenty vitamins and minerals present in the original wheat grain are reduced by half or more, according to the official bible on the composition of foods. Concern that this refining might be leaving humans malnourished compared to their livestock was first expressed in 1919. It was not until 1940 that the government decided to do something about it. The tussle between private profit and public interest in the food industry was evident even then. When Lord (then plain Mr) Boothby rose to his feet in the House of Commons to announce that vitamin B1 would be added to bread for the sake of the nation's health, he reassured the Honourable Members that he had resigned as chairman of the company that made the vitamins when he was first appointed a junior minister.

The government now requires millers to put back two of the B vitamins, B1 and B3, and iron and calcium. But they are not restored to the levels found in wholemeal flour. Calcium is whacked back in generous proportions – chalk is cheap – and goes in at nearly four times the level in the original wholemeal. The more expensive B vitamins, however, along with iron, are only restored to a percentage of the levels present in wholemeal.

John Lister is the miller serious chefs and bakers turn to for their flour. He runs Shipton Mills, a company which works from a restored watermill in the Cotswolds, producing some of the country's finest flours. Ancient stones still grind his wholemeal and his white flour is matured by careful storage, not by additives and enzymes. He believes a country's bread is a barometer of its culture. By this measure the state of ours is none too healthy.

Lister explained the significance of good milling to me.

'When you stone-grind flour the grain goes in at the top and comes out the side twenty seconds later. You know you've got the whole lot.' For thousands of years flour was ground in this way. It's a relatively gentle process that leaves most of the nutrients intact. But a pair of stones can only grind 250kg of flour an hour. In 1834 a new method was invented which made mass production possible – the steel roller mill. Now the vast majority of bread flour is ground in roller mills. A steel roller can make 20 tonnes of flour an hour passing wheat up and down through a sequence of rollers that gradually get bigger and bigger. As the grain passes through, the bran, wheat germ, white and finer white parts are separated and collected in different bins. 'You can use roller mills more softly and have fewer rollers, but for CBP flour you do an enormous amount of grinding under huge pressure, to break open all the starch molecules. The flour ends up very fractured and grey. Then it absorbs water like a sponge. It's critical to modern baking to get lots of water in.'

When you make wholemeal on a roller mill, you go through the same process, taking the wheat right through to white flour and then mixing all the different grades back in, but you don't necessarily end up with exactly the whole grain and you get much more damaged starch than you do from a stone-grinding. That's why stoneground wholemeal tastes different and one of the reasons why a CBP wholemeal loaf can vary so much from a traditionally made one.

Like so much of our industrialized food system, CBP amounts to a great experiment. 'It didn't take 2,000 years to develop the process of making bread for us just to bin it without consequences. The question is, have we made our staple indigestible?' Lister says.

He has done some work with local doctors on gluten allergy, the prevalence of which seems to be growing alarmingly. 'It's the fermentation time that makes wheat digestible. When we made bread that had been given thirty-six to forty-eight hours to ferment, it did not cause a reaction in people who suffer from gluten allergies. We know we also have many more yeast-related illnesses today than in the past.

'We have factories turning wheat into its constituent parts – pure starch, pure powdered gluten. Pure gluten is like chewing gum, they add it to give the flour enough strength to survive the factory process. We have bred wheat varieties for the dominant CBP processes in which the proteins are not as malleable as they used to be. Year on year since the introduction of the Chorleywood process, bread consumption has declined. At the end of it, the bread just isn't nice any more.'

Industrial bakers have tried to respond to the renaissance of interest in proper bread by expanding what they called the 'bread with bits' market, and supermarkets have increased their offering of 'artisan-style' loaves. The suffix '-style' is the giveaway here. Many still use improvers and the Chorleywood process. Although the description 'wholemeal' is protected by regulation, there are no legal definitions of what terms like 'artisan' and 'wholegrain' mean, as the Real Bread Campaign points out. It found loaves in supermarkets sold using 'wholegrain' claims that were 20 per cent wholemeal flour or less.

The industry view is that people wouldn't buy white sliced bread if that were not what they wanted. But of course it's not that simple. The economics of the bread market are so distorted that for many people there is no real choice.

The baking industry, despite being so concentrated in so few hands, has been at the mercy of the big retailers. Its products were used over an extended period by supermarket groups as one of the key weapons in their war to win control of the high street. Bread was, through the late 1990s and early 2000s, a 'loss leader', sold for so little by the big chains, who were able to cross-subsidize any loss of profit with higher margins on other goods, that other independent shops could not compete. Loss-leading helped squeeze the life out of high streets and markets. The unintended effect was that many of the most vulnerable in society ended up with little access to fresh wholesome food.

Supermarkets were not solely responsible for the change, but they were one of the main driving forces behind it.

It is illegal and deemed predatory pricing in most European countries to sell goods below the price of production. France, Belgium, Greece, Italy, Luxembourg, Portugal and Spain banned the practice. Other European countries including Germany, Austria and Ireland placed tight restrictions on it. An inquiry by the UK's Competition Commission into the British supermarkets found the practice operated against the public interest in the UK. But it did not make any recommendations to stop it.

For supermarkets it has worked like this: everyday groceries, such as bread, butter, milk and sugar, are classified as KVIs – known value items. These are the key purchases whose price shoppers know and by which they judge which shop offers the best value. Most prices are no longer marked on packets but only appear on the shelves, where we notice them briefly. They change frequently. As a result, most of us have no clue what other items cost when asked.

Supermarkets cut their prices on the known value items to bring people into their shop rather than anyone else's. Loss-leading was used to build up their image as retailers offering the best value and has the same effect as predatory pricing: it knocks other shops, particularly small specialist shops, such as bakers, butchers and greengrocers, and convenience stores, out of business. Professor Paul Dobson of the Norwich Business School at the University of East Anglia made a study of the practice in 2002. Leading UK supermarkets were operating then with about 100–200 items being sold below the price they paid for them at any one time. A further 370 lines were typically being sold at a gross margin of less than 5 per cent – in other words below a price which would generate a decent profit for the store. Sainsbury's told the Competition Commission inquiry into supermarkets in 2000 that 25 per cent of its own-label products were sold below cost. On a sample day, Asda had 215 items for sale below cost. Tesco had 160.

White sliced bread was used as one of the supermarkets' key competitive weapons. In July 2003 the cheapest white sliced bread on sale in the major multiples was being sold at 19p when the cost to the retailer was between 22p to 26p. If the supermarkets had been selling it with a typical retail margin, it should have cost 28p to 33p. The price had dropped as low as 7p in 1999. Bread in England was half the price of similar bread in France and a third of the price in Germany. The cheapest bread was and is still nearly always an own-label loaf, which gives the supermarkets more bargaining power over the suppliers, since it undermines the manufacturers' own brands by making them look bad value and increases competition between suppliers.

All of which sounds fine at first hearing – good healthy competition which apparently gives us cheaper food. Except that retailers are in the business of making profits, and their losses on known value items are made good in higher prices elsewhere – on those items we can't remember the cost of. Ironically the practice reduces competition as people are encouraged to compare the price only of loss leaders between supermarket stores rather than looking across the whole range of things they buy.

Bread was not the only food affected. The brands started to fight back with heavy investment in advertising. The categories used by supermarkets to suck people in moved on. Milk was used as a loss leader for a while, as were baked beans. Before the baked beans war broke out between retailers and manufacturers, the cheapest own-label beans sold at between 16p and 19p and accounted for 13 per cent of the market. Prices fell to 9p, increasing the own-label share to 37 per cent of the market, undermining the more expensive brands. At one point they went as low as 3p per tin. Nestlé told the Competition Commission that at this level it literally could not can fresh air for the price supermarkets wanted. The end result was that Nestlé closed its Crosse and Blackwell canning operation and withdrew from that area of its business. Just one example of how loss-leading tends to produce more concentrated markets that favour large retailers not more competitive ones. Certain categories of meat have been used as loss leaders too. More recently alcohol has been a favourite draw, but the explosion in alcohol-related diseases has led the government to act and it may no longer be sold at a loss.

Without the benefit of forced disclosure to the competition authorities, it is impossible to know how many products supermarkets are selling at a loss currently, but Professor Dobson, who has tracked prices for over ten years now, working at various universities, is in no doubt that significant numbers of own-brand known value items are still being sold at prices that are so low that net margins are likely to be negative.

An indication of where the balance of power lies came in 2010 when Premier Foods and Tesco got into a dispute over who should take the hit for the rising cost of wheat and energy. Neither side would comment on their commercial agreements but Premier was reported to have tried to negotiate for most of what it said was a 14 per cent rise in its costs to be passed on to the retailer. Tesco refused to accept the rise and instead 'delisted', that is stopped selling, most of Hovis's products. The trading dispute between the two spread to Premier's other brands including Mr Kipling, Branston and Oxo, with the manufacturer claiming that 160 of its product lines had been removed from stores for a period, costing it around £10 million in lost sales. The dispute has since been resolved.

People on low incomes spend a much higher proportion of their money on cheap staples such as bread, milk and baked beans than more affluent households. If loss-leading effectively subsidized the things poor families bought most at the expense of a few manufacturers and richer people's tastes we might see it as a useful if unintended piece of wealth redistribution. In fact it is those on low incomes who suffer most.

Loss leaders and promotions are skewed towards the least healthy purchases – over-refined cereals and other highly processed products full of salt, fat and sugar. Healthy foods, such as fruit, vegetables and wholemeal bread tend to have the highest

retail margins. As Dobson points out, the introduction of persistent selling of white bread below cost was accompanied by a
decline in the consumption of wholemeal bread. Deep discounting generally drives a race to the bottom. It undercuts
quality foods by so much that it distorts the market in favour of
the cheapest and unhealthiest.

It is perhaps the loss of other places to buy food that hits the
poorest hardest however. The supermarkets' practice of loss-leading
took custom away from other shops and alternative distribution
systems such as doorstep milk deliveries, so that they have been
unable to survive.

Sometimes the effect was rapid and obvious. When the insti-
tution of the universal milkman died out, as shoppers increasingly
switched to the cut-price pinta available in the supermarkets,
there was a wave of nostalgic regret. But it seemed a little half-
hearted. People mourned the loss of the social function – the
milkman who knew everyone, checked up on the old ladies
each day, noticed the burglars. But we didn't stop patronizing
those who ruthlessly undercut him.

A senior director of one of the leading chains admitted to me
privately that the late opening hours adopted by his company
were not profitable ones – that wasn't the point. You opened late
to stop people shopping elsewhere. Late opening is a way of
making sure you are the biggest beast in the jungle, of mopping
up the opposition, however small. Supermarkets' discounts don't
just take away a bit of business, they have a habit of taking away
the whole lot. The milkman was just the beginning. Where every
high street once had a butcher, a baker and greengrocer, now
only a fraction of the post-war numbers of these specialist shops
remain. Pharmacies and newsagents were the next target. Supermarkets lobbied hard and won the battle to scrap retail price
maintenance on certain proprietary medicines and started dispensing prescriptions. In 2002 Asda started slashing the price of
magazines.

Since the 1940s around 100,000 small shops have closed and

every year their number drops by a further 10 per cent. Between 1995 and 2060, independent fresh food specialists, including bakers, butchers, fishmongers and greengrocers, saw their sales drop by 40 per cent as supermarkets consolidated their grip on the food sales.

Nearly 60 per cent of high street butchers disappeared between 1985 and 2000. Seven out of ten English villages are without a shop.

By 2011 over 97 per cent of all grocery sales were in the hands of the big retail chains and just 8,000 supermarket outlets. Nearly one in six shops on high streets were vacant and less than half of retail spending was in town centres. Independent retailing in the UK looked to be in a crisis that was terminal. The prime minister David Cameron commissioned a review by TV celebrity Mary Portas, who had starred in popular series about the instant makeover of shops, to recommend action to save our high streets. Her report was published, small grants were made to councils to reverse the trend, but they proved surprisingly hard to spend effectively, and the deep structural problems identified, problems that would require big political decisions to change, were largely left unaddressed.

The independent think-tank the New Economics Foundation had warned of all this a decade earlier: that high streets would reach a 'tipping point', as supermarkets were allowed to grow almost unchecked, which for many would be a death knell. Once the number of local shops falls below a critical mass, the amount of money circulating within the local economy plummets to the point where people can no longer do a proper shop locally and are forced to travel elsewhere.

The dynamics worked in a way few of us imagined. If a new supermarket opened on the edge of town and half the residents did one third of their shopping there, retail revenue could drop by about 17 per cent in the town-centre shops. The people who were going to the supermarket might still do two thirds of their shopping in the town, and the other half of the population might do all its shopping in the town centre, but a fall in revenue of 17 per cent was enough to start killing off the high street shops. Once that happens more people feel forced to switch to the supermarket, because they cannot get everything they need in the centre, and the town begins to shut down. As individuals we feel helpless to buck the trend. But it was not that we chose this.

It didn't take many people changing their habits to force a change on a whole community that no one really wanted. The loss has not been confined to the process of buying our food. Local shops perform dozens of social functions. They are where acquaintances who might not otherwise meet bump into each other and talk, they are somewhere for the elderly or those stuck at home with young children to go; by using them we find familiar faces that make us feel safe in our areas, or, as one American author writing about the death of US cities puts it, these encounters at the local level create a web of public respect and trust. When they go out of business we are left with boarded-up shopping parades or high streets full of fast-food outlets and betting shops, covered in graffiti and litter. Whole areas can become deserts where there are almost no shops selling decent fresh food or other goods. This was not what we foresaw when we leapt into our cars to do our weekly shop where known value items are cheapest.

Other European countries were much quicker to spot the damage done to the social fabric by allowing big supermarkets to acquire a stranglehold on retailing. It was the end of the 1990s before the UK tightened up its planning laws to stop new out-of-town developments. In France, by contrast, local authorities were given the right to veto the construction of supermarkets over 1,000 square metres in 1973. In 1996 the French government introduced a law that required a public inquiry for any outlet of 6,000 square metres to protect 'the social and economic cohesion and the fabric of society'. Supermarkets were also banned from advertising on TV in France until the EU forced the country to lift its restriction at the beginning of 2004.

Supermarkets argue that customers have chosen what kind of shopping suits them best. It has to be acknowledged that for many working people, without the convenience of a weekly one-stop shop, life would be virtually impossible. And of course latterly the rise of internet shopping made a big contribution to the decline of the high street too. Supermarkets have also been able to offer much wider choice. Many of the small grocers they have replaced had become pretty depressing places, with tired and unimaginative offerings.

Those sufficiently well-off to own a car or to shop in bulk or pay online delivery charges may feel that the loss of the high street shops is sad or mildly inconvenient, but that the benefits outweigh the disadvantages. But for people on low incomes, many of whom have no cars, and the growing numbers of elderly with limited mobility, the disappearance of other shopping outlets has often represented a devastating loss of a basic service. When I first wrote *Not On the Label* there were many deprived areas that had become food deserts. Since then the big retailers have moved back into the vacuum they created in many places, opening smaller city centre stores in convenience formats. These are often welcome, despite prices that may be 3–4 per cent higher than in their larger stores, but they do not replace the choice that has been lost – the butcher where you could buy the sort of cheap reliable cuts of meat no longer available in the big stores for all their horse-burgers; the bakers of real bread; the vegetable stalls where you could find knock-down fresh food that was not cosmetically perfect but affordably good to cook with.

My interest in the politics of food was first sparked nearly thirty years ago by a pioneering public health nutritionist, Caroline Walker. In between working for government advisory committees she was involved in a project in the East End of London to tackle the disproportionate rates of cardiovascular disease suffered among its poorer communities. They were living in one of those food deserts and could not afford decent food, so were filling up on junk instead. Caroline's warning that a debased, industrialized diet was taking a terrible toll on the nation's health, and that the government needed to act to change what we ate, was dismissed by the industry as food Leninism. Two decades later, as epidemics of obesity and diabetes take hold and the relation between diet and other diseases such as heart disease and cancer becomes clearer, her warnings and those of other experts were harder to dismiss. Caroline died young, so it was something of a pilgrimage for me to go back to the East End and the areas that had been her stamping ground. The government had designated them as food and health action zones.

Outside West Ham station the Dolphin fish bar's windows were obscured behind the small mesh of security grilles that characterize so many areas in decline. The convenience shop next door selling Wall's ice cream and lottery tickets had a few tired vegetables on its half-empty shelves. Further along, a video shop selling wine and fizzy drinks offered photocopying. A new small convenience store, built in the station under the footbridge over the main road to catch returning commuters, was better stocked but expensive. These were the only shops within easy walking distance of a whole network of housing estates in the London borough of Newham.

Lilian Rowley had lived nearby in West Ham for thirty-eight-and-a-half years. She was a widow on two pensions – her husband's occupational one and the state pension, so she counted herself better off than many of her fellow septuagenarians. She spent £10 a week on food, eating lunch at a pensioners' club. She remembered shopping round the corner just after the war, at Mr Jones's grocery where the assistant was called Doris or at Mr and Mrs Shannon's the greengrocers where they would always pick out a nice Laxton for her and sell her 'scrumpy ones for cheap'. 'Of course, as a child, everybody knew everybody and we'd go out to shop on our own. The manager of the shop would be on the step making sure everyone behaved. There was a baker – I can remember the smell. They used to sell off stale loaves so you could have a bread and butter pudding very cheaply. But that's gone, it's all gone. We've still got a few shops but they're expensive convenience places. The butcher's closed.'

Lilian was active and enjoyed nothing better than a weekly dance, but like the majority of her friends she had no car. 'I have to get the bus to Stratford to the nearest supermarket four or five times a week because I can't carry heavy loads. That's twenty-five minutes, but at least the bus is free. It gets me out but it's not sociable at all now. I smile at people in the supermarket but I think they think you're a bit funny, you know. The trouble is I'm five feet tall and I just cannot reach the top shelves. There are staff somewhere around but not where you want them. I've thought of taking one of those clipper things on a handle you get to help you put your socks on, but I'd feel foolish. The fruit is so expensive – I always bought apples but not any luxury items. The peaches were forty-nine pence each last week! I don't buy cheap bread. I like good seed bread, the other stuff's like glue. I do drink a lot of milk. On a budget it's a good way of getting cheap food, but my doctor's told me to cut down on the fat.'

Lilian's lifeline had been a new food co-op set up on a nearby estate. It had enabled her to increase dramatically the amount of fresh food she could buy locally. It was also a place to go and help, and get to know new people.

The co-op scheme was started here by Eric Samuel, a Caribbean-born Pentecostal minister who had made this food desert his unofficial parish. He took me on a tour, providing a commentary on what we saw delivered with preacher's zeal but at rapper's speed. 'Come here, come, come with me, look at this. It's a total food desert. There's a tiny parade. It cannot compete with the supermarkets. The prices the supermarkets charge for fresh healthy food are wicked. We have terrible rates of diet-related disease here but it has become impossible for ordinary people to live well.' The co-op started when he decided to go to

Spitalfields at the crack of dawn each morning to buy good cheap fresh fruit and vegetables and bring them back for those people who had no cars or could not afford to shop elsewhere. His temporal reward has been an honour and the attention of a whole posse of government advisers and their schemes.

With the help of money from the Labour government's new deals for regeneration and action on health, the co-op project had expanded. Ironically, it was the taxpayer who was now picking up the bill for successive governments' failure to tackle the power of the supermarket retailers and to protect the public from the consequence of the demise of high streets and town centres.

Lita Webb, another East End dynamo, helped run the food co-ops and supplied fresh fruit and vegetables to the school breakfast clubs so that children can start the day with something good in their stomachs. She also dropped bags off to the elderly who couldn't get out. Local doctors prescribed fresh fruit and vegetable vouchers from the co-op for those diagnosed with diabetes, heart disease and cancers, to help them change their eating habits.

The hub of the West Ham scheme was an old community shed, with those ubiquitous mesh grilles and a spiked metal fence, that turned into the local greengrocer once a week. It was the sort of place where neighbours came to gossip, where Lita would say hello to everyone, and if you found yourself £2 short you could owe it till next week. Lita and I chatted over a cup of coffee while people filled their baskets. Some of the people who came to use the co-op were people on benefits; many were working in low-paid jobs in social services or were students.

Love Anderson arrived with two of her four children. She was a care worker with the elderly, bringing home £200 a week while her children were at school. She stocked up on staples at the co-op – plantains, sweet potatoes and fruit. When I asked her what difference it had made to her and where she used to shop before, she dissolved into emotion. 'I'm speechless. It's made such a difference. It would cost much more before. We had to walk to Canning Town. Food takes all my money. I used to go hungry and we used to live on white bread and rice. The children don't like them any more, they can have all this.'

Isaac Hewett was a twenty-one-year-old dental student, with an income of £12,000 a year, £7,000 of it made up of debt in the form of student loans. When he came in at the end of the day, he was dressed all in black from his shirt and tie to his trousers and big shoes, and with his shoulder-length ginger hair he looked the archetypal student, except for the buggy from which his sixteen-month-old son Hudson stared out with huge eyes and a pale, sleep-bleary face.

'My wife and I spend £18 a week on food for the three of us,' Isaac said. 'I live in Stratford so I'm near shops, but I walk down here to get the weekly supplies of fresh fruit and vegetables. We can eat them now. We used not to. We can't afford the fresh stuff in the supermarkets. And I like the idea of it. Stratford was one of the homes of the early Co-operative Movement. There have been times when you go without because you want the best for your child. It's not that we're completely desperate, but it may be that we've chosen to have a bit of a social life and have gone out together for once in a while. Then we can't afford fresh fruit and vegetables, and we have to fill up on white sliced bread and the cheapest things.'

I walked to Canning Town afterwards to see the loss of shops and the degeneration they had all talked about. It had become a desolate high street, with the pillars of the A13 flyover marching right through the community. The old Kwiksave building was being gutted, and shuttered shops along the high road were interspersed with takeaways advertising themselves with the smell of cheap fat and fried chicken and trails of debris. 'Two pieces of chicken and chips, only £2.29. Kid's meal of nuggets and chips and fizzy drink only £1.50.' The Rathbone market was just a car park when I passed, but sold mostly clothes, not much food, when it did splutter to life, according to an office cleaner emptying bins. Nail bars and pawnbrokers had filled the gaps between run-down shops selling yams and plantains. The Titanic Café was left to speak of the neighbourhood's ambitions, in between the Light of This World Church and hairdressers flogging cornrows and braid. The only beams of light were the golden arches of the McDonald's beyond the traffic lights, illuminating a road sign to Becton, and its superstore, 3 miles away.

Which socio-economic class you are born into is still one of the most significant determinants of how healthy you will be. Sharp inequalities can be clearly mapped, even short distances apart, according to Dr Tim Lobstein, director of the childhood research programme at the International Association for the Study of Obesity. Travel the eight stops on the Jubilee line tube from central London's Westminster to Canning Town and you will find a decrease in life expectancy of nearly one year for each station going east.

A child born in one deprived Glasgow suburb can expect a life twenty-eight years shorter than another living only 13 kilometres away in a more affluent area, a three-year investigation for the World Health Organization found. Commenting on one of the key factors, the WHO report concluded: 'Obesity is caused not by moral failure of individuals but by the excess availability of high-fat, high-sugar foods.' The marketplace can generate wealth but it can 'also generate negative conditions for health', which will only be resolved by tackling 'the inequitable distribution of power, money and resources', it went on.

Right across the country, those on low incomes suffer higher incidence of a whole range of illnesses relating to poor diet. Lobstein catalogued them for me. Higher rates of anaemia caused by lack of iron, especially in pregnancy. Mothers from low-income groups are more likely to have children of low birthweight who, in turn, are likely to suffer poor health and educational prospects as a result. Poorer families have more dental disease and more childhood eczema and asthma. They are more likely to suffer from obesity, both as children and as adults. They have higher rates of raised blood pressure, thanks to excess salt in their processed-food diets. They are more likely to suffer diabetes, heart disease, vascular disease and strokes. They suffer more cancers of the lung, stomach and oesophagus. They have more cataracts caused by poor nutrition than those in other classes. And the protective role of good nutrition is missing. A survey of men and women living on benefits found that a third ate no fruit at all during the week their diets were recorded.

It's not just diet, of course – alcohol and tobacco consumption are implicated, too, as poverty ties a Gordian knot of health problems. Over half of younger children in low-income groups are inactive almost all day as well, with two- to ten-year-olds getting less than thirty minutes of physical activity daily.

Elizabeth Dowler, professor of food and social policy at Warwick University, who was recently involved in the government's Low Income Diet and Nutrition survey, says the class differences are stark but complicated. 'If you live for more than six months on the minimum wage or on benefits there is growing evidence you cannot afford to buy the food you need for health. Food is the flexible area that you cut back on when you are on a low income. Unlike council tax or utility bills, no one fines you if you don't spend on food and no one takes your children away, so that's what you cut, and you have a fag because that takes the hunger away.'

When you are on a low income you buy the kind of food that fills you up most cheaply. What may seem ignorant choices to others are in fact quite rational. Lobstein has calculated the cost of 100 calories of food energy from different types of food. The cheapest way to get your 100 calories is to buy fats, processed starches and sugars. A hundred calories of broccoli costs 51p, but 100 calories of frozen chips only cost 2p. Good-quality sausages that are high in meat but low in fat cost 22p per 100 calories, but 'value' fatty ones are only 4p per 100 calories. Poor-quality fish fingers are 12p per 100 calories compared with 29p for ones made with fish fillet that are higher in nutrients. Fresh orange juice costs 38p per 100 calories, while the same dose of energy from sugary orange squash costs 5p.

There's nothing here that hasn't been raised for decades, centuries even. When George Orwell wrote *The Road to Wigan Pier* in the middle of the 1930s depression, he set out to record the lives of the English working class in the industrial north. He was appalled by the quality of their diets. 'A man dies and is buried and all his actions forgotten but the food he has eaten lives after him in the sound or rotten bones of his children.' Orwell wrote down detailed accounts of how unemployed working-class people on welfare spent their money. He doubted it was even theoretically possible to live on their allowance. 'The basis of their diet is white bread and margarine, corned beef, sugared tea and potatoes. Would it not be better if they spent more money on wholesome things like oranges and wholemeal bread?' Yes it would, he answered, but 'no ordinary human being is ever going to do such a thing. A millionaire may enjoy breakfasting off orange juice and Ryvita, an unemployed man doesn't … When you are underfed, harassed, bored and miserable, you don't want to eat dull, wholesome food. You want something a little bit tasty. Let's have three-pennorth of chips! Put the kettle on and we'll all have a nice cup of tea!'

Yet today the language of class has been almost removed from the political discourse. In Thatcherite, Blairite and Cameroonian Britain, it has been framed instead in terms of 'choice'. There is talk of the need to give people opportunities, but after that, it's down to individual responsibility.

Situated on the edge of the 2012 London Olympics development, Newham and Canning Town had seen money pour in to large-scale regeneration projects in the area. As if to underline their overwhelming dominance, the council had given planning permission for a large retail distribution centre in one major development, along with a big supermarket. When I returned recently, smart flats with smart London prices were being built where there had previously been desolation. The big four supermarkets had opened a proliferation of convenience branches. It was no longer a food desert. It was more of a mirage, for many residents. They were surrounded by the sight of food and drink now, but many couldn't afford it. Eric Samuel was still running his food co-op, driving fresh fruit and vegetables in mobile vans to housing estates to sell cheap healthy food to those who would otherwise go without. 'Wages are too low, benefits are being capped; the infrastructure has changed beyond recognition, but so many people in Newham still can't afford decent food. A nice big supermarket will come but the only good deal will be on bananas when they are sold as a loss leader. The rest will beyond the reach of many we serve.'

6. Apples and Bananas

The apple trail through Kent, Garden of England, was perhaps the most famous of the old guided orchard tours, although Hereford and Worcester were also known for the beauty of their fruit trees in flower. Late spring would bring the show – clouds of white and carmine petals set against emerald buds, or twigs flushed their length with pink, depending on the apple type: James Grieve, Crispin, Chivers Delight, St Edmund's Pippin, Cox and D'Arcy Spice – the names of the traditional varieties as poetic as the blossom along the bough.

Nick Swatland's apple farm near Sittingbourne used to be as fine a sight as any. But no more. The Kent Tourist Board no longer runs the blossom trail, since so many of the orchards have been grubbed up. And in 2002 Nick packed up his apple business. His last year, 2001, was ironically one of the best ever, with a huge and good-quality crop, but he saw little from it. He was supplying the supermarkets through a marketing organization, but the prices just kept getting lower and lower. 'We were being given twenty to twenty-one pence a kilo, they were selling them in the stores at twice that, and we needed thirty-two pence to break even. The prices would change by the day, and then they'd take sixty to ninety days to pay you, when you'd already paid your labour. If you were a very good boy you'd get some money eventually. It was not good for the heart. It was a combination of things, I suppose, that finished us: the global economy, dominant supermarkets and the strength of the pound.' It was a wrench selling most of the farm – his father had started out in 1941, but in the end he, like Nick, was just relieved to be out of it.

John Dickson was a farmer in Cambridgeshire. He was hanging

on with his apples, pears and plums, but only just. He averaged a seventy-hour week for an income of about £18,000. His farm had orchards with 10,000 trees, that were home to owls, hawks and much other wildlife, but he hadn't earned enough to pay income tax in three of the previous five years. He used to supply the big supermarkets direct but got delisted, for complaining, he said. Most people are too afraid to speak out. He was supplying smaller supermarkets through a packhouse.

'You'd agree a price at the beginning of the season, then the week after it would be cut, then it would be cut again, till you say, very sorry but I can't take that kind of money, and you get dropped. Most of the time you feel you have no choice about going along with them, because once you've been dropped you can't get back in at a decent price. And you've got all their bloody packaging and have had to pay for it.

'Last year, I had to do a "promotion" on apples, three pounds for the price of two pounds, and I had to take the loss. I also had to pay two-and-a-half pence extra for each sticker that went on the pack boasting about the offer. The supermarket said they knew I was making a loss on the apples but no one would pay more and they could always get them somewhere else abroad if I didn't want to do it.'

But perhaps the most maddening thing was the beauty parade. A supermarket apple must look good in front of the camera or risk rejection.

A Dutch company provides packhouses with the machines, which cost hundreds of thousands of pounds, to measure cosmetic perfection. The 'Greefa Intelligent Quality Sorter' has cameras that take up to seventy colour pictures of every apple as it passes along a conveyor belt to determine the 'blush of non-equally coloured fruit', and to grade it by size. It can detect deviations of as little as one square millimetre. So if the supermarket specification says that an apple of a particular variety must be 15–17 per cent blush red on green, for instance, it can 'grade out' or reject any apples that are 18 per cent red on green or a miserable 14 per cent red on green. Its promotional literature cheerfully explains the reason for the beauty parade: 'Nature has many surprises ... Buyers, however, require uniform fruit and vegetables of standard size.'

The beauty parade often means the difference between profit and loss for the farmer. Anything 'graded out' for failing the test ends up, if the farmer is lucky, as fruit for juice at giveaway prices of 3–5p a pound, but as often as not it will just go to waste.

Then there's the penetrometer. It's a spring-loaded little tool that measures the resistance of the fruit. John Dickson was eloquent on the subject of the penetrometer. 'I had the buyer round and he said my pressures were out. He admitted my Coxes were the best he'd tasted, but they weren't hard enough for his shelf life, and he told me I'd have to pick the fruit earlier,' he said. 'All the ripe ones have to come off when we go through the grader. No wonder people complain fruit doesn't taste of anything. They also get tested for starch and sugars and all that. I test mine the traditional way, with my front teeth. I can't get very excited about all this.'

The triumph of appearance over flavour had gone so far that the World Apple and Pear Association had announced that it was considering drawing up 'an international organoleptic standards' label. Fruit that tasted of something would qualify for the new logo.

It was the same with the plums. John grew thirty-two varieties, could start picking on his wedding anniversary, 13 July, and still have plums at the end of October. But the supermarket English season only lasts a few weeks, and they would only take three varieties. 'The market for Victorias used to work really well. The largest went to the fruit market, the middles to canning and the smalls for jam. Now the smalls get thrown away, and most of the middles do too. They've got to be thirty-eight millimetres, unmarked, with stalk, to pass muster. The specification covers two sides of A4. The shape must be "typical", they must be more than fifty per cent coloured but they've also got to have a four-day shelf life. Well, that means they've got to be picked rock-hard. Plums need to be picked and eaten within a day or two to taste good. I can see an enormous supermarket from my fields. I asked if I could supply it direct with plums that were actually ripe, in peak condition. It can't be done.'

Size matters too. Assuming the fruit can survive the penetrometer, it must conform to the supermarkets' vital statistics. For John this presents its own problems. 'When I was a boy, sixty millimetres was considered the ideal size for an apple – that would be five or six apples to a pound; you'd sell larger sixty-five-millimetre ones for a premium. But sixty-five millimetres gave you four apples to a pound. Now the supermarkets want a minimum of seventy-millimetre apples from me, so you only get three to a pound. Which of course means most customers end up buying more: to get four apples now you need to buy one-and-a-quarter pounds rather than the traditional pound.

'But to achieve those bigger apples I have to prune my trees much harder, and overfeed them. The apple is less well balanced because of the excess fertilizer; it loses its flavour. Then you get bitter pit – that's brown spots – and I have to spray all the time with calcium to prevent the markings.' A Cox may have been sprayed up to sixteen times by the time it reaches the shops.

The supermarket 'grade out' has become a source of great dread to farmers around the world. Enormous quantities of food go to waste because they do not meet the very narrow specifications now demanded by most big supermarkets. I have watched smallholders in Kenya's Machakos hills grading green beans for export to the UK supermarkets. They stood in a simple traditional building on the edge of a triangle of rough ground, shaded by mango, jacaranda and pepper trees, measuring the vegetables against wooden slats to check that they conformed to the requirement that a green bean should be 95mm in length and between 5 and 7.5mm in diameter. And they had to be straight; curved green beans would not do. The packer and exporter, Homegrown, explained that 35 per cent of beans failed to make the supermarket grade, and while a few of the rejects went to cattle feed, or into the local market, most went to waste, even in a country where people go hungry.

A leading Lincolnshire supplier of Brussels sprouts to the supermarkets was allowed two sizes for his crop, 25–30mm or 30–35mm. A neighbouring supplier who grew carrots for the supermarkets told me that his typical waste figures were even higher. For every 30 tonnes of carrots harvested, just 10 tonnes were used. As well as the vegetables rejected because they are marked or damaged in some way, anything that is bent, or has a slightly green top, gets graded out.

Organic farmers have been hit particularly hard by this demand for cosmetic perfection, since they cannot resort to heavy chemical use to achieve it. No one is immune, as I discovered on a trip to Highgrove, to see the Prince of Wales's organic farm.

'You are entering a GMO-free zone,' reads the sign on the track as you swing into His Royal Highness's estate near Tetbury in the rolling Cotswold hills. Prince Charles bought the land here in the 1980s and gradually converted it to organic farming two decades ago. Home Farm is run, as has long been the tradition on rich landowners' estates, as a model farm where new ideas and enlightened agriculture may be tried out. The Prince is opposed to genetic modification. He is also patron of the British organic farmers' organization, the Soil Association, showing guests around Home Farm to persuade them of the cause. 'All the things I have tried to do in this small corner of Gloucestershire have been the physical expression of a personal philosophy,' he has said. The traditional crop rotations are used to maintain soil fertility and health. Hedgerows and trees have been planted with an artist's eye. The farm manager, David Wilson, who had farmed conventionally before he worked with the Prince of Wales to convert to organic farming, says that now he has tried both methods, organic farming 'just makes complete sense'. He looks back with amazement at his agricultural college textbooks with their adverts for the agrochemical companies. It would be hard not to be converted by the well-tended beauty of the place that HRH has 'put heart and soul into'.

Like guests at a Jane Austen tea party, we gathered in the sunshine for our tour of farm and gardens followed by picnic lunch, in the absence of the patron himself. The charabancs pulled up one by one on the gravel outside a large barn, as beautifully preserved as a National Trust tea room. Few had been able to resist the excitement of the outing. There was the adviser from Number Ten, the top civil servant from the Department of Health, the man in charge of 'better regulation', various leading lights from the organic movement, a big cheese from a French food multinational. They emerged from their vehicles, all as instructed by the invitation wearing sensible boots, some of which looked suspiciously clean. Then came the school-dinner lady who had transformed meals at St Peter's primary school in Nottinghamshire, the corporate but socially responsible face of a large supermarket, and my friend from the bakers' federation, together with an OAP who was saving allotments in Hastings.

First we had tea and talk with Duchy biscuits, then David Wilson led the party off through the grounds. We admired the Highgrove Ayrshire dairy cows, chosen he said partly because HRH didn't want to see any more black and white Friesians blotting the landscape, and partly because he is troubled by the overbreeding for high yields that has narrowed the gene pool, made animals prone to sickness, and diluted traditional breeds. Home Farm has had considerable success with its experiments in bovine homeopathy. These low-yielding cows glowed with good health. They were brown and white and becoming against the gentle rise of the pasture. But commercial reality intruded here as everywhere. The Highgrove farm had been hit like all other dairy farmers by the collapse of the milk price. But for the power of his own brand, Prince Charles would have been selling his organic milk at less than the cost of production.

We ambled back down the fields to the vegetable areas where

the onion beds had just been hand-hoed, though it's hard to get the staff these days. 'We had to get a gang in on Monday, Iraqis and Indians in a minibus from Birmingham. Of course we can't get messed up with anything illegal,' Wilson said, sparking a discussion among the farmers in the party about the price of casual manual labour and the difficulty of competing against others who might be tempted to cut corners. Anyone working on the Duchy farms is very carefully vetted.

Foursomes and couples were forming now, breaking up, coming together again, rearranging themselves in the ritualized dance of a day's networking, and I found myself catching a curious jumble of half-absorbed snippets: government health policy priorities being addressed ... nitrogen imbalance ... public sector procurement rules framed within EU parameters ... slug egg predators ... unravelling regulatory red tape ... worm resistance ... the role of the American soy bean association in setting subsidy levels ... clean sheep bottoms ...

We paused to inspect a field of winter wheat, where poppies are allowed to flourish and long grass margins give shelter to small mammals and teeming insect life acting as natural predators to pests. And my, what a lot of insects there were this summer, we agreed, as we flicked them away.

And now, just as the party was flagging a little in the midsummer heat, a 4×4 carriage appeared, drawing a trailer behind it, with bales of straw arranged in two rows as rustic seats, to pull us up a small incline from where we could admire the royal carrots and potatoes. The party safely installed, we proceeded at a sedate pace up the hill, waving cheerily to the Iraqis resting next to the carrot field they had been weeding that day, while an Indian ganger drew on his fag next to his B reg minivan. The gangmaster, I learned later, was Zad Padda (see Chapter 3: Salad). When we were level with the potato fields, the talk turned to the dreaded 'grade out'.

Prince Charles had had his vegetables rejected by the supermarkets too. In fact the Highgrove grade outs were currently running at about 40 per cent. Sometimes the rejection was justified but sometimes it seemed not, it might be just that the skin on a potato was a little ugly ... whereas the odd scab was acceptable a few years ago, now it isn't, the quest for perfection has gone too far. As an organic farmer you can only get rid of scab by doing things that damage the soil or use too much water. Prince Charles had been asking for his rejected vegetables back – he wanted to feed them to his cattle. He also made Duchy crisps (£1.59 a pack at Sainsbury's or Waitrose), but once the rejected potatoes had gone into the system it was rather hard to find them again.

Later, in the formal kitchen garden, where fragrant roses grow in among decorative herbs and summer vegetables, I chewed over the state of the rural nation with the then director of the Soil Association, Patrick Holden. The imbalance of power between producers and retailers was having a devastating effect on organic farmers. It was a conversation we had had before. 'It's not a food chain so much as a fear chain. The supermarket directors live in fear of losing market share and not being able to deliver endless growth to their shareholders, the supermarket buyer lives in fear of not meeting his or her targets and always wants to buy cheap and sell expensive, the packer lives in mortal fear of being delisted by the supermarkets, the grower lives in mortal fear of having his goods rejected or the price falling below the cost of production. How do you rebuild trust in a chain which is dominated by aggressive players and practices? This is what happens with the twin pressures of globalization and concentration of power. It's a crisis affecting every farmer in the land.'

The impact has been widespread. Britain has suffered from an agricultural slump. Figures from the Department of Environment, Food and Rural Affairs and the National Farmers' Union show that in England over 17,000 farmers and workers – or nearly 5 per cent of the workforce – left the land in the twelve months to June 2003. Total job losses for the farming industry since 1996 exceeded 80,000. The numbers working the land stabilized a little after but the nature of employment and income showed the alarming trend continuing. In 2000 a quarter of UK farm holders were under forty-five years of age, but by 2010 that had fallen to just 14 per cent. A third of farm owners were old age pensioners. The total number of farms being run commercially dropped by a further 26,000 between 2005 and 2012. To survive you had to become bigger or have an alternative source of income.

Not only have rural incomes collapsed, traditional landscapes, wildlife and biodiversity are under threat. The demise of the English orchard is just one typical case. You could see similar patterns in many other sectors – from dairy farming to poultry production. We lost nearly two thirds of our apple orchards in less than thirty years. There are 6,000 varieties of dessert and cooking apples and hundreds more cider apples, but many of them have been lost to commercial production and survive only in the national fruit collection. By the end of the twentieth century just ten varieties accounted for nearly all the eating apples in UK orchards, with 70 per cent of production being Coxes and Bramleys.

Supermarkets increasingly buy their apples abroad, even at the height of the English apple season. A survey of supermarkets by Friends of the Earth in 2001 found that in late October and early November most were importing the majority of their apples and pears, despite a bumper English harvest. British farmers had meanwhile received EU grants to grub up their trees, as retailers switched to global sourcing.

The crisis affecting farmers in Europe is in part the shake-down from the post-war productionist era. Before the Second World War, there were about 500,000 farms in Britain, the vast majority of which were small and mixed, raising both crops and livestock and using rotation to maintain soil fertility and contain pests and disease. Spending on feeds or fertilizers from agrochemical companies was minimal. Manure from animals was used instead to feed the crops which in turn provided fodder for the animals in a sustainable pattern of land management that was centuries old. By planting different crops each year the life cycle of pests was disrupted and diseases were by and large prevented from building up in the soil. Where that failed, labour-intensive husbandry was needed to nip problems in the bud.

But then the war brought shortages and rationing as Britain was cut off by Hitler's U-boats. The Ministry of Agriculture, working with the National Farmers' Union, took control of producing the nation's food, including its price and distribution. An all-out drive to boost farmers' incomes and maximize production began. Emergency measures were introduced to increase yields. After the war, these were formalized in the 1947 Agriculture Act, which gave farmers both guaranteed prices and guaranteed markets. The government was determined that Britain should never face food shortages again. Farmers were paid subsidies, first by the British government and then by the Common Market, for the quantities of food they produced. To obtain maximum yields, farmers started to specialize. Livestock were moved indoors where their conditions and feeding could be controlled. Mixed farming was gradually replaced by monoculture. With prices fixed, farmers were freed from the need to grow different crops as an insurance policy against glut or disaster. They were set on the path to industrialization.

The war had also seen the rapid development of chemical works to process nitrates for the manufacture of explosives. In peacetime, these companies were looking for a new use, and so the mass marketing of nitrate fertilizers for agriculture began. Organophosphates, developed as poisonous nerve agents against the enemy, could be marketed as new pesticides.

The Green revolution made it possible to produce much more food. But the combination of subsidies and the intensification it encouraged soon led to oversupply, as farmers became disconnected from their markets. Prices could only be maintained by expensive interventions. European farmers showed they could be highly efficient, using new technologies and agrochemicals to replace labour and boost yields phenomenally, but the legacy has turned out to be one of environmental degradation and decline in rural economies.

Each cow may produce twice as many litres of milk a year, each chicken may grow twice as fast, and each hectare of wheat may yield nearly three times as many tonnes as fifty years ago, but in that time, 60 per cent of ancient woodlands, 97 per cent of meadows with their rich flora and fauna, and 50 per cent of birds that depend on agricultural fields have gone, as have nearly 200,000 miles of hedges. Not only has intensive farming polluted water courses (see Chapter 3: Salad), it has also created problems of soil erosion and flood. Its industrialization of livestock has left animals prone to devastating epidemics of disease.

Meanwhile, other countries with more propitious climates, cheaper labour and sometimes differing standards have been able to undercut the prices offered by British farmers. But the distorting effects of subsidies are only half of the picture.

Bill Vorley, senior research associate at the International Institute for Environment and Development, studied the underlying causes of the slump in farm incomes. The cause was partly oversupply, but he argued that one of the most important factors, concentration of power in processing and retailing, had slipped under the radar.

Attention had been focused on the way protectionist trade policies, such as farm subsidies and tariffs in the USA and the Common Agricultural Policy in Europe, have distorted markets and penalized poorer farmers. But in his report on agribusiness, *Food Inc.*, Vorley pointed out that 'even if unjust trade rules were to be reformed, disparities in bargaining power, scale, market access or information [would remain]'. Farmers are playing to the rules of the new global market and 'perfect competition' in which profits are supposed to go to the most efficient, but their customers, the food processors and retailers, are now part of oligopolies or complex monopolies which enable them to set the rules of the game and suck all the profit out of it.

The crisis has not been unique to Britain. It has hit rural economies across industrialized countries. France lost half its farmers between 1982 and 1999. In Germany the number of farmers has declined by a quarter in the ten years to 2004 alone. The USA has lost over 4 million farmers since the 1930s. And of course the slump is not confined to the developed world but has affected developing countries even more severely.

In less than half a century, the food chain has been turned upside down. The money made from it has shifted dramatically from the millions of producers at the bottom of the chain to a few corporations at the top. With about 2.5 billion people out of a global population of 7 billion dependent on agriculture around the world, the distribution of profits in the chain is not just an academic matter but of vital importance to global stability and development. Food processing and retailing are vastly profitable today, but across Europe farmers are going bankrupt despite their vast subsidies, while in developing countries farmers can barely keep alive.

By mid-2013, just four supermarket groups controlled three quarters of £32 billion worth of grocery sales in the UK. Tesco's share was 30 per cent, Asda-Wal-Mart's 17 per cent, Sainsbury's 16.5 per cent and Morrisons' almost 12 per cent. Add in the next two supermarket chains by size, the Co-op with a share of 6.4 per cent and Waitrose with 4.8 per cent, and some 87 per cent of the total market is taken care of by just six players. The drive to greater concentration has been relentless. Unless a supermarket group can keep up with the buying power of the dominant players, it cannot hope to survive.

The concentration of retail power has not just taken place in the UK. It is a global phenomenon. By the mid-2000s the top thirty grocers in the world controlled an estimated third of all food sales. Supermarkets chains had rushed to expand into other countries and strengthen their position, generally by merger and acquisition. Wal-Mart was not just the world's largest food retailer, it was one of the world's largest companies by sales.

When Not On the Label was first published its sales were $245 bil-
lion, making it bigger than all but thirty of the world's largest
national economies. Nearly a decade on, in the year to January
2013, the US-headquartered company recorded net sales of
$466 billion, highlighting its staggering rate of expansion. As Ira
Kalish, global director of Deloitte Research, put it, 'There is
nothing like Wal-Mart. They are so much bigger than any retailer
has ever been that's it's not possible to compare.' The company
is nearly four times the size of the next biggest retailer, the
French chain Carrefour, and the UK-headquartered Tesco,
which are both awesomely large, and have been two and three
in the world rankings with revenues around the £65–75 billion
mark in recent years. Not far behind are the Seven & I Holdings
group with its 7-Eleven stores, then Costco, Kruger, Schwartz,
AEON, Aldi and Auchun. Sainsbury's is the only other British
supermarket group in the top twenty-five globally, typically ranking around 20–23.

Tesco, which has expanded rapidly in central and eastern Europe, south-east Asia and China, was operating in eleven countries
in 2013, having abandoned its attempt to set up in the US. The
global buying power of Asda, through Wal-Mart, and of Tesco,
with chains in several countries, undoubtedly helped these companies consolidate their positions as Britain's leading retailers.

The battle of the bananas is a classic example of how the dynamics of this globalized retail concentration and buying power have
worked.

In 2002, Wal-Mart [the world's largest retailer which owns
Asda in the UK] renegotiated its banana buying. It invited the
biggest distributors of bananas to bid for a global contract to supply
its stores in several countries. Control of banana trading had been
taken over by the end of the 1990s by an oligopoly, with three
quarters of global trade in the hands of just five companies, Chiquita (26 per cent of the market), Dole (25 per cent) and Del Monte
Fresh Produce, Fyffes and Noboa (8 per cent each).

Bidding for the international Wal-Mart contract was ferocious. The size of the contract meant that it alone would dramatically alter market shares in favour of the winners. Del Monte Fresh Produce, sourcing bananas from Latin America, won a large chunk of it and, because of the scale of the business on offer, promised Wal-Mart a deal that would enable the retailer to slash its prices to customers, including its Asda shoppers.

Bananas are British retailers' largest-selling and most lucrative item. According to the fair trade non-profit organization, Banana Link, for every £1 of bananas sold at retail, the supermarkets keep 40p while growers receive just 10p. Bananas are, like bread, known value items, one of the few items whose price shoppers remember and use to make comparisons between different shops and whether they offer good value or not. So if you cut prices on bananas you put intense pressure on your competition. As the price of bananas in Asda shops fell from £1.08 per kilo in the summer of 2002 to 81p per kilo in March 2003, other retailers were forced to scramble to keep up.

Sainsbury's said it was losing £22 million a year on bananas as it tried to match Asda prices. Its orders could not touch the scale of Wal-Mart operating globally, and it could not extract the same deal from suppliers. Moreover, it had been sourcing many of its bananas from the Windward Islands, where the fruit is produced on family farms with fewer chemicals but correspondingly greater labour costs. The Windwards could not match the prices offered by Latin American countries, where bananas for export are produced on large-scale plantations which depend on routine aerial spraying of pesticides and where infringements of labour rights and environmental abuses are both notorious and well documented. Nowhere have abuses been greater than in Ecuador, from where some of the bananas for the supermarket price war were to come. Banana Link calculated how much money would be left for other links in the food chain if bananas were being sold in shops in the UK at 81p per kilo. At this price it is impossible for a grower in Costa Rica to be paid the set legal minimum for a box of bananas, and impossible in turn for that grower to pay his labourers a legal minimum wage. 'International buyers are in effect obliging all banana-exporting countries to reproduce Ecuador's poor labour and environmental conditions,' it says.

Fair trade campaign groups have documented the conditions that were behind that price. In 1999, Del Monte sacked all 4,300 of its workers on one of its biggest plantations in Costa Rica, the country that supplied much of UK demand. They re-employed them on wages reduced by 30–50 per cent, on longer hours and with fewer benefits.

This model was subsequently rolled out across the industrial banana sector. Aid organizations say that deterioration in conditions for workers has accompanied each banana war. That around 50 per cent of workers on these plantations are now migrants within Latin America is a reflection of how poor pay and conditions became. The UK supermarkets say that when they cut the price of bananas in a promotion they fund it themselves and take the hit on their margins. But for all their protestations that the cuts are not passed on, the fact remains that the world price of bananas has been driven down relentlessly since the 1970s, as have working conditions. On the ground, fair trade campaigners say they still find evidence of poverty wages, excessive hours, poor health and safety standards, intimidation of union members and environmental degradation.

Under pressure from bad publicity about these conditions, the big global banana traders – Del Monte, Chiquita and Dole – were pushed into working with aid organizations and local unions to do something about them. They seemed concerned to distance themselves from the trade's banana republic legacy. But aid agencies feared that successive price wars between the supermarkets over the fruit risked jeopardizing progress.

In 2009 the supermarkets entered another round of battle over banana prices. They went down to 38p per kilo in Asda and then 35p per kilo in Tesco. Once again they said they were not passing the pain on down the supply chain. I decided to analyse some data on what was going on with other prices at the time. Some of Asda's biggest-selling brands had seen steep rises, and these were goods that had not been on special offer.

There had been a 72 per cent increase in PG Tips tea, a 45 per cent rise on some Colgate top-selling toothpastes, a more than 100 per cent increase on some Pringles crisps, 38 per cent on Rich Tea biscuits and 85 per cent on single cream.

Industry experts told me it looked remarkably like a supermarket increasing its margin to build a war chest of cash. Could I or they be sure? No. Like most shoppers, I find it impossible to keep track of supermarket pricing because it is so variable and opaque. Even the competition authorities have admitted they do not have the resources to monitor what the big picture is. But it's a fair bet that what supermarkets give back to us with one hand they are taking, or have already taken, with the other. In the short term, cutting the price of bananas and selling them below the cost of production is a paper exercise in shifting profits around, designed to grab publicity, pull shoppers in to spend on other highly profitable goods, and squeeze their competitors.

But in the medium and long term, it has been no game for the rest of the banana industry. A phony supermarket price war is a real war for them – one in which they tend to suffer the collateral damage. We know from the bitter history of such price wars that the costs have been passed down the chain, if not immediately, then over the subsequent months.

For all but the biggest players this sort of war is a zero-sum game, eroding their profits alarmingly. Sainsbury's and Waitrose had decided to stop playing it and made a commitment to buy all their bananas from fair trade sources in 2007. The race to the bottom by the others put enormous pressure on them as they had to subsidize the difference in costs.

When the price war of 2013 saw bananas down to 68p per kilo, Sainsbury's made a complaint to the Advertising Standards Authority that Tesco was marketing itself with a promise to repay the difference if rivals sold a basket of popular foods for less than it did. Sainsbury's argued that it was not comparing like with like, and that fair trade bananas were not the same as those sold without the promise to pay producers fairly. The ASA rejected Sainsbury's complaint, saying that the values behind a product's sourcing were not a relevant measure in comparing quality.

The competition authorities have similarly adopted a narrow definition of public interest when judging whether the concentration of power in the leading supermarkets has been anti-competitive. This has been equalled by the narrowness of their definition of what the market is. When big chains started wanting to acquire convenience store companies, they were judged to be a separate market and so the takeovers were unopposed.

The stranglehold that supermarket buyers had acquired over the food chain was graphically illustrated by analyst Jan-Willem Grievink in 2003. He drew an hourglass with a wide line at the top to represent the 160 million consumers making decisions about purchasing in Europe, and another wide line at the bottom representing the 3.2 million farms and producers who grew food for them at the time. But the lines connecting the two ends of the food chain, the consumers and the producers, were not direct. They narrowed to a tiny pinch-point in the middle of the hourglasss, where just 110 retail buying desks decided what manufacturers might sell to us and what would be available in the shops for us to buy. He highlighted this pinch-point in the diagram with a large arrow marked 'Power'.

The impact of this stranglehold was subject to various competition inquiries and yet very little was done to stop it tightening further.

The 1990s saw a flurry of activity. During this time, supermarkets were accused in the press of being responsible, together with banks and car manufacturers, for a 'rip-off Britain'. Complaints that prices were higher in the UK than in neighbouring

European countries or the USA grew louder and louder. When New Labour came to power in 1997, both Tony Blair and Stephen Byers, who was trade secretary from 1998, took up the cause. The Office of Fair Trading (OFT) was asked to look into the grocery market. By spring of 1999, it had asked the Competition Commission to conduct a full-scale inquiry. That same spring, the chief executive of Wal-Mart visited England, and explored how a takeover bid for Asda would be received politically. He and his team were invited to tea at Downing Street. When criticized for entertaining them, the prime minister said he made no apology. 'We are overpriced compared to the USA and the reason, in part, is that there is too little competition.' Welcoming in a price-cutting US giant was seen to be championing the cause of the people. Within a month or two, Wal-Mart had announced its takeover of Asda and triggered a shake-up of the whole supermarket sector.

The main complaint over supermarkets had been the disparity between prices they paid to farmers and prices they charged consumers in the shops. When the Competition Commission published the results of its inquiry in late 2000, they ran to some 1,200 pages of detailed analysis. Needless to say, few people managed to wade through all of them, and it was the summary of findings that was widely reported. The headlines showed that the retailers were off the hook. 'Supermarkets given the all clear,' said the BBC. 'Shoppers getting a fair deal,' announced another press report. The large supermarket chains had spent about £20 million in legal and other costs defending themselves. The Commission found that there had been a decline in the real price of food of 9.4 per cent from 1989 to 1998. It concluded that the retailers were broadly competitive and did not make excessive profits.

Prices in the UK supermarkets were higher than some European counterparts, as much as 12–16 per cent higher than in France, Germany or the Netherlands, but land and building costs were higher and together with exchange rates helped account for the difference.

Byers defended the two-year investigation, saying that since it

started there had been significant changes in the industry, notably the entry into the UK market of Wal-Mart which had led
to price cuts worth about £1 billion to customers.

A senior member of the government later admitted to me
privately that there was disappointment that the Competition
Commission had not come down harder on the supermarkets.
This lingering sense that they had got off lightly may have been
behind an outburst by Tony Blair six months later. It came at the
height of the foot and mouth crisis that had engulfed much of
the country and was crippling English farming. Meeting farmers
on a tour of the West Country, he blamed the supermarkets for
much of the pressure on British agriculture. 'We all want cheaper
food in our shops, but on the other hand the supermarkets have
pretty much got an arm-lock on you people at the moment.'

The letters to Downing Street from supermarket bosses came
thick and fast, as did the government backtracking. The retailers
had pretty much got an arm-lock on the government. They
could point out that the exhaustive Competition Commission
report had cleared them. The government's Curry Commission
into sustainable food and farming, set up in the wake of the foot
and mouth disaster, looked extensively at agricultural subsidies,
but barely touched on retailer power.

However, a closer look at the full 1,200-page Competition
Commission report showed that the Commission already had
some serious concerns about power, despite its overall findings.
It had not only said that some pricing practices pursued by the
supermarkets were 'against the public interest', in particular the
practices of selling certain products below the cost of production and of charging different prices in different stores depending
on the strength of local competition. It also reported that there
were a 'substantial number of serious concerns' about the relationship between supermarkets and their suppliers, that is, about
how they used their enormous buying power. Astonishingly, it
recommended no action on the first two problem areas. It did
recommend a code of practice to regulate the way supermarkets

dealt with suppliers, and went so far as to say it would have to have legal force in order to work. However, once the inquiry had started, the supermarkets, who could see which way the wind was blowing, rapidly developed their own codes of practice to pre-empt its findings. A voluntary code was introduced. A year later, the consensus among suppliers was that the code was so weak as to be useless.

Buried in the dense economic analysis of the report were some extraordinary insights into how the business was working these days.

The Commission had heard many allegations about the way the big supermarkets treated their suppliers. It found 'a climate of apprehension among many suppliers founded on their view that there is an imbalance of power between them and the multiples'. It had also proved a struggle for the Commission to extract information despite its statutory powers. Suppliers, even large multinational manufacturers, were extremely reluctant to come forward for fear of being delisted, and needed absolute guarantees of confidentiality. Even with those guarantees, many suppliers still refused to give evidence for fear of the consequences. This climate of fear is one that journalists were familiar with. It remains hard to get anyone to go on the record about how they are treated by the big multiples.

According to the report, 'many suppliers commented on the purchasing power of the [main supermarkets] and their ability to drive down prices to uneconomic levels and what they saw as their general high-handedness.'

A small supplier commented: 'The power of the multiples, especially of young buyers [aged twenty-five to twenty-eight] without experience, is frightening. [They have] the power to dictate prices and margins, display or not, allocate space and threaten covertly.'

One supplier organization said the supermarkets 'talk about partnerships but these do not exist, and they ruthlessly erode suppliers' margins with no consideration of the damage they are

doing to that company or its employees. Multiples switch their
buyers around every six to twelve months in order that loyalty
to suppliers can be avoided. The new buyer is given carte blanche
to delist suppliers who are frequently treated with complete
contempt.'

Another supplier said that it had been asked by one multiple
to make three separate cash contributions to the supermarket's
profits. The third, requested by telephone, was for a sum over
£100,000 and was claimed as 'a contribution towards profits'.
The same supplier said the multiple had introduced other
charges, none of which had been negotiated and all of which
had been deducted from their next payments without agreement. They felt that if they complained they would 'upset the
relationship'.

The Commission investigated fifty-two alleged 'coercive and
abusive business practices' used by the supermarkets. It found
that twenty-five of them operated against the public interest.
Not all the main supermarkets were guilty of operating all the
anti-competitive practices, but the practices were widespread
and all the supermarkets practised several of them. The practices
gave rise to 'a second complex monopoly situation', the report
concluded.

To outsiders some of the practices and lack of action to stop
them were mind-boggling. Suppliers are asked to pay listing fees
just to get their products on the shelves. They are also asked to
pay extra for better positions on the shelves.

Promotions and price cuts are often funded by suppliers and
produce for special offers is often predominantly paid for by
suppliers. Suppliers can face threats of delisting if they do not
agree to price reductions. They had restrictions put on trade
with rival supermarkets. Elsewhere suppliers were also found to
have been asked to 'contribute to the costs of store refurbish-
ments or openings'.

Among the most controversial of practices was the supermarkets' demand for 'overriding discounts'. These are discounts on

the agreed price if sales reach certain volumes. Discounts were also often sought retrospectively, yet there appeared to be no corresponding sharing of risk, for supermarkets also demand compensation from suppliers if sales were less than expected. Suppliers complained of having amounts deducted from their invoices without agreement, and of having the cost of complaints from shoppers passed automatically back to them without investigating who was at fault.

Asda and Morrisons were found to sell produce with labels which might be taken to indicate that the produce came from the UK when it in fact came from overseas, putting genuine UK produce at a disadvantage.

When you find yourself in the company of any supplier, it never takes long for the conversation to turn to these practices and the devastating impact they have. I had been told of a major supermarket requesting £1 million up front from a large dairy co-operative in order for negotiations about listing its milk to begin. One South African wine supplier had said that it was required to pay £100,000 to have its bottles moved up just one shelf. A food manufacturer with a turnover of several hundred million pounds a year told the supermarket it supplied that since its costs – wages and raw materials – had gone up, it needed to increase its prices by 1 per cent. The reply was that not only was a price rise unacceptable, a cut of 3 per cent was in fact needed and if it wasn't forthcoming, the manufacturer could clear its products off the supermarket's shelves immediately. Pea farmers in the north of England, who had contracted to supply a supermarket at an agreed price at the beginning of the season and planted accordingly, were told on the eve of harvest that their price would be halved.

Some of the requests were surreally funny. A Tesco letter several years ago became legendary. It told its suppliers that its Dudley Moore TV advertising campaign promoting chicken had been so successful that it would like a contribution for it. Nick Howell, a fish supplier in Cornwall, received a letter saying his contribution would be £2,000. 'I wrote back saying I don't supply chickens and we've never discussed this, get lost. Then a letter came saying "Thank you, we will be deducting it from your monthly payments." And they did.' Tesco said the issue was raised at the time of the Competition Commission report, when it had refuted it. 'We do not require suppliers to contribute to advertising retrospectively. Positive long-term supplier relationships are key to our business and we work hard to maintain them,' a spokesman said. The Competition Commission said it had not always been able to resolve the differences between suppliers' and supermarkets' accounts of how business was conducted. But for most suppliers, the way power was exercised over them was anything but funny.

They were bearing the brunt of the price war between the big supermarkets as the retailers battled for dominance of the UK market. Even some of the largest suppliers were beginning to say publicly that it could not go on. The chairman and chief executive of Nestlé UK, Alistair Sykes, complained of 'the real danger that the competition between the major retailers has become too focused on short-term unsustainable price cutting', which could destroy the profitability of brands.

Writing in the trade magazine the *Grocer*, the sales director of Unilever Bestfoods UK talked of 'the spectre' of this practice. 'If too much profitability is sucked out of the chain, it will fundamentally damage the quality of the offering to the consumer by adding to the pressure felt by farmers and primary producers.' The Association of Frozen Food Producers warned the Competition Commission inquiry into the Safeway takeover that any further strengthening of the top three retailers would 'severely damage the viability of food manufacturing in the UK'.

The *Grocer* also conducted a survey in 2003 of top manufacturers about so called 'trade investment'. This is a euphemism for the direct payments required by supermarkets. Almost half the manufacturers said that 'trade investment' accounted for between

15 and 25 per cent of their turnover. A £200 million supplier would expect to have a 'trade fund' of between £30 million and £50 million a year to cover such things as price cuts demanded by the retailers after a price has already been agreed, the cost of special offers, and other promotions in the stores not built into their original negotiations. The manufacturers felt much of it was going on 'wasteful promotions' and price-cutting which simply served the retailer's interest. 'Most is going towards the current in-fighting between the retailers,' one top own-label executive said.

Such is the power of the big retailers that despite the fact that they thought it was money poorly spent, most manufacturers expected to have to find more for this 'trade investment' in the following twelve months. They could not afford not to, since there was almost nowhere else to go if they wanted to reach the mass of consumers. The suppliers were in effect being forced to subsidize the supermarkets' fight for control of our spending.

Increasingly, supermarket profits were coming not from margins on food sold but from direct contributions. Studies in Australia suggested that over half the gross profit of the big retailers was coming from direct payments made by suppliers to supermarket head offices. These payments are not calculated as part of the retailers' margins on produce, enabling them to argue that they are highly competitive and work on very tight margins.

The voluntary code in the UK proved as ineffective as most producers had feared. Eventually there was sufficient pressure for a second inquiry by the Competition Commission to be ordered in 2008. It proposed a strengthened code to protect suppliers, which should be enforced by an independent supermarket ombudsman. In 2009 the head of the Competition Commission was still talking about the climate of fear that existed among suppliers. With the retailers arguing against it all the way, it was not until 2013 that the legislation was put in place and an adjudicator was finally appointed. As she travelled around the country preparing to take up her role, she reported being told of three instances in which suppliers had been asked to pay more than £1 million if they wanted their products stocked. The trade press was still reporting cases of suppliers complaining that supermarkets were asking them to fund promotions. Industry bodies told me that while some of the practices prohibited in the code of practice had stopped, their members were still suffering delays in payments and still experienced the levying of fines where target margins had not been met. Farmers had told a select committee of MPs in 2013 that they had no contracts and were working to a system of 'margin buckets', whereby the supermarkets set a target for how much profit they expected to make and expected suppliers to make up any shortfall, even though it was not the supplier who had control over the price at which goods were sold.

It was no surprise that in the depths of a recession suppliers' profits would be squeezed but the *Grocer*'s analysis in 2012 showed that the margins of Britain's top 150 food and drink manufacturers had been squeezed to a fourteen-year low and had contracted 0.8 percentage points, while supermarkets' margins contracted less, by just 0.3 percentage points.

The supermarkets have become the gatekeepers who control access to us, the customers. Manufacturers and farmers are being required to pay for that access.

The big supermarkets argue that they offer people convenience, value for money and unprecedented choice. It is indisputable that hundreds of products that were not widely available before are now commonplace. But it is questionable whether it is really consumers who want many of them. In Europe 10,000 new food products are launched every year, but 90 per cent of them fail to make it into their second year.

The concentration of power has narrowed our choice in other ways too. By 2004 Wal-Mart already had 32 per cent of the US nappy market, 30 per cent of the market in hair-care products, and 26 per cent of toothpaste sales. Despite the fact that large numbers of its US stores sell guns, it had decided to act as moral and cultural gatekeeper by not stocking any CDs or DVDs with parental warning stickers. It removed 'lad' magazines from sale for a period and started obscuring the covers of *Cosmopolitan* and *Marie Claire*. The big music companies responded by supplying sanitized versions of CDs to the stores, because you can't reach your audience if the biggest player won't stock your products.

The choice of Tesco's buyers has an enormous effect on what gets sold too. It sells more chart CDs than Virgin and more toiletries than Boots and Superdrug combined. Over the Christmas period of 2003, the supermarkets fought a price war over beer, using cheap alcohol to draw custom into their shops. As they slashed prices on a couple of the leading brands, others were cleared from the shelves to make space. What we are allowed to purchase, from the type of music to the variety of tomato or brand of beer, is being determined by buyers operating in the supermarkets' interests rather than the consumers'.

The inexorable logic of such concentrated power in retailing is that suppliers must consolidate too, which erodes our choice still further. The competition authorities are caught in a bind here. Unless suppliers merge and combine they may not be able to survive the pressure from retailers. The takeover of Express Dairies by the Danish giant Arla meant that there were only three major milk suppliers to the supermarkets in the UK: Robert Wiseman, Dairy Crest and the new Arla Food UK. Yet the takeover was given a smooth ride. As one analyst said to the *Grocer*, 'It doesn't surprise me the Commission was as timid as it was. The general consensus is the retailers don't need protecting, they're more than capable of bashing these businesses around on their own.' But none of that is good news for small suppliers or anyone new who imagined they might be able to enter this concentrated grocery market.

If buyer power enables supermarkets to buy goods more

cheaply and pass the savings on to customers, does it matter that only a handful of companies control so much of the global food system? For a long period prices generally did fall, so the argument was that it must be good for ordinary people.

It proved naive however to think this would be true in the long term. Even in 2000 the Competition Commission report showed that supermarkets already charged higher prices in areas where there was less competition. There was plenty of evidence, not just from manufacturers with vested interests, that their food pricing strategy was not sustainable but a reflection of a market in which players were digging deep into their pockets to win supremacy.

Sainsbury's told the Competition Commission inquiry into the takeover of Safeway that by its calculations Tesco derived 73 per cent and Asda 100 per cent of their profits from their non-food business, and that by 2005 they would be making 'an economic loss' on food if current trends continue. Asda dismissed this as untrue. Tesco also denied that it had been cross-subsidizing its food business with profits from its household goods and clothes sector, but the company's commercial director for non-food, Richard Brasher, told a food retailing conference that 'the competition that is Wal-Mart has introduced a tension that makes margins thin and oxygen low'.

Moreover, the price levels were being sustained by cut-price labour, much of it working below the legal minimum wage (see Chapter 3: Salad).

By 2010 prices were changing so much it was almost impossible for the ordinary shopper to know what was best value. To work out what was happening, I decided to analyse thousands of prices with some expert help, and published my findings in the *Guardian*. In the run up to the previous Christmas, Tesco and Asda had engaged in the customary marketing war over prices. When I looked in detail, it turned out that a majority of price cuts were just 1p. In contrast, the majority of price increases imposed by the two retail giants during the same period were more than 10p.

I asked Professor John Bridgeman, who had conducted official inquiries into the supermarket sector as director general of the Office of Fair Trading from 1995 to 2000, what he thought it meant.

He said it was 'price flexing' which showed a 'cynical manipulation of the language of value'.

'They are not in reality cutting prices but flexing prices, making them go up and down and destabilizing the price structure,' Bridgeman said. 'All they are doing is introducing so much volatility no one can tell whether prices are going up or down. It can only be to consumers' detriment and it does [the supermarkets'] image no good.'

Data taken from Asda's website by third-party analysts indicated that it cut nearly 800 prices between 16 and 23 December, with two thirds of the cuts being just 1p and 80 per cent of the total number being less than 10p. It also increased more than 850 prices that week. In contrast, only 6 per cent of the rising prices went up by the same small increment of 1p; 53 per cent of the rises were more than 10p.

The pattern was repeated in data taken from the Tesco website: between 16 and 23 December it cut about 930 prices, 70 per cent of which were by just 1p. It also increased just under 1,000 prices in the same period: 7 per cent of these rises were by the small increment of 1p, and more than 600 – or 60 per cent – of the price increases were by more than 10p.

Both supermarkets said the majority of price increases in that period could be explained by products which had been discounted coming off promotion.

In Bridgeman's view, the scale of price changing and the relative size of the cuts and rises is both confusing and misleading to consumers. 'The most dangerous thing [for] competition in this sector is price volatility,' he said. 'It confuses consumers, deters investors and has driven corner shops out of business because they don't know what price they have to compete on,' he said.

The rise and fall in price of a leading brand of cleaner, Cif

Anti-Bacterial, provided a 'perfect example of price volatility designed to confuse consumers', according to Bridgeman.

In June 2009 the Cif cleaner was being sold at £2.50 in both Asda and Tesco. In August it went on promotion briefly at Asda at £1 before going up to the price of £2.60. Tesco dropped the price to £2 in September before putting it back up to £2.50, and then discounting it again in November to half price at £1.25. By December Asda had put it up to £2.80 and higher, and the week before Christmas Tesco increased its price to £2.80. By the end of the year, both retailers had increased the price by what Bridgeman called an 'aggressive' 12 per cent over the price shoppers paid for the same product at the beginning at the summer. Discounts had disguised a rise, he said, and you could see the same pattern with some types of breads.

The net effect of these rises and cuts on consumer bills is hard for anyone outside the industry to calculate. Whether you benefited or lost out would have depended on what you put in your basket over that period.

Professor Paul Dobson, who had studied bread prices (see Chapter 5: Bread) said the pattern I had identified before Christmas matched the overall pattern. Researchers at Loughborough and at Warwick University found that, overall, price cuts made by the big four UK supermarkets – Tesco, Asda, Sainsbury's and Morrisons – tended to be small and price rises larger.

His research found the most common price cut among the big four over five years was 1p. Such low cuts have little impact at the checkout, but introducing them on large numbers of goods enables the supermarkets to claim they are cutting thousands of prices. According to Dobson, over the five-year period these small cuts have been used to mask serious price hikes on a smaller number of lines with a big net effect on bills. 'In the big inflationary period of 2008, there were two and a half times the numbers of price cuts in the big four as price rises, but in fact prices overall were rising very rapidly,' he said.

Dobson said his research showed that, of the big four UK

supermarkets, Tesco was the most prolific user of 1p cuts, and Asda the second most prolific. He also said Tesco changed its prices more than the other retailers.

Asda did not challenge the figures but said the explanation for the large number of 1p cuts was 'straightforward'. 'We won't be beaten on price. So if a competitor goes lower than us on a comparable product, even by just a penny, we will always try and match or beat that price,' said a spokesperson. 'Whichever way you look at the numbers, Asda is the undisputed lowest price supermarket – as independently verified by mysupermarket.com.'

Tesco also rejected Bridgeman's interpretation of the significance of the number of small and large price changes. In a statement, the company said: 'We do not manipulate prices in this cynical way. The *Guardian* and Professor Bridgeman are using data we do not recognize and his conclusion that we are deliberately confusing customers is nonsense.

'This is a competitive market and prices are lower this year than last year. Our customers know us, shop with us every week, trust us and are not confused. Instead of trying to find product price changes to fit a half-baked theory, Bridgeman and the *Guardian* should look at what has happened to the overall price of customers' baskets. As the current head of the Office of Fair Trading said last month, the sector is "highly competitive" and prices have "come down enormously".'

Professor Dobson's more recent work shows the strategy of yo-yoing prices continues. And we seem to have been bamboozled by the latest application of this sophisticated piece of retail psychology. Forty per cent of the supermarket food we buy in the UK is now on 'special offer'. We are spending over £50 billion a year on offers, in fact. Price promotions accounted for over half of all spending on alcohol and soft drinks. They were also heavily used on ready meals, confectionery and snacks. Fruit and vegetables were less promoted. We find ourselves putting things in our basket we had not set out to buy. The big retailers offer promises to 'match' the prices in rival shops if they turn out to be cheaper. Few shoppers actually bother to check so retailers do not have to pay out much on their price guarantees. Meanwhile our till receipts tell us we have 'saved' huge amounts on these discounted goods when we check out. They make us feel savvy, and every retailer manages to seem the cheapest. 'It's very smart. We have become promo junkies. We have been in a deep recession and yet their profits remain very handsome. It's a reflection of the fact the market is too concentrated.' Where is the force that will come to stir it up? Dobson wanted to know, and why do many promotions remain skewed to the least healthy foods, high in salt, fat and sugar?

Professor Lang, the man who started the food miles debate (see Chapter 4: Beans and Asparagus), predicted much of what has happened over the last thirty years when he first realized that supermarkets were changing the whole economic landscape. 'At the time it was considered totally deviant to say supermarkets were getting too powerful. They were seen as a force for public good because they had taken on and tackled the excessive power of manufacturers that had emerged post-war as well as the vested interests of the farmers. The supermarkets were the middle classes' friend. People would talk with excitement about a branch of Sainsbury's opening near them. They couldn't wait for all the cosmopolitan foods. But time has shown we were right. They now have unprecedented power over the distribution of food and determine the shape of the entire supply chain. They have so crushed any alternatives that now consumers dance to their tune, and consumers are uneasy – they are aware they have to get in cars to shop and the experience is one of drudgery, queuing, carrying vast amounts, struggling in car parks. The mood is changing but there's almost nowhere else to go now,' Lang says.

He has watched with interest as his arguments have been taken up by the sort of mainstream economists who dismissed them earlier.

In February 2003 the Organization for Economic Co-operation

and Development (OECD), the heartland of the economic establishment, held a conference in The Hague on 'Changing Dimensions of the Food Economy' and invited Lang to lecture. Top government officials, senior food industry executives, leading experts from universities and competition authorities from all round the world gathered to contemplate the future under what the Dutch minister of agriculture Cees Veerman described as a 'new economic order ... that has an enormous impact on not only the community but on our lives as individuals'. The impact of this new food economy was greater, he said, than the traditional instruments designed to control it. The food economy was now dominated by global parties when competition authorities have no jurisdiction at that level.

In his speech to open the conference Veerman explained that 'the balance of power in the chain [has] been completely turned upside down. Retailers and processors now rule the chain, not the farmer.' The result is that consumers can have their choice of foods from an array that is more varied than ever before and prices are lower, 'but there is a downside to all this', he told the gathering. The issue was politically sensitive but they had to ask, were the profits being fairly divided over the chain, or could the new market structure result in the misuse of power? If they were not, the effects would be felt in policy areas across the board – in environment, labour, health, agriculture, trade and competition.

The smaller conventional supermarket and even the middle-sized chain has become a relic of the past. In order to compete with the growing power of retailers, manufacturers have had to concentrate on marketing and development of new products. The actual business of making food has become almost peripheral to profit, and is increasingly 'outsourced'.

Professor John Connor, an expert in industrial economics and cartels, from Purdue University in Indiana, warned the assembled OECD worthies that global concentration in food retailing, food manufacturing and raw materials for food was already at levels 'high enough to generate significant departures from effective competition'. He predicted that price-fixing scandals would become more common: 'We've entered an era when transportation and communication appear to facilitate global price fixing.'

Evidence of various investigations into alleged price fixing has proved him right to worry. The Office of Fair Trading accused the major UK dairy groups and supermarkets of colluding to fix the price of milk, butter and cheese between 2002 and 2003. It agreed fines with them of £116 million at the end of 2007 following provisional findings from a three-year investigation. Sainsbury's, Asda, Safeway, Dairy Crest and Robert Wiseman all admitted to anti-competitive practices and to colluding to raise the price of milk in the shops. Arla escaped fines having been granted immunity in return for providing information to the inquiry. Tesco fought the allegations and in 2013 a court finally ruled it should pay £6.5 million for communicating its pricing to rival retailers through a supplier.

The supermarkets and processors said in their defence that they had put up prices to shoppers to help farmers, but the farmers' unions said farmers had seen little long-term benefit.

The European Commission has acted twice, once in 2008 and again in 2011, to break up price-fixing cartels among traders in the banana sector.

Another week, another high-level conference. This time at the UN's Food and Agriculture Organization in October 2003, where experts had been asked to prepare reports from thirty-five developing and middle-income countries on the impact on health of shifts in diets and urbanization. Most of the reports were coming back saying that the same pattern – rapid concentration of power in the hands of a few supermarket groups, small and medium enterprises and family farms squeezed out of business, collapse of agricultural incomes – was being seen everywhere from Latin America to China and south-east Asia.

The FAO meeting of experts was being warned that the consequences were devastating. More than half the population in the developing world is rural and dependent on subsistence agriculture or farm work. They are losing their livelihoods as processors consolidate and favour larger producers and as supermarkets take over control of the supply chain. If prices are so low that the 2.5 billion people around the world who depend on agriculture for their livelihoods cannot survive on the land, they are forced into migration, as so many British packhouses bear witness.

The political influence of the supermarkets in the UK has often been blamed for government's failure to check their growing power. There is no doubt that they have had access to the heart of government. The revolving door between Downing Street and the retailers has seen a supermarket owner, Lord Sainsbury, become a minister; a supermarket chief executive, Sir Peter Davis, also of Sainsbury's, chair government taskforces and sit on the policy commission on food; and senior executives move from Downing Street and the Cabinet Office to Tesco and back for taskforce and steering-group duty.

But a senior former member of government pointed out to me another reason why there was no political will in the UK to address the power of the supermarkets. The price war between the big retailers had for a while prevented inflation in food, which had kept down inflation figures overall. Retailers had expanded and provided new jobs, more jobs, for a time, than were being lost in companies that had felt the supermarket squeeze (Boots, for example, who cut 900 jobs at their Nottingham headquarters). For a Labour party taunted with a history of economic incompetence, nothing was more important than that. The same could have been said of the USA, where economists referred to the 'Wal-Mart effect'. Wal-Mart's relentless pressure on suppliers and wages had driven productivity across the whole economy and suppressed inflation.

It was not to last, of course. By the time of the post-crash global recession, food inflation was running ahead of headline inflation. Locked into a model that depended on intense energy use, supermarket costs rose as the price of fuel soared and stayed stubbornly high. By then so much capital had been invested in an infrastructure built on this model, to change direction would require seismic upheaval.

Governments in middle-income countries that were the next target for supermarket acquisitions seemed barely to have woken up to the significance of the trend. International giants such as Tesco, Carrefour, Ahold, Metro and Delhaize controlled 75 per cent of the Czech grocery market in 2004. There were emerging reports of complaints of pressure on manufacturers and of high listing fees and late payments. Large retail chains were expected to have gained control of nearly 50 per cent of Poland's total food sales within two years, and the top ten retailers in that country were all owned by big foreign groups, including Tesco and Carrefour. Supermarkets already controlled 50–60 per cent of food sales in Latin America. The way they operated was forcing thousands of small and medium farmers, traders and truckers out of business, yet their acquisitions were largely unopposed.

And yet a few years into the downturn after the financial crisis and cracks in the edifice were appearing. There was much talk when I met supermarket directors privately of needing governments to take the lead on stopping unsustainable practices. They were facing what they called a 'decoupling' of the usual relationship between falling incomes in recession and falling costs. Their costs, driven by commodity inflation and energy prices, were rising rapidly when incomes were stagnating or falling. Almost all their supply chains for raw materials were throwing up problems as climate change was biting, from cocoa to coffee, from maize to soya, from dairy to fish.

Rocked by the horsemeat scandal, Tesco started shifting the thrust of its marketing from price to quality.

The phrase 'choice editing' had entered their lexicon. Whisper it, but customers might have to get used to the idea that they could not have everything from wherever whenever. Some foods might simply be too harmful – to our health, to the environment, or too depleting of resources – or just too expensive to be stocked.

7. Coffee and Grains

Martin Luther used to wonder what people actually do in heaven. For most participants in the intensely competitive food manufacturing industry, contemplation of Nestlé's soluble coffee business must seem like the commercial equivalent of Luther's spiritual meditation. This is a market where Nestlé has a global share of 57 per cent, sales three times the level of its nearest competitor, and margins which we estimate at 26 per cent. Nothing else in food and beverages is remotely as good.

   This Deutsche Bank analysts' view of the rich pickings in the coffee market in 2000 would have come as a surprise to coffee growers at the time. They were in the middle of a deep five-year crisis which saw the price of coffee beans slump to a thirty-year low. Many of the 25 million coffee farmers around the world ended up selling their crops at a loss. There was, however, almost no corresponding fall in the price consumers paid for their coffee, as you might expect in a properly functioning free market. Not surprisingly, the profits of the companies who controlled the processing of the world's coffee beans remained very healthy. For while the income from coffee to the countries that grow it halved, the retail value of the same coffee in industrialized countries more than doubled.

   Nestlé's Nescafé is one of a clutch of global 'A-brands' powerful enough to stand up to the increasing dominance of the transnational retailers. This is where you can see the other half of the picture in the battle for control of our food. The coffee supply chain has become highly concentrated. What has happened in the coffee sector is mirrored in the trade in and processing of other agricultural commodities.

A handful of players have acquired control of around half of the international trade in coffee beans – in 2009 they were ECOM Agroindustrial Corporation, Louis Dreyfus, Neumann, VOLCAFE and Olam International. As well as coffee, these giant traders have huge interests in other agricultural products, from sugar to cocoa, edible oil, cotton and grains. They are what Olam International describes as 'global integrated supply chain managers of agricultural products and food ingredients'. They have established their positions with a series of mergers and takeovers, which look set to continue, since size is crucial to market power. Olam and Louis Dreyfus were said to be in merger talks which were abandoned in 2011.

Then at the next point in the chain just five roasting companies buy between half and three quarters of the world's total supply of green coffee beans in most years. Figures vary, but some analysts have estimated that the two largest coffee corporations alone – Nestlé, and what was until recently Kraft, restructured and renamed Mondalēz International in 2012 – buy close to half the supply.

Just five companies meanwhile control half the global market in retail sales of coffee – the list here is topped by Nestlé and Mondalēz again. As well as owning Cadbury, Mondalēz markets coffee under the Kenco, Jacobs, Carte Noire and Maxwell House brands. It describes Jacobs as one of its $1 billion a year 'power brands'. Keeping these two giants company was, from 2013, the German private investor group that had bought Douwe Egberts and its other coffee brands, Cafitesse, Maison du Café and Café Pilao; the US-based ice cream, jam and drink manufacturer Smucker, which sold Folger and Millstone brands in the US; and Tchibo, which sold mainly in Germany.

As the supermarkets have become more and more powerful, manufacturers have become bigger and bigger to hold their own. Scale here has also come through a flurry of mergers, acquisitions and demergers in the last three decades as big companies have swallowed up their rivals, and rationalized their portfolios to focus on core superbrands. They spend heavily on marketing and advertising, for it is by making their brands consumer 'must-haves', A-listers, that they maintain their leverage with the big retailers in the price wars.

The exact profits the roasting and processing companies make from coffee are hard to pin down since they are reported as part of their larger group earnings or, where they are private, not at all. But Nestlé's trading profit on its beverages section, not including bottled water, was $4.9 billion in 2012. The restructuring of Kraft/Mondalēz and allocation of debt made its profits for coffee in the same period difficult to see, but back in 2001, during the coffee slump, Kraft's beverages, desserts and cereals division earned $4.9 billion.

Just as with other raw materials, the money made from coffee has shifted dramatically from those at the bottom of the chain, in this case in developing countries, to those at the top in the industrialized world. Now less than 10 per cent of the retail value of coffee stays with the countries that grow it, whereas in the 1990s they might have expected to keep 30 per cent of it.

By 2011 the price of arabica coffee had swung to a thirty-four-year high and the price of robusta beans had soared too, despite that year seeing the largest world production of coffee on record. Global consumption was growing in part thanks to emerging economies, but supply and demand were narrowly in balance. Intense speculative trading on the commodity markets was blamed for helping to keep prices artificially high. Most coffee producers saw little of the benefit from this extreme volatility. They had carried the impact of falling prices and yet did not gain in full from rising prices. And such increases in prices as they did receive were largely wiped out by huge rises in their costs of fuel, fertilizer, transport and food. Climate change, moreover, was already bringing a dramatic increase in pests and disease.

The transfer of power and wealth from those at the bottom of the chain to a small number of players at the top mirrors what has happened to farmers in Western countries (as we saw in Chapter 6: Apples and Bananas). Half a century ago, 50–60p of every £1 spent on food and drink in the UK went to farmers. Now less than 10p in every £1 goes back to them. While the shift has taken a heavy toll on rural communities across Europe, for some poor countries it has meant the devastation of their whole economies.

The significance to developing countries of fluctuations in agricultural commodity prices would be hard to exaggerate, as a few examples using coffee show. In Ethiopia coffee accounted for 30 per cent of export earnings in 2010–11, and nearly a fifth of the population depended on coffee for their livelihood. In Burundi, the figure was 60 per cent of export earnings, in Honduras it was a quarter, in Nicaragua nearly a fifth. In Uganda almost a third of the population was dependent on coffee sales at the time of the crisis in the early 2000s. Countries across Central America and East Africa were left severely exposed by the slump as export earnings plummeted from $10 billion to $6 billion and hundreds of thousands of farmers were forced out of business into migration.

Until 1989, the market for coffee was, like many other commodities, managed with quotas for each producing country set by the International Coffee Agreement, rather in the way OPEC works for oil. The idea was to keep the price of coffee relatively high and stable within a band of prices. The Agreement broke down in 1989. There was a certain amount of corruption in administering the scheme and backdoor exporting to get round quotas. But the US desire to win a bigger share of the market and in theory greater economic and political stability for Central American producers in its own backyard was also a major factor. Once the Agreement had collapsed, the market became flooded and prices dropped dramatically, except for brief spikes when frosts in Brazil led to a shortage.

The flooding of the market was largely due to Vietnam. Ten years previously, Vietnam barely counted as a coffee producer.

Then, in the 1990s, came liberalization. Encouraged by the World Bank and International Monetary Fund to restructure its economy, open up its markets and invest its energies in generating foreign exchange, the Vietnamese government began an aggressive programme to encourage its farmers to move out of domestic production of rice (the price of which was volatile in part thanks to dumping of subsidized harvests from the USA) and into growing cash crops for export, particularly coffee.

Vietnam is not ideally suited to coffee production and nearly all its crop is of the lower-quality robusta type used either for instant coffee or in blends with the more expensive arabica type of beans. But by 2000, with the heavy use of fertilizers and pesticides, Vietnam had turned itself into the second largest coffee-producing country in the world after Brazil. Kraft, which bought heavily from Vietnam, expressed concern at 'severe quality and environmental problems at all stages of the coffee production process' in that country. Rapid expansion of coffee growing had been accompanied by 'severe deforestations' and 'negative ecological effects caused by over-fertilization and widespread irrigation', the company said. And all this to produce an oversupply, just as the Brazilians were also bumping up their yields by mechanizing and intensifying production with a greater use of agrochemicals.

For despite its impact on quality and the environment, intensification had been encouraged by international aid donors, in Latin America as well as Vietnam. In addition to the greater use of agrochemicals, strip-picking the coffee cherries in clusters, as opposed to traditional hand-harvesting of individual cherries, became common practice. That tends to mean that a high percentage of immature green cherries, which give bad black beans, are picked along with ripe ones, reducing the quality of the coffee and increasing the risk of a particular cancer-causing fungus forming.

With dreadful irony, the net result of the efforts of the international institutions and their free market ideology to help poor countries develop, had been environmental damage and a collapse in their incomes from coffee. Oxfam, which produced a detailed report on the coffee crisis, described it as 'a development disaster whose impact will be felt for a long time'. Families dependent on money generated by coffee were pulling their children out of school, could no longer afford basic medicines and were cutting back on food. The crisis was so deep that banks in developing countries were in trouble, and governments which depended on export earnings from coffee were unable to repay debts or cover their budgets for education and health.

I went to Uganda in 2003 to see the impact of the crisis at first hand. I was particularly interested in that country because it had become the Western aid donors' darling. Its authoritarian leader, Yoweri Museveni, was credited with turning from Marxist guerrilla to prudent economic manager to put the country's bloody past behind it. Just a few years before, despite corruption and an alarming rise in military spending, Uganda was being hailed as 'a beacon in a dark continent'. It was one of the few African countries which, thanks to an enlightened programme of public health education, seemed to be getting to grips with its AIDS crisis. It had largely done what the World Bank and International Monetary Fund told it to do. It had restructured its economy, opened its capital markets, and privatized. It had produced a strategy to reduce poverty. It was rewarded by being made the first country to qualify for debt relief under the Highly Indebted Poor Countries debt relief initiative. But then came the collapse of coffee prices.

In 1994/5 when the price of coffee was high, Uganda earned $433 million from the crop. In 2000/2001 its revenues from coffee slumped to $110 million even though it sold more beans. The value of the debt relief, paid by Western taxpayers and intended as a helping hand out of poverty, was wiped out by the collapse of coffee revenues.

In Kampala I first visited the Uganda Coffee Development Authority, housed in a down-at-heel 1960s-style block near the centre of town. Once past the armed guard on the narrow concrete stairwell, I climbed up several floors to the office of William Naggaga, the board secretary of the organization. A sophisticated former diplomat who had lived in London for many years, he agreed that in one way the root of the crisis at the time was quite simple.

'Global excess production, that's the problem. More coffee is being produced than is being drunk. It's very comfortable for the roasters. There is a carry-over from each year and they have accumulated stocks, which have now become the punishing stocks. Vietnam was encouraged to go from one million bags of coffee a year to fourteen million bags a year by the World Bank and the US government. It was encouraged to produce for a market which was already balanced. Nobody seems to have thought about it. Would you like a cup of coffee?'

He brought a tray to the table and I had my first taste of African coffee on East African soil. It was milky and very weak. 'Our earnings have fallen by more than fifty per cent,' Naggaga continued. 'It's a vicious circle: when the price goes down, the level of care farmers put into it depreciates. They don't tend their crops; the quality is low. By some coincidence the excess in production is the same as the volume of low-quality coffee being produced. But there are roasting techniques now that allow them to make use of low-quality beans. Before the liberalization of the coffee market here there was no export of black beans. We destroyed them. They don't taste good. But now they blend them to get rid of the taste, and they use new steaming methods to reduce the bitterness. We had to go to the minister to allow us to include them as an export, because they were not exportable grade in Uganda. We actually had to seek permission and a change of regulations to export black beans.'

But of course, the problem, both then and now, was about more than just supply and demand out of kilter. 'The roasters are taking too much out. They are so powerful they can determine the price. This is a monopolistic situation, not a free market. Just think of it, five men from the big companies – they are all men, I wish they were women, things might be different – sitting in a room and deciding the fate of twenty-five million coffee farmers around the world.'

One way developing countries could increase their share of the final value of the coffee sold would be to process more of it themselves. But breaking into that so-called added-value market is almost impossible. Once processed or manufactured, agricultural goods generally face punitive tariffs when imported into the West. Coffee imported from many countries faces EU tariffs that escalate the more it is processed. Parts of Africa have preferential terms, so this is not the obstacle with Ugandan coffee, but there are other barriers. 'The brands are so powerful, they control the distribution chains. They've worked out their deals and discounts with the retailers. It is very difficult for anyone else to penetrate that part of the market where the value is added,' said Mr Naggaga.

I asked him if he was against globalization. 'No, globalization is good, but taken in this way it is madness. A few men should not decide what millions of people eat and drink. I'm telling you, it is us today. But it may be you tomorrow. Make some noise.'

In the streets outside, a pleasant, cooling breeze had got up from the capital's seven hills. The central hill is famous for its parks and extraordinary birds. Here the flat tops of the acacia trees have been colonized by giant Maribou storks. Like vultures with their scavenging appetites and flesh-coloured wattles, their oversized bodies seem impossibly large for the slender branches of the trees on which they have made their comfortable nests.

I took a taxi next to Ugacof, the Ugandan coffee exporters' association. Like many of the taxis in Kampala, the suspension in this one was on its last legs, and as we headed for the outskirts of the capital, it felt as though the bottom had dropped out of the car and we were bumping along the ground. Meanwhile, most of the road ahead had been taken up by a huge convoy of new

Toyota pick-up trucks, each fitted with giant hoardings and pumping out music advertising Pepsi. We were forced to stutter along in its wake.

When we reached the headquarters of Ugacof, beyond the containers being loaded and unloaded with coffee beans, they looked like a colonial relic, a long verandahed building shaded by palm trees and surrounded by immaculate grass and flowering shrubs. The exporters here send coffee to the big roasters, but their margins are tiny, squeezed like everyone else's down the chain.

One of the managers, Claude Auberson, had agreed to see me, and while I waited, I flicked through the technical manuals on coffee production in the reception area, wondering what to make of them. 'High roasts are preferred in the US because they mask poor blending, dirty machines and stale coffee ... bitterness is reduced by the addition of sucrose, sodium chloride or citric acid ... Hydrocolloids in general decrease the perception of bitterness ... The bitterness is weakened when polyphenols are introduced ...'

Eventually I was ushered into the airy office of M. Auberson, a tall, mustachioed Frenchman, who was studying the market prices on his screen. 'The [coffee commodity trading] markets, in New York for arabica and London for robusta, were meant to help stabilize prices for producers by setting the price, but now they are the playground for speculators who have nothing to do with the industry. It's added to volatility but you can't stop people trading,' he said, shrugging and motioning me to a seat.

Auberson had worked in Africa for thirty years and was frank about the extent of corruption and its effect on any efforts to introduce stabilization mechanisms. But, as he saw it, the real problem was that nearly all the money was going somewhere between the point at which the beans are imported to Europe and the point at which the product reaches the shelf. 'If you ask the roasters what their excuse is, they will say that thirty per cent of the retail price goes on advertising and packaging. But where is the rest going? We are too small. We have no power. These large roasters have immense power and they are pushing most of the risk down the chain. Have you heard of "vendor-managed inventories"? This is how it works now. Suppliers have to keep huge stocks available near the roasters' factories ready for just when they want them, without commitment on their side, so the manufacturers can order "just in time". The suppliers carry all the risk and cost. It's outrageous, well, I suppose it's smart business if you can get it. And they can, because they are big transnationals, so no one can stop them.'

'What about fair trade, doesn't that help?' I asked.

'It's a drop on a hot stone.'

Nestlé told me that it was not in favour of volatile coffee prices. It argued that when the price drops, roast ground coffee became cheaper in relation to its instant brands and made them less competitive. Furthermore, its costs are only partly made up of raw materials. It has much more invested in capital-intensive processing machinery and spends heavily on advertising and marketing. It has supported international efforts to stabilize the price. But the main problem, it argued, was fluctuations in supply and demand.

The following day I drove down to the coffee-growing areas near Lake Victoria, with my guide from Oxfam, Monica Asekenye. This was where the cheaper robusta coffee is grown, to be used in blends with the better-quality arabicas or in instant coffee. We followed the thin strip of road between the oxide-red dust edges on either side. It stretched ahead, straight and empty all the way to the Congo. First came the papyrus swamps with their feathery foliage and pythons, then scenes of breathtaking tropical beauty as we passed through wooded hills and mile upon mile of smallholdings. Small shacks by the road offered handfuls of fruit. Everywhere women were tilling their patches, planting sweet potatoes, hoeing their yams, or tending the cassava growing beside their sugar cane.

After a few hours we reached Mgipi Epicenter, a tiny cluster of shacks on the road, and turned off the tarmac on to a red dirt track. Dozens of birds rose up in front of us – lilac-breasted rollers, doves, red bishops, little brown jobs too quick to identify, fleeing the rare motorized disturbance. Long-horned cattle glanced up briefly from their grazing. We rattled for half an hour along tiny, endlessly forking tracks in our own cloud of dust until eventually we reached a clearing that was Kituntu village and found the adobe hut of coffee farmer John Kafuluzi.

His coffee was organic by default, manured with cow dung and hand-weeded and hand-harvested, since he could not afford agrochemicals. The bushes were interplanted with bananas, sweet potatoes and other subsistence crops on which he and his family lived.

John's mother, children and his sister's family came out to greet us and we sat on wooden boxes to talk. On John's knee, a listless child, his youngest at just eighteen months old, drifted in and out of fevered sleep. She had malaria, as did three of her siblings. Her brother standing nearby had the tight, swollen belly of the malnourished. At the other end of the track a strange caterpillar appeared. Four small pairs of scurrying legs sticking out from under an upturned 1960s sofa were making their way towards us. Some of John's other children had been to a neighbour's to borrow seating for the foreigner.

Our translator was trying to explain to John how much a cup of coffee sold for in a London café. 'One cup, five thousand Ugandan shillings?' A confused smile flickered across his face, registering disbelief, but then his eyes filled with tears. 'No, you mean one kilo, no, no, this is painful to hear. I only got two hundred shillings a kilo for my coffee this year.' John's eldest sons Bruno and Michael had to drop out of school when prices fell because the family could no longer afford the fees. They had hoped to train to be doctors or accountants. In the good years the cash from their small coffee crop was enough to send everyone to school. Now the children were taking turns to go to school instead. Their clothes were torn and stained. Some of the coffee bushes were neglected; no longer worth the effort of tending.

Inside the hut, just visible through the half-open door, an old man was lying on the floor on a thin mattress, the fragile bones of his wasted back rising prominently each time he took a shallow breath. Peter Kafuluzi, John's father, who had farmed coffee here for forty-five years, was dying, but the family could not afford medicine for him. They had spent their savings the previous year on his treatment. Medicine for the children's malaria would have cost them up to 5,000 shillings.

The soil here is fertile and alluvial, capable of producing surplus. It has ample rainfall and needs no irrigation or fertilizer. The vegetation is so lush, the birdsong so rich, it is hard to understand how people can be going hungry. In good times, the coffee made enough money for families to pay for the essentials: education, medicine, clothes and roofing materials and extra food to supplement their limited subsistence diets with a bit of meat or milk. But without coffee they had nothing to sell for cash.

John didn't know why he got so little for his crop but thought the local middlemen must be cheating. In fact, Oxfam studied the chain and discovered that at the beginning of 2002, a Ugandan farmer received 14 cents (US) for 1kg of beans. The local middleman who transported it to the mill took 5 cents profit, as did the miller, and the cost of transport to Kampala added a further 2 cents, making the cost of the coffee when it arrived at the exporter's warehouse 26 cents. The exporter, operating on a tiny margin and minimal return on his capital-intensive machinery to dry, grade and pack the beans, added 19 cents to the kilo, taking it up to 45 cents. Freight, the importer's costs and margins took the price to $1.64 when it reached the factory of one of the giant roasting companies. By the time that same kilo was sold in the shops in the form of instant coffee it was worth $26.40, or 7,000 per cent more than the farmer got for it.

On our way back to Kampala, we dropped in at a nursery

which raised coffee seedlings. A young man approached me to say he wanted to go to school. He'd had to drop out because there was no money. 'I am very disappointed. This was my future.' Soon there was a small crowd of children around us saying the same thing.

Arabica coffee, grown at high altitudes and with a finer taste, fetches higher prices than robusta, but that had done little to insulate its farmers from the crisis. The drive up to one of the main arabica areas of Uganda took us in the opposite direction, along the road to Kenya and the foothills of Mount Elgon, the volcanic mountain that straddles the border. The road this side of the country runs past the Coca-Cola factory, built with government approval, in what was a 'preserved wetland' area, despite a hunger strike protest by a local MP, then through the old colonial estates of tea and sugar plantations, where monoculture had created a sea of emerald green.

Eventually you come to Mbale, the small outpost at the base of Mount Elgon. As we approached the town, the usual roadside procession of bare-footed women in African dress carrying firewood on their heads gave way to one of heavily veiled women in Muslim burqas. This is the home of the Islamic university, supported by Saudi money. Uganda has been predominantly Christian since nineteenth-century Western Church missionaries came proselytizing and offering not only religion but also free medicine and education. But Mbale also has a Muslim community which is attracting converts. 'A different god has more money than yours now and offers free education,' our driver explained.

On the edge of Mbale, near the shaded streets of the faded old colonial town, we found the mill and warehouse of the now privatized Bugisu co-operative union to which many of the coffee growers of the area deliver their beans.

We arrived towards the end of the day, the hour when children file along the roads carrying their yellow jerrycans to fetch water from the wells. The notices on the door of the office next to the milling factory were not encouraging. 'Anyone opting to do industrial research here should try elsewhere because we have already had enough of them,' said one. Beneath it was another: 'Hitherto every Tom, Dick and Harry have been making personal calls using office telephones. Such calls are henceforth prohibited and non-compliance or complicity shall lead to stern punishments of the culprits, by order of the admin manager.' Peering through the window, I could see battered filing cabinets, overflowing with yellowing cardboard files, and papers and invoices stacked in dusty piles on top, but the chair behind the tin desk was unoccupied. The manager, Wamutu Samuel, had attended a funeral that week, and had been in court over a land dispute. We were told to come back tomorrow.

When we met the following day, Wamutu looked exhausted, the whites of his brown eyes covered with a yellowy film. He mumbled through his figures on prices before and after liberalization and I had to strain to hear him above the sound of constantly falling coffee beans from the mill behind. But the message was the same. The quality had declined, the multinationals had arrived at the farm gate, fair trade and organic coffees gave them a premium and offered hope to some farmers, but so far the quantities involved were small.

Finally Wamutu said he would find someone to introduce us to the arabica farmers and we set off, following the road that winds steeply up into a gorge on the edge of Mount Elgon. Under a bright blue sky, streaked with thin cloud, we climbed up to the wooded hills. The slopes of the mountain were planted with bananas and 'Irish potatoes', the staple crops, and everywhere was verdant. George Sakwa, his wife Topista and their family live near the top of the mountain in the tiny remote village of Buginyanya.

They had been up since before dawn, seven of them labouring in the steep terraces of their coffee garden for five hours, before returning to their hut for breakfast of half a cup of tea with a little sugar. They used to employ casual labour to help with the coffee, but couldn't afford it now and anyway, since there was no money to send them to school any more, the children were free to work. In a good year, George had been able to get 1 million Ugandan shillings for his high-quality arabica, but the previous year he had got less than half that. All the spare money was then spent on his elder son Boniface's school fees. The other children were sent home because he couldn't pay.

The Sakwas sold a bit of land in 2001 to keep the children at school but that reduced their ability to earn money even further. 'We have no other source of income, which is why my house is in such bad shape,' George told me. He took me inside. One room was given over to the goats, another to his stores of coffee. He was hanging on before selling the year's harvest, hoping the price would pick up. It was dark apart from the light glinting through holes in the tin roof.

The house leaked, the timbers were beginning to rot, and the mud plaster had come off the walls in large chunks. They had patched the roof where they could with papyrus, but the children still got wet when it rained and were suffering from respiratory problems. Their clothes and blankets were so worn they had nothing left to cover themselves with at night to keep the mosquitoes off. Several of the children had malaria. They did not have enough to eat. They had also had to give up buying soap, George explained, though without a trace of anger or self-pity. He had a fine young wife, Topista – his third – and sixteen children. They would help him survive.

To the side of the house in a circular mud hut that was the family kitchen, an eight-year-old girl was feeding the tiny twigs she had gathered from the woods into a fire over which she was making a maize-meal porridge, their meal for the day. Behind the hut under the dappled shade of a stand of trees, I noticed the mounds of four tiny graves. Topista was mother to nine of George's children, but four had died already. Malaria claimed two, another died in an accident with hot water in the hut, and another of an unexplained fever. Their nearest hospital was in

Mbale. They had no money for transport, none for medicine either.

Driving back to the airport the following day, I passed a government billboard, a sign erected in more optimistic times, proudly declaring, 'Coffee eradicates poverty.'

A decade on, and with Uganda experiencing the impacts of climate change, farmers had suffered both extreme rainfall and drought, higher temperatures and unprecedented levels of pests, which they feared could threatened the survival of the industry in coming years. The discovery of oil reserves brought the promise of exciting new revenues, but with Museveni increasingly shifting from constitutional government to a prolonged rule based on patronage, few believed growing political and social tensions would be removed without wider development. Decent sources of livelihoods for the rural poor were still needed. The 2.5 million people, or 8 per cent of the population, who depended on coffee for their main income were still impoverished.

When I got back to England, I bought a jar of instant and punctured its tight paper seal. A rich smell of fresh coffee wafted up. When coffee is made into instant, it is brewed, concentrated and then dried. In the process, much of the aroma is lost, but manufacturers are allowed to add volatile oils that carry the smell back into the jar. Contemplating this ingenious and perfectly legal deception, I wondered whether what I had seen could really be as simple as it seemed.

These were markets that were not working, in which too much of the value had been sucked out from the bottom and transferred to the top. Our complicated system of subsidies, tariffs and other trade distortions had helped create this new architecture.

The shift in the distribution of power in the coffee chain can be seen in most food sectors where clusters of agribusiness corporations now rule the roost. This has not happened by accident but by design, and has been the corollary of post-war government policy.

Perhaps the most significant of these complexes is that which dominates trading and processing in grains and oilseeds, that is corn, wheat, soya, rice and palm. This is where the largest quantities of commodities, the building blocks that go into nearly all processed foods, are bought and sold. Although a handful of companies account for the lion's share of these markets, their names have largely slipped under the radar of most European consumers. They supply most of the food industry with its raw material for manufacturing; they play the markets, have vastly complicated corporate structures to enable them to shift transactions and profits from subsidiary to subsidiary, while also trading in futures and derivatives; they control refining and crushing plants, and organize shipping and storage, but without their own brand names and retail presence we have mostly been unaware of them. They prefer it that way.

Nevertheless by mid-morning snacktime you will certainly have encountered their products several times wherever you are in the world, whether it is the corn in your flakes, the wheat in your bread, the orange in your juice, the sugar in your jam, the chocolate on your biscuit, the coffee in your cup. By the end of the day, if you've eaten beef, chicken or pork, consumed anything containing salt, gums, starches, gluten, sweeteners or fats, or bought a ready meal or a takeaway, they will have shaped your consumption even further.

Four giant transnationals dominate the raw materials of the global food system. Known as the ABCD group for the alphabetic convenience of their initials, ADM, Bunge, Cargill and (Louis) Dreyfus, account for between 75 per cent and 90 per cent of the global grain trade, according to estimates. Figures cannot be given with confidence, however, because two of the companies are privately owned and do not give out market shares. Scale, reach and secrecy are part of their weaponry. The detailed knowledge they have of what is being produced and held where is part of their commercial advantage when trading and negotiating price.

A fifth name has been added to their ranks more recently. Swiss-based Glencore, better known for its activities in crude oil and other extractive industries, was revealed to be a grain and oilseed trader on a scale previously not fully understood when the private company published figures for the first time as it prepared for a £37 billion flotation on the London stock exchange in 2011. It does not process agricultural commodities but accounted for 9 per cent of traded volumes in grains and 4.5 per cent of oilseeds that year.

US-based Cargill is the largest private company in the world – and famous for its secrecy. Its headquarters is a mock-Tudor meets mock-French chateau in Minnetonka in the US Midwest, where the company was founded by a family of grain traders in 1865. Today, it is still majority-owned by descendants of the family. Its main commodity-trading operation is run out of the tax haven of Switzerland. Its sales were $137 billion in 2013, and its net earnings were $2.3 billion.

As well as being a leading player in the trading, processing and transporting of the most important agricultural commodities, from soya to corn, wheat, cocoa, sugar and meats, it is one of the world largest hedge funds. It makes starches, gums, proteins, sweeteners, and animal feed and biofuels. Its interests have also included fertilizers. When Gordon Brown, as prime minister, convened a summit of movers in the food system in London to discuss the 2008 food crisis, Cargill was invited. When Walkers crisps had an image problem with the saturated fats in its products, Cargill came to the rescue, having a large acreage of land in eastern Europe planted with a new variety of 'Sunseed' sunflowers to produce a different fat profile.

Cargill is responsible for about half of all McDonald's chicken products across Europe. It sells bulk fats to Unilever. It makes low-calorie sweeteners for big brand colas and high-fructose corn syrups for soft drinks.

When the US wanted to appoint someone to lead the reconstruction of agriculture in Iraq, it turned to former Cargill

executive Dan Amstutz. In China, where Cargill has a joint ven-
ture with Monsanto, to whom it sold its enormous seed interests
a decade ago, it has trained over 2 million farmers in the
American way of agriculture. Over that same decade, Cargill,
ADM and Bunge are thought to have acquired about 80 per
cent of China's soya processing capacity. More recently, Cargill
has been moving up the food chain into high-value, hi-tech
additives and what it calls 'food solutions', mixes of flavouring
and texturizing additives for the manufacturing industry.

Louis Dreyfus, established in 1851, is also private and still family owned, headquartered in Paris but again trading largely out
of Switzerland. It gives no figures and never comments to the
media, but its estimated revenues in 2009 were £34 billion. As
well as its large presence in coffee bean trading, it has enormous
grain, sugar and energy trading interests around the world,
although in recent years it has concentrated on financial aspects
of commodity trading.

Bunge, which expanded through the late nineteenth century
as a grain trader in South America, is now incorporated in the
tax haven of Bermuda but its headquarters are in the US. Its net
revenues in 2012 were $61 billion, and net earnings were down
from a high of $2.3 billion in 2010 to $64 million in 2012, following a series of write-downs in parts of the business it was
intending to sell. It is a leading processor of oilseeds, and producer and trader of grains, sugar and bioenergy. It has also been a
key player in the global fertilizer market.

ADM, or Archer Daniels Midland, is incorporated in the US
tax-haven state of Delaware and headquartered in Illinois. Its
revenues in 2012 were $89 billion and its earnings were $1.2 billion.
ADM's origins go back to a US seed-crushing business begun
in 1902. It has built up vast interests in trading, processing and
transporting soya and other oilseeds, and corn, wheat, cocoa and
other agricultural commodities. It is a leading manufacturer of
oils, corn sweeteners, flour, biofuels, food additives from gums to
gluten, lecithin, soya isolates and animal feed ingredients.

These companies dominate the processing industry that divides soya beans into oil for food manufacturing and protein meal for animal feed. The latter has made the livestock revolution, in which animals are fed intensively on a fast-food diet of grains rather than grass, possible. Without their concentrated protein feeds, cheap industrialized chicken would not exist. They take corn and turn it into the myriad forms of sugars and starch from which highly processed food products are built.

To add to the concentration of power, Cargill, ADM and Bunge have strategic alliances and joint ventures with the seed and agrochemical companies that dominate the agricultural inputs part of the global food system. Four firms, Monsanto (incorporated in Delaware, HQ in Missouri), Dupont (incorporated and HQ in Delaware), Syngenta (incorporated and HQ in Switzerland) and Limagrain, a French-based international co-operative, account for over 50 per cent of global seed sales, for example.

In agrochemicals, six firms, DuPont, Monsanto, Syngenta, Dow (incorporated in Delaware, HQ in Michigan), and the two German chemical giants Bayer and BASF, control three quarters of the market. The predominance of tax haven locations in these lists is no accident.

(For more information on how these companies shape the food system and determine what we eat, see my book *Eat Your Heart Out*.)

It was seeing the physical scale of this agri-industrial complex on the ground in Latin America that helped me to understand its significance.

The Pampas of Argentina are just as my old geography textbooks described them: vast flat plains stretching to distant horizons, white heads of tall grasses catching the early light. A great empty road ploughs a furrow from Buenos Aires through mile upon mile of fertile lands towards the ports on the great South American waterway, the Paraná river.

The Argentinian beef cattle I learned about at school and which used to be synonymous with this region – it makes up one of the world's most expansive grazing lands – were not much in evidence when I visited in 2011, however. Instead you could see the transnational grain complex everywhere.

The way-markers now were not cattle ranches but grain silos, agricultural hangars for harvesting machines, and banner adverts across nearly every field for agrochemicals and genetically modified soya seed.

Occasionally, the green and orange logo of Monsanto's Roundup glyphosate herbicide gave way to an election poster for the Perónist president, Cristina Kirchner, or to a rival chemical or seed company's billboard. But there was no question who dominated the landscape here.

Less visible at first were the big transnational exporters. But when, after hours of monotonous driving, I reached the ports of Rosario and San Lorenzo-San Martín they were unmissable: Cargill, ADM, Bunge and Dreyfus, with their dozens of crushing plants, biodiesel refineries, docks, grain terminals and elevators towering above the wide expanse of muddy river.

This is where about 55 million tonnes of soya a year, worth $24 billion, starts a journey through the docks to the importing countries – China, India and Europe. So much grain passes through these ports that traffic jams of some of the world's largest container ships have built up which are two weeks long.

The trade here had become a key battleground in the fight over the global food system. For in South America, those who control the food chain, make money from it and determine what we eat were at the heart of a fierce political debate.

The Argentinian authorities had taken the dramatic step of suspending all four big transnational traders from their export register that year, accusing them of tax evasion. Then it expelled Bunge from the register altogether.

The industrial soya complex arrived in Argentina from North America with a bang when the government approved the planting of genetically modified crops for the first time in 1996. Since then soya production had gone from about 6 million hectares to 17 million, and 60 per cent of productive land had been given over to the monocrop.

Many of the beef cattle had been squeezed into US-style feed-lots to be fattened on grain instead of grass, and 2.5 million hectares of woods had been lost.

More recently, the Chinese had arrived. They had signed a deal in 2011 with the government of Patagonia's Río Negro province giving them access to an area of land larger than Cornwall. It put in place the framework for the Chinese state-owned agribusiness company Beidahuang to acquire hundreds of thousands of acres of privately owned farmland, along with irrigation rights and a concession of the huge San Antonio port. Beidahuang, based in the north-eastern province of Heilongjiang, is the leading soya producer in China and one of the country's five largest soya processors. It also raises more than 600,000 cows, 1.3 million pigs and more than 6 million chickens at any one time. It had been acquiring tracts of land in the Philippines too, and buying palm plantations and grain terminals as it pursued the Chinese government's policy of securing food supply lines from abroad.

The province was pleased with what it saw as an important agreement to develop its economy, but Argentinian environmental groups and constitutional experts were outraged. Eduardo Barcesat, a top constitutional lawyer, had been helping the federal government of the Argentinian president draft legislation that would restrict foreign ownership of Argentinian land. The laws would also provide, for the first time, a full register of all landholding so that authorities could keep track of who owned what.

'Chinese and Indian people have been coming to Argentina over the last five years and would be happy to buy all our land, whatever the price. American businesses have been buying access to our water,' Barcesat told me. 'We need our own people to eat well first, and after that we can feed the rest of the world. We want more small and middle-sized owners, we don't like the excessive concentration, and we want farmers who will be careful with the land, not exploit it.'

Environmentalists in Río Negro feared the Chinese arrival would mean the heavy use of agrochemicals and ecological degradation and would place severe strain on the region's water resources. Some of the land in question was virgin forest that would be deforested.

The campaigners said that since soya cultivation was highly mechanized it would prompt unemployment in the area, as it had elsewhere in the country, where many rural communities had seen an increase in deep poverty as jobs had been lost with the arrival of soya farming. They were worried too about the emergence of superweeds resistant to pesticides and the impact on human health of such heavy use of agrochemicals.

But soya had turned Argentina into a global agricultural powerhouse alongside Brazil. These two countries are now, along with the US, the largest exporters of soya in the world.

Back in the capital I had arranged to meet Ricardo Echegaray, head of the Argentinian revenue service (Afip), and a close ally of the president. Soya planted on top of soya, with no pause to till the soil, had without question helped pay farm debts since Argentina's financial collapse in 2001 but, according to the revenue boss, the transnational traders were exporting not just the soya but much of their vast profits out of Argentina as well.

The companies all denied the allegation of tax evasion and said they would defend themselves vigorously. At the time of writing, some two years later, the battle between them and the state was still ongoing. The Argentinian government's assessment was that grain traders, including the big four and other regional players, owed nearly $1 billion in tax that should have been paid in previous years.

Echegaray detailed the charges for me in a remarkably frank discussion in the grand surroundings of the presidential offices.

He said he had begun investigating Argentina's large business taxpayers towards the end of 2008, cross-checking information given to his authorities with that from other countries where their exports were destined, by making use of tax information exchange treaties – some of which had been newly signed in the wake of the global financial crash. He also cross-checked declarations made to Argentinian customs with corporate income tax returns.

He said he had evidence from his detailed inquiry that all four traders had submitted false declarations of sales and routed profits through tax havens or their headquarters, in contravention of Argentinian tax law. He also alleged they had on occasion used phantom firms to buy grain. He further alleged that they had inflated costs in Argentina to reduce taxable profits or claim tax credits there.

'These companies have descended into criminality. The agro-exporters have extracted the most profit from the economy here in recent years, and our policy is that those who gain most should pay most. We have noticed the companies with the biggest sales show the least profits here. But all the work is done here. The soil is Argentinian, the harvest is done with Argentinian machinery by Argentinians, it is transported on Argentinian roads, through Argentinian ports. It uses Argentinian services and resources – so why are all the gains made in Argentina appearing on paper in other countries?'

The Afip inquiry focused on the traders' sales to Uruguay, among other low-tax jurisdictions.

Echegaray said Bunge had set up an office in the tax-free zone of Montevideo through which it began routing its exports after 2007, from which point it declared no gains in Argentina. He alleged his checks had revealed that Bunge employed only a handful of people in Uruguay's capital, and that it had no real imports or exports from that office other than small items for those staff. Bunge denied the allegations absolutely and was adamant it had broken no laws or tax rules. 'We believe that we have done nothing wrong and that our past tax payments are complete. This is an issue that is not unique to Bunge, or even our industry. We will continue to take the appropriate legal steps to defend ourselves,' it said in a statement.

Echegaray alleged that Cargill had also used Uruguay and Swiss subsidiaries to evade taxes in Argentina. Cargill said: 'All the allegations made about Cargill are false. Cargill complies with all Argentine tax and customs regulations. We are vigorously defending various tax and customs audits and litigation.'

ADM responded that it 'conducts business in accordance with the laws, including those governing tax obligations, in the countries where we operate. We are co-operating with Afip to successfully resolve this situation.'

Dreyfus declined to comment, but according to Ciara, the grain exporters' trade association in Argentina, it too denied all the charges. Ciara's president, Alberto Rodriguez, described the government's claims of tax evasion as political posturing.

The neoliberal consensus of the last two and a half decades, in which emerging economies have been encouraged to open up their agricultural markets and export raw materials while the US and EU have maintained their farming subsidies, is under powerful challenge in South America.

Left-wing governments, including Kirchner's in Argentina, are reclaiming food sovereignty and a greater share of the profits. Part of that has involved taking on the big concentrations of corporate power that characterize many parts of the global food system – 'the untouchables', as one Argentinian official described them.

Eduardo Barcesat, the constitutional lawyer, agreed that the tax moves were a political decision. 'The US big traders control most of the storage and the price,' he said. 'This is a move to put things in order: no more cheating. Argentina is not getting enough of the value of its resources. We are colonized and we have to be free.'

★

This extraordinary clustering of power and money in the global food trade has been identified by aid agencies and academics as one of the structural flaws of the current system. At each stage a handful of players dominate, not just in primary agriculture but in food manufacturing and retailing. The result, according to Oxfam in a major report in 2011 warning that staple food prices are likely to more than double by 2030, is that 'they extract much of the value along the chain, while costs and risks cascade down on to the weakest participants, generally the farmers and labourers at the bottom'. The resources of the least developed countries – land, water, soil, plantation labour – are taken up by production but the benefit accrues not to them but instead to the most developed economies, in patterns familiar from colonization.

Oxfam was just the latest in a long line of critics to highlight this corporate concentration as a root cause of hunger and poverty. The ABCD group said they welcome informed debate but that, as far as they were concerned, their operations were the vital waters that kept food and its finance flowing from those who can grow it to those who need to consume it. Scale enables them to be highly efficient. The grain trade is capital intensive; their profits reflect the fact that they invest heavily in storage facilities, port and transport infrastructure, and the crushing and grinding facilities that extract food's constituent parts, and they also take the risk from changing prices when they trade.

The emergence of this agri-industrial complex did not occur by chance but was fostered by Western governments with the billions of dollars, euros and pounds allocated by them to US and European agricultural subsidies. Before the Second World War, western Europe had largely depended on food surpluses from eastern Europe to supplement its own production, but its agricultural lands had been devastated by the war and the Iron Curtain was descending to the east. The surviving populations of both east and west faced acute food shortages. The US had encouraged its farmers to maximize production to help its allies during the war. It emerged with its agricultural base intact in 1945, and took on the role of feeding the world. It announced the Marshall Plan to rebuild shattered Western economies with financial aid. As well as playing a vital role in reconstruction and relieving the threat of a humanitarian crisis, the plan set the new terms of trade with the non-communist world. Tariff barriers for American goods were removed and a large part of the $13 billion in financial aid paid under the Marshall Plan between 1947 and 1952 was spent by European countries on imports of US food, animal feed and fertilizer. US farmers were given subsidies to deliver greater surpluses, so that in the five years following the war in Europe, the US supplied half of the world's total wheat trade, setting a pattern for grain trading for the decades to come. The American exports the plan delivered also created whole new patterns of consumption and drove the development of markets for the processed products of US surpluses, particularly of corn and soya.

With memories of food shortages and rationing still seared on to the minds of Europeans, their governments were determined to maximize production too. Most had already subsidized some of their farming before the war and taken over production during it; in the aftermath subsidies were used to encourage greater production. After the Treaty of Rome was signed in 1957 and the Common Market was formed, the European Community placed agriculture policy at its core. Farming subsidies were developed that aimed to make food plentiful and affordable, while also making sure farmers were paid well enough to prosper. By the 1980s, despite several changes to the system, this subsidized production was generating huge surpluses and enormous waste, and agriculture was accounting for 70 per cent of the whole EC budget. Much of the excess was dumped at prices below the cost of production on world markets where it undermined farmers in poor countries.

From 1947 to 1994 the General Agreement on Tariffs and

Trade (GATT) was the forum for global negotiations about trade rules. The World Trade Organization (WTO) came into being at the beginning of 1995, at the end of the Uruguay round of GATT talks, which were held between 1986 and 1994. WTO has been the forum since then for negotiating international trade rules. Agriculture was included in the original GATT talks but the Uruguay round's agreement specifically committed countries to lifting trade restrictions and abolishing distorting subsidies.

Poor countries were forced to open up their markets, and the international financial institutions made doing so a condition of loans and aid. Yet rich Western countries kept their quotas and continued to subsidize their agriculture, so that when poor countries did liberalize, cheap subsidized goods would flood in and put local food producers out of business. Import tariffs meanwhile have made it harder for poorer countries to switch their production to more lucrative processed food. The obvious answer for a Ugandan coffee farmer faced with volatile prices is to grow something else, but in reality their choices are limited. They might grow sugar but then find themselves undercut by Western imports. And, as William Naggaga said, breaking in to the more valuable instant coffee market is almost impossible.

Countries in the OECD, the club of affluent economies, have in fact continued to spend over $250 billion a year supporting their farming sectors. Despite repeated reforms, the EU spent €55 billion in 2012 on its common agricultural policy. Consumers paid twice, once in higher taxes to fund subsidies and a second time through high food prices; it has been estimated that the Common Agricultural Policy (CAP) costs a typical British or European family of four an extra €1,000 a year.

Despite a commitment to reduce farm subsidies President Bush's controversial Farm Bill in 2002 actually promised to raise them and allocated over $190 billion over a ten-year period to protect US agriculture.

Ten years later, intense political wrangling over the 2012 Farm Bill left it still being debated in 2013. Republicans wanted to see a deep cut in the element of food stamps paid to the poor while Democrats wanted the amount paid to rich farmers and agribusiness reduced – the top 10 per cent of companies have accounted for around 75 per cent of the agricultural subsidies according to some analyses. Although direct payments to farmers looked set to be cut, around $20 billion a year would still be transferred from US taxpayers to its agricultural sector via various subsidy mechanisms.

The latest Doha round of WTO negotiations was meant to be the 'developing' round in which tariffs would lowered and subsidies to agricultural produce would be cut to help poorer countries. But talks have been deadlocked and the process stalled, as industrialized countries argued for extending WTO influence to new issues such as freer foreign investment while the developing nations said they would like the changes they had been promised on subsidies and tariffs first. Meanwhile individual countries have increasingly got on with making 'bilateral' trade deals between themselves, in which the rush to secure supplies was more evident than concern about free unfettered trade. These would see China doing deals to buy more than two thirds of Brazil's soya exports in recent years.

For a long time the popular conception, encouraged by political rhetoric, was that Western agricultural subsidies went to keeping farmers in business. Information about who actually received the money was kept secret. Campaign groups both sides of the Atlantic had to fight hard to force details of where taxpayers' money was going out into the open. But eventually it became clear that agricultural subsidies were by and large corporate welfare. They have done precious little to protect small and family farms. (For a fuller account of the impact of farm subsidies on what we consume and who benefits from them, see *Eat Your Heart Out*.)

US Department of Agriculture figures show that the average

American corn farmer lost about $230 for each acre of corn planted over the five years to 2005. However nearly three quarters of the market value of US corn exports was being covered by payments in the form of various subsidies, from crop insurance payments to export refunds, from the US government. The figure for rice was even higher, according to analysis by Oxfam. Just five crops accounted for 90 per cent of the money paid out in US agricultural subsidies between 1995 and 2005: corn, rice, wheat, soya beans and cotton. Sugar, dairy products and tobacco have also been heavily subsidized, but most fresh fruit and vegetable production has received minimal support. What subsidies have done, even as farmers have been driven off the land in their thousands, is keep agricultural commodities cheap for the transnational food corporations that use them to 'add value'.

Adding value means moving consumers up the food chain, from eating simple unprocessed foods that have low margins to eating processed products with far higher margins. You can add value to grain by turning it into higher value proteins to feed to animals for meat and dairy foods that you sell at greater margins. Or you can add value by taking subsidized commodity crops, breaking them down into their constituent parts and making them into long-life ingredients for snacks and ready meals that you can sell for far more than the sum of their parts. Added value here is added shareholder value, not nutritional value, which as a very rough rule of thumb I reckon is stripped away from whole foods in this process in inverse proportion to the shareholder value added.

The pattern has been the same in Europe. Until 2004, the names of those receiving payments under the Common Agriculture Policy had been, outrageously, kept secret. A campaign using new Freedom of Information (FoI) legislation briefly forced them out into the open. (A recent court judgment in Europe has ruled that making the information public infringes recipients' right to privacy, however, so once again several countries are refusing access to the information.) When I analysed

the data that was available for 2004 for the *Guardian* it became
clear that the bulk of the UK's CAP money was going to a very
small percentage of the largest farms and farm companies, and
nearly a third of the total CAP budget was being paid out in
export refunds to large companies and in BSE payments to
large-scale abattoirs and renderers contracted to clear up the
consequences of intensive production and its recurring outbreaks of disease.

The largest individual payments were going to transnational
food companies, and in the UK included companies such as
Tate & Lyle, Nestlé, Cadbury, Kraft and exporters of processed
dairy products. Suppliers of bulk sugars and concentrated fats to
processed food manufacturers were creaming it. Further freedom of information requests revealed a similar pattern, the
largest individual payments going to transnationals in other
European countries.

In 2009, transnational sugar companies were the largest bene-
ficiaries of CAP agricultural subsidies across Europe, according
to analysis from farmsubsidy.org, the campaign group behind
the original freedom of information battle. They were being
compensated as part of reforming the EU sugar regime of
subsidies.

Subsidies have in other words given an oligopoly of transnationals fixed prices for an extended period. They have provided
cheap raw materials for manufacturing the highly processed
foods sold for such high margins around the world.

By the 2000s this period of extravagant surplus was coming
to an end, however. Having promoted diets created from what it
could produce in abundance for export, the US wanted its food
surplus back to put into its cars as fuel. Europe, to a lesser extent,
wanted food for biofuels too. A growing and increasingly urbanized global population was shifting towards a more Western diet,
and increasing demand. We were moving rapidly from an era
taken up with the disposal of surplus to one characterized by a

scramble for resources and record prices, as Argentina's experience of foreign investment showed.

The scale of land grabs since the 2008 food crisis has been a barometer of the pressure on capacity to feed the world. Deals like those done by the Chinese in Patagonia have been proliferating. Research from the International Land Coalition, and Oxfam Novib, the Netherlands affiliate of Oxfam International, has identified more than 1,200 international land deals covering more than 80 million hectares since 2000 – the vast majority of them after 2007. More than 60 per cent of the land targeted was in Africa, often in countries where hunger is endemic. (The UN Food and Agriculture's director general warned in 2012 that private investors had turned parts of Africa into the 'wild west' in urgent need of a sheriff to restore the rule of law as they bought land to produce food or biofuels for export in countries where hunger and food security were serious problems.)

The context had changed dramatically and commodity prices were soaring, but agribusiness remained hooked on the subsidized ingredients upon which its economic model had been built. Persuading the populations of emerging economies, and even of those in the poorest countries living on less than $2 a day, to buy processed food was part of their strategy for maintaining growth, even as it became clearer and clearer that the planet would not be big enough to feed the world this way. But who could instruct globalized food systems to change direction? The problem now is that, having rigged markets for decades to help transnationals acquire their positions, they are too big for any individual government to control.

In 2013, no more than 500 companies controlled 70 per cent of the key decisions in the food system globally, according to Oxfam's research. They decide how key resources such as land, water, seeds, technologies and infrastructure are developed and used. They are able to set the rules around prices, costs and standards. They are the principal distributors and users of the commodity fats, sugars, starches and proteins our system delivers in such abundance.

In food manufacturing, whether for sales via supermarkets or fast-food restaurants, a dozen or so giant global players own the brands that feature so large in industrialized diets. The Forbes 2000 ranking in April 2013 lists Nestlé as the largest, with annual global sales of over $100 billion from brands that span breakfast cereals, confectionery, coffee and chocolate, baby milks and foods, bottled water, sauces and pet food. It is followed by Unilever (sales $67.7 billion), with its portfolio of brands including ice cream, margarine and spreads, mayonnaise, teas, soups and sauces as well as soaps. Mars (an estimated $52 billion in sales – as a private company it does not publish full accounts) is best known for its confectionery and chewing gum but also owns Dolmio, Uncle Ben's rice, Seeds of Change, and hot chocolate and coffee brands.

In drinks and snacks, at the time of the ranking, PepsiCo had sales of $65.5 billion a year (it owns Tropicana juices and Walkers crisps as well as its cola and other snack brands). Coca-Cola came in with sales of $48 billion.

Mondalēz (sales $35 billion) is now the corporation behind Cadbury, Suchard, Green & Black's, several leading brands of biscuit, chewing gum and coffee, and Philadelphia cream cheese.

The best-selling yoghurts and yoghurt drinks Actimel and Activia belong to Danone (sales $27.5 billion), along with bottled water brands and processed desserts. Associated British Foods (sales $19.8 billion) through its subsidiary Allied Bakeries owns bread brands Allinson, Kingsmill and Sunblest, as well as sugars, teas, vegetable oils, ice creams, corn starches, soup bases and sauces. Kraft Foods (sales $18.3 billion) is now the US segment of sales, split off from the rest of Kraft and its brands, which have been renamed Mondalēz.

General Mills (sales $17.4 billion) and Kellogg's ($14.2 billion) both produce leading breakfast cereal brands while General Mills also has ice cream, baking products, snacks, soups and yoghurts and desserts in its portfolio.

McDonald's sales were $27.6 billion, while Compass Group, the catering giant that supplies restaurants, schools and other institutions around the world, topped $27.3 billion.

These companies are so big their scale is hard to absorb from a catalogue of revenues and profits. But to put them in context, Nestlé's revenues in 2012 were larger than the GDP of all but seventy of the world's countries. Its $100 billion in sales was very nearly double the GDP of Uganda ($51 billion), and comfortably exceeded the GDPs of other coffee producing countries such as Guatemala ($78 billion) and Costa Rica ($59 billion).

These processed food manufacturers enjoyed uninterrupted growth between the Second World War and the 1980s when the supermarkets became sufficiently powerful to challenge them. As Professor Tim Lang has pointed out, the number of people living in cities grew from 10 per cent to 50 per cent of the global population in that period, and the trend is accelerating. The global population is both growing in number and living longer, providing food companies with a natural target for their convenience products. But they are also increasingly under pressure as it becomes clear that junk diets high in energy-dense but nutrient-light over-processed foods are the vectors of a global epidemic of diet-related disease.

Although most have sought to diversify and add healthier products to their portfolios, they are in a bind here, as a detailed investigation by JP Morgan's financial analysts made clear.

In a report in 2006 on how the food industry was responding to the obesity crisis, they explained that:

The profitability of the vast majority of food and beverage categories usually regarded as healthy (for example, water, dairy, fruit/vegetables) is below industry average. This certainly creates a dilemma for companies who enjoy above-industry-average margins (e.g. confectionery, hot beverages, snack producers) and would like to enter the healthier segments of the market.

The simple unprocessed foods we need to eat more of – staples such as fruit, vegetables, whole grains and pulses – only give manufacturers and processors a 3–6 per cent operating margin. You don't make big margins selling humble oats in a plain package for porridge. Relatively simple processed foods like cheese or plain yoghurt give 9–12 per cent margins. Highly processed cereals, snacks, biscuits, soft drinks, desserts and confectionery, on the other hand, give brand manufacturers more than 15 per cent margins. Even higher margins can be gained from specialist nutrition products such as baby food and sports drinks. There's little incentive for manufacturers to move into selling products that are less processed. They have to stay high up what industry describes as the 'value chain' by developing new products within their existing categories which can command premium prices because they claim to be healthier. That's why in the three years to the beginning of 2006 two thirds of product launches within the food industry fell into the category of foods that were 'light', 'diet', 'better for you' or those labelled 'enriched with', or that made other health claims. These can be priced at a premium of up to 400 per cent, according to the analysts.

This for me is the crux of the problem. What the rest of us need is for these unhealthy categories simply to wither. We don't need processed foods made from the same old commodity ingredients dressed up with the odd added nutrient for which great claims are made. We need to return to whole foods and eat less processed food, full stop. And we need a redistribution of the money made in the food chain, away from the transnational traders and manufacturers and back towards the primary producers and those who are employed in the factories they own or to which they outsource. Or, as Olivier de Schutter, the UN's Special Rapporteur on the Right to Food, put it when presenting his report to the UN Human Rights Council calling for the overhaul of subsidies, the taxing of unhealthy processed foods and drinks, and a crack-down on marketing of junk diets:

Our food systems are making people sick. One in seven people globally are undernourished, and many more suffer from the hidden hunger of micronutrient deficiency, while 1.3 billion are overweight or obese. Urbanization, supermarketization and the global spread of modern lifestyles have shaken up traditional food habits. The result is a public health disaster. Governments have been focusing on increasing calorie availability, but they have often been indifferent to what kind of calories are on offer, at what price . . .

We have deferred to food companies the responsibility for ensuring that a good nutritional balance emerges. Voluntary guidelines and piecemeal nutrition initiatives have failed . . . the odds remain stacked against the achievement of a healthy, balanced diet.

Heavy processing thrives in our global food system, and is a win-win for multinational agri-food companies. Processed items can be produced and distributed on a huge scale, thanks to cheap subsidized ingredients and their increased shelf life.

But for the people, it is a lose-lose. Children become hooked on the junk foods targeted at them. In better-off countries, the poorest population groups are most affected because foods high in fats, sugar and salt are often cheaper than healthy diets as a result of misguided subsidies whose health impacts have been wholly ignored. The West is now exporting diabetes and heart disease to developing countries, along with the processed foods that line the shelves of global supermarkets. We should not simply invest our hopes in medicalizing our diets with enriched products, or changing people's choices through health warnings. We need strategies [which] will only work if the food systems underpinning them are put right.

In fact some of the big food corporates have started talking themselves about the need for change. Paul Polman, CEO of

Unilever, has talked with almost evangelical fervour of the need for businesses to become good corporate citizens. The company announced its Sustainable Living Plan in 2010 which aimed to double the size of its global business by 2020 while shrinking its environmental footprint radically at the same time. He has described his company as a 'solutions provider, a co-creator with the consumer of mainstream sustainable living'.

Presenting the company's results in 2013 he said: 'The biggest challenge is the continuing threat to "planetary boundaries", resulting in extreme weather patterns and growing resource constraints. These have an increasing impact on people's lives.

'Put simply, we cannot thrive as a business in a world where too many people are still excluded, marginalized or penalized through global economic activity, where nearly one billion go to bed hungry every night, 2.8 billion are short of water and increasing numbers of people are excluded from the opportunity to work.'

Nestlé's website, in common with those of most big food companies, carries a description of a raft of commitments it has made recently to become more sustainable and to improve the nutritional content of its products. Its CEO Paul Bulcke has said, 'We recognize that our position in society brings not only opportunities, but also responsibilities. We can play a valuable leadership role in support of concerted action.'

The obstacles to turning this rhetoric about good corporate citizenship into reality are considerable, however, not least because of the pressure on public companies to maximize growth and returns to shareholders, and on private companies to produce quick returns for their equity investors who typically want to exit after a few years. Manufacturing sectors have not been immune to the sort of driving forces that have produced unfeasible returns in the financial sector. When US-based Kraft, as it then was, took over Cadbury and subsequently announced job cuts in England, there was outcry in the UK, where many clung to a sentimentally nationalist view that manufacturing

British brands might still be about making things and making them at home.

In fact, for the previous decade, 'growth' in the food and drink sector had, as elsewhere, involved freeing up more and more cash to be handed out to shareholders and top executives in the form of share buy-backs, dividends and bonuses. It had been achieved by taking on debt, closing factories, even profitable ones, selling off assets and eliminating direct employment. In the upside-down world of impatient finance capitalism, manufacturers' 'growth' had actually required the destruction of companies' productive capacity. Manufacturing itself is almost becoming peripheral as production is outsourced and the companies themselves concentrate on marketing and sales.

Between 2000 and 2004, for example, Kraft Foods' 'Sustainable Growth Plan' involved 6,000 job cuts and the closure of twenty factories around the globe. That was followed by thousands of further job cuts and a dozen or so more factory closures between 2006 and 2008, which the company promised would generate additional cash flows of $3.4 billion for share buy-backs, dividends and acquisitions. Many US jobs were outsourced to Mexico, where subcontractors were able to make such famous brands as Grahams crackers.

Despite all the sentimentality expressed about the iconic British brand Cadbury, it had been doing this too. Cadbury, historically an employer offering good wages, benefits and pensions, introduced its 'Fuel for Growth' plan in 2003. That was followed by fourteen factory closures in a twelve-month period. It became the 'Vision into Action' plan of 2008–11, which promised the further closure of 15 per cent of manufacturing sites around the world and a cut of 15 per cent, or around 7,000, in the directly employed workforce. A key aim: to generate more cash flow for shareholders.

In 2000 Unilever launched its 'Path to Growth' strategy. It promised enormous restructuring to release over €45 billion 'surplus cash' to shareholders over the decade to 2010. About

Not On the Label

300,000 people were employed by Unilever when the plan was announced. By 2010, according to the international food unions, only around half that number were directly employed by it. Many tens of thousands of workers were now instead outsourced labourers for its contractors and their agencies, often in non-unionized workplaces.

Nestlé, the world's largest food manufacturer, led the way in giving this new meaning to growth. It dramatically increased outsourcing of jobs to contractors to cut costs, and cut its number of factories, thereby delivering returns to shareholders over the decade to 2010 that were far higher than those traditionally expected in manufacturing sectors. This model of downsizing and distributing the money freed up enabled it to release more than £20 billion in cash to shareholders through share buy-backs between 2007 and 2010.

Job cuts have not been straightforwardly about eliminating waste or increasing productivity. They have not in the food sector even been about replacing jobs in affluent countries with work in poorer and therefore more competitive countries, since most food production remains local or regional. Outsourcing has swept away permanent jobs in developing countries too. The cuts have delivered lower costs by reducing terms and conditions, and by transferring risk to those who are now only casually employed, on and off, at the bottom of the chain. Peter Rossman, who has tracked all these new routes to growth for the IUF trade union association in Geneva, has shown how they resulted in lower investment, and potentially sacrificed the long-term health of companies to the demands of the global financial markets for quick profits. Hedge fund and private equity investors in food companies have demanded annual rates of return to match the unsustainable speculative ones they have found on the raging bull markets.

The result has been a huge transfer of wealth, at the expense not just of employees but of most national economies. In parallel with maximizing the return to shareholders, food companies have been minimizing the tax they pay through restructuring. The cash that has been sucked out from companies that took decades, even centuries to grow, has not found its way back as increased contributions to national exchequers. Food corporations typically now run their businesses through structures that put brand ownership and licensing offshore, and locate procurement of raw materials and management in tax havens such as Switzerland and the US state of Delaware. The hedge funds and private equity shareholders driving the trend take their profits offshore too.

The battle over who should benefit from the profits in the food system being fought in South America has been engaged in the UK and Europe too.

Tax avoidance (which is legal, as opposed to evasion, which is illegal) is one of those arcane and technical subjects it can be hard to get to grips with, but the case of Walkers crisps, owned by the US transnational giant PepsiCo, vividly brought home to me what this flight of capital meant when I was researching a series of articles, The Tax Gap, with colleagues at the *Guardian*.

A curious thing happened to the UK profits of Walkers Snack Foods in 1999. They fell off a cliff, as did the UK tax bill that went with them.

Walkers still manufactured its crisps in Leicester at the world's largest crisp factory, as befits the top brand in a country whose potato-snack habit is one of the largest in the world. Its sales, boosted by that footballing symbol of middle England, Gary Lineker, remained by and large as healthy as his image, despite nutritionists' best efforts. And yet Walkers' UK profits took a dive from which they have not recovered.

The explanation was quite simple. Walkers had been 'restructured' by its owners. This shifted much of its profits to a tax haven in Switzerland.

In June 1999, PepsiCo transferred ownership of its Walkers

brands, built up in the UK over the decades since it first began frying in 1948, out of England and into a Swiss subsidiary, Frito-Lay Trading Company GmbH. Walkers carried on making the crisps that millions of Britons eat daily at its sites in England. It also carried on employing roughly the same number of production workers, about 3,000, and its marketing still boasted that 'we're proud our crisps are made from 100 per cent British potatoes, and we love our home'. But for all Walkers' Britishness, its 'intellectual property' and 'business functions and risks' had quietly migrated to the low-tax canton of Bern. The British factories were reduced from a major profit centre to mere contract manufacturers, paid a margin over their costs by PepsiCo's Swiss trading company.

On paper Walkers no longer owned at any point the raw materials or products it made; it did not own the potatoes that went into the factory nor the crisps that came out. Its sales and marketing company did not own what it sold to the supermarkets and pub chains. It just collected commission like the Avon Lady. PepsiCo's Swiss-registered entity owned the goods remotely instead.

What did this surreal arrangement mean for the UK exchequer?

The year before it happened, Walkers Snack Foods was turning over £469 million. This generated profits in the UK of £91 million and a tax bill of £28 million to hand over to the British Inland Revenue. But in 1999, the year the brands were sold, Walkers Snack Foods turnover almost halved, as did its profits, and its UK tax bill went down to £14.7 million.

The original Walkers operation in Britain had by now been split into three separate components: Walkers Snack Foods, the original manufacturing arm; Walkers Distribution; and Walkers Snacks, a sales and marketing entity. Adding all their tax charges together, the Walkers total came to just £18.3 million – nearly £10 million less than the previous year's tax bill. By 2000, the first full year after restructuring, the total UK tax contribution from the new group had plummeted further to just £11.4 million. Profits were piling up in low-tax Switzerland, in what was presented as now essentially a Swiss-managed operation. The Walkers companies were said merely to be making and distributing the crisps, and collecting the money from UK supermarkets, on behalf of the real managers abroad.

There were some strange features to the newly devised 'sales and marketing' entity, Walkers Snacks. A large chunk of the old Walkers' turnover was allocated to it. The average pay of the 170 employees also allocated to it in 1999 was exceptionally high, suggesting some expensive people might work there.

There turned out to be much room for argument with HMRC about just how 'Swiss' the Walkers crisps operation had really become.

In shifting a substantial chunk of the profits from its operations out of the UK to Switzerland in this way, PepsiCo became one of the earliest adopters of the sort of business restructuring that Inland Revenue sources have described as the biggest threat to the UK tax base. Industry calls it 'tax efficient supply-chain management'.

Dozens of large companies have followed the PepsiCo route. Tax authorities around the world struggle to keep up with them. Transnational food companies are not the only ones to have shifted profits to low-tax jurisdictions but they have been among those leading the way.

It took two more years for the UK authorities to blow the referee's whistle on PepsiCo. By that time the UK tax bill from the restructured companies had shrunk to around £8 million. Corporations, just like individuals, submit their returns in arrears. Walkers' auditors, KPMG, recorded the Inland Revenue's challenge to its tax returns. 'The tax authorities have queried a number of historical transactions,' they said. However, the auditors added that 'management are confident that the treatment which has been adopted is correct'. Nevertheless, the company started making a provision in the next few years for a bigger tax bill but without disclosing it in its statutory accounts. It did this 'on the grounds that it might be prejudicial to the company's interests in its dealings with the tax authorities'. Eventually, PepsiCo did a deal, and gave around £40 million back to Britain.

But the dispute moved at glacially slow speed. It took until October 2009 for a final settlement with HMRC to be agreed and revealed in the small print of the Walkers accounts. The UK had managed to claw back less than a third of what it might have received had an unchanged structure continued producing the same sort of level of UK profits and tax as Walkers Snack Foods had in 1998.

Invited to comment, New York-based PepsiCo told me: 'PepsiCo manages its tax affairs in a prudent and lawful manner.'

An immediate problem for the biggest manufacturers of processed foods is that their economic model depends on cheap raw materials. As we move from surplus to shortage in a globalized world, these raw materials are no longer cheap, just as the supermarkets' economic model has been built on crude oil and energy that is no longer cheap.

A glimpse of these tensions could be seen in a Consumers' Association study in 2013 of big-name food brands: it found that several had shrunk pack sizes by as much as a quarter while at the same time pushing up the price. When the researchers asked the makers of these products why they had shrunk them, they were generally told that in the face of rising costs they chose to downsize products rather than increase prices beyond what the market would stand. Some said they were reducing portion size to meet targets set as part of the battle against obesity.

It has become easy to find examples of industry boasting it has removed salt and saturated fat by the tonne, and 'renovated' products by the thousand. The difficulty of course is that all this reformulation highlights the extent to which we have been subject to a sort of food Fordism, sold the mass production of standardized commodity parts, bolted together to make various models of the same thing in snacks, drinks, sweets and ready meals.

It raises the uncomfortable question: what were all those things they were removing doing in our diets in the first place?

8. The Ready Meal

It is over thirty years since Marks and Spencer first brought the ready meal into our lives and set in train a revolution in our eating habits. About a third of us used these supermarket meals more than once a week until the horsemeat scandal dented our faith and led to a 20 per cent drop in purchases. Britain has in fact been the largest consumer in Europe of ready meals, a reflection no doubt not only of its position at the top of the league for long working hours, but also of changing patterns of family life. The trade has a phrase for it: 'in-home meal solutions for single-person eating occasions'.

Instant, effortless meals provided by factory kitchens have been a theme of literary utopias since the early twentieth century but in those brave new worlds the convenience meal was celebrated for its efficiency or its capacity to liberate from drudgery rather than for any sensory experience. There have been frozen versions of instant dinners before, but for today's eaters, the genius of the new ready meal that has spread to all retailers is that it promises freshness and pleasure too.

The last time I cruised down the ready-meal aisle of a supermarket, a vast array of dishes, placed next to the fruit and vegetable section, offered liberal sprinklings of 'fresh' this or 'hand-selected' that. The outer packs were all gorgeous colour photography. Key words, picked out in fashionable typography, hinted at the care and quality that had gone into their preparation. Top chefs from around the world appeared to have been labouring personally to provide me with a choice of exotic meals. I came back with a lamb dish, a 'favourite recipe', with what sounded like a delicious gravy and stuffing.

While it reheated, I had time to read the label. The ingredients of my lamb dish, described in such mouth-watering prose on the front of the pack, were listed in long and minute detail in the small print on the back. By law, ingredients must be listed in order of weight. This is what it contained:

Lamb (23 per cent), water, fried potato (21 per cent), carrot (6 per cent), peas (6 per cent), red wine, onion

So far so good, although rather heavier on the potato and lighter on the lamb than I had realized at first sight, then as the bold letters slipped into fainter and harder-to-read type, it became more and more intriguing:

Pork sausage meat (pork, water, rusk, wheat flour, salt, herbs, ground spices, preservative: sodium acetate, sodium sulphite; dextrose, stabilizer: polyphosphate, antioxidants: ascorbic acid, sodium citrate; spice extract, glucose syrup)

Breadcrumb (wheat flour, water, yeast, soya flour, salt, rapeseed and palm oil, vinegar, sugar, wheat gluten, emulsifiers: mono and diglycerides of fatty acids, sodium stearoyl lactylate; preservative: calcium propionate; flour improver L-ascorbic acid; dextrose, flavouring)

Redcurrant jelly (3 per cent) (sugar, water, redcurrant concentrate, lemon juice, citric acid, gelling agent: pectin; acidity regulator: acetic acid, preservative: potassium sorbate)

Lamb stock (concentrated lamb broth, vegetable concentrate, tomato concentrate, glucose syrup, salt, flavourings, yeast extract, dextrin, lamb fat, sunflower oil)

Modified maize starch, tomato purée

Lamb bouillon (salt, dextrose, yeast extract, lamb, skimmed milk powder, onion powder, potato starch, flavourings, hydrogenated rapeseed oil, white pepper, malt extract, citric acid, paprika)

Rapeseed oil, salt, margarine, wheat flour, garlic purée, mint, rosemary, dextrose, white pepper.

Now, in case I lost you half-way through, that was at least eight mentions of different kinds of sugars and sweetening agents, seven of fats in various forms, four of preservatives and three of chemical flavourings, not to mention thickeners such as starch in different guises.

I could have gone instead for the Mediterranean flavours of a vegetarian lasagne ready meal. As well as water (the main ingredient by weight), that contained cooked pasta, various vegetables, cheese, cream, fats which included margarine, rapeseed oil and butter, starch, salt and sugar, and herbs together with a vegetable bouillon of:

Salt, dextrose [*a form of sugar*], potato starch [*a thickener*], sugar [*what, more?*], lactose [*more sweetening*], yeast extract, flavouring, hydrogenated rapeseed oil, onion powder, citric acid, herbs, dehydrated celery, malt extract [*more sweetening*] and turmeric extract [*for that Mediterranean feel or possibly handy colouring*].

That ready meal managed to be made up of 15 per cent sugars.

These are not quite the ingredients I would reach for when making a lamb casserole or a vegetarian lasagne. But otherwise there was nothing exceptional about the contents of the ready meals described above. I could find others like them in any supermarket.

Frozen-food manufacturers point out that a weekly basket of prepared fresh chilled meals like this costs 40 per cent more than a basket of frozen meals made with similar ingredients. Yet many of the constituent ingredients of fresh chilled meals have been previously frozen, and fresh chilled meals often contain more additives and preservatives than frozen. Such is the power of packaging and marketing, however, that we have all bought into the illusion sold by these industrialized products of the factory line.

Ready meals, like other processed foods, have typically been high in processed fats – generally derived from soya, palm or rapeseed oil – and processed sugars – derived not just from sugar but also from corn. Large numbers of them contain processed starch – also generally derived from corn. In fact, a quarter of all processed foods are made with corn in some form and two thirds of all processed foods contain soya or its derivatives.

In the last few decades, considerable research effort in the food industry has been devoted to finding ways to break soya and corn down into their constituent parts and discovering new uses for them. As the US Corn Refiners' Association explained on its website, 'Corn refining is today's leading example of value-added agriculture. Refiners separate corn into its components, starch, oil, protein, and fibre, and convert them to higher-value products.'

The ready meal is the incarnation of 'added value'.

The protein from corn, as we have seen, goes to feeding intensively reared animals, to create 'added-value' meat, leaving the oil and starch. Starches are thickening and bulking agents, and are often used to replace more expensive ingredients. Starch in its natural form has technical limitations, so food technologists have devised ways to treat or modify it with various acids, enzymes or oxidizing agents to improve its resistance to heat, make it more soluble in cold water and better able to produce gels, pastes and other textures required by the food industry. (Because modified starch has been altered at the molecular level, it is banned in organic production.) Highly processed starches are low in nutritional value and most are also high in calories. But this component of corn is used widely in ready meals and processed meats.

In an article in *Innovative Food Ingredients* magazine, entitled 'Innovative uses of corn starch in food', the American Corn Refiners' Association explained the many different ways food manufacturers could make use of starch. 'Starches are a vital element in today's diet, used in practically every category of processed food.' When modified by enzymes to produce cyclo-dextrin for instance, starch can 'mask off-flavours and unpleasant odours'. When chemically modified to make 'resistant starch', it has 'excellent expansion qualities' and can be used 'as a bulking agent in reduced-sugar or reduced-fat food formulations'.

The list of merits appeared endless.

Several innovative applications of corn starch involve the replacement of other ingredients that may be expensive … pre-gelatinized starch can be used to replace tomato solids or fruit solids. Granular or flaked starch can provide texture and bulk to simulate the pulpy characteristics of the solids they replace at a reduced cost to the manufacturer. These types of textural starches are used effectively in tomato sauces, fruit fillings, fruit drinks, instant hot cereals, potato products and baby foods. In addition, the starch can add to the product's shelf life by efficiently binding water during storage … Imitation cheese manufacturers can cut costs by replacing [milk ingredients] with specially modified thin boiling starches …

The piece went on to conclude that 'The diversity and sophistication of food products that are available is attributable in part to the imagination of the carbohydrate chemist.'

Evidence of the carbohydrate chemist's imagination has been everywhere. In October 2003, Shropshire trading standards officers decided to test the office workers' staple: the sandwich. They bought chicken sandwiches from all the major high street retailers. 'These sandwiches are described as chicken. Some boast they contain 100 per cent chicken breast … In many, the very small print … tells another story,' their report concluded. Many of the sandwiches contained chicken which had been adulterated with starch, water and flavourings. A typical example was as follows: a 'roast chicken and salad sandwich with tender roast chicken breasts' whose label declared its chicken contained water, salt, dextrose, stabilizer, E450, E451, E452, modified maize starch and whey protein. David Walker, then chief trading standards officer of Shropshire County Council, explained: 'Starch has no technological function other than as a meat adulterant. It soaks up water. The adulterated chicken industry has grown up in the last two years. Very few people know. The Food Standards Agency didn't know about it. My colleagues didn't know about it. But the problem is, the technology is moving so fast, we'll never keep up with it.' My own random trawl of supermarket prepacked 'roast chicken slices' and 'roast chicken sandwiches' in 2013 revealed some ingredients lists where the 'chicken' contained cornflour or cornflour, rice flour and dextrose. Things had moved, but not far.

The low-fat yoghurt is another classic example of the use of starch to add value. Often marketed as a healthy food, a typical strawberry yoghurt version contains not just yoghurt and strawberries, but also starch to thicken it and replace the texture of fruit; gelatine, gums, or pectin to glue it together and make it gel; colouring and flavourings; and some form of fructose (i.e. corn syrup). (It helps to know your labelling law here: a strawberry yoghurt must contain some real strawberry. A strawberry-flavoured yoghurt has had a briefer encounter with the fruit. A strawberry-flavour yoghurt, on the other hand, has not been within sight of a strawberry.)

Perhaps the most lucrative product of the carbohydrate chemist's imagination, however, has been the corn sweetener, and in particular high-fructose corn syrup (HFCS). It was food scientists in Japan who first found a way to produce this syrup, a sweetener that can be up to eight times sweeter than sucrose from cane sugar. By the late 1970s the industry was able to mass-produce it. Greg Critser describes the effect of these technological advances in his book *Fat Land*. In the early 1980s, Pepsi and Coca-Cola in the USA switched completely to HFCS, saving them 20 per cent in sweetener costs and enabling them to increase portion sizes dramatically as they looked to give their products a market edge. (In the UK, Coca-Cola is sweetened with sugar.) HFCS became the commonest form of sweetener in soft drinks around the world. Soft drinks are another classic example of added value.

A manufacturer of an alternative brand of cola was kind enough to share his production costs with me in 2003. As a rule of thumb, only one third of the cost of production of processed foods is the cost of ingredients – one third is the cost of packaging and one third the cost of processing. The higher the quality of the product, the higher the percentage of the costs devoted to ingredients. But sometimes the costs of ingredients are negligible.

For example, in a can of cola retailing at that time for between 40p and 50p, the metal can itself cost 7–8p, and the ingredients less than 2p. Sugar or sweetener makes up 10 per cent of the recipe; colouring and flavouring and other additives account for a tiny percentage more; the rest is water. The most expensive ingredient is the sugar or sweetener. A can of cola contains 30g of sugar or the equivalent in corn syrup, which cost just 1.3p.

So much for the sugars and starches. One of the other characteristics of processed foods is that they are high in fats. These tend to be soya, rapeseed and palm oil. Manufacturing processes need fats with slightly different properties to soya oil extracted from soya beans, and so for a long time much of it was hydrogenated. Hydrogenation was developed in the 1920s as a way of artificially hardening liquid oils so that they would function more like animal fats. The oil is heated to 200°C and held at that temperature for several hours with a metal catalyst, usually nickel, while hydrogen gas is pumped through it. The hydrogen atoms penetrate the oil molecules, forming trans fats. Hydrogenated fat is exceptionally hard and plastic-like when cooled which has made it particularly useful in food processing. Rapeseed oil can be treated in the same way. But the very property that makes the hydrogenated fats so useful to manufacturers also made them a health risk for consumers. It is now accepted that it is safest to avoid hydrogenated fats, because they have a similar effect on your arteries to other hard fats. They were long banned in organic production. The FSA advised that 'trans fats have no nutritional benefits and because of the effect they have on blood cholesterol they increase the risk of coronary heart disease ... evidence suggests that the adverse effects of trans fats are worse than saturated fats'.

Research in the US in 1993 had confirmed fears about the risks associated with artificial trans fats in food. It was then that Unilever started removing them from its brands, it told me. Flora spread, sold as a healthy heart food, had contained on average 10 per cent trans fats but was free of them by 1994. The process of removing them from its other brands, which averaged 25 per cent trans fats, took longer. By 2004 the level of trans fats had been reduced to less than 0.5 per cent in all its fat spreads. By 2006, 8,000 of Unilever's products, or about half of its total portfolio, had been reformulated to make them more healthy, it said, with a resulting decrease of 30,000 tonnes of trans fats in its products between 2004 and 2006.

Long after the risks of trans fats and hydrogenation were known, many manufacturers continued to use them widely in processed foods such as ready meals, margarines, fat spreads, crisps, bakery products, biscuits and cakes. It was the threat of litigation and class actions against manufacturers in the USA, combined with a requirement there that they should be labelled from 2006, that pushed much of the industry into action. Use of the law and regulation, although out of fashion, generally works.

Most reputable brand names have now eliminated trans fats or reduced them to very low levels, although the legacy of the impact of their use on our health will take time to work through. The harder, saturated fractions of palm oil have generally replaced hydrogenated oils in many products (see Chapter 5: Bread).

Since I first wrote about these tricks of the trade, a consumer backlash and demands from the FSA for the UK industry to reduce unhealthy levels of salt, fats and sugar in its foods have exerted a combined pressure on manufacturers. The FSA had been particularly effective forcing through reductions in the

industry's use of salt by setting strict targets and naming and shaming companies' products. From the early 2000s there appeared to
be a change of attitude and manufacturers started to reformulate.

But it was easier for some economically than for others.

As a retailer that only stocks its own brand of food, Marks and
Spencer had greater control over what it sold than the larger
supermarket chains. But the extent to which it had to change
was a reflection of how much needed to improve. The company
started reducing salt in products in 1998 and banned five controversial additives. Even so, it was caught on the hop by the Sudan
1 scandal in February 2005. When the FSA announced that the
illegal carcinogenic red dye had been used to adulterate chilli
powder, fifteen Marks and Spencer products were among the
500-plus that had to be recalled from leading supermarkets and
fast-food chains. There were few manufacturers or retailers not
caught up in the scandal. At the time, an M&S shepherd's pie
had been typical of most ready meals, containing 57 ingredients,
many of them additives buried in compound ingredients such as
stock and sauce, and several of them things no cook would ever
use at home. An internal inventory of hydrogenated fats found
they were present in 1,200 out of a total of roughly 4,000 Marks
and Spencer lines. The technical director, David Gregory, decided
they all had to go as quickly as possible.

At the gleaming new RF Brookes factory near Newport the
scale of the shake-up became clear when I visited. If you have
bought food at Marks and Spencer, you will have eaten something from here, the largest ready-meal factory in Europe. It
supplies over £100 million worth of 'meal solutions' in 143
varieties a year, including soups and sauces, and Indian, Italian
and British ready meals.

The order to clean up ingredients meant culling the E numbers consumer groups were most worried about, removing
processed starches, malt and yeast extracts, gums and stabilizers
from chilled foods and replacing hydrogenated vegetable fats.
Over 450 recipe changes were needed to 267 products.

'Historically, as price became more of an issue you would use stocks or yeast extract to provide flavour that was not achieved through the quality of ingredients or proper cooking. Malt extract used to be added for colour to make meat look as though it had been cooked for longer, but when we removed it we realized it also masked a lot of the flavour,' a Marks and Spencer technologist who worked on the project told me.

Modified starches give higher yields than plain cornflour and freeze better but consumers are rightly suspicious of them. They are still widely used, but the buzz in the industrial ingredients sector became 'clean label' technology. Blends of cornflour and wheatflour that could fulfil the same bulking and stabilizing functions as modified starch but sounded less scary were developed.

Marks and Spencer decided to restrict its suppliers to using 123 EU-approved additives. It also worked on a new range of meals from which additives would be removed altogether, 'even from the ingredients of the ingredients of the ingredients'. The shepherd's pie came down to twenty-four ingredients.

By moving fast, Marks and Spencer was able to claim a competitive advantage over other retailers: it had removed hydrogenated fat from 98 per cent of its food by 2006. Others followed more slowly.

During those turbulent years in the food industry, when its secrets were being revealed by what it declared was its past, Martin Paterson was its public voice as deputy director of the trade lobby group, the Food and Drink Federation (FDF). A former Ministry of Defence press officer, he had been master of the combative response to any criticism in his FDF role.

He admitted to me that there had needed to be a change in attitude among food manufacturers. 'There used to be a sense in the industry that the public didn't need to know what you put in your food. You played up to the regulations. That's no longer good enough.' But he said that it would get harder and harder for companies to move further on health. Removing salt was relatively easy, although even that had been strongly resisted. (About 75 per cent of salt in our diets comes from processed foods, according to the FSA.) As ever it was because of the economics.

Salt provides flavour to cheap food at around $150 a tonne. Real spices cost up to $2,000 a tonne. 'The problem with fat and sugar,' Paterson pointed out, was that 'they are often what make up the bulk of the product. And some products just are sugar boiled through hydrogenated fat. Take those out and you are left with a wrapper or a stick.' Fat and sugar have also, thanks to subsidies, been cheap. The analysts JP Morgan estimated that the cost of industrial fat had fallen by 50 per cent in the fifty years up to the millennium, whereas the cost of a healthy ingredient such as fruit had increased by a third. Where manufacturers have reduced fat levels in products and marketed them as low fat or 'light', all too often the sugar content has risen to take fat's place. A 'light' strawberry yoghurt I found boasted that it was virtually fat-free but it was 7 per cent sugars, with not only added fructose but extra artificial sweetening too. Breakfast cereals, repeatedly criticized for being high in salt and sugar have made progress reducing salt, but many, especially those aimed at children remain high in sugar, as a Consumers' Association survey in 2012 revealed.

With many products the response to the consumer backlash was simply to push the ingredients shoppers didn't want down as far as possible.

An upmarket 'premium' supermarket ready meal of chicken in wine and bacon sauce now may present a 'clean label' until you get down to the fine print and its compound ingredients, when it turns out the bacon has both added sugar and dextrose, and the chicken stock contains sugar, salt and cornflour.

The truth is that we need to move away from many types of processed food, yet no company can honestly want its market to shrink.

★

To turn the products of highly subsidized commodity agriculture, the cheap fats, sugars and starches, into acceptable foods, you need additives.

Over $22 billion is spent each year by the food industry on chemical additives to change the colour, texture, flavour and shelf life of our food. Over $1 billion a year is spent on food colourings alone, to deceive our senses. Manufacturers wanting to create the impression of fruit or vegetables or other expensive ingredients without the bother of paying for the real thing have 4,500 different flavouring compounds at their disposal.

Colours are still liberally used to disguise the absence of real ingredients but they are as likely to be additives derived from 'black carrot' or red cabbage now as artificial colourings. Industry was spurred to find substitutes for artificial colourings by a UK study in 2007 that linked mixtures of colourings and the preservative sodium benzoate to hyperactivity in children. The EU proposed requiring companies using the colourings to label their products with a warning that they might have an adverse effect on children. Industry consultants Leatherhead Food International estimated that natural colours accounted for around 30 per cent of the global colourings market in 2008.

Other flavourings and colourings replace the natural flavours and colours that are either absent because of the lack of real ingredients or because they have been lost in processing; emulsifiers and stabilizers bind water and fat together and stop them separating out again.

Some additives are necessary to help the ingredients survive the factory process. In cheap yoghurt manufacture, for example, high-speed machinery pumps the yoghurt along miles of pipes. This breaks its delicate structure, which traditionally comes from the natural thickening associated with the incubation of bacteria. So gums are added at the beginning of the process to make the product 'bullet-proof', as one manufacturer described it. (More expensive yoghurts are not pumped to such an extent, and have their fruit added by hand to preserve the structure, but that adds to labour costs.)

Erik Millstone, reader in science policy at Sussex University, has studied the additives industry for many years. He points out in *The Atlas of Food* that consumers in industrialized countries now eat 13–15lb (6–7kg) of food additives a year.

The food industry often defends the use of additives by saying that they protect consumers from food poisoning, but additives used as preservatives or to stop fat going rancid account for less than 1 per cent by weight of all the additives used. About 90 per cent of additives in processed food are cosmetic. The vast majority are used to make cheap fat, constipating starch and subsidized sugars look and taste like natural food.

Food manufacturers have always cut corners and substituted cheap alternatives for expensive ingredients. In 1429, the Guild of Pepperers battled to stop people mixing gravel and twigs with pepper. But the first mass adulterations came with the Industrial Revolution, and as with labour conditions, the historic parallels are instructive. Feeding cities with their newly urbanized populations required new supply systems. Whereas previously most people would have grown their own food or bought from their immediate neighbours, city dwellers were dependent on much longer chains and soon became ignorant of how their food was made. With no legal obstacles and fierce competition, adulteration became commonplace. Whereas before, an unscrupulous butcher or baker might have been restrained by the knowledge that any shortcuts he chose could poison his neighbours and friends, now he could hide in the anonymity of distance and the city.

Analytical chemistry was still in its infancy in the eighteenth and early nineteenth centuries, and there was little fear of detection until Frederick Accum developed methods to examine food. His work, *There is Death in the Pot*, as it was popularly known, or more properly, *A Treatise on Adulterations of Food and Culinary Poisons*, was a bestseller when it was published in 1820.

Its subtitle was 'exhibiting the fraudulent sophistications of bread, beer, wine, spiritous liquors, tea, coffee, cream, confectionery, vinegar, mustard, pepper, cheese, olive oil, pickles and other articles employed in domestic economy, and methods of detecting them'. Accum fled the country after a minor scandal but the cause was taken up by Dr Arthur Hassall who first used the microscope to show that coffee was being routinely adulterated with roasted chicory, peas and wheat. Thomas Wakley, owner and editor of the medical journal the *Lancet*, told Hassall that he would never achieve anything until he defied the libel lawyers and named and shamed the perpetrators of the adulterations. With government apparently uninterested in action, the two men agreed to work on a series of articles analysing samples of food and drink bought from shops around London and exposing the fraud, together with the names and addresses of the shops involved.

Their work revealed a scandal of immense proportions as Hassall reported fortnightly in the *Lancet* on samples of coffee, sugar, water, bread, milk and a whole range of other foods and found lead, water, dyes, alum and flour all being used to debase food. The scandal eventually led to the 1875 Sale of Food and Drugs Act which made it an offence to sell adulterated food. Early food branding emerged as a response to the anxiety that surrounded the adulterations. Before then, most food was sold loose. Brands were the customer's guarantee of the quality and provenance of the ingredients.

With each generation the adulterations have changed but the elements have followed a pattern: ignorance among the consuming public, an assumption among the producers that what they are doing is entirely acceptable, the lure of large profits, and weak law or weak enforcement.

In her 1931 book, *The Suffragette Movement*, Sylvia Pankhurst gave as an example of sweated labour the work of women whose job it was to rub pieces of wood into seed shapes so they could be added to raspberry jam made without the aid of raspberries.

Outraged, she helped open a factory making jam from real fruit at affordable prices to create jobs for pacifist women during the First World War.

After the Second World War, fruit squashes entirely devoid of real fruit were made with sugar, citric acid and flavourings. Starch was added to give the impression of cloudiness created by fruit, cellulose imitated pith, and tiny bits of wood were made to look like pips.

The adulteration of twenty-first-century food adheres to the pattern. The difference, however, is that today it is being practised by some of the world's largest manufacturers entirely within the law. Adulteration now takes place on an unprecedented scale and is of unparalleled sophistication. The food industry's response in the early nineteenth century has a familiar ring to it. It claimed then that people wanted cheap food, and that the added ingredients were not adulterants but made food look and taste better. It argued that the poor couldn't afford anything else and therefore richer people's interventions were misguided. It said that if people didn't like what was being sold they wouldn't buy it.

Real food does cost more. Legal adulteration trades on this, but the evidence is that when people do understand what is happening they are in fact very concerned indeed.

In 1983 new European legislation required manufacturers to list additives in food by E numbers for the first time. As they started to see how their processed food was made, consumers become increasingly suspicious about these additives. Then, as if by a miracle, E numbers started to disappear. The E numbers were still there in the food of course but manufacturers stopped using them on labels. The pork sausage bit of my lamb casserole, for instance, contained E262, E221, either E450 or 544 or 545, E300 and E331, but there's not an E number in sight. Listing the additives in full might seem helpful, but actually I end up knowing less. Which polyphosphate is it? Is it the one that may prevent the absorption of vital nutrients such as iron, or the one associated with bowel disorders, or neither? Polyphosphates are used to make meat absorb water, saving manufacturers' costs, so why is it there anyway? E221, incidentally, is one of the sulphite group of preservatives which act ultimately as sulphur dioxide. They destroy vitamin B1, have been shown in animal studies to increase the incidence of tumours and are commonly associated with adverse or allergic reactions. Sulphites are permitted in high concentrations in many foods and are therefore easy to consume in worrying amounts.

While some additives started declaring themselves by another name, others simply went underground. Food legislation helps manufacturers here. Additives used as 'processing aids' do not have to be declared. Nor do the individual ingredients of all 'compound ingredients' have to be declared on the label, unless they make up more than 2 per cent by weight of the total product. Since in weight terms only a small quantity of additives may be needed to achieve the desired results, this still leaves room for hiding. So, for example, if I want to make a drink for children without having to mention preservatives on the label, I can buy some 'natural lemon flavouring' (which incidentally does not mean that the flavouring is natural, merely that if it has been chemically synthesized, it is 'nature-identical') and make sure the natural flavouring has a hefty dose of preservative added to it. The preservative, which will be surplus to the flavouring's requirements, will also have a preservative effect on the whole product.

For a glimpse behind the façade of the food industry today, there is no better place than Paris, the culinary capital of the world. Every second year, the food industry gathers here for a trade fair to which members of the public are not invited. Le Salon International de l'Alimentation (SIAL) is where manufacturers and processors, retail buyers and product development managers, catering suppliers and exporters from some 100 countries gather to do deals. Spread over six vast exhibition halls on the outskirts of the city are displays of the latest innovations in our convenience-meal existence.

I went to the fair with an undercover team from *Panorama* when we were investigating the scandal of Dutch chicken adulterated with beef waste, for this is where the agents for chicken pumped full of water and additives take orders from takeaway restaurants and ready-meal manufacturers around the world. While the BBC reporters were being told by Dutch exporters how they could turn water into money, I visited other alchemists' stalls. Everywhere there was evidence of a vast and wondrous scientific effort to turn base materials into lucre.

Endless display fridges showed the possibilities: frozen meat ready-chopped and flavoured for convenient ready-meal manufacture, Chinese spice, tikka- or chargrilled-style; Mediterranean vegetables premarked with even black grill lines for that instant barbecue feel; frozen prawns with added water and polyphosphates to keep it in, or not, depending on the price; ready-frozen industrial sauce pellets; puréed cubes of sugared, coloured and flavoured frozen kiwi, mango and raspberry for desserts. One giant banner advertised 'industrial cheese'; another boasted a miracle soft cheese that is 'always fully ripe'.

A section on new trends gave its assessment of the industry's efforts to create its own upmarket added-value brands, an assessment which would certainly be disputed by the retailers: 'All supermarkets have introduced premium brands ... on average these are 75 per cent more expensive for the same quality ... this sector is showing strong growth ...'

I wandered off into a stand that resembled a Victorian perfume shop. Its olde worlde wooden shelves were full of silver vials that looked like exquisite aromatherapy bottles. An assistant offered me a sprayer and invited me to sample the essences. I gave one a quick squirt and the stand was immediately filled with the delicious smell of wild mushroom. These 'natural extracts' were being marketed to restaurants for chefs to spray on to dishes as they left the kitchen, effortlessly conjuring up the intensity of basil or truffle with only a metal canister for a prop.

I decided to join the lecture tour on additives titled 'Additives are everywhere. Discover them'. I learned that consumers were becoming 'more sophisticated', they wanted cleaner labels, they wanted things to 'nourish their intellects' as well as their taste-buds, and they were preoccupied with 'nomadism'. The tour took in several new neutraceutical products. This is where the drugs industry meets the food industry and where many believed the money of the future would be, with vitamins and minerals added to highly processed foods so that they can be sold as healthy. Then we visited a company that has devised a way to distil oak smoke into a liquid to add to wine. Is that legal, I asked. 'Everyone accepts the taste very happily, but legislation is a problem.' On another stand, scientists were explaining how they hydrolyze fish flavour from crab shells for ready meals.

The use of additives is one good measure of the industry's performance in making our food healthier. If the manufacturers of the additives themselves are feeling the chill, there must be progress. But in fact the $22 billion global additives market grew by 2.4 per cent a year between 2001 and 2004, the period when the food industry would have us believe it was transforming itself. The research group Leatherhead Food International predicted that it would grow further by 2–3 per cent a year over the following years.

At a specialist additives conference in 2006, I heard ingredients manufacturers explain how innovations in sweeteners, starches and fat replacers could help the industry acquire 'cleaner labels' at no extra cost. A scientist from France who specialized in fats and was expert in the chemistry of mayonnaise shared his pain with us. Mayonnaise is really fat and a bit of egg. People want to eat less fat, but what happens when you take the fat out of mayonnaise, he asked.

You add water instead. Lots of water. The mayonnaise stops clinging to the salad you are trying to cover. It turns grey. It doesn't taste so nice. He wound himself up to the natural conclusion. 'You can't actually make low-fat mayonnaise,' he said. But if you are a mayonnaise manufacturer, you have to make reduced fat mayo and that requires additives. 'If I wanted to do this at home,' said the scientist, 'I would use yoghurt and make tzatziki instead.'

Just as the additives market has continued to grow, so has the whole new category of highly processed foods called neutraceuticals or 'functional foods' that are supposed to confer specific health benefits. The leading manufacturers see this market as the key to growth. It was worth $9.9 billion globally in 2003 and was predicted to keep growing by 16 per cent a year. In the UK, the market grew 32 per cent by value between 2006 and 2011 to reach over £750 million.

There has been one slight hitch, however. New rules were finally approved by the European Parliament in 2007, after years of consumer campaigning and in the face of fierce lobbying from the industry against them, to prevent food companies selling products with health claims unless they had proved them first, and unless the products had been judged healthy enough overall to merit carrying a health claim, that is if they were not too high in salts, sugars or fat. Member states were asked to submit lists of health claims on foods to the European Food Safety Authority with dossiers of scientific evidence to be assessed. A barrage of thousands of claims was submitted, with the result that it was 2010 before rulings began to come through in earnest. But as they did, more than three quarters of health claims submitted by the food industry were rejected as unsubstantiated. Among the high profile, high margin casualties were the claims made for 'probiotics'. Marketing based on the idea that they boosted the immune system or reduced gut problems was found to be based on unsound science.

All this would be serious enough if we were just being ripped off, but debasement of our food is having a profound effect on our health. The fresh foods which provide vital nutrients, the vitamins, minerals and essential fatty acids we need for health, are being replaced by large quantities of hardened fats, sugars and salt. Our industrialized diet is now known to be a major contributor to disease. We are being fed junk and it is making us sick.

The scale of the problem has in fact been widely accepted for years, but when *Not On the Label* was first published, many in the food industry were still arguing about it, insisting there was no such thing as junk food, only poor diets.

The WHO, summarizing the situation in its 2000 report, found that 60 per cent of deaths around the world were 'clearly related to changes in dietary patterns and increased consumption of fatty, salty, and sugary foods'. Cardiovascular disease (CVD), diabetes and cancer accounted for about 30 per cent of the burden of ill-health. Conservative estimates suggest that around one third of the risk of CVD was related to 'unbalanced nutrition' and 30–40 per cent of cancers could be prevented through better diet, the report concluded.

As Western diets high in fats, sugars and salt are adopted in developing countries, the same Western patterns of disease emerge. The dramatic rise in consumption of fats and sugars in China and India that has crept in with industrialization and urbanization, for example, is mirrored by an equally dramatic and alarming rise in cardiovascular disease, obesity and diabetes in those countries.

By 2011 the global epidemic of diet-related disease was so serious that the UN called a special summit of world leaders, only the second such it had ever convened, to 'combat heart disease, cancers, diabetes and lung disease' by setting targets to cut smoking and 'slash the high salt, sugar and fat content in foods that caused them'. It calculated that 36 million preventable deaths had been caused by non-communicable or so-called 'life-style' diseases around the world in 2008, and that the number would reach 52 million by 2030. In Mexico, for example, 70 per cent of the adult population is overweight or obese and the average adult requires medical treatment for eighteen years for related diseases such as diabetes. China too has reached a tipping point, where 10 per cent of the population is overweight or obese, matching for the first time the numbers of its citizens who are undernourished.

The director general of the WHO called the epidemic 'a slow-motion disaster' that would 'break the bank'. Diabetes care already accounted for 15 per cent of some nation's health budgets. A Harvard University study projected that, unchecked, these diseases would cost the global economy more than $30 trillion, or very nearly half of the total global GDP in 2010. Globally more than 1 billion people are already overweight and at least 300 million are obese.

Despite the urgency of the crisis, determined industry lobbying behind the scenes at the summit saw proposals to set targets for action watered down.

In the UK, the latest NHS figures in 2011 show a marked increase in obesity rates, with nearly a quarter of all men and just over a quarter of all women classed as clinically obese. One in ten reception class children aged four to five years old were also obese. Around half of all adults who were obese also had high blood pressure.

Nutrition is still a poorly understood science, but there is no longer room for any doubt that industrialized diets, combined with declining physical activity, are the vectors of disease, encouraging the consumption of too much of the wrong sorts of energy-dense food, saturated and processed fats, highly refined carbohydrates and sugars, which load us with calories without providing nutrients. These energy-dense foods have replaced the unrefined ones that we need to provide the essential vitamins, minerals and fats vital for health – fresh fruit and vegetables, fish, nuts and seeds, and unrefined carbohydrates. It is hard to get fat on unrefined foods, because their natural bulk fills us up. When we eat highly processed energy-dense foods, however, our bodies may fail to realize when we have had enough. And a product like high-fructose corn syrup may even be metabolized in a different way to other foods. It appears not to need to be broken down in the way that other sugars are, but to be delivered straight to the liver and turned into fat.

The International Obesity Taskforce has described obesity as 'the most critical public health issue of the twenty-first century'. For the first time in 100 years, medical experts are predicting, life expectancy in developed countries will fall. Thanks to obesity, our children face the prospect of dying at a younger age than us.

There is also a clear link between poverty and obesity. Some 30 per cent of girls and 36 per cent of young women are obese or overweight in the most deprived areas of the country, compared to 23 per cent of girls and 27 per cent of young women in the most affluent areas. The government's Health Development Agency has talked of a 'timebomb'.

Obesity goes hand in hand with other diseases. Type 2 diabetes, which used to be called adult-onset diabetes and is caused by poor diet, is being found increasingly in children in the UK. Being diagnosed with diabetes is the equivalent of having had your first heart attack. It reduces your life expectancy by several years. Diabetes is not only linked to heart disease, but also affects the eyes, kidneys and circulation. More than 300 million people around the world are believed already to have impaired glucose tolerance, the precursor to diabetes. Diabesity, as the Americans call it, could undo the progress made in health in Europe since the war.

Obesity is the disease that has finally pushed the panic button over diet and health, although there have been plenty of reasons to activate it before now. The relationship between industrialized diets and the largest causes of premature death and morbidity in the UK, heart disease, strokes and cancer, is compelling and has been generally agreed for much longer. The British government has at last woken up to the costs of diet-related diseases. The Wanless report on the National Health Service, commissioned by the Treasury, estimated that diet-related diseases cost the NHS £6.2 billion a year. But because the aetiology of these diseases is complicated, it has been easier for the food industry to dispute the connections.

Coronary heart disease is the biggest killer in the UK, and

40 per cent of premature deaths in men – that is, men dying before the age of retirement – are caused by heart disease and stroke. The rates of death have in fact fallen dramatically since the 1970s as treatments have improved, but the numbers suffering heart disease have not. The UK still has one of the highest rates of heart disease in the world. Immigrant populations soon show the same patterns of diet-related disease as they adopt Western lifestyles.

The same processes that are causing furring up of the coronary arteries appear to be going on in the circulatory system in the brain. There is increasing evidence that dementia is linked to diet.

Although there has been much dispute over the years on the relationship between diet and cancer, the UK Department of Health and the World Cancer Research Fund have both concluded that diets which include large amounts of fruit and vegetables will cut cancer rates. And conversely, a diet which is high in saturated fats and processed meats, but poor in antioxidant vitamins, particularly A, C and E, puts you at greater risk. Yet few people in the UK eat the amount of fresh fruit and vegetables recommended. Children do particularly badly. On average, they eat only two portions of fruit and vegetables each day. One in five children never eats fruit in an average week, and more than half never eat green leafy vegetables.

But it doesn't end there. The part played by some nutrients in good health is still being uncovered. Some of the most interesting new work at the moment is being done on the role of essential fatty acids. The brain, vascular system and to a lesser extent every cell in the body relies on essential fats for its construction.

Professor Michael Crawford, who in the 1960s and 1970s worked on essential fats and their role in Western degenerative diseases, points out that one of the most dramatic changes in the composition of food that has taken place in the last fifty years as it has become industrialized is the shift in the balance of fatty acids in the diet. He explained the role of essential fatty acids in his 1972 book, *What We Eat Today*.

Mammals cannot make essential fatty acids but must find them in their food. In plants there are two kinds of essential fatty acids, alpha-linolenic (found mostly in leaves, but also in the seed of some leguminous plants), and linoleic (found in seeds). These are polyunsaturated and when animals eat them they build on them, making longer-chain fatty acids, which are used in brain construction. Alpha-linolenic acid is converted into the omega-3 family of essential fatty acids, including EPA and DHA. Linoleic is converted by the body into the omega-6 family of essential fatty acids, particularly arachidonic acid. Crawford showed in 1972 that both arachidonic and DHA acids were specifically used in the brain. The DHA is particularly concentrated in the synaptic junctions and signalling systems of the brain and retina. The requirement of the brain for DHA has since been confirmed by many research papers. The richest source of DHA and EPA is fish.

Polyunsaturated compounds such as these are unstable and susceptible to oxidation, but luckily in nature they are present in plants together with antioxidants such as vitamin E, which acts as a natural preservative. Flavones, responsible for the bright colour in fruits such as tomatoes, are also antioxidants.

When seed oils are processed, any alpha-linolenic acid is generally selectively removed because it is unstable. When rice is polished or when wheat is processed into white flour, the germ of the seed and its essential fats are removed. When corn is made into breakfast cereal, the essential fats are also purified out. Palm oil, meanwhile, has almost no essential fats.

The essential fatty acids are vital for reproduction, for neural, vascular and immune system function, for food metabolism, and for the regulation of cell growth and regeneration. The body's inflammatory response, created to deal with injury or microbial attack, is regulated by omega-3s. The reduction of omega-3s in the diet leads to chronic inflammation and plays a significant part in degenerative diseases.

The omega-3 family of fatty acids plays a particularly important role in brain structure and function. About 60 per cent of the brain by dry weight is fat.

Whereas our ancestors would have eaten wild game, green leaves, nuts, seeds and fish which are all high in omega-3 fatty acids, we now consume much more omega-6. And whereas in the past, our diets would have provided a roughly equal balance of omega-3 and omega-6, now manufacturers who are looking for long shelf life use mostly processed soy, corn, palm and cotton seed oil which provide high amounts of omega-6 fatty acids and very little omega-3. Hydrogenating oil also wipes out polyunsaturated omega-3.

The ratio of omega-6 to omega-3, instead of being 1:1, as in the brain, is now thought to be between 10:1 and 20:1 in the American diet. The annual consumption of soya oil in the USA has increased a thousand-fold in less than 100 years, with the average American knocking back 11kg of soya oil in various forms a year. In the UK today we probably eat sixteen times as much omega-6 as omega-3, whereas a century ago we would have been getting amounts much closer to 1:1. Intensive farming has played a part in the changes too. The meat of cows fed grass has omega-3 in it but intensively reared grain-fed cattle have higher levels of saturated fats and little omega-3. Wild fish are high in omega-3 essential fatty acids, but in farmed fish omega-3s are displaced by omega-6s. Moreover, some of the vital trace elements and vitamins needed to metabolize essential fatty acids and other foods are being depleted.

Soils fed only with artificial fertilizers containing nitrogen, phosphate and potash (NPK) gradually lose their vital trace elements. Anne-Marie Mayer of Cornell University has charted the reduction in the vitamin and mineral content of food grown in Britain between the late 1930s and the 1990s. She found significant falls in the levels of calcium, magnesium and copper in vegetables and in magnesium, iron, copper and potassium in fruit. Her findings have been replicated by the geologist David Thomas, who analysed data from the bible of nutrition, *The Composition of Foods*, and found a huge dip in mineral content over the last sixty years. In just a few decades, the zinc content of seven common foods fell by nearly 60 per cent. Between the beginning of the Second World War and the early 1990s, the mineral content of vegetables dropped by 27 per cent in iron, and 24 per cent in magnesium, for example. Overall, levels of minerals have declined between a quarter and three quarters in fruit and vegetables. Scientific understanding of some of these nutrients and their biochemistry is very new. Selenium, for instance, was only recognized in 1957 but it is needed to metabolize essential fatty acids, and deficiency is now known to be linked to heart disease and other illnesses.

A whole range of studies is now being conducted into the effects of essential fatty acid deficiency on mental health, behaviour, and developmental problems. It is too early to say with certainty what the links are between dietary imbalance and these other disorders that appear to be rising dramatically in industrialized countries, but increasing numbers of scientists believe there is a connection. Joseph Hibbeln, a biochemist and psychiatrist from the National Institutes of Health, Washington, DC, has looked at the links between essential fats and depression to see if there could be a nutritional factor behind the soaring rates of depression in affluent countries. In the USA, people born after the Second World War are twice as likely to develop depression as their parents, and the age at which it first strikes is falling. In the UK the number of prescriptions for antidepressants rose by one third in just ten years.

Hibbeln explained the mechanisms to *New Scientist* magazine. All chemical and electrical signals must pass through the outside wall of the brain. This membrane is composed almost entirely of fats. Neural cell membranes are in fact 20 per cent essential fatty acids. If their composition and therefore their shape changes, their function is impaired. Fatty acids have also been linked to the neurotransmitter serotonin. Hibbeln has found that people with little omega-3 in their spinal fluid seem to have low levels of serotonin (some antidepressant drugs work by boosting serotonin levels).

Cross-cultural studies show a strong link between national consumption of essential fatty acids and levels of depression. As a Western diet full of processed foods and animal fats infiltrates a culture, the rate of depression rises accordingly. Other studies have found that some patients with manic depression respond to supplements of fish oils.

In the UK, scientists have been exploring the link between essential fatty acid deficiency or imbalance and developmental conditions. There is mounting evidence that deficiencies are involved in dyslexia, dyspraxia, attention deficit and hyperactivity disorder and autistic spectrum disorders. The incidence of these disorders has risen dramatically in recent decades.

Even more startling are the implications of a randomized, double-blind, placebo-controlled trial conducted by Bernard Gesch, senior research scientist in the Department of Physiology at Oxford University, and his colleagues. During the study, which took place in one of Britain's maximum security prisons, where inmates reported some of the highest levels of prison violence in the country, prisoners were randomly assigned a placebo or a course of supplements containing essential fatty acids and key vitamins and minerals necessary to metabolize them. The number of serious offences including violence committed by the prisoners fell by nearly 40 per cent in those taking the supplements but not at all in those not taking them.*

---

* The idea that nutrition might be a key factor in anti-social behaviour is not new. Dr Hugh Sinclair persuaded the wartime British government to supplement the diet of all pregnant mothers with cod liver oil and orange juice because he had found blood levels low in many vitamins and essential fatty acids in much of the population and speculated that this could cause illness and bad behaviour.

Gesch began his work when he was a probation officer in Northampton working with juvenile offenders. He was seeing young girls and boys who were committing strings of burglaries or violent offences. 'They'd turn up with bags of sweets, or junk, and they looked so unhealthy.' Nutritionists were asked to look at the children's diets and by improving them managed to reduce reoffending. The local court started using diet as a component of its sentencing, but critics said the improvements in clients could be explained by other factors. The attraction of conducting a properly scientific trial in a prison was that in such a controlled environment, exact intakes could be measured and other potentially confounding factors removed to see if there was a link. To Gesch, the case was 'just bleeding obvious'.

The brain is a metabolic powerhouse, which despite being only 2 per cent of our body mass, consumes around 20 per cent of available energy. To metabolize this energy requires a range of nutrients, vitamins, minerals and essential fatty acids. These are essential for the normal functioning of the brain, which means there may be consequences if we don't get enough of them from our diet.

Gesch was certainly not suggesting that nutrition is the only cause of antisocial behaviour. He also admitted he was entering the realms of speculation when he pointed out that the dramatic rise in notifiable criminal offences in the UK from 1,100 per 100,000 people in 1950 to 9,400 per 100,000 people in 1996 coincided with dramatic changes in diet post-war. It may just be coincidence that the greatest levels of criminal behaviour are seen in male youths in late adolescence, just at the point when their accelerated growth puts their brains in competition with their bodies for nutrients. But for Gesch, one of the most powerful drivers to finding out more was the response from the prison inmates whose behaviour appeared to have improved. He started receiving little thank-you notes from some of the country's most feared and violent offenders.

There is a long way to go before we fully understand the links between diet and mental processes, but one of the reasons all these lines of research are so appealing is that they are intuitive and suggest cheap, non-invasive remedies. They confirm what many parents and teachers now experience, that children fed a diet of junk are often unmanageable. Growing children, who need the best food, nowadays nearly always eat the worst. A study by the Consumers' Association (CA) showed the scale of the problem we are building for the future. Researchers asked 246 primary and secondary school children to keep food diaries in an effort to draw a picture of the average diet of today's children.

Zoë, aged fifteen, started day one with a slice of white toast and butter and a mug of tea. During mid-morning break at school, she had a bag of Walkers salt and vinegar crisps. School lunch was a plate of chips and gravy with two small sausages. At mid-afternoon break at school she had a Chupa Chups 'orange flavour' lollipop. After school she had more crisps, Golden Wonder crispy bacon flavour, a bar of Terry's chocolate orange, a packet of sweets and a bottle of 'toothkind' Ribena with blackcurrant flavour. Tea-time at home provided home-made shepherd's pie with baked beans and a glass of sugar-free lemonade. During the evening Zoë consumed a small packet of wine gums and six chocolate sweets. Before bed she had a glass of skimmed milk. Day two was similar, except that the white toast and tea for breakfast was supplemented with a small tin of macaroni cheese on toast and more Ribena. Mid-morning snack was crisps again with a small bottle of diet lemonade. Lunch was chips and gravy again, this time accompanying a turkey product. The afternoon lollipop and after-school crisps were followed by supper at home of chips, gravy and chicken nuggets, with a small portion of mushy peas and lemonade. During the evening Zoë consumed two Aero chocolate bars, before a bedtime glass of orange juice. And so on through the week.

Lynne, aged eleven, had even less variety in her diet, eating the same sweetened processed cereal with milk each morning for breakfast, having the same packed lunch of peanut butter sandwiches, crisps and flavoured yoghurt, and cheese and tomato pizza for tea each day, either with cola or water to drink, and the same cake during the course of each evening. She regularly ate four bags of crisps in the course of a day, having them at both school break-times, at lunch-time and after school. Large numbers of foods targeted at children remain poor quality.

The contents of the typical cheap chicken nugget were revealed in Chapter 2. A well-made pizza, with a dough of flour, yeast, olive oil and salt, is both healthy and delicious. But cheap ones get up to 2 per cent sugar added, along with modified starch, corn syrup and flavourings. The same goes for the tomato sauce: the wholesome ones are made with tomatoes, oil, garlic and not much else; the cheap ones are made with sugar, starch and flavourings to disguise a light touch on the tomatoes. Cheese can be good cheese or industrial cheese analogue made with vegetable oil, proteins, starch and flavourings. And sausages and burgers have always provided a licence to adulterate, legally or otherwise. The horsemeat scandal showed us the delights of the economy burger. A typical economy sausage's list of ingredients, found in my local supermarket in 2013 was as follows:

Pork (42 per cent), water, pork fat (10 per cent), rusk, potato starch, soya protein concentrate

Salt and flavourings had been included to make it taste of something, diphosphates and gum had been added to hold it together, cochineal colouring had been added to give it a pink meaty look, and it had three different types of preservative.

For years school meals were as nutritionally depleted as the worst junk food. Then TV chef Jamie Oliver began a hugely successful campaign to shock parents and government into changing them. (His producer said she had been prompted in part by my articles in the *Guardian* on chicken nuggets and a colleague's on Bernard Matthews' Turkey Twizzlers.) Oliver's programmes also built on the work of campaigners who had been struggling to draw attention to the poor quality of deregulated school food for years. The impact of energetic and entertaining celebrity support was enormous and immediate. The government introduced new standards and what children eat at school has improved dramatically since. But take-up remains a problem – 57 per cent of school-aged children were not eating school dinners in 2013, instead bringing in packed lunches, snacking or going off site to buy fast food. The coalition government had also decided that the standards introduced in the wake of the TV campaign would not be mandatory for new academies or free schools.

Sadly, packed lunches still left a lot to be desired. Favourite ingredients included ham sandwiches made with white sliced bread, packets of crisps, sweet drinks and sugary cereal bars. Even the ham is often not what it seems. Most of what we buy these days is sold pre-sliced and packed. It is nearly all either 'formed ham' or 'reformed ham'.

Formed ham is made by dissecting the muscle meat from the leg bone of a pig and roughly chopping it. Then it is either passed under rows of needles on hydraulic arms which inject it with a solution of water, sugars, preservatives, flavourings and other additives or put into a giant cement-mixer-like machine to be tumbled or massaged with a similar solution. The machinery is the same as that used to adulterate chicken. Both technologies enable the processors to pump large quantities of water into the meat. Many hams contain up to 20 per cent added water.

The tumbling process dissolves an amino acid called myosin in the meat which becomes very sticky, so that when the pork is next put into D-shaped or ham-shaped moulds and cooked, it comes out looking like a whole piece of meat. If the ham is to be presented sliced as a traditional cut, a layer of fat is stuck round the edge of the mould to make it look as though it has just been cut off a whole leg. Ham made this way is uniformly wet. It must be labelled 'formed from cuts of legs'. It should be made from muscle meat but does not have to have been made from cuts from the same animal.

Moving down a grade, 'reformed' ham is made from chopped-up or emulsified meat which is not necessarily all muscle meat. During the process of making 'formed' ham, a gunge of scraps gathers at the bottom of the machines and this may be used in making 'reformed ham', as can mechanically recovered or mechanically deboned meat. The process is the same as that for 'formed ham' but the ingredients of 'reformed ham' are even cheaper.

Few of the 246 children's diaries in the CA study mentioned fresh fruit and vegetables; most described diets high in fat, sugars and salt and lacking many vital nutrients. The nutritionist who analysed them found many were low in iron, zinc, folate, vitamins A and C and calcium.

Children today also consume thirty times the amount of soft drinks and twenty-five times the amount of confectionery they did in 1950. Overall consumption of soft drinks had doubled in the twelve-year period between the official National Diet and Nutrition surveys of 2002–3 and its predecessor.

The food industry argues that parents decide what their children eat and are responsible for their diets. It says that if they are not providing balanced ones, it is a question of education.

But the children in the CA survey are not peculiar, nor are their parents negligent. For most parents it has become a struggle to make sure their children eat well. Although our food in the West is more plentiful and varied than ever before, anxiety about what we eat has probably never been higher.

How did we become so removed from good food? Why, if the experts' advice is now so clear, have governments done so little to ensure that we eat what we need for health?

Part of the explanation is certainly cultural. Since the war, working hours have lengthened, more women have gone out to work, and family structures have changed. As societies in the

West have become more affluent, the proportion of income spent on what we eat has declined. We have chosen to spend our new wealth not on better-quality food but on other pleasures. The time we give to food has also declined dramatically. In the 1930s we spent over three hours preparing food each day. By the 1970s that had dropped to one hour. Today we spend on average less than fifteen minutes a day cooking. As individual gratification has taken over from the communal, the home-cooked family meal has become an endangered species.

But our choice of food is also powerfully influenced by advertising. The food and drink industry spent £838 million on advertising in the UK in 2007, according to the Department of Health, and in typical years about three quarters of that is spent marketing to children.

The biggest spender in 2012 was Coca-Cola with a budget of £19 million. Mars, Kraft/Mondalēz and Nestlé helped make confectionery the sector that accounted for the largest proportion of advertising spend in the fast-moving consumer goods category that year.

The biggest categories of food advertised are sugary breakfast cereals, confectionery, soft drinks, potted desserts and yoghurts, and savoury snacks such as crisps. Advertising of fast-food brands comes next. The figures are hard to come by, but *The Atlas of Food* records that the world's biggest food advertisers in 1999 were Nestlé, Coca-Cola, McDonald's, Mars, Pepsi, Danone and Kellogg's. In 2010, according to the UN Special Rapporteur on the Right to Food, US companies spent $8.5 billion advertising food, drink, and confectionery, and the vast majority of the money went on foods high in salt, fat and sugar.

The foods advertised are not exactly the sum of what is recommended for a healthy diet. Exposure to this manipulation of our appetites starts young; the techniques used have become increasingly sophisticated.

Marketing experts have worked out ways to engage with children from a very early age using psychological techniques.

Studies have shown that children do not discriminate between television programmes and adverts until some time between the ages of four and seven. They don't recognize bias until the age of eight. But jingles, graphic symbols and repetition are used to catch their attention.

Animated characters children recognize have been used to endorse products; sporting heroes have been used to associate products with social acceptance; and repeat purchases have been encouraged with collectable free toys. A psychologist who has led several public health education campaigns for the Department of Health, Dr Aric Sigman, explored how marketing is designed to exploit children's basic needs. He identified four 'vulnerabilities that advertisers aim for': the need for peer group acceptance, the need for stimulation, the need for role models and the need for nurture and protection. He believed that advertising disrupts the normal process of child-rearing, subverting a child's needs when they are most vulnerable and pliable. Many advertisements make appeals to pester power, that phenomenon that is most subversive of parental control. The fight to curb marketing to children in the UK has been prolonged. The techniques used to find target audiences kept changing. Each time a new one was exposed, manufacturers agreed to take a responsible line, but new methods would be devised.

The independent campaign group the Food Commission charted how soft drinks companies had focused their attention on the teenage market. It highlighted methods of reaching children that slip under the radar of parents – the internet and text messaging. Companies sponsor music and pay for links with the most popular pop singers, sports celebrities and film stars.

The brilliance of the techniques has not been in any doubt. The team that marketed the launch of Kellogg's Real Fruit Winders described some of them in detail in their submission to the Institute of Practitioners in Advertising's Advertising Effectiveness Awards in 2002. 'Communications worked by getting on to kids' radars ... by creating the desired sense of

"cool" . . . we went to toy fairs, we studied the success of Poke-
mon . . . we would have to give kids ownership of the brand and
not let Mum in on the act . . .' To do this, the advertisers created the world of the Chewchat gang, whose pranks centred
round winding up terrified fruit and squishing it into Real Fruit
Winders. They invented a language to 'spread the word about
the brand virally' and placed it on websites children use to get
music news and celebrity gossip. Measured by acceptance among
young people, and volume of sales, the campaign was a huge
success. Mothers were also impressed by the 'fruit' message, seeing these products as healthier treats than sweets.

When children are receiving this sort of subliminal education,
it can be very hard for parents to counter it.

Cadbury was severely criticized in 2003 for its marketing campaign aimed at children in schools. (Walkers crisps had been there
before it with a school scheme to swap crisp packets for books.)
Like most of the food industry, Cadbury's argued that the crisis of
obesity was more to do with the fact that children today are less
active than they used to be than with what they eat. It launched a
£9 million marketing drive to get children to exchange chocolate
wrappers for free school sports equipment and persuaded the UK
sports minister, Richard Caborn, to give his endorsement to the
scheme, which it said would help tackle obesity.

But the Food Commission calculated that to earn one netball
worth about £5, primary schoolchildren would have to spend
nearly £40 on chocolate and consume more than 20,000 calories. A ten-year-old child eating enough chocolate to earn a
basketball through the scheme would need to play basketball for
ninety hours to burn off the calories consumed. A junior basketball team would have to play twenty-seven full-length games to
burn off the calories. Cadbury defended the promotion, which
it said was 'a genuine attempt . . . to encourage greater physical
activity among young people', inactivity being 'the greatest
cause of obesity among young people'. The FSA subsequently

said that it had not been consulted about the sports minister's endorsement of the scheme, but had it been, it would have advised against what it deemed to be conflicting messages.

Growing pressure to ban or at least control much more tightly food advertising to children was fiercely resisted by the industry. It argued that advertising encouraged brand loyalty, not consumption in itself. To settle the issue, the FSA commissioned a comprehensive review of research on the effects of advertising food to children from Professor Gerard Hastings of the University of Strathclyde. His team found that not only did advertising influence what food children choose but also what they feel about it. 'The debate should now shift to what action is needed,' Professor Hastings concluded.

The big guns from the manufacturers in these sectors were summoned before the House of Commons health select committee inquiry on obesity to account for themselves at the end of 2003. Top executives from McDonald's, PepsiCo (which owns the Walkers brand as well as Pepsi), Kellogg's and Cadbury Schweppes were grilled by MPs in a room packed with journalists, campaigners and industry representatives.

It was hard to ignore the parallels with the tobacco industry. The committee's chairman, David Hinchliffe MP, had been a leading political figure in the fight to ban cigarette advertising. On the other side, the food industry was marshalling many of the sorts of arguments used by the tobacco lobby. Obesity would not be tackled by restricting freedom of choice. Its advertising did not increase sales which were really 'pretty flat' but simply encouraged brand loyalty. The scientific evidence was unclear. Education about good diet and greater physical activity – calories in, calories out – were more important than controls on the industry. Tim Mobsby, President of Kellogg's Europe, told the committee for example that he had not seen anything that clearly demonstrated that there is a link between sugar and obesity and that he would be quite happy if children ate his Coco Pops most days of the week. There are no such things as bad foods, only bad diets, the companies agreed.

But Andrew Cosslett, the managing director of confectionery for Cadbury Schweppes in Europe, the Middle East and Africa, unintentionally made the campaigners' own point while trying to defend his chocolate. He had bought a low-fat yoghurt thinking it would be healthy, he said, and had taken it home, only to find to his amazement, when he examined the label, that it contained more calories than a large Crunchie bar. 'Yoghurt, you would assume, has a certain health profile and when you see a low-fat yoghurt with a clear statement drawing attention to the fact that it is low-fat, you would be doubly convinced and it would reinforce your instinct that this is a good food product. It is only when you get it home and examine the calories that you find it has two hundred-plus calories in it, which was a surprise to me and I have been in the food industry for a long time.' In fact, Mr Cosslett went so far as to say, there are people being deluded on a daily basis about what they are buying.

To be fair, in a free market, and in the absence of tighter controls, the advertising and manufacturing industries are only doing what industries do, selling themselves as hard and effectively as possible.

The industry lost that round of the battle in theory when the broadcasting regulator in the UK, Ofcom, announced new measures in 2006 to restrict television advertising to children of foods and drinks high in salt, fat and sugar, to be phased in over two years.

I made a freedom of information request and found that it had been lobbied on twenty-nine occasions by the food and advertising industry in the run-up to publishing its proposals. It had met health and consumer groups on four occasions.

Advertising aimed specifically at children on TV did fall. But in practice the industry was able to work round the ban, which was limited in its scope. It did not cover many of the programmes watched by children that were classed as adult programmes, such as soap operas and talent shows, nor did it cover the increasingly significant world of digital marketing. A systematic review of evidence published in the scientific journal *Obesity Review* in 2013 looked at children's exposure to adverts for foods and drinks high in sugar and fat across Europe, Asia, Australia and North America, and found that it had changed little in the previous five years. Industry surveys by contrast showed that companies had complied with voluntary pledges to limit this sort of marketing. The author of the review, Dr Tim Lobstein, found the discrepancy was due to what was measured. 'Companies don't look at the family TV programmes watched by children, only children's TV. And they use their own criteria for judging what is appropriate to advertise to children. Ofcom has banned junk food advertising during children's TV programmes, and this is effective, according to the review, but only during children's TV.' Advertising of junk food during family television in the UK has actually increased since the ban on ads during children's television came in, undermining the benefits the rules might have had, he explained.

Industry lobbying to protect its interests continues to be highly effective. When the FSA looked as though it might become too successful in its measures, it was subject to lobbying that helped eviscerate it.

It was a Friday afternoon in May 2009 when Andrew Lansley's Public Health Commission met, as usual, in the newly restored 1930s splendour of Unilever House on Victoria Embankment in London. It was gathering for its final plenary session, having been tasked by Lansley, later to become health secretary but then in opposition, to come up with new policies for the Conservatives to tackle the big public health crises of obesity, diet-related disease and alcohol abuse.

The commission's job was to assess Lansley's idea that a deal between business and government should form the basis of his health strategy after the election. It was about to produce its report: We're All in This Together, Improving the Long Term Health of the Nation.

The chair of the commission, by invitation of Lansley, was Dave Lewis, UK and Ireland chairman of Unilever, one of the largest processors of industrial fats in the world.

With him were Lucy Neville-Rolfe, then corporate affairs director of Tesco, the supermarket that had been a leading opponent of the traffic light food labelling scheme favoured by the FSA, and Lady Buscombe, Conservative peer and former head of the Advertising Association, where she had established herself as a formidable political champion of the advertising industry's right to operate free of restrictions.

Asda's corporate affairs director, Paul Kelly, formerly PR head of Compass, the school meals company of turkey twizzler fame, had to send his apologies. Mark Leverton, policy director of Diageo, manufacturer of leading vodka, whisky and beer brands, joined them by phone.

Diageo, in fact, had closer links with the Lib Dems than the Conservatives – its corporate relations director, Ian Wright, was one of three people who paid donations directly into Nick Clegg's personal bank account to fund a researcher – but that would come in useful later once the election results were known. Bolstering the alcohol industry's presence in person was Jeremy Beadles, chief executive of its lobby group, the Wine and Spirit Trade Association.

The area of increasing physical activity to fight obesity was covered by Fred Turok, chairman of the Fitness Industry Association, the group representing private gyms and professional personal trainers. Public interest groups were represented at the meeting by a handful of health and consumer charities and two leading liver and alcohol specialists.

The secretariat for the Public Health Commission that day was, as usual, provided by Unilever and its marketing team. They were led by Unilever's public affairs director George Gordon, and joined by Martin le Jeune, director of the corporate PR agency Open Road (its clients include Unilever, Sky and the alcohol industry's Portman Group). Le Jeune is former public affairs director of Sky, a former director of Fishburn Hedges PR agency (clients Diageo, Nestlé), and is a member of a group calling itself the 'progressive conservatives', who are dedicated to 'progress achieved by maximizing liberty in both economic and social fields'.

The commission's fifth meeting in Unilever House had 'set the scope for progress' on the contentious issues for the industry of food and alcohol labelling, and portion sizes.

It must have felt like a new dawn for the food and drinks industries. After more than four years of determined and co-ordinated lobbying, they were about to achieve the corporate PR agency dream: being invited to write the policy themselves. And, if the Conservatives won the election, in Lansley they would have a health secretary who understood them.

He not only subscribed to the libertarian view that public health should be more a matter of personal responsibility than government action, he bought into the whole pro-business PR view of the world. (At that time, Lansley was a paid director of the marketing agency Profero, whose clients have included Pepsi, Mars, Pizza Hut and Diageo's Guinness. He gave up the directorship at the end of 2009.)

Lansley in fact attached huge importance to public health, believing that too much emphasis had been put on treating illness in the NHS rather than preventing it in the first place. He talked about the ageing population and rising costs adding to the economic imperative to rebalance prevention and cure – but said change would come through a partnership between individuals, business, charities and local and national government, and by understanding behavioural science.

By the time he outlined his vision for public health as a responsibility deal between business and government in 2008, Lansley had already adopted several of the industry's favoured approaches to the food, drink and health crises, promising that if he were in office 'government and FSA promotion of traffic light labelling will stop'; that there would be no mandatory extension of advertising restrictions; and that alcohol strategy would focus on responsible drinking messages and improved labelling which the industry preferred to regulation.

Lansley also committed to avoiding a narrow focus on 'fear of junk foods' that might demonize individual manufacturers' products, and to talking instead in terms of diets as a whole, of the balance of energy in and energy out, and of portion size. He had said the government and the FSA would 'highlight the continuing contribution made by business to improving diet by reformulating its products'.

And so the FSA, the regulator that had caused food and drink manufacturers and retailers so much irritation, was about to have its comeuppance. Government policy on public health and nutrition would soon be taken away from it and placed back in political hands.

The work of the Public Health Commission was not only setting out a strategy for a new Conservative government, it had created a working group of industry partners who could be drafted in effortlessly to the new administration's public health structure once Lansley had become secretary of state for health.

After the election, and a few months into the new coalition government, with Lansley due to publish his white paper on public health, I discovered that the same cast of characters had been invited into Whitehall. They made up the bulk of new so-called 'responsibility deal' networks the health secretary had set up to be at the heart of his public health policy. Alongside them were McDonald's, KFC, PepsiCo and Compass. They were drawing up deals between the Department of Health and business, having been asked to volunteer measures to tackle obesity, diet-related disease, alcohol abuse and lack of exercise.

In a reversal of normal government process, recommendations were not being prepared by civil servants before the meetings, but by the working groups themselves and then sent to civil servants and the wider group for comment, according to sources close to the deals. A senior corporate source welcomed this, saying it was recognition by the new government that a lot of the best expertise lies within industry and voluntary sector groups.

Co-chair of the alcohol deal, with Lib Dem health minister Paul Burstow, was the Wine and Spirit Trade Association head, Jeremy Beadles. The Fitness Industry Association's Fred Turok was in the chair of the physical activity deal with Conservative minister Simon Burns.

The food deal was chaired by Lansley himself and Dr Susan Jebb, the leading Medical Research Council obesity academic, known for her pragmatic approach to working with industry and for endorsing the methods of Weight Watchers.

The over-arching board, set up and chaired by Lansley to oversee all of these business responsibility deal networks, also included many of the contributors to the health commission at Unilever House. As well as local government representatives, health charities and a regional health director, there were Unilever, Tesco, and Asda from the industry lobbies – plus other leading retailers, Diageo, the Wine and Spirit Trade Association, the Advertising Association, the Fitness Industry Association, Compass and Mars.

Lansley's special adviser on policy development at the Department of Health, meanwhile, had worked previously at Mandate Communications, a corporate PR agency whose clients had included health organizations as well as Kraft/Cadbury, Dominos Pizza and drug companies.

In early meetings, these commercial partners had been invited to draft priorities and identify barriers, such as EU legislation, that they would like removed. They had been assured by Lansley that he wanted to explore voluntary, not regulatory, approaches, and to support them in removing obstacles. Using the pricing of food or alcohol to change consumption had been ruled out. One group was told that the health department did not want to lead, but rather hear from its members what should be done.

Looking back, senior FSA sources identify those Unilever

House meetings as the 'beginning of the FSA abolition movement'. They could see the writing on the wall for their traffic
light labelling scheme, despite the research that showed it was
the most helpful one for consumers.

When it came to power the coalition announced that the
FSA would have its powers much reduced as its role in setting
nutrition policy would be taken over the Department of Health.

Relations between the agency as regulator and the food
industry it regulated had been severely strained for some time.
The FSA's successful move, with broadcast regulator Ofcom, to
introduce restrictions on TV advertising of foods high in salt, fat
or sugar to children had already hit food companies hard. The
breakfast cereal industry was particularly affected, with the vast
majority of its marketing effort falling foul of the new rules.

The FSA's proposal to introduce traffic light food labelling
on processed foods that would put a red light on foods high in
salt, sugar or fat was where many companies drew their line in
the sand. They thought a red light would be understood by consumers as 'stop', and were not prepared to negotiate on a device
that would damage their sales.

Although some retailers such as Sainsbury's, Asda and Waitrose accepted the FSA's scientific research supporting the value
of traffic lights and introduced a version of them, Tesco and
Morrisons were adamantly opposed at the time.

The response from manufacturers to all these public health
measures was a lobbying effort of unprecedented intensity, both
in the UK and in Europe, according to senior sources from the
regulator and Whitehall. Tesco, Kellogg's, Unilever and Kraft led
a campaign to derail the FSA's labelling scheme by launching
their own rival system based on guideline daily amounts (GDAs).
FSA research showed consumers found GDAs harder to understand than the system they were proposing.

The industry also spent hundreds of millions of euros lobbying against traffic lights at European level.

'It was appalling the way manufacturers and Tesco conspired to defeat traffic light labelling despite the willingness of other retailers to give it a shot,' Richard Ayre, a member of the FSA board for seven years, told me, adding that tensions between the FSA and the Department of Health had existed from the beginning.

By the end of their term, Labour ministers had in fact become impatient with the FSA's independence too.

When it came to power, the Conservative–Liberal Democrat coalition formally announced that the FSA would lose a large part of its remit. Around seventy nutrition experts from the FSA moved to the Department of Health, along with their files. Labelling was dispatched to the Department for Environment, Food and Rural Affairs. The splintering of responsibility for our food would be felt when the horsemeat scandal occurred.

Professor Philip James, who produced the blueprint for the FSA at the personal invitation of Tony Blair, and later became chair of the International Obesity Taskforce, traces much of the problem today back to the late 1970s. Until then the food standards of many foods were tightly regulated. But many of the standards were outdated – specifying, for example, that ice cream had to contain a certain percentage of fat. Power blocs built around the old farming lobbies maintained them. The new mood of consumerism that swept in with Mrs Thatcher demanded they should be abolished and replaced by free choice. So food standards were deregulated. Manufacturers were allowed to make what they liked so long as it was microbiologically safe and so long as it was labelled so that consumers could make that choice. 'Choice', the Conservative mantra of the 1980s and 1990s, remained the prevailing philosophy in food through the Labour years and still endures today.

The trouble with this notion is that choice is so often illusory. Children bombarded with advertising and left with a vending machine do not make informed choices. Nor do adults who practically need a PhD to decipher food labels. Nor do families whose pay is so low they cannot afford fresh, whole food. Nor do chief executives at the mercy of impatient shareholders.

Who will concern themselves with whether we are sold junk? We must look to ourselves. It will take a coalition of interests in which the public, as in previous centuries, takes the lead. Change will come when ordinary people, realizing that our current food system is environmentally, ethically and even biologically unsustainable, exert their buying power, and above all their political power, and finally say, 'Enough is enough.'

Afterword to the Revised Edition

The deep structural faults in the current food system have become clearer than ever since *Not On the Label* was first published. The financial crisis of 2008 brought the underlying problems into sharp focus. The impact of climate change and crises of resources of which environmentalists had warned have come upon us far sooner than even the pessimists predicted.

There have been stirrings of official recognition: the UK government, which had determinedly pursued a policy of letting the market and international trade provide, began changing its tune. A report in 2011 on the future of food and farming noted that as the global population increased from 7 billion to around 9 billion by 2050 there would be increased demand for food, competition for land, water and energy would intensify, while the effects of climate change would accelerate. Any one of these pressures would present substantial challenges to food security; together they constituted a major threat that required a strategic reappraisal of how the world is fed. This solemn sounding of that alarm came not from the Department for Environment, Food and Rural Affairs, which is still in thrall to laissez-faire, but from the Foresight programme which reported direct to the prime minister and cabinet office.

It would have been hard not to come to this conclusion. Dramatic rises in the price of staple foods sparked riots in twenty-three countries across the Middle East, North Africa and South Asia in 2008, and protests in dozens more. Governments were given a wake-up call as to the scale of the challenge. Spikes in the price of bread and civil disturbance have been historic bedfellows. There were knee-jerk reactions – a panic wave of protectionist measures from food exporting countries to keep

their own harvests at home and their urban poor off the streets –
which exacerbated price volatility. We were given an indication
of how future shortages might play out: the international markets cannot be counted on to provide; other countries will put
their own citizens first. Maximizing production in farming in
our own country would seem a no-brainer. Food, like energy, is
a strategic issue, not one where we can afford to say other countries can produce it cheaper than us so let's not bother. The war
generation understood that but subsequent generations have
forgotten.

The violent unrest of 2008 did not lead to any overhaul of the
fundamentals of power and distribution in the global food business however, and so by 2011 rises in food prices at unprecedented
rates were once again the trigger for uprisings, this time in the
Arab Spring.

An equitable food system is vital to global stability. Instead, all
the progress in science and technology, all the globalization of
trade, all the industrialization of production and distribution
and neoliberal opening up of markets have brought us only as
far as this: the profoundly troubling paradox that close to 1 billion people around the world go to bed hungry every day while
at the same time over 1 billion are overweight or obese.

Was the horsemeat scandal of 2013 one of a first wave of
shocks that warn of system failure? It demonstrated that the economics of the current model were bust. The impact is being felt
even in rich countries; it is magnified tenfold in poorer parts of
the world.

Even in a country as affluent as Britain you can now find the
daily experience of hunger re-emerging alongside the effects of
excess, as I discovered when I visited a church in one of the capital's wealthiest streets handing out food parcels in 2012. By the
time most visitors reach the doors of the Hammersmith and
Fulham foodbank in West London, run by the charity the Trussell Trust, they have not eaten properly for days.

Those who come here must be referred by a recognized public authority – it might be a school that has noticed children are not being fed, a GP who has noticed signs of malnutrition, or a social worker who finds a mental health patient is not eating. The food that is distributed is donated by the public. The Trussell Trust had seen a huge surge in demand for centres around the country since the recession; it fed 41,000 people in 2009–10 but by 2013 half a million people were being given emergency food like this. More and more, it was helping people who were in work but struggling with stagnant wages and soaring food and fuel bills. Behind the undoubtedly good private work to relieve this hunger was a devastating public moral failure.

The Hammersmith and Fulham foodbank is located in one of those London streets that have become enclaves of stratospheric City wealth in the last three decades. People have become intensely relaxed about being filthy rich here: huge SUVs, the so-called 'Chelsea tractors', on parade outside nineteenth-century red-brick villas worth £2–3 million, home cinemas displayed in immaculate architectural extensions of sheet glass. Next door to the foodbank is the Hurlingham Clinic, where a different manifestation of our dysfunctional relationship with food can be seen in adverts for expensive 'aesthetic procedures', from injectable fillers to cellulite management, in order to achieve the unreal physical perfection peddled by marketers everywhere. By dreadful irony, one of the clinic's specialties is solving weight problems, as described in its literature: 'There can be few of us that have not tried to lose a few pounds at some time or other . . . But for some of us getting weight off and keeping it off seems to be an impossible dream. If you have tried everything and nothing seems to work, well, there is a solution. Feel satisfied after small meals, lose the desire to snack between meals, feel healthier, be healthier and lose those extra pounds for good. This solution is the only proven method of effectively controlling your weight permanently. The solution lies in surgery.' Wealth is no barrier to falling victim to the ills of the food system.

I watched the parcels go out at the foodbank one afternoon. Audrey, shedding tears of shame, had given most of her pension cheque to her daughter and grandchildren following a fire that destroyed their home. The daughter, a pharmacist – retraining as a teacher so she could look after the children in the holidays – had not been able to afford insurance, so had been left with nothing. Audrey was having the grandchildren for the weekend but had no money to feed them. She had herself been living on a diet of breakfast cereal and crackers with small pieces of cheese.

A pregnant mother with two children and no food for their supper, husband at work, was too distressed to talk; a young man with mental health problems, moved from a hostel to a flat and waiting for his benefits to be transferred, who'd had no food for nearly three days and no money for heating … the litany of hardship was humbling.

Of the visitors who come to the foodbank, over a fifth were on incomes so low, whether in jobs or on benefits, that the smallest upset tipped them into crisis, the manager told me. Meanwhile capping benefits so that recipients should not be better off than the average working family was casting poverty once more in the eighteenth-century language of Malthus, which saw hunger as a necessary spur to the idle to work.

João, from Portugal, had been fully employed in catering jobs since 2004 and paid his share of tax and national insurance. This sector, like so many parts of the food economy, had depended on migrants paid little for long shifts, and successive governments had turned a blind eye to illegal employment that undercut proper jobs when it became a convenient wages policy. But João had been made redundant. He had fallen into debt because he was not allowed to escape his mobile phone contract. He had applied for the two vacancies at the Jobcentre that morning, but they had been filled. He had been going two to three days at a time without food, going to bed to conserve energy. It was hard to see how hunger might spur him to greater efforts to work when there were no jobs.

But even those who came to the foodbank who were in work were on wages so low they could not afford to feed their families.

As food and fuel inflation roared away, the national minimum wage was out of kilter with living costs. There were proposals to allow regional variations in the minimum wage that would cut it further, and the Agricultural Wages Board, which had set living standards for many rural workers in the lowest-paid farming jobs, was being abolished.

To see this sort of hunger in Britain was a shock. In developing countries, where malnutrition has never gone away, we are less surprised to find it, assuming it is some inevitable part of national poverty or the unfortunate consequence of some shortage produced by drought or war. But in fact by the end of the first decade of the twenty-first century it looked as though something much more disturbing was going on – the pressures in the food system risked sending development into reverse. People are increasingly going hungry not because of cyclical famine or conflict, but because the money to be made in the food system is being sucked out by those at the top of the chain.

I went to Guatemala in 2011 to try to understand how a country that is one of the world's leading producers of food for the global markets could also have one of the highest rates of malnutrition in the world. Half of all children under five there are malnourished, yet it is the fifth largest exporter of sugar *and* of coffee *and* of bananas. Its rural areas have been witnessing a largely unregulated palm oil rush – the area given over to plantations of the crop had increased by 146 per cent between 2005 and 2010 – as international traders have sought to cash in on demand for biofuels created by US and European mandates and subsidies and rising demand for palm oil for processed food. How can so many be hungry when surrounded by so much food?

The new palm frontier is in the north of the country, where what were protected tropical forests have nevertheless been cleared for plantations. Land grabs here for the oil rush have often involved dispossession of peasant farmers. Smallholders who used to grow their own food have given frequent accounts of agribusinesses sending land agents to negotiate buying or renting their farms. If they refuse, the agents tell them they 'will return later to negotiate with your widow'. Land deeds are often unclear, and in many cases only those with money for lawyers have been able to register their claims. Claims made by businesses often go unchecked. Land grabs like these have been recorded by aid agencies across South and Central America and Africa in the last few years as private foreign investors see sky-high agricultural commodity prices as an opportunity for making money. State enterprises have joined the scramble for territory and water too, as the Chinese government and Arab countries look to secure food for their populations. These are not the sort of investments that take care of food security for the local people. In Guatemala, palm producers had been leasing land for just ten years for plantations, since that is the period over which the monocrop cultivation is expected to exhaust the soil. Then they will move on.

Agribusiness has expanded palm and sugar plantations for ethanol, and diverted rivers to irrigate the trees and cane, threatening food security in another way. Climate change has already resulted in more extreme hurricanes and intense unseasonal rain in the region. The diverted rivers try to revert to their natural courses during storms, washing away the land in between. Smallholders around the plantations were increasingly experiencing floods that destroy their subsistence crops and ruin their houses.

Half the population live in extreme poverty on less than $2 a day. The money to be made from the food chain here, as in most poor countries, has been captured by elites and transnational corporations, leaving them excluded.

Domingo Tamupsis was working as a harvester on a Guatemalan sugar plantation when I met him, for a firm that exports bioethanol to fill the fuel tanks of cars in the US. He was working ten to twelve hours a day, six days a week.

His settlement, Willywood, in the fertile Pacific coastal area, is surrounded by industrial farms but he was earning so little his family could not afford to eat every day. Some days he survived his shift of hard physical labour on nothing but the mangoes that drop from trees by the roadside.

His wife Marina was twenty-three, but so slight she might be mistaken for a girl. She had two daughters, Yeimi, aged six, and Jessica, aged two. Jessica was the size of the average European one-year-old, her distended stomach a sign of chronic malnutrition. When she smiled, hollow creases formed in her cheeks, betraying her semi-permanent state of hunger.

The year before I met them, Marina had given birth in the eighth month of pregnancy to a stillborn child. She had been ill and hungry throughout, then felt severe pains one day at breakfast time. When she finally reached the nearest medical help, a hospital forty-five minutes away, staff told her the baby was dead. They returned the body to her, but she and Domingo had no cash for the return bus. A doctor gave them the fare, and a friend in town lent money for a coffin. So it was that their third child, Marvin Orlando, a brother for their two little girls, came home to be buried.

Tamupsis could see no way out of his dilemma. 'The money I make is not enough to feed us,' he told me. 'We feed the children first because the girls cry so much when they are hungry, but it's not enough and I think that's why they get ill and don't thrive. I don't know where to get more money: I can't work any harder and I can't steal because they shoot you if you steal.'

The food was there but there was no access to it: the main problem is distribution. Land is concentrated in very few hands. The transnational exporting companies pay very little tax. Labour conditions on plantations are at best poor, and often appalling. Wages are too low to cover the cost of basic food as prices rise. Efforts to organize and demand better wages, or a bigger slice of the large cake, have been brutally repressed.

Meanwhile the economic policies favoured by the international financial institutions in the last few decades have here, as in so many developing countries, weakened food security.

In the 1980s a structural adjustment programme imposed by the International Monetary Fund on the debt-laden nation led to the slashing of technical assistance provided by the agriculture ministry to small farmers, the sort of help they need to adapt their farming methods to climate change. Guatemala, which had been self-sufficient in grain, was encouraged to pursue growth through agricultural exports. Local production of staples declined.

The free trade agreement approved in 2005 between the US and Central American states had undermined farmers further. Subsidized US grains had poured in under the agreement, putting small producers out of business. The pattern has been repeated in developing countries around the world. Guatemala had become dependent on imports of staple foods, and so was at the mercy of increasingly volatile food prices internationally. When a food price spike occurred in 2008, the price of corn locally was 240 per cent higher than the year before. The average poor rural Guatemalan family spends 80 per cent of its income on food; when world prices rise sharply, families simply cannot eat.

Reordering a food system as dysfunctional as this so that it works for the majority of us, rather than for the minority, requires root and branch reform. The politics of food is, in other words, the politics of modern global capitalism itself.

Thoughts on what that root and branch reform should cover come easily enough: breaking up the oligopolies that have become too powerful; ending distorting agricultural subsidies and rethinking instead what sort of support farming needs to make it sustainable, not just in a narrow economic sense, but in a way that protects the environment and our health; an end to subsidies that divert food to fuel; a redrawing of the lines between the competing interests of labour and capital; re-regulation of the agricultural commodity markets, deregulated after intense lobbying from the financial sector in 2000 to allow new forms of speculation that have contributed so damagingly to volatility; a clamp down on tax havens so that governments can collect a fair share of the profits; wages policies that promote a living wage, and proper enforcement of labour regulations that have been widely flouted; fiscal measures to shift consumption away from products that we know contribute to ill-health; curbs on marketing of junk foods, particularly where aimed at children . . .

But while a wish list might easily be agreed, seeing how it might be implemented is far harder.

For the late twentieth century has seen not just the deregulation of markets but the weakening of the institutions that have traditionally mediated between the excessive power of those markets and the individual. The power of unions, and of the professional bodies that used to represent individuals and help shape policy, has been eroded. The many collectives, from co-operatives to faith groups, that used to bring their moral force to bear, have been in decline. Moreover transnational institutions with the clout to tame the globalized commercial forces that have been allowed to build mostly do not exist. Globalization has left mere states impotent.

For the modern globalized corporation is not, as it is so often called, a state within a state so much as a power above and beyond the state. International development experts stopped talking about 'multinationals' years ago in fact, preferring instead the tag of 'transnational corporations', because these companies now transcend national authorities.

While traditional multinationals identified with a national home, transnationals have no such loyalty. Territorial borders are no longer important. This had been the whole thrust of World Trade Organization (WTO) treaties in the past decades. Transnationals can now take advantage of the free movement of capital and the ease of shifting production from country to country to choose the regulatory framework that suits them best. If restrained by legitimate legislative authorities – which might want to tax or ban the branding of harmful products such as tobacco or sugars, say – they can appeal to WTO rules to enforce their rights or bring a legal case for violation of their intellectual property.

Transnationals can and do locate their profits offshore to thwart any individual country's efforts to take revenue from them. The ability to raise taxes to provide services is a core function of democratic government, yet governments have been reduced to supplicants, cutting their tax rates further and further to woo corporates. Meanwhile transnationals have used patents and intellectual property rights to create their own system of private taxation.

If local labour laws or environmental regulations become too onerous for them, they can move operations to less regulated jurisdictions. So globalized food manufacturers can move to cheaper centres of production when governments introduce minimum wages or unions win workers' rights.

Developing countries, dealing with corporations whose revenue often exceeds their own GDP, have long been aware of their own lack of power. They are familiar with the way world trade rules have been written to benefit business and limit what any one country can impose on them. They know about the transnationals' tendency to oligopoly; they know too about their ability to penetrate the heart of government with lobbying and to capture the regulatory process. In an affluent country like the UK, we are still reluctant to recognize this.

So who will hold power to account?

The most effective checks on transnationals are as likely to come from NGOs and consumers as from individual governments these days. Campaigners have found new forms of asymmetric engagement that enable them to take on the power of corporations. Harnessing the same advances in technology and instant globalized communication that transnationals have used to build up their control, activists have mobilized shared interest groups across borders to challenge them. Direct action groups such as Greenpeace have been able to connect protesters against the alleged role of agribusiness in deforestation of tropical rainforests with activists across European countries in highly effective simultaneous campaigns against the brands that buy from them.

Grassroots political movements have used social media to create new forums for political debate and to summon up effective protest. The UK Uncut movement, for example, has succeeded triumphantly in changing the agenda around corporate tax by staging occupations and inflicting damage to the reputations of those companies that fail to pay it.

Many of us have felt disenfranchised by the failure of the main political parties to produce policies bold enough to tackle the real issues, but the invitations I receive to give talks from different groups around the country leave me in no doubt that there is a wealth of social capital ready to invest its time and energy in change. These groups cover the political spectrum from conserving right to radical left. They are mirrored in grassroots organizations around the world. As William Naggaga, the coffee expert in Uganda said, we need to 'make some noise'. It will take political engagement, and long hard slog, to bring about reform.

We all also eat and buy food. The politics of food was never about shopping alone, but the choices we make have an impact, if only to send a powerful message to those in government and industry. We connect too with other institutions that we can try to influence, from schools to colleges, from hospitals to care homes, from workplaces to local government. It is from a thousand small rebellions that the beginnings of movements are built.

What you do will depend on your circumstances, where you live and what you can afford, not only in money but in time and effort. My personal rules are simple enough and are mostly followed, but with lapses allowed when the pressures of modern life or competing interests overwhelm: fresh whole foods and few highly processed products; nothing that claims to be a new food or that makes a marketed health claim; nothing with ingredients on the label I do not recognize; more whole grains, pulses, fresh fruits and vegetables, less but better-quality meat and animal produce, fish from sustainable sources; more fair trade, more organic, more local and seasonal, less global summer time, and more from independent shops or direct from producers at the market. The quality of my staples has become very important to me. My journeys around the food system over the years have taught me that following these rough over-arching principles means I am more likely to be buying from types of production that are less damaging to the environment, are less likely to exploit people and the world's limited resources and are more likely to protect my family's long-term health. These are not certainties. We do need governments to take action, and we need a new politics to make them take it. But we also need to make this cultural shift ourselves if we are to give moral legitimacy to our demands for change.

Having enough to eat and access to food that is good enough to be properly nourishing is a basic right. Food is also one of life's great pleasures. Shopping for it, preparing it and eating it has bound people together for centuries. In the end, it's about what kind of society we want.

Acknowledgements

Much of my research and writing on globalization and the politics of food has been carried out in my role as special correspondent for the *Guardian*. It is one of the few remaining media groups to invest in the expensive business of investigative journalism. I owe an enormous debt to the editors there who have supported me over nearly two decades. In particular I should like to thank Alan Rusbridger, David Leigh, Paul Johnson, Becky Gardiner and Lucy Lamble. I am also grateful to its formidable team of libel lawyers, without whom it would not have been possible to publish serious critique of transnational corporations, which all too often respond to challenge with threats of legal action. Many of my fellow correspondents have also been generous in sharing their expertise over the years.

My interest in the politics of food was originally sparked by Caroline Walker and her husband Geoffrey Cannon, who first taught me how to investigate. Professors Tim Lang and Aubrey Sheiham have explained the system to me over many years. Tim Lobstein, Jane Landon, Jeanette Longfield, Kath Dalmeny, Andrew Simms, Alistair Smith and Patrick Holden have been a constant source of information and inspiration.

Few of my journeys could have been accomplished without the activists on the ground or the insiders who shared information, sometimes at considerable personal cost. Publicly I can thank Don Pollard, Dave Richards, Miles Hubbard, 'Dan', Spitou Mendy and Edilberto Sena. The late Angela Hale, Nuno Guerreiro, Andy Jones and Carlos Arguedas Mora were all courageous campaigners against the system who not only greatly furthered my understanding of it but were also warm companions on the way.

I am grateful too to the many staff at the aid agencies Oxfam, Christian Aid, Action Aid, Banana Link and Greenpeace who helped to organize trips or provided detailed background briefings, and to press officers and officials who have answered my questions with such forbearance.

At Penguin, I should like to thank Juliet Annan and Helen Campbell who first commissioned and edited *Not On the Label*, and the current team, Mary Mount, Jillian Taylor, Nicola Evans, Keith Taylor, Debbie Hatfield and David Hirst. My agent and friend Bill Hamilton has been a wise editor. Matthew Bullard, my husband, opened my eyes to the developing world, and has been my sounding-board as always.

Finally I should like to thank all those who shared secrets but who cannot be identified, but without whom much of the original book and this latest edition could not have been written.

Notes and References

CHAPTER I: HORSE

My investigations into the horsemeat scandal began at the *Guardian*. Thanks are due to Dan Sabbagh and Nick Hopkins who have helped edit my findings, John Domokos who filmed for them and Mike Burke who gave extensive legal advice.

In parliament, I should like to thank Barry Gardiner and Mary Creagh and her team. Staff at the Food Standards Agency FSA dealt with enquiries with unfailing patience. Many in the food and retail industry shared knowledge but have needed to remain anonymous.

p. 1 *Lumps of horse are fine but*: European Commission, Regulation (EU) No 206/2010 (www.ec.europa.eu/food/animal/animalprod-ucts/meatproducts/minced_meat).

p. 1 *A well known Amsterdam steakhouse: Het Parool*, 14 February 2013.

p. 2 *The unflappable head of the Irish Food Safety Authority*: Oral evidence taken before the Environment, Food and Rural Affairs Committee inquiry into food contamination, 23 April 2013.

p. 2 *Of course, to lead a body called Horse Sport Ireland*: Horse Sport Ireland press release, Patrick Wall appointed new chairman of Horse Sport Ireland, 31 January 2013.

p. 2 *A company that had supplied beef adulterated with horsemeat*: L. Ridley, *Event* magazine, 25 February 2015; D. Batty, the *Guardian*, 14 March 2013.

p. 2 *The dealer was an elected member of the corporation of the City*: For a list of members of the City of London see www.democracy cityoflondon.gov.uk/mgMemberIndex.

p. 3 *Meanwhile one Dutch trader*: the *Guardian*, 13 February 2013.

p. 3 *via a French trading group, Spanghero*: G. Montague-Jones, the *Grocer*, 14 February 2013; J. Glotz, the *Grocer*, 19 March 2013.

p. 4   *The department's report*: report on Equine DNA & Mislabelling of
Processed Beef Investigation, 14 March 2013, Department of Agriculture, Food and the Marine, Ireland (www.agriculture.gov.ie/
media/migration/publications/2013/EquineDNAreportMarch
2013190313.pdf).

p. 4   *Farrell had been supported at the committee*: minutes of the Irish
National Parliament Joint Committee on Agriculture, Fisheries
and Food debate, 31 March 2010 (http://debates.oireachtas.
ie/AGJ/2010/03/31/00003.asp).

p. 6   *The raw material for a decent beef burger*: F. Lawrence, the *Guardian*,
10 May 2013.

p. 6   *index of meat prices*: Meat price surge fuels fears of food inflation,
J. Farchy and G. Meyer, *Financial Times*, 1 September 2010.

p. 6   *Beef prices were up again*: Figures from the English Beef and
Sheep Industry (EBLEX), (www.eblex.org.uk/markets/market-
intelligence-publications.aspx).

p. 7   *livestock being estimated to be responsible for 80 per cent of agricultural
emissions*: Figures from UNEP Global Environmental Alert Service
newsletter, October 2012 (www.unep.org/pdf/UNEP-GEAS_
OCT_2012.pdf).

p. 7   *Globally, 15 per cent of maize production*: 'Agrofuels and the Right
to Food' Q&A from Olivier De Schutter, UN Special Rapporteur
on the Right to Food, 17 October 2012.

p. 8   *Despite high global prices*: EBLEX market intelligence briefing
with analyst Debbie Butcher, May 2013.

p. 8   *The average UK farm income*: 'Agriculture in the United Kingdom,
2012' report, Department for Environment, Food and Rural Affairs
(Defra), (www.gov.uk/government/publications/agriculture-in-the-
united-kingdom-2012).

p. 8   *It was not that the price of meat to consumers had not gone up*: 'Horse
meat scandal: the economics', analysis by Edmund Conway, 13
February 2013 (www.edmundconway.com); Office for National Statistics (ONS) data for Consumer Prices Index (CPI), March 2013,
(www.ons.gov.uk); and EBLEX data (www.guardian.co.uk/global-
development/datablog/2011/jun/07/rising-cost-of-food).

p. 9   *The Irish ABP Food Group*: See ABP Food Group website (www. abpfoodgroup.com/about-us/our-company); and the *Irish Times* (www.irishtimes.com/business/sectors/agribusiness-and-food/good-man-s-meat-empire-stretches-from-ireland-to-poland-1.1042691).

p. 9   *Dawn Meats held the contract*: RTÉ News, 24 May 2012

p. 9   *Other businesses owned by the Queally family*: Q. K. Cold Stores Limited (www.duedil.com/company/IE065788/q-k-cold-stores-limited);Dawn Meats Group (www.duedil.com/company/IE214173/dawn-meats-group).

p. 10   *The average duration of shareholding*: 'Empowering' shareholders won't revolutionize corporate culture, Prem Sikka, *The Conversation*, 18 January 2012.

p. 10   *The way Tesco's financial results*: Z.Wood, the *Guardian*, 3 October 2012.

p. 11   *Processors trade bodies*: Personal communication, Association of Independent Meat Suppliers, May 2013, Meatinfo, passim.

p. 11   *By 2012, the total number of cattle*: Figures from EBLEX (www. eblex.org.uk).

p. 12   *I asked a key player in the business of supermarket meat*: The secret of the 'special offer' economy burger, F. Lawrence, the *Guardian*, 24 January 2013.

p. 12   *Manufacturers used to use desinewed meat*: EU bans production of desinewed meat, *Meat Trades Journal*, 5 April 2012 (www.meatinfo. co.uk/news/archivestory.php/aid/13874/EU_bans_production_of_desinewed_meat.html).

p. 14   *Here's a list of the benefits claimed for barley malt*: Information taken from Munton's Ingredients (www.muntonsingredients.com/products/food-beverage-producers/products-for-food-beverage-producers).

p. 15   *The labels on bargain-basement burgers found to contain horse*: Food Standards Agency Ireland (FSAI): (http://www.fsai.ie/uploaded-Files/News_Centre/Burger_results_2013_01.pdf)

p. 15   *Not all supermarket and fast-food beef burgers are made this way*: Back to the future: how company takes beef from farmer to burger, F. Lawrence, the *Guardian*, 10 May 2013.

p. 18   *frozen burger prices fell*: See analysis by Edmund Conway, as above.

p. 18   *The attraction of horse as the form of this fraud*: Oral evidence taken before the Environment, Food and Rural Affairs Committee inquiry into food contamination, 14 May 2013.

p. 18   *The opportunities for fraud*: Equine DNA report, 14 March 2013 (www.agriculture.gov.ie).

p. 19   *The consultancy ... KPMG pointed out*: KPMG press release on the supply chain, 13 February 2013.

p. 19   *the size of the war chest*: Tesco agrees £25m deal with British beef and pork farmers, *Evening Standard*, 8 November 2012.

p. 19   *The Food Standards Agency Low Income Diet and Nutrition survey*: Low Income Diet and Nutrition survey, M. Nelson, B. Erens. B. Bates, S. Church and T. Boshier, FSA, 2007.

p. 22   *The USPCA had warned*: Ulster Society for the Protection of Animals, 16 January 2013 (www.uspca.co.uk/the-truth-about-irish-horsemeat).

p. 23   *In October 2012 they secured the conviction*: Judiciary of Scotland, sentencing statements, HMA v Laurence McAllister and Kieran Joseph Murphy (www.scotland-judiciary.org.uk); and Scottish SPCA, Man convicted of illegal horse transport, 31 October 2012.

p. 23   *The US horse trade has been bedevilled*: J. Rodolico, *Latitude News* (www.latitudenews.com/story/the-shady-trade-in-american-horsemeat).

p. 24   *The EU stopped collecting data*: Horsemeat: EU imports and exports data, the *Guardian,* 13 February 2013.

p. 24   *One of the targets was the Food Standards Agency*: Who is the government's health deal with big business really good for?, F. Lawrence, the *Guardian*, 12 November 2010.

p. 25   *Plants over a certain size are also required*: UNISON press release, Unison calls for reintroduction of meat cutting inspections, 8 February 2013.

p. 26   *Local authority budgets had been slashed*: Cuts and deregulation fostered horsemeat scandal, says Labour, M. Taylor and J. Meikle, the *Guardian*, 18 January 2013; and UNISON press release.

p. 27   *The FSA had suspended*: FSA press release, Action taken against animal abuse in slaughterhouse, 19 January 2013.

p. 27   *A man claiming to be part of a criminal gang*: BBC News, 6 March 2013 (www.bbc.co.uk/news/uk-england-stoke-staffordshire-21681291).

p. 28   *The company that owned Red Lion*: F. Lawrence, the *Guardian*, 22 April 2013.

p. 32   *The scandal had burst in to the open*: Food Safety Authority of Ireland press release, FSAI Survey Finds Horse DNA in Some Beef Burger Products, 15 January 2013; Tesco beef burgers found to contain 29 per cent horse meat, R. Silverman and A. Phillipson, the *Telegraph*, 15 January 2013.

p. 33   *Liffey Meats was owned by*: the *Evening Herald,* 16 January 2013.

p. 33   *Waitrose tests on beef products*: the *Guardian*, 13 February 2013.

p. 34   *Co-op beef burgers ... Burger King's offering*: the *Grocer*, 21 February 2013; and the *Guardian*, 31 January 2013.

p. 34   *It was not the first time the company had been caught up*: the *Evening Herald*, 16 January 2013.

p. 35   *the Department of Agriculture concluded*: the *Grocer*, 16 January 2013.

p. 35   *ABP at first*: the *Grocer,* 21 January 2013; report of the Tribunal of Inquiry into the Beef Processing Industry, Dublin Stationery Office 1994.

p. 35   *ABP said it had bought meat*: the *Grocer*, 6 February 2013.

p. 36   *Some of the boxes of meat had no labels*: Interview with Gerry McCurdy, Director of Northern Ireland FSA, RTÉ News radio broadcast, 5 February 2013.

p. 37   *According to the Irish Department of Agriculture*: report on Equine DNA & Mislabelling of Processed Beef Investigation; and the *Grocer*, 17 March 2013.

p. 38   *The French authorities seemed to have been able to unravel*: A. Chrisa-falis, the *Guardian*, 15 February 2013.

p. 38   *Officials and meat buyers hoping for a full flow of information*: F. Lawrence, the *Guardian*, 10 May 2013.

p. 39   *The place many of these tensions were played out*: Oral evidence taken before the Environment, Food and Rural Affairs Committee inquiry into food contamination, 23 April 2013; see *Meanwhile*

Back at the Ranch, by Fintan O'Toole,Vintage, 1995; personal communication, Fintan O'Toole.

p. 45   *The Efra committee ... wanted to ask questions*: Oral evidence, Efra enquiry, 23 April 2013, as above; Report of the BeefTribunal, as above.

p. 46   *it emerged that Goodman secretly owned*: National Parliament of Ireland report on Value for Money Examination – Performance Measurement in Teagasc., 6 April 2000 (debates.oireachtas.ie/ACC/2000/04/06/00004.asp).

p. 49   *The company had lost its order*: Meat Trades Journal, 6 February 2013 (www.meatinfo.co.uk/news/fullstory.php/aid/15175/Horsemeat:_Asda_removes_Freeza_Meats_burgers.html).

p. 50   *the curious incident of the Asda fresh beef Bolognese*:The *Grocer*, 16 February 2013.

p. 51   *sales of frozen burgers had slumped*:The *Grocer,* 18 February 2013.

CHAPTER 2: CHICKEN

The work for much of this chapter was carried out in my role as a special correspondent for the *Guardian*. I am grateful to the editors and legal team at the paper who gave me great support, in particular Ian Katz, Harriet Sherwood and Siobhain Butterworth. David Leigh guided me during the investigation at Lloyd Maunder, which was published on 6 December 2001. Rob Evans helped gain disclosures under the European open government code.

At *Panorama*, I should like to thank Betsan Powys, Howard Bradburn and Andy Bell.

Several sources acted as whistleblowers at considerable personal risk. Their number grew as my investigations went on and I would like to thank them anonymously. Names of workers have been changed to protect them.

Several people gave me the benefit of their detailed knowledge: John Sandford of Hull trading standards on the water in chicken scandal; Richard Young on antibiotic use in farming; Sue Sonnex, Lewis Coates and Steve Haslam on the recycling of condemned meat; Peter Bradnock of the British Poultry Council and Peter King of the National Farmers' Union on the chicken industry.

p. 63   *The owner of Denby Poultry, Peter Roberts*: The *Guardian*, 30 August 2003.

p. 64   *Meat from the companies involved in the recycling*: FSA food hazard warning, 11 April 2001, and statement, 24 April 2001.

p. 67   *When Leicester trading standards received a complaint*: Leicestershire County Council Trading Standards, Chicken nuggets complaint prompts investigation, January 2002.

p. 69   *The FSA announced the results of the tests*: FSA, press release, Survey uncovers added water in restaurant and takeaway chicken, 11 December 2001.

p. 70   *The baton had passed to Ireland*: Food Safety Authority (Ireland), press release, Food Safety Authority finds some imported chicken fillets in breach of food labelling laws, 21 May 2002.

p. 71   *The English FSA's public response*: FSA, letter to the *Guardian*, 10 July 2002, from David Statham, director of enforcement.

p. 71   *They caught a Dutch additive supplier and a German protein manufacturer*: BBC *Panorama*, The Chicken Run, 22 May 2003.

p. 72   *At first the FSA maintained the line that it was a labelling issue*: FSA water in chicken update, 21 May 2003; F. Lawrence, Move to halt tainted chicken, the *Guardian*, 20 June 2003.

p. 72   *A study by the FSA in 2008*: Survey reveals chicken being pumped with water is still being sold, www.foodmanufacture. co.uk, R. Pendrous, 4 March 2006; and *Daily Mail,* 25 June 2007.

p. 73   *A chicken farmer, who may also have invested £1 million or more in chicken units*: Personal communications with the National Farmers' Union and chicken processors.

p. 74   *The modern broiler chicken*: Sustain, *Food Facts*, No. 9: Fowl Deeds, 1999 (www.sustainweb.org); RSPCA, Behind closed doors – the truth about chicken bred for meat, 2002 (www.rspca.org.uk); Compassion in World Farming, *Chicken, How Come It's So Cheap?* and *The Detrimental Impacts of Industrial Animal Agriculture* (www.ciwf. co.uk); Farm Animal Welfare Council, *Interim Report on the Animal Welfare Implications of Farm Assurance Schemes* (Defra, 2001).

p. 74   *maximum stocking densities*: CIWF factsheet, Meat Chickens, 2010 (www.ciwf.org.uk).

p. 74　*In fact a survey conducted by Compassion in World Farming*: CIWF, *Supermarkets and Farm Animal Welfare*, 2001.

p. 76　*A study in 1992 by the University of Bristol*: S. Kestin *et al.*, Prevalence of leg weaknesses in broiler chickens and its relationship with genotype, *Veterinary Record* (1992, 131, 190–9).

p. 76　*A 1996* Which? *survey of chicken on sale in leading supermarkets*: How safe is chicken?, *Which?*, October 1996.

p. 77　*In 1999 the government's Advisory Committee on the Microbiological Safety of Food (ACMSF) said*: ACMSF, *Report on Microbial Antibiotic Resistance in Relation to Food Safety* (The Stationery Office, 1999); R. Young *et al.*, *The Use and Misuse of Antibiotics in UK Agriculture* (The Soil Association, 1999).

p. 77　*But by 2003 it had become clear that one in five producers*: J. Meikle, the *Guardian*, 27 May and 6 June 2003.

p. 78　*By 2013 the UK's chief medical officer was warning*: The *Guardian*, 3 January 2013; and the Soil Association, CIWF and Sustain report for the Alliance to Save Our Antibiotics: Antibiotic Resistance – the impact of intensive farming on human health (www.soilassociation.org).

p. 80　*The UK poultry industry escaped*: World Health Organization, press release, 23 January 2004; Avian influenza, the threat looms, the *Lancet* (24 January 2004, 363, pp. 257ff).

p. 81　*In 2007 it was the UK's turn*: Bird flu found at Bernard Matthews farm in Suffolk, BBC News, 17 April 2013; and www.foodmanufacture.co.uk, 19 April 2013.

CHAPTER 3: SALAD

The information in this chapter has come from dozens of interviews with individual workers, with government and police officers, and with employers, most of whom cannot be identified. Some fear for their contracts or jobs, others for their safety. Most names have been changed. I am grateful for the many hours these people gave to explaining the system to me.

For information about the UK, I am able to thank publicly: Don Pollard, formerly of the T&G Union; David Jackson and other officials from Operation Gangmaster; and the late Nuno Guerreiro of the Portuguese Workers' Association.

For explanation of the issues surrounding pesticides, I am grateful to David Buffin and Barbara Dinham of the Pesticides Action Network UK, Sandra Bell of Friends of the Earth and Dr Vyvyan Howard of the University of Liverpool.

I am also indebted to many people who helped me on my trip in Spain, some of whom cannot be identified.

Hector Gravina of Amicos de la Terra gave me the benefit of his extensive knowledge and facilitated introductions. Viktor Gonzalves and SEAE, the Spanish ecological society, welcomed me to their conference; Jorge Pajares Miravalles acted as translator in conversations with Manuel Ariza. Nicholas Bell of the European Civic Forum provided background studies on migrant labour. Thanks also to Pedro and Cello Garcia of ANSE.

I am particularly grateful to the members of SOC, the Spanish rural workers' union, who introduced me to workers in Almeria and helped with translations: Mari Garcia Bueno, from the head office, and Abel Cader, Gabriel Ataya and Mustafa Ait-Korhci from the Almeria office.

Cecy Bullard helped with initial research on the conditions among migrants in southern Spain. Maggie O'Kane commissioned further work that led to a film for the *Guardian*, which was directed by Matt Haan.

p. 82   *The value of the UK salad vegetable market*: UK Salad Market Report *2003* (The Greenery Information Service, London W1T 6BT).

p. 82   *Modified-atmosphere packaging (MAP) can now increase the shelf life*: Li Xiong, *Modified Atmosphere Packaging, A Fact Book* (Department of Food Science, Pennsylvania State University, 1999); A. B. Smyth *et al.*, Modified atmosphere packaged cut iceberg lettuce: effect of temperature and CO_2 partial pressure on respiration and quality, A. B. Smyth *et al.*, *Journal of Agricultural Food Chemistry* (1998; 46, 4556–62).

p. 83   *this new invention to prolong shelf life*: M. Serafini *et al.*, Effect of acute ingestion of fresh and stored lettuce on plasma total antioxidant capacity and antioxidant levels in human subjects, *British Journal of Nutrition* (2002; 88, 615–23).

p. 84   *When the results of this trial*: Packing is OK, but not the water: letter from Jon Fielder, Waterwise Technology, to the *Grocer*, 29 March 2003.

'With a chlorine rinse, there is also a long-term possible risk associated with carcinogens'. Mary Ellen Camire, Head of Food Science, University of Maine, USA, quoted in *Progressive Grocer*, May 1998 (www.progressivegrocer.com/news/0511998).

p. 84   *There appears to be good reason for supermarkets selling prewashed salads to worry*: S. K. Sagoo *et al.*, Microbiological study of ready-to-eat salad vegetables from retail establishments uncovers a national outbreak of Salmonellosis, *Journal of Food Protection* (col. 66, no. 3 (2003), 403–9).

S. O'Brien *et al.*, The microbiological status of ready-to-eat fruit and vegetables, discussion paper, ACM/510 of the Advisory Committee on the Microbiological Safety of Food, 2001 (www. good. gov.uk/multimedia/pdfs/acm510.42m.pdf).

PHLS 2000, Outbreaks of Salmonella typhimurium DT 204b infection in England and Wales and elsewhere in Europe, *Communicable Disease Report Weekly* (10:349); and PHLS 2000, Case control study links salad vegetables to national increase in multi-resistant Salmonella typhimurium DT 104, *Communicable Disease Report Weekly* (10:333, 336).

p. 87   *Labourers are often needed at very short notice*: *Gangmasters*, House of Commons, Environment, Food and Rural Affairs Committee, 14th report of session 2002/3 (Stationery Office, tel. 0870 600 5522; http://tso.co.uk/bookshop).

p. 88   *The exceptionally hot weather*: Personal communication, salad growers.

p. 90   *Don Pollard, who did extensive research for the T&G union*: D. Pollard, report of UK survey on gangmaster labour, Rural Agricultural Workers' Trade Group, T&GWU, between 1998 and 2000.

p. 90   *Operation Shark, a pilot investigation into illegal labour*: First reported in the *Guardian*, Food: The Way We Eat Now series: F. Lawrence, The New Landless Labourers, 17 May 2003.

p. 94 *Both supermarkets' representatives and the farmers' union denied*: *Gangmasters*, House of Commons, Efra committee, as above.

p. 95 *If you wanted evidence of the impact of supermarkets' price wars on wages*: Is Wal-Mart too powerful? *Business Week*, 6 October 2003 (www.businessweekeurope.com).

New York Times, leader, 15 November, 2003: 'Wal-Mart's prices are about 14 per cent lower because the company is aggressive about squeezing costs, including labour ...'

p. 102 *One of the local doctors*: Personal communication with Dr Giles Smith, Thetford, and letter to Efra committee, 3 April 2003.

p. 106 *the GLA moved in to liberate*: Gangmasters Licensing Authority press release, Seven arrested in joint operation, 25 April 2013 (www.gla.defra.gov.uk); and F. Lawrence, the *Guardian*, 29 October 2012 and 31 October 2012.

p. 111 *The nitrate problem is not confined to Spain*: J. N. Pretty *et al.*, An assessment of the total external costs of UK agriculture, *Agricultural Systems* (65 (2), 113–36).

p. 111 *Some 55 per cent of the country has recently been designated as 'nitrate vulnerable zones'*: The figure would have been much higher but for intense lobbying from the National Farmers' Union. Water companies estimate that over the next five years UK customers will have to pay £25 a year on their water bills to cover the cost of removing nitrates from drinking water. In the past the utilities have diluted drinking water with high concentrations of nitrates with water that has lower levels to meet safety limits, but now they are finding it increasingly difficult to find uncontaminated supplies. Personal communication, the Environment Agency.

P. Brown, Nitrate pollution raises water bills, the *Guardian*, 11 August 2003.

p. 113 *Lettuce appears on the 'persistent offenders list'*: Avoiding pesticide residues, *Which?* magazine, September 2003 (www.which.co.uk/which). See also The List of Lists, PAN UK catalogue of particularly harmful pesticides (www.pan-uk.org).

p. 114 *The agrochemical industry has seen rapid concentration*: Agrochemical sales worldwide and market share, compiled from *Agrow's Top*

20, 2003 edition, Richmond UK, 2003, by Barbara Dinham, Pesticides Action Network, UK (www.pan-uk.org). See also (www.transparencymarketresearch.com/agrochemical-market.html) and F. Lawrence, Poverty Matters, the *Guardian*.

p. 115   *the government programme of tests for pesticide residues*: Pesticides Action Network (PAN) database (www.pesticideinfo.org); and Defra Pesticides Usage Survey report 243 and 244, 2011; Pesticides Residues in Food (PRiF) report 2011 (www.pesticides.gov.uk).

p. 116   *The Pesticide Action Network has drawn up its own list*: Disrupting Food press release, 6 April 2012 (www.disruptingfood.info).

p. 117   *The FSA's advice is*: FSA, *Pesticides, Your Questions Answered* (www.foodstandards.gov.uk/safereating/pesticides/).

p. 117   *the so-called 'cocktail effect'*: WiGRAMP, Risk Assessment of Mixtures of Pesticides and Similar Substances, Committee on the Toxicity of Chemicals in Food, Consumer Products and the Environment (COT), September 2003 (www.food.gov.uk/multi media. pdfs/report(indexed)pdf).

Royal Society Working Group report on endocrine-disrupting chemicals, chair Professor Patrick Bateson, June 2000 (www.royal soc.ac.uk/files/startfiles/document_111.pdf).

Vyvyan Howard *et al.*, *Endocrine Disrupters*: *Environmental Health and Policies* (Environmental Science and Technology Library, Kluwer Academic Publishers, June 2001).

J. Blythman, Bite the dust, in the *Guardian*, Food: The Way We Eat Now series, 10 May 2003.

p. 118   *The problem for the supermarkets is*: Friends of the Earth press release, 17 September 2003 (www.foe.co.uk).

'A briefing paper for Defra on the Spanish Horticulture industry', Horticulture study tour to southern Spain, March 2000 (www.adas.co.uk/horticulture/govreports/spain00.htm).

See also Sustain, Salad Days, *Food Facts*, 8, 1999 (www:http:// users.charity.vfree.com/s/sustain/).

p. 130   *So I returned to the area once more*: Spain's salad growers are modern day slaves, say charities, F. Lawrence, the *Guardian*, 7 February 2011.

p. 132   *The industry wrote pointing out local academics and the industry*:
María José Pardo Losilla, managing director of Andalucian trade
organisation Hortyfruta, Letters to the Editor, the *Guardian*, 2
March 2011; and C. Elliott, the *Guardian*, 7 March 2011

CHAPTER 4: BEANS AND ASPARAGUS

The late Dr Andy Jones, formerly of the Stockholm Environment
Institute at the University of York, and Caroline Lucas both did copi-
ous work on food distribution and its impact, and I am indebted to
both of them.

Tara Garnett also provided expert research papers and statistics.

The food miles debate was started in 1992 by Tim Lang and the SAFE
Alliance with its 1994 report on the environmental and social implications of the rapid escalation in the distance food was travelling. SAFE
became Sustain, the alliance for better food and farming, which has published a series of inspiring *Food Facts* booklets. Vicki Hird and Jeanette
Longfield of Sustain both helped with many of my investigations.

Nicola Ellen, Dave Timpson, Peter Ferguson, and Roy Attree of
Safeway generously gave several hours to explaining distribution systems to me on my trips to Aylesford. Kevin Hawkins of Safeway
facilitated the trips and has remained good-humouredly open, even
when he knows my views are opposed to his. I am also grateful to the
press office of Tesco for organizing a trip to its distribution centre at
Chepstow, and to Martin Tate and Bob, and to the Asda press office, for
facilitating the lorry trip.

The Austrian Consumers' Association provided data on the impact
of transport on the nutritional content of food.

Additional statistics came from the Institute of Grocery Distribution,
Retail Logistics; Department of Transport, *Transport Statistics, Great Britain*; Achieving the UK's Climate Change Commitments, e3 Consulting,
2002, quoted in T. Garnett, *Wise Moves*, Transport 2000 Trust, 2003.

On Global Warming, see: *Climate Change. The UK programme, Defra;
First Assessment Report*, Intergovernmental Panel on Climate Change,

Geneva, 1990; IPCC special report, *Aviation and the Global Environment*, Geneva, 1999.

The study of asparagus was conducted by Progressio for its report *Drop by Drop*, published by Progressio, CEPES and Water Witness International, September 2010.

p. 136   *Between 35 and 40 per cent of heavy goods vehicles on UK roads today*: A. Jones, *Eating Oil* (Sustain, 2001); Department of Transport, *Transport Statistics: Great Britain, 2002*.

p. 144   *International trade in food*: C. Lucas, *Stopping the Great Food Swap* (The Greens/European Free Alliance, European Parliament, 2001).

p. 145   *Live animals have not been spared*: CIWF, *Live Exports*, 2000.

p. 145   *A ready-made lasagne can contain around twenty different ingredients*: T. Garnett, *Wise Moves* (Transport 2000 Trust, 2003).

p. 145   *'Central government is in favour of it but local government isn't'*: London considers lorry ban, *Cycling Weekly*, 11 April 2013.

p. 148   *The FSA advised that frozen broccoli*: BBC News, 31 March 2003.

p. 148   *Their comments followed research by the Austrian Consumers' Association*: VKI, April 2003 (www.konsument.at).

p. 149   *Over 80 per cent of organic food now comes from abroad*: The Soil Association, 2001.

p. 149   *Ironically, the baby potatoes are quite likely to have been in store*: personal communication with potato buyer.

p. 150   *the UK was importing 750,000 tonnes of potatoes*: *Farmers Weekly*, 2 January 2013; market information from British Tomatoes website.

p. 151   *The way we produce and distribute food*: Food Matters: Towards a Strategy for the 21st Century, Cabinet Office, July 2008 (http:// webarchive.nationalarchives.gov.uk).

p. 151   *The Intergovernmental Panel on Climate Change (IPCC)*: IPCC, Geneva, 1990.

p. 151   *Since the Industrial Revolution*: For figures on atmospheric carbon dioxide, Sir David King, chief scientific adviser, Climate change science: adapt, mitigate or ignore? *Science* magazine, 9 January 2004; for figures on global warming, The Hadley Centre, *Climate Change, Observations and Predictions* (The Met Office/Defra, December 2003).

p. 152   *Reporting in the middle of 2013, the United Nations*: Unprecedented climate extremes marked last decade, A. Kirby, the *Guardian*, 3 July 2013.

p. 155   *A quarter of household waste*: WRAP, Courtauld Commitment Phase 2 Progress Report December 2011 (www.wrap.org.uk/ sites/files/wrap/CC2_Interim_Report_AUG_2012.pdf); and www. gov.uk/government /policies/reducing-and-managing-waste/ supporting-pages/food-waste.

p. 156   *the late Dr Andy Jones put all this into context*: A. Jones, *Eating Oil*, (Sustain, 2001).

p. 157   *The market in fresh asparagus*: *Drop by Drop*: Understanding the impacts of the UK's water footprint through a case study of Peruvian asparagus, Progressio, in association with Centro Peruano de Estudios Sociale and Water Witness International, September 2010; How Peru's wells are sucked dry, the *Guardian*, F. Lawrence, 15 September 2010; Implementation of the United States-Peru Trade Promotion Agreement, hearing before the Committee on Ways and Means, US House of Representatives, 12 July 2006.

p. 162   *The case for cutting out meat consumption*: Is it time we cut down on meat? F. Lawrence, the *Guardian*, 10 September 2011.

p. 165   *The government was caught on the hop*: V. Elliott, *The Times*, 14 September 2000.

p. 165   *In the end it was not a question of days*: personal communications with John White, Federation of Bakers, and anonymous sources.

p. 166   *extreme weather event . . . led to the supply of root vegetables*: the Guardian, 15 January 2010.

CHAPTER 5: BREAD

Elizabeth Weisberg and Rachel Duffield of the Lighthouse Bakery instructed me in the art of real breadmaking in the course of many visits. John White of the Federation of Bakers was generous with his knowledge and kindly organized my visit to the bread factory. Elizabeth David's *English Bread and Yeast Cookery* (Penguin Books, 1979) has said it all before, and is particularly eloquent on the ills of factory bread. I am also indebted to the work of Geoff Tansey and the Agricapital Group of the British Society for Social Responsibility in Science, which produced the report *Our Daily Bread*, sadly no longer in print; however, Tansey's book *The Food System*, co-authored with Tony Worsley (Earthscan, 2000), is in print. The New Economics Foundation provided detailed analysis of the crisis facing independent grocery shops. The Food Standards Agency helped with information on legislation. On food poverty, see E. Dowler and S. Turner with B. Dobson, *Poverty Bites: Food, Health and Poor Families* (Child Poverty Action Group, 2001), and Sustain, *Hunger from the Inside: The Experience of Food Poverty in the UK*.

p. 171   *Like much of food manufacturing today, the bread sector has become highly concentrated*: Figures from the Federation of Bakers (www.bakersfederation.org.uk). See also Keynote report, *Bread and Bakery Products*, March 2003.

p. 171   *By 2013 production had been consolidated*: personal communication, Federation of Bakers.

p. 173   *Then in the early 1960s a method evolved*: Information on the Chorleywood Bread Process from Campden and Chorleywood Food Research Association, *The Master Bakers' Book of Breadmaking*, published by the National Association of Master Bakers, 21 Baldock Street, Ware, Herts, SG12 9DH, and the Federation of Bakers.

p. 174   *the addition of a fat with a high melting point*: Information taken from http://gbr.bakels.com/product/?show=page&id=4493.

p. 174   *Now they mostly use a fractionated fat*: personal communication, Campden and Chorleywood Food Research Association (CCFRA).

p. 175   *Its hardness is double-edged*: Malaysian Palm Oil Board, *Health and Nutritional Aspects of Palm Stearin, Perceptions and Facts* (www.mpob.gov.my/article/nut_stearin.htm).

p. 175   *The most commonly used group of emulsifiers*: Personal communication, CCFRA.

p. 175   *Double the amount of yeast*: *The Master Bakers' Book of Breadmaking*, as above.

p. 176   *It took from 1927*: *Our Daily Bread*, British Society for Social Responsibility in Science, 1978; Bread and Flour regulations 1998;

D. J. Jukes, *Food Legislation of the UK* (4th edition, Butterworth-Heinemann, 1997); Food Law pages maintained by David Jukes at the University of Reading (www.fst.rdg.ac.uk/foodlaw).

p. 176   *Since the 1980s, however, companies have been using genetic modification*: J. Elkington and J. Hailes, *The New Foods Guide* (Gollancz, 1999); European Food Information Council, *Applications of Food Biotechnology: Enzymes* (www.eufic.org/gb/tech/); personal communication, CCFRA.

p. 176   *A report in the technical journal* New Food: T. Sharp, CCFRA, *Baking*, Issue 4, 2001. See also the technical news on the bakery industry website (www.bod.bakery.co.uk/bodpages.nsf/Enzymes in Baking).

p. 177   *Getting water into the dough*: *The Master Bakers' Book of Breadmaking* notes: 'The extra water needed in [CBP] is usually about 3.5 per cent more on flour weight than used in a three-hour bulk fermentation process.' For the increase in percentage water added to bread, see the London Food Commission, *Food Adulteration: Water in Food* (Unwin Hyman, 1988).

p. 178   *The Rank Hovis McDougall milling and bread group . . . was bought*: Premier Foods strike threat as factory closures proceed, www.foodmanufacture.co.uk, 2 August 2013; and A. Cave, the *Telegraph*, 16 February 2013.

p. 181   *The diet*: R. Atkins, *Dr Atkins New Diet Revolution* (Vermilion, 2003).

p. 182   *The GI takes glucose as the benchmark*: For a full list of GI values, see K. Foster-Powell *et al.*, International Table of Glycemic Index and Glycemic Load Values, *American Journal of Clinical Nutrition*, (2002; 76, 5–56).

p. 184   *During the milling of white flour*: Food Standards Agency, *McCance and Widdowson's The Composition of Foods* (6th edition, 2002, Cambridge: Royal Society of Chemistry).

p. 184   *When Lord (then plain Mr) Boothby rose to his feet*: *Our Daily Bread*, as above.

p. 184   *The government now requires millers*: CCFRA, as above.

p. 185   *That's why stoneground wholemeal tastes different*: The big millers admitted that the proportion of germ and bran varied in wholemeal when they told a government advisory committee in the early 1980s that they could not give precise figures for the amount of dietary fibre in bread; see C.Walker and G. Cannon, *The Food Scandal* (Century, 1984).

p. 186 *there are no legal definitions*: Real Bread Campaign, Sustain, 27 February 2012 (www.sustainweb.org/news/feb13_real_bread_wholegrain_truth).

p. 187 *An inquiry by the UK's Competition Commission*: The Stationery Office, *Supermarkets*, Competition Commission report, October 2000 (www.ukstate.com).

p. 187 *Professor Paul Dobson*: P. Dobson, *The Economic Effects of Constant Below-Cost Selling Practices by Grocery Retailers* (Loughborough University/Federation of Bakers, July 2002).

p. 187 *Sainsbury's told the Competition Commission*: Competition Commission, *Supermarkets*, as above.

p. 188 *In July 2003 the cheapest white sliced bread on sale*: Figures from P. Dobson, as above, and Federation of Bakers.

p. 189 *An indication of where the balance of power lies*: the *Grocer*, 1 July 2011; and *British Baker* magazine (www.bakeryinfo.co.uk), 22 October 2010; and the *Telegraph*, 7 October 2011.

p. 191 *Independent retailing in the UK looked to be in a crisis that was terminal*: Centre for Food Policy Research, Thames Valley University, *The Crisis in UK Local Food Retailing*, July 2000; New Economics Foundation, *Ghost Town Britain*, 2002.

CHAPTER 6: APPLES AND BANANAS

Tim Lang, professor of food policy at City University, London, shared much of his academic research on supermarkets for this chapter. His book *Food Wars* is published by Earthscan, with co-author Michael Heasman. I am also grateful to Bill Vorley of the International Institute of Environment and Development in London for his insights into concentrations of power in the food and agriculture sectors.

Joanna Blythman has been a source of support and inspiration. Sandra Bell of Friends of the Earth provided information from FoE surveys.

I am grateful to Patrick Holden, formerly of the Soil Association, who, as well as taking me to Highgrove, explained many aspects of the food system; and to David Wilson, farm manager of Highgrove. John Breach, chairman of the British Independent Fruit Growers' Association provided expert practical knowledge. John Vidal of the *Guardian* enlightened me on some of the environmental impacts of intensive farming.

The *Grocer* magazine is the source of some of the details about trade investment and manufacturers' attitudes to supermarkets. Thanks to Julian Hunt. Professors John Bridgeman and Paul Dobson have been generous with their knowledge.

I have also talked to many farmers, packers, manufacturers and their trade associations, and occasional supermarket buyers, to understand how supermarket buying works. Most fear that if they were identified their ability to continue to do business or their jobs would be compromised. Some names have been changed.

p. 203   *A Dutch company provides packhouses with the machines*: www.greefa.nl.

p. 209   *Figures from the Department of Environment, Food and Rural Affairs*: See *Food and Farming: A Sustainable Future*, report by the Policy Commission on the Future of Farming and Food, chaired by Sir Don Curry, January 2002, (http://www.cabinet-office.gov.uk).

p. 210   *The numbers working the land*: Figures from Defra/ONS, Agriculture in the UK 2012.

p. 210   *We lost nearly two thirds of our apple orchards*: Safe Alliance, *How Green are Our Apples?* (London, 1999).

p. 210   *Supermarkets increasingly buy their apples abroad*: Friends of the Earth, *Survey of Apples and Pears in UK retailers*, November 2001 (www.foe.co.uk/campaigns/real_food).

p. 212   *Each cow may produce twice as many litres of milk a year*: Figures on loss of wildlife from J. Vidal, in the *Guardian*'s The Way We Eat Now series, 17 May 2003.

p. 212   *But in his report on agribusiness*: B. Vorley, *Food Inc.: Corporate Concentration from Farm to Consumer* (UK Food Group/IIED, London, 2004, www.iied.org).

p. 213   *The crisis has not been unique to Britain*: Figures from *Food Inc.*, as above.

p. 213   *Just four supermarket groups*: Kantor Worldpanel Grocery market share, July 2013.

p. 213   *The top thirty grocers in the world controlled*: Top 25 Global Retailers, Supermarket News, (www.supermarketnews.com/top-25-global-food-retailers-2012).

p. 213   *Wal-Mart was not just the world's largest food retailer*: Wal-Mart corporate and financial facts (www.news.walmart.com); Tesco plc Annual Review 2013 (www.tescoplc.com); Carrefour Q4 2012 sales growth (www.carrefour.com).

p. 214   *The battle of the bananas*: Personal communication, Bernard Cornibert, Windward Bananas; F. Lawrence, Unfair Trade Winds, the *Guardian*, 17 May 2003; Banana Link (www.bananalink.org.uk); *Food Inc.*, as above.

p. 216   *In 2009 the supermarkets entered another round of battle*: F. Lawrence, the *Guardian*, 12 October 2009; and R. Ford, the *Grocer*, 7 June 2013.

p. 218   *The ASA rejected*: ASA rules for Tesco in spat with Sainsbury's, *Reuters*, 30 July 2013.

p. 218   *The concentration of power*: See M&M Planet Retail (www.planetretail.net) for figures on supermarket market share. For concentration in Europe, see also P. Dobson, *Retailer Buyer Power in European Markets* (Loughborough University Business School, research series paper 2002: 1).

p. 218   *The stranglehold that supermarket buyers had acquired*: J. Grievink, *The Supply Chain Funnel in Europe* (Cap Gemini/OECD 2003), lecture at the OECD conference on Changing Dimension of the Food Economy, The Hague, February 2003.

p. 219   *When New Labour came to power*: See, for example, the speech by Stephen Byers, Labour Party Conference, 29 September 1999.

p. 219   *That same spring, the chief executive of Wal-Mart visited England*: BBC News, Blair aims for enterprise economy, 6 July 1999.

p. 219   *When the Competition Commission published the results of its inquiry*: *Supermarkets*, a report on the supply of groceries from multiple stores in the UK, by the Competition Commission, October

2000; and *Safeway Merger Inquiries: Remedies Statement*, by the Competition Commission, June 2003 (the Stationery Office, PO Box 29, Norwich NR3 1GN, www.competition-commission.org.uk).

p. 220   *'We all want cheaper food'*: BBC News, 2 March 2001.

p. 224   *The chairman and chief executive of Nestlé UK*: the *Grocer*, 4 October 2003.

p. 224   *Writing in the trade magazine the* Grocer, *the sales director of Unilever Bestfoods UK*: 4 October 2003.

p. 224   *Almost half the manufacturers*: the *Grocer*, 15 October 2003.

p. 225   *Studies in Australia*: www.pag.com.au/articles/strat.htm, quoted in *Food Inc.*, as above.

p. 225   *The voluntary code*: Draft Groceries Code Adjudicator Bill, 14 June 2011, Efra (The Stationery Office: www.publications.parliament.uk); the *Grocer*, 19 January 2013; *Farmers Weekly*, 4 April 2013; Groceries Code adjudicator to tackle illegal kickbacks, www.foodmanufacture.co.uk, 29 April 2013.

p. 226   *It was no surprise that in the depths of a recession suppliers' profits would be squeezed*: F. Lawrence, the *Guardian*, 12 February and 22 February 2010; and the *Grocer*, 27 October 2012.

p. 226   *In Europe 10,000 new food products are launched every year*: T. Lang, the *Guardian*'s The Way We Eat Now series, 17 May 2003.

p. 226   *The concentration of power has narrowed our choice*: The *Grocer*, 1 November 2003.

p. 227   *The takeover of Express Dairies*: The *Grocer*, 18 October 2003.

p. 228   *the company's commercial director for non-food, Richard Brasher*: the *Grocer*, 1 November 2003.

p. 228   *By 2010 prices were changing so much*: F. Lawrence, the *Guardian*, 22 February 2010; Professor Paul Dobson, University of East Anglia, *Supermarket Offers*, 21 November 2012 and other papers on supermarket pricing.

p. 232   *In February 2003 the Organization for Economic Co-operation and Development*: http://webdomino1.oecd.org/comnet/agr/food eco.nsf/view/html/index/'file/confdoc.htm.

p. 233   *Professor John Connor*: J. Connor, *The Changing Structure of Global Food Markets: Dimensions, Effects, and Policy Implications* (paper given to the OECD conference on Changing Dimensions of the Food Economy, The Hague, February 2003, by John M. Connor, professor of industrial economics, Purdue University, West Lafayette, Indiana, USA). See also *Competition Policy and Food*, a lecture given to a conference at City University, 24 September, 2003, by Professor John Cubbin, economics department, City University, available on UK Food Group website.

p. 234   *Tesco fought the allegations*: *Financial Times,* 10 August 2011; and the *Telegraph* (Tesco to pay £6.5m fine . . .).

p. 234   *The European Commission has acted twice*: BBC News, 12 October 2011.

p. 234   *This time at the UN's Food and Agriculture Organization*: FAO Urbanization Working Party, Globalization of Food Systems workshop, 8–10 October 2003 (www.fao.org/es/ESN/nutrition/national_urbanization_en.stm).

p. 236   *Governments in middle-income countries*: For details of grocery market shares, see the *Grocer*, 22 March 2003; *Food Inc.*, as above; M&M Planet Retail, as above.

CHAPTER 7: COFFEE AND GRAINS

I am grateful to all the staff of Oxfam in the Kampala office who helped organize my trip to the coffee areas of Uganda. Monica Asekenye was a knowledgeable and companionable guide, and many of her colleagues were generous with their time. In the UK, Lys Holdoway also helped facilitate my trip.

Oxfam's 2002 report on the coffee crisis, *Mugged: Poverty in Your Coffee Cup* by Charis Gresser and Sophia Tickell, is the source of much of the detailed analysis, and I am grateful to them for permission to use it here. Updates are available on Oxfam's websites: www.maketradefair.com and www.oxfam.org.uk.

Thanks also to ActionAid for their studies on the impacts of subsidies and WTO investment agreements on development: *Farmgate* and *Unlimited Companies* (www.actionaid.org).

Food Inc. by Bill Vorley (UK Food Group/IIED, London, 2004, www.iied.org) has detailed analysis of concentrations in commodity trading and manufacturing.

Some of my research on agricultural subsidies was originally conducted as part of writing my second book, *Eat Your Heart Out*, and more detailed accounts are contained there of both these and the activities of big transnational grain traders. My trip to South America and subsequent investigations were originally carried out for the *Guardian*. Gloria Beretervide helped me extensively on the ground and acted as translator.

Analysis of recent statistics on the coffee market comes from the Fairtrade Foundation's 2012 Coffee report. Peter Rossman of the International Union of Food workers pointed me at the 'financialization' of the food industry. Analysis of companies' tax practices was part of work for the *Guardian* series The Tax Gap. A huge thank you to those tax experts who taught me to read accounts and calculate what companies were paying. They prefer to remain nameless but I am very grateful to them for their rare ability to translate the arcane and technical into everyday language, and for their even rarer willingness to work pro bono.

p. 238 *'Martin Luther used to wonder.* Deutsche Bank AG, *Soluble Coffee: A Pot of Gold?*, analyst report by J. Parker and A. Erskine, 2 May 2000, quoted in Oxfam coffee report, *Mugged*, as above.

p. 238 *Nestlé's Nescafé is one of a clutch of global 'A-brands'*: Figures on global brands and global food manufacturers from Leatherhead Food International, *Global Food Markets*, and OC&C Strategy Consultants, *Global Giants Index*.

p. 238 *This is where you can see the other half of the picture*: Cap Gemini, Ernst & Young/Reed Elsevier, *State of the Art in Food: The Changing Face of the Worldwide Food Industry*, 2002.

p. 239 *Olam and Louis Dreyfus were said to be in merger talks*: *Financial Times,* 24 September 2010.

p. 239 *Figures vary, but*: Fairtrade Foundation, Commodities report, May 2012 (www.fairtrade.org.uk).

p. 240   *The money made from coffee has shifted*: Oxfam report *Mugged*: *Poverty in your Coffee Cup* 2002, World Bank World Development report 2008, quoted in Fairtrade and Coffee report.

p. 240   *By 2011 the price of arabica*: wwww.agritrade.cta.int/Agriculture/ Commodities/Coffee/Executive-Brief-Update-2012-Coffee-sector

p. 241   *The significance to developing countries*: Oxfam, *Mugged*; Fairtrade Coffee report.

p. 243   *The significance to developing countries of fluctuations*: Oxfam, *Mugged*, as above.

p. 243   *Its authoritarian leader, Yoweri Museveni*: See, for example, J. Stiglitz, *Globalization and Its Discontents* (Allen Lane, 2002); FT World Report, *Uganda* (FT.com, 15 April 2003).

p. 243   *It was rewarded by being made the first country to qualify for debt relief*: personal communication, DIFD.

p. 243   *In 1994/5 when the price of coffee was high*: Figures from Uganda Coffee Trade Federation, *The Coffee Yearbook, 2000–2001*.

p. 245   *Coffee imported from many countries face EU tariffs*: International Trade Centre, The Coffee Guide (www.thecoffeeguide.org/coffee-guide/the-markets-for-coffee/Tariff-barriers).

p. 247   *Nestlé told me that it was not in favour of volatile coffee prices*: Nestlé position paper, 18 September 2002, and personal communications.

p. 250   *The road this side of the country runs past the Coca-Cola factory*: *East African Weekly*, 4 March 2002.

p. 253   *When coffee is made into instant*: personal communication, Food Standards Agency.

p. 254   *Perhaps the most significant of these complexes*: F. Lawrence, Poverty Matters blog, the *Guardian* (www.theguardian.com), 2 June 2011.

p. 255   *Swiss-based Glencore*: The *Telegraph*, 15 April 2011.

p. 255   *US-based Cargill*: www.just-food.com/news/annual-profits-almost-double-at-cargill_id124074.aspx

p. 256   *ADM ... has built up*: Securities and Exchange Commission (SEC) report, Form 10-K, 2012 (http://pdf.secdatabase.com/106/ 0000007084-12-000034.pdf).

p. 258   *The trade here had become a key battleground*: F. Lawrence, the *Guardian*, 1 June 2011.

p. 260 *some two years later, the battle between them and the state*: Bloomberg, 25 March 2013; and the *Australian*, 2 July 2013.

p. 263 *according to Oxfam in a major report*: 'Growing a Better Future: Food justice in a resource-constrained world', R. Bailey, Oxfam, 31 May 2011.

p. 264 *the European Community placed agriculture policy*: www.euromove.org.uk/index.php?id=6514; and www.europa.eu/rapid/press-release_MEMO-13-631_en.htm.

p. 264 *From 1947 to 1994 the General Agreement on Tariffs and Trade*: For an introduction to international trade rules, see G. Tansey and T. Worsley, *The Food System* (Earthscan, 2000); the Consumers' Association, *Unwrapping the WTO* (2 Marylebone Road, London NW1 4DF); Save the Children Fund briefing papers on WTO and the International Monetary Fund (www.savethechildren.org.uk); and the Bretton Woods Project (www.brettonwoodsproject.org).

p. 265 *rich Western countries kept their quotas and continued to subsidize*: OECD Producer Support Estimate in 2006 was $252, 508m, see www.oecd.org; OECD (2009) 'Agricultural Policies in OECD Countries: Monitoring and Evaluation 2009'.

p. 265 *CAP costs*: Ö. Legrain, 'Beyond CAP: Why the EU Budget Needs Reform', the Lisbon Council e-brief, Issue 09/2010.

p. 265 *President Bush's controversial Farm Bill*: BBC News, 10 May 2002.

p. 266 *the 2012 Farm Bill*: S. Kirchgaessner, www.ft.com, 14 July 2013.

p. 268 *The largest individual payments*: F. Lawrence, the *Guardian*, 8 December 2005.

p. 268 *In 2009, transnational sugar companies*: J. Chaffin, *Financial Times*, 5 May 2010.

p. 269 *turned parts of Africa into the 'wild west'*: M. Tran, the *Guardian*, 29 October 2012.

p. 270 *The Forbes 2000 ranking in April 2013 lists*: www.forbes.com/global2000/list

p. 271 *larger than the GDP of all but seventy of the world's countries*: http://en.wikipedia.org/wiki/List_of_countries_by_GDP_(PPP).

p. 272 *as Olivier de Schutter … put it*: F. Lawrence, the *Guardian*, Poverty Matters blog, 9 March 2012; UN report by the Special

Rapporteur, Olivier de Schutter, 26 December 2011 (www.ohchr. org); see also www.srfood.org/en/five-ways-to-tackle-disastrous-diets-un-food-expert.

p. 274   *Presenting the company's results in 2013, he said*: Unilever Sustainable Living Plan, April 2013 (www.unilever.com/sustainable-living/news/news/Paul-Polman-Volatility-and-uncertainty-the-new-normal.aspx).

p. 274   *[Nestle's] CEO Paul Bulcke has said*: 14 March 2013: www.foodnavigator.com/Financial-Industry/Nestle-outlines-sustain-ability-and-nutrition-goals.

p. 280   *A glimpse of these tensions*: Household brands slash size of goods, the *Telegraph*, 21 March 2013.

CHAPTER 8: THE READY MEAL

Caroline Walker, who died in 1988, first explained the relationship between modern adulterations of food and ill-health to me. I am indebted to her pioneering spirit. Craig Sams first opened my eyes to the relationship between subsidies and cheap ingredients for processed foods. Tim Lobstein and Kath Dalmeny of the Food Commission have shared their research over the years. David Walker, formerly of Shropshire County Council has acted as a walking dictionary of food adulteration and meat processing. David Gregory, and his successor Paul Willgoss, technical directors at Marks and Spencer, and Paul Kelly of Asda-Wal-Mart have been generous in engaging in a dialogue. Thanks also to the press office of the Food Standards Agency for details on legislation.

p. 282   *Britain has in fact been the largest consumer in Europe of ready meals*: Mintel, February 2001; www.readymealsinfo.com.

p. 284   *Frozen food manufacturers point out*: The *Grocer*, 21 June 2003.

p. 285   *In fact, a quarter of all processed foods*: US Corn Refiners' Association (www.corn.org); Economic Research Service, US Department of Agriculture, briefing room: corn (www.usda.gov); Institute of Food Research, Norwich, *Soya* briefing paper (www.ifr.ac.uk).

p. 285   *As the US Corn Refiners' Association explained*: www.corn.org/web/tapping.htm.

p. 285   *In an article in* Innovative Food Ingredients *magazine*: S. F. Shoesmith, Innovative Uses of Corn Starch in Food, *Innovative Food Ingredients* (business briefing, World Markets Research Centre, 2002, www.wmrc.com).

p. 286   *In October 2003, Shropshire trading standards officers*: Shropshire County Council Trading Standards Service, *Chicken Survey*, 17 October 2003.

p. 286   *A strawberry-flavoured yoghurt has had a briefer encounter with the fruit*: F. Lawrence (ed.), *Additives* (Century, 1986); J. Meek, the *Guardian*'s The Way We Eat Now series, 17 May 2003.

p. 287   *Breakfast cereals*: *Which?* report, 15 February 2012.

p. 288   *Hydrogenation was developed in the 1920s*: Sustain, *Fat of the Land*, 2000; C. Sams, *The Little Food Book* (Alastair Sawday Publishing, 2003).

p. 288   *It is now accepted that it is safest to avoid hydrogenated fats*: US Food and Drug Administration, *Revealing Trans Fats*, September–October 2003; FSA, *Healthier Eating, Ask an Expert, Hydrogenated and Trans Fats* (www.foodstandards.gov.uk).

p. 290   *It was easier for some economically than others*: F. Lawrence, the *Guardian*, 25 April 2006.

p. 292   *Greg Critser describes the effect*: G. Critser, *Fat Land* (Penguin, 2003).

p. 293   *Over $22 billion is spent each year by the food industry on chemical additives*: *Innovative Food Ingredients*, as above; T. Lang & E. Millstone, *The Atlas of Food* (Earthscan, 2003).

p. 293   *Colours are still liberally used*: 'Coloring Food, Naturally', *Chemical & Engineering News*, Vol. 86, no. 50, December 2008.

p. 294   *Erik Millstone*: see *Atlas of Food*, as above; also, E. Millstone, *Food Additives* (Penguin, 1986) and *Additives: A Guide for Everyone* (Penguin, 1988).

p. 294   *Food manufacturers have always cut corners*: E. P. Thompson, The Moral Economy of the English Crowd in the Eighteenth Century, *Past and Present*, 50, 1971; T. Smollett, *Humphry Clinker* (Penguin, 1967); C. Walker and G. Cannon, *The Food Scandal* (Century, 1984).

p. 294 *His work,* There is Death in the Pot: F. Accum, *A Treatise on Adulterations of Food and Culinary Poisons,* 1820 (Longman, Hurst, Peel, Orme and Brown).

p. 295 *Thomas Wakley:* F. Bing, Frederick Accum: A Biographical Sketch, *Journal of Nutrition,* 89, 1966; E. Gray, *By Candlelight: The Life of Dr Arthur Hill Hassall* (Robert Hale, 1983); A. Amos, *Pure Food and Pure Food Legislation* (Butterworths, 1960).

p. 296 *The pork sausage bit of my lamb casserole:* F. Lawrence (ed.), *Additives* (Century, 1986).

p. 297 *Nor do the individual ingredients of all 'compound ingredients':* Personal communication, Food Standards Agency; Directive 2003/89/EC of the European Parliament and of the Council, 10 November 2003; C. Sams, *The Little Food Book,* as above.

p. 297 *Le Salon International de l'Alimentation:* SIAL (Paris, 2002, www.sial.fr).

p. 300 *The market grew by 32 per cent:* http://oxygen.mintel.com/display/545240/

p. 300 *There has been one slight hitch:* F. Lawrence, the *Guardian,* 19 October 2010 and 23 November 2010.

p. 301 *The WHO, summarizing the situation:* WHO, *The Impact of Food and Nutrition on Public Health* (Regional Office for Europe, Copenhagen, 2000), and WHO/FAO, *Report of the Joint Expert Consultation on Diet, Nutrition and the Prevention of Chronic Diseases,* 916 (Rome, 2003).

p. 301 *As Western diets high in fats, sugars and salt:* WHO/FAO, 916, as above.

p. 302 *The director general of the WHO called the epidemic 'a slow-motion disaster':* Non-Communicable Diseases Deemed Development Challenge Of 'Epidemic Proportions', 19 September 2011, UN (www.un.org/News/Press/docs/2011/ga11138.doc.htm).

p. 302 *determined industry lobbying:* S. Boseley, www.guardian.com, 30 August 2011.

p. 302 *the latest NHS figures show:* Obesity figures update 2013, NHS, based on figures from 2011 (www.nhs.uk/news/2013/02February/Pages/Latest-obesity-stats-for-England-are-alarming-reading.aspx).

p. 302 *When we eat highly processed energy-dense foods*: A. M. Prentice, S. A. Jebb, Fast foods, energy density and obesity: a possible mechanistic link, *Obesity Reviews*, 28 October 2003 (as announced at www.mrc.ac.uk/txt/public-22_october_2003); see also Dr Jebb on supermarket ready meals in the same link.

p. 302 *And a product like high-fructose corn syrup*: Evidence presented to the House of Commons Health Committee inquiry into obesity, 27 November 2003; Critser, *Fat Land*, as above.

p. 303 *The International Obesity Taskforce*: press briefing, London, 11 November 2003.

p. 303 *There is also a clear link between poverty and obesity*: DoH/NCSR/Royal Free, as above.

p. 303 *Type 2 diabetes, which used to be called adult-onset diabetes*: S. Boseley, Diabetes creating world catastrophe, warns leading doctor, the *Guardian*, 25 August 2003; see also International Diabetes Federation.

p. 303 *The Wanless report on the National Health Service*: HM Treasury, *Wanless Review: Securing Our Future Health*, April 2002.

p. 303 *Coronary heart disease is the biggest killer*: British Heart Foundation statistics (www.heartstats.org).

p. 304 *Although there has been much dispute over the years*: Department of Health, *Nutritional Aspects of the Development of Cancer*, 1998; World Cancer Research Fund, *Food, Nutrition, and the Prevention of Cancer: a Global Perspective*, 1997.

p. 304 *Children do particularly badly*: Report of the Policy Commission on the Future of Farming and Food (Cabinet Office, January 2002).

p. 304 *Professor Michael Crawford*: M. & S. Crawford, *What We Eat Today* (Neville Spearman, 1972).

p. 306 *The ratio of omega-6 to omega-3*: M. Small, The Happy Fat, *New Scientist*, 175, 24 August 2002.

p. 306 *Soils fed only with artificial fertilizers*: A.-M. Mayer, Historical Changes in Mineral Content of Fruits and Vegetables, *Agricultural Production and Nutrition* (Tufts University School of Nutrition Science and Policy, May 1997); replicated by D. Thomas, *The Loss of Minerals in Our Food between 1940 and*

1991 (Cleave Lecture, delivered to the McCarrison Society, 20 November 2003).

p. 307 *Joseph Hibbeln*: Small, The Happy Fat, as above; D. Horrobin, Omega-3 Fatty Acid for Schizophrenia, *American Journal of Psychiatry* (2003; 160: 188–9).

p. 308 *There is mounting evidence that deficiencies are involved*: See, for example, A. J. Richardson and B. K. Puri, A randomized, double-blind, placebo-controlled study of the effects of supplementation with highly unsaturated fatty acids on ADHD-related symptoms in children with specific learning disabilities, *Prog Neuropsychopharm Biol Psychiat* (2002; 26 (2) 233–9); A. J. Richardson, Fatty Acids in Dyslexia, Dyspraxia, ADHD and the Autistic Spectrum, *Nutrition Practitioner* (2001; 2(3), 18–24); and www.durhamtrial.org.

p. 308 *During the study, which took place in one of Britain's maximum security prisons*: B. Gesch *et al.*, Influence of Supplementary Vitamins, Minerals and Essential Fatty Acids on the Anti-Social Behaviour of Young Adult Prisoners, *British Journal of Psychiatry* (2002; 181, 22–8).

p. 310 *A study by the Consumers' Association*: School Dinners, *Which?* magazine, March 2003.

p. 312 *take-up remains a problem*: http://www.schoolfoodplan.com/wp-content/uploads/2013/07/School-Food-Plan-2013.pdf

p. 313 *Children today also consume thirty times the amount of soft drinks*: School Dinners, *Which?* magazine, as above.

p. 314 *The time we give to food*: Figures from Unilever.

p. 314 *The food and drink industry spent £838 million*: The Children's Food Campaign, Junk Food Marketing (www.sustainweb.org/childrensfoodcampaign/junk_food_marketing).

p. 314 *The biggest spender in 2012*: the *Grocer*, 17 May 2013.

p. 314 *The biggest categories of food advertised*: Food Standards Agency, *Review of Research on the Effects of Food Promotion to Children*, by Professor Gerard Hastings *et al.* (University of Strathclyde, September 2003).

p. 314 *In 2010, according to the UN special rapporteur*: Olivier De Schutter, www.srfood.org/en/five-ways-to-tackle-disastrous-diets-un-food-expert.

p. 314   *Marketing experts have worked out ways*: M. K. Lewis and A. J. Hill, Food Advertising on British Children's Television, *International Journal of Obesity* (1998; 2, 206–14).

p. 315   *Dr Aric Sigman*: *Blackmail*, Co-op inquiry into the Ethics of Food and Drink Advertising to Children (The Co-op, July 2000).

p. 315   *the independent campaign group the Food Commission*: K. Dalmeny, E. Hanna, T. Lobstein, *Broadcasting Bad Health* (International Association of Consumer Food Organizations, July 2003).

p. 315   *The brilliance of the techniques*: Advertising Effectiveness Awards, Institute of Practitioners in Advertising, 2002.

p. 316   *Cadbury was severely criticized*: The Food Commission, press release, 29 April 2003.

p. 317   *The big guns from the manufacturers*: Oral evidence presented to the House of Commons Health Committee inquiry into obesity, 27 November 2003.

p. 318 *Ofcom announced new measures in 2006*: The *Guardian*, 17 November 2006.

p. 318   *lobbied on twenty-nine occasions*: F. Lawrence, the *Guardian*, 22 April 2006.

p. 319   *A systematic review*: briefing to the International Association for the Study of Obesity, July 2013.

p. 319   *It was a Friday afternoon in May*: F. Lawrence, the *Guardian*, 12 November 2010.

p. 325   *Professor Philip James traces much of the problem*: P. James, *Nutrition and the Future*, (Lecture given to the Caroline Walker Trust, 1997).

Index